Real World Economics

Anthem Development Studies and Globalization

Chang, Ha-Joon (ed.) *Institutional Change and Economic Development* (2007)

Rangaswamy, Vedavalli *Energy for Development* (2007)

Ringmar, Erik *Why Europe was First* (2006)

Ellman, Michael (ed.) *Russia's Oil and Natural Gas* (2006)

Buira, Ariel (ed.) *Reforming the Governance of the IMF and the World Bank* (2006)

Ringmar, Erik *Surviving Capitalism* (2005)

Saquet, Anne-Marie *World Atlas of Sustainable Development* (2005)

Ritzen, Jozef *A Chance for the World Bank* (2005)

Buira, Ariel (ed.) *The IMF and the World Bank at Sixty* (2005)

Assayag, Jackie & Fuller, Chris (eds) *Globalizing India* (2005)

Standing, Guy *Promoting Income Security as a Right* (2004)

Chang, Ha-Joon (ed.) *Rethinking Development Economics* (2003)

Chang, Ha-Joon *Kicking Away the Ladder* (2003)

Real World Economics

A Post-Autistic Economics Reader

Edited by
Edward Fullbrook

ANTHEM PRESS
LONDON · NEW YORK · DELHI

Anthem Press
An imprint of Wimbledon Publishing Company
www.anthempress.com

This edition first published in UK and USA 2007
by ANTHEM PRESS
75-76 Blackfriars Road, London SE1 8HA, UK
or PO Box 9779, London SW19 7ZG, UK and
244 Madison Ave. #116, New York, NY 10016, USA

British Library Cataloguing in Publication Data
A catalogue record for this book is available from the British Library.

Library of Congress Cataloging in Publication Data
A catalog record for this book has been requested.

ISBN-10: 1 84331 236 0 (Pbk)
ISBN-13: 978 1 84331 236 9 (Pbk)

1 3 5 7 9 10 8 6 4 2

Printed in EU

CONTENTS

Part 6:   Case histories

Part 7:   Is anything worth keeping in microeconomics?

CONTRIBUTORS

Frank Ackerman Global Development and Environment Institute, Tufts University, US

Trond Andresen The Norwegian University of Science and Technology, Norway

Asatar Bair Doctoral Candidate, University of Massachusetts at Amherst, US

Ana Maria Bianchi Universidade de Sao Paulo, Brazil

Jorge Buzaglo University of Gothenburg, Sweden

Bruce J Caldwell University of North Carolina, US

Nathaniel N Chamberland graduated 2002 from Trinity College, US

Ha-Joon Chang Cambridge University, UK

Robert Costanza University of Vermont, US

Herman E Daly School of Public Policy, University of Maryland, US

James G Devine Loyola Marymount University, US

Peter Dorman The Evergreen State College, US

Steve Fleetwood Lancaster University, UK

Edward Fullbrook University of the West of England, UK

James K Galbraith University of Texas at Austin, US

Daniel Gay PhD student at the University of Stirling, UK

Yves Gingras University of Quebec, Montreal, Canada

Bernard Guerrien The Sorbonne, Paris, and Université Paris I, France

Geoff Harcourt Cambridge University, UK

Shaun Hargreaves Heap University of East Anglia, UK

Robert Heilbroner New School University, New York, US

Geoffrey M. Hodgson University of Hertfordshire, UK

Goutam U Jois JD Candidate at Harvard University, US

Steve Keen University of Western Sydney, Australia

J E King La Trobe University, Australia

Reiner Kümmel Institute of Theoretical Physics, University of Würrzburg, Germany

Robert E Lane Yale University, US

Dietmar Lindenberger Institute of Energy Economics, University of Cologne, Germany

Robert Locke US

Anne Mayhew University of Tennessee, US

Matthew McCartney School of Oriental and African Studies, University of
    London, UK
Deirdre McCloskey University of Illinois at Chicago / Erasmus University
    Rotterdam, Netherlands
Poul Thøis Madsen Aalborg University, Denmark
William Milberg New School University, New York, US
Alex Millmow Charles Sturt University, Australia
Jamie Morgan The Open University, UK
Claude Mouchot Centre Walras, Université Lumière-Lyon2, France
Julie A Nelson Global Development and Environment Institute, Tufts University,
    US
Juan Pablo Pardo-Guerra National University of Mexico, Mexico
Kevin Quinn Bowling Green State University, US
Gilles Raveaud co-founder of Austisme-Économie, École Normale Supérieure de
    Cachan, France
Jacques Sapir L'École des Hautes Études en Sciences Sociales, Paris, France
Esther-Mirjam Sent University of Notre Dame, US, and Netherlands Institute for
    Advanced Study in the Humanities and Social Sciences (NIAS), Netherlands
Alan Shipman UK author of *The Globalization Myth* (Icon Books, 2002)
Kyle Siler Department of Sociology, Cornell University, Ithaca, NY, US
Sashi Sivramkrishna Foundation to Aid Industrial Recovery, India
Peter Söderbaum Mälardalen University, Sweden
Mehrdad Vahabi Université Paris 8, France)
Olivier Vaury École Normale Supérieure, Paris
Charles K Wilber University of Notre Dame, US
Richard Wolff University of Massachusetts, Amherst, US
Stephen T Ziliak Roosevelt University, US

INTRODUCTION

Edward Fullbrook

With the new millennium came post-autistic economics. Sparked by a rebellion of French economics students in the summer of 2000 (see Appendix I), the improbably named movement spread globally among academic economists, growing exponentially until today its *Post-Autistic Economics Review* has nearly 10,000 subscribers (Appendix III).

Rather than being a school of thought, post-autistic economics is a response to what economists identify as a state of decadence prevailing in their profession. Economics is now so sick that even members of its inter-sanctum publicly admit it. For example, six winners of the Bank of Sweden Prize for Economics, alias "Nobel Prize for Economics", have written as follows.

> ... economics has become increasingly an arcane branch of mathematics rather than dealing with real economic problems. (Milton Friedman, 1999, p. 137)

> It is a peculiar fact that the literature on economics and economic history contains so little discussion of the central institution that underlies neoclassical economics – the market. (Douglass North, 1977, p. 710)

> Page after page of professional economic journals are filled with mathematical formulas [...] Year after year economic theorists continue to produce scores of mathematical models and to explore in great detail their formal properties; and the econometricians fit algebraic functions of all possible shapes to essentially the same sets of data. (Wassily Leontief, 1982, p. 104)

Existing economics is a theoretical [meaning mathematical] system which floats in the air and which bears little relation to what happens in the real world. (Ronald Coase, 1999, p. 2)

Today if you ask a mainstream economist a question about almost any aspect of economic life, the response will be: suppose we model that situation and see what happens ... modern mainstream economics consists of little else but examples of this process. (Robert Solow, 1997, p. 43)

Economics as taught "in America's graduate schools ... bears testimony to a triumph of ideology over science." (Joseph Stiglitz, 2002)

Post-autistic economics aims to rectify the desperate state of affairs identified by Friedman, North, Leontief, Coase, Solow and Stiglitz. The movement has four primary demands.

1. Economics should become reality based

Since the 1870s economics has been bedevilled by the idea that it should give itself the appearance of resembling Newtonian physics. This belief came as a natural consequence of economists' craving for scientific respectability. By mimicking classical physics, which was the popular model of high science, they hoped to be perceived as serious scientists. This sham shaped the works of the two principal founders of neoclassical economics, the variety upon which today's "mainstream" is based. One founder, the Englishman Stanley Jevons, wrote as follows:

> . . . all branches and divisions of economic science must be pervaded by certain general principles ["the general principles of mechanics"]. It is to the investigation of such principles – to the tracing out of *the mechanics of self-interest and utility*, that this essay has been devoted. The establishment of such a theory is a necessary preliminary to any definite drafting of the superstructure of the aggregate science. (Jevons 1970, p. 50, emphasis added)

Jevons's injunction, which was echoed by his French cofounder Leon Walras, constituted a bizarre methodological turning for economics that persists to the present day. It was bizarre because economics' attempt to make its formal structure resemble physics' meant adopting a methodology that was exactly upside-down from that of its idol. Physics is pre-eminently an empirical science, meaning that its "general principles", including those of classical mechanics, are based on observations of the physical world, their formal correspondence with those observations being the sole basis of their legitimacy. But the project launched by Jevons and Walras meant that the general principles of economics were to be established not through observations of the economic world, but rather by substituting economic terminology into the formal structures of Newtonian physics. In this way economics set about developing a model that had the same formal properties as Newton's model of the physical universe. Whether the economic and physical universes do in fact have the same formal properties was never an issue. Whereas *empirical research* had identified the fundamental properties of the physical universe that Newton and others then modelled, the founders of neoclassical economics merely *defined* a set of concepts that lent themselves to being combined in a model with the same formal properties as Newton's model. In doing so they disconnected theory generation from empirical observation, thereby turning it into a purely formalist operation.

But a craving for the prestige enjoyed by natural scientists is not the only reason for economics' misuse of mathematics. The complexity of the economic and social world poses enormous difficulties for understanding that world schematically and makes its reduction to simple laws impossible. This theoretical intractableness makes it tempting to escape into imaginary worlds, especially mathematical models that look wonderfully sophisticated, but have little or nothing to do with economic reality. These models, without any concrete data, lend themselves to unending mathematical developments and everlasting speculations, thereby forever postponing a return to "dealing with real economic problems" and leaving economics stranded in an autistic world.

The post-autistic economics movement seeks to liberate economics from that world. But before there can be a return to reality, economists must learn to choose their methods to fit the problem rather than the other way around.

2. Economics should be problem led, not method led

Neoclassical mainstream economists have made a metaphysical commitment to a particular method of investigating the economic realm. Rather than choosing the individual *and* society or institutions as its theoretical foundation, it has chosen the individual alone. All economic phenomena is studied only as if it were the result of individual choices made with given preferences, scarcities and constraints, and always tending toward equilibrium and being always not only of a quantifiable nature but also one reducible to functional relations of the form "whenever event (or state of affairs) *x*, then event (or state of affairs) *y*".

Not withstanding the obvious limitations of this method, the placing of any method ahead of subject matter is contrary not only to common sense but also to practice in the natural sciences. Whereas other disciplines define themselves in terms of a phenomenal realm to be studied and then seek methods appropriate to that realm, economics has come to define itself in terms of its methodological approach. Tony Lawson describes the situation as follows:

> Rather than starting with a question about an aspect of social reality and determining an appropriate method, modern economists usually start with a particular type of method and presume, mistakenly, that it must be appropriate to all social contexts. The result is that, in their conceptions, modern economists end up distorting social phenomena just to render them open to treatment by their chosen approach. (Lawson 2004, p. 22)

But the situation is even more complicated. Because of the very nature of conceptual thought, any one method of inquiry offers only a partial view of the object of enquiry. From this awkward fact stems the third and most radical demand of the post-autistic economics movement.

3. Economics should, like physics, be pluralistic, not monistic

Today physicists have two theories for describing the universe, the general theory of relativity and quantum mechanics. Not only do the conceptual frameworks of these theories differ fundamentally, but also *their basic concepts directly contradict each other*. (Bohm, 1983, p.176)

- General relativity conceives of space and time as continuous; quantum theory conceives of them as discontinuous.
- General relativity conceives of matter as particulate; quantum theory conceives of it as a wave-particle duality.
- General relativity conceives of physical objects as having actual properties; quantum theory describes them as having only potential properties within the given physical situation.

- General relativity conceives all physical reality as determinate and all events as in principle having a causal explanation; quantum theory admits indeterminacy and events incapable of causal explanation.

Conceptual differences greater than these are scarcely imaginable. This radical pluralism is physics' response to the complexity of the object, the universe, which they wish to understand. The physicist David Bohm explains the pluralist case as follows:

> One may indeed compare a theory to a particular view of some object. Each view gives only an appearance of the object in some aspect. The whole object is not perceived in any one view but, rather, it is grasped only *implicitly* as that single reality which is shown in all these views. (Bohm 1983, p. 8)

This idea of pluralism was at the centre of the French students manifesto that sparked the Post-Autistic Economics movement. It included the following:

> Out of all the approaches to economic questions that exist, generally only one is presented to us. This approach is supposed to explain everything by means of a purely axiomatic process, as if this were THE economic truth. We do not accept this dogmatism. We want a pluralism of approaches adapted to the complexity of the objects and to the uncertainty surrounding most of the big questions in economics (unemployment, inequalities, the place of financial markets, the advantages and disadvantages of free-trade, globalization, economic development, etc).

The phrase "approaches adapted to the complexity of the objects" is an in-your-face radicalization of the demand for a pluralist economics because it inverts the traditional but implicit philosophical idealism of economics, whereby the approach takes precedent over the object of inquiry, the reality of the latter being admitted only to the extent that it is illuminated by the former. In the past this disposition has characterised not just neoclassical economists, but the various schools generally. In the context of this tradition, the naked spirit of empiricism in the students' petition was, and for many economists continues to be, shocking. If accepted it deprives every school of the dream of representing "THE economic truth" and makes communication among different approaches *essential* to any broad advancement of economic knowledge. It requires a completely new ball game, including new textbooks. Many of the articles that have appeared in the *Post-Autistic Economics Review* and collected for this volume represent attempts to come to terms with the conceptualizations and practicalities of this fundamentally different approach to the doing and teaching of economics. I want to say a few things about the thinking and concerns that lie behind this pluralism.

Every scientific pursuit launches itself from a conceptual framework, a set of presuppositions about the nature of reality that, *by providing a radical simplification of reality*, makes investigation possible. These include such things as a classification of entities, which properties of those entities are taken into account, the types of connections recognized, whether all events are determinate or not, the nature and direction of causal relations, and whether or not there exist structural relations as well as aggregate ones. In this way a conceptual framework defines a particular point of view toward its object of enquiry. Inevitably, different conceptual frameworks offer different points of view. What one sees when one looks at Michelangelo's statue of David depends on where one is standing. No one visiting David would refuse to walk around and view him from different vantage points. But this is what economics has essentially come to do with the economy. The "mainstream" today refers to the study of the economy from an essentially neoclassical viewpoint. Various assumptions of that viewpoint may be dropped one or two at a time, like the viewer of David leaning to the left or right, but the primary vantage point remains fixed.

All anti-pluralism is epistemologically dangerous. But it is especially so when it takes the form of allegiance to economics' neoclassical make-believe world. Here everything, like in a fairytale, works wondrously well. There is never any unemployment; markets of all kinds always clear instantly; everyone gets exactly what they deserve; market outcomes are invariably "optimal"; everyone maximizes their potential; and all citizens possess a crystal ball that infallibly foresees the future. In this axiomatic paradise (without messy things like social beings, institutions, history, culture, ethics, religion, human development and the indeterminacy that always accompanies freedom) there is no government ownership, no regulation, no corporate accountability, no building codes, no health and safety laws, no collective bargaining rights, no food standards, no controls on oligopoly and monopoly, no welfare, no public health departments, no universal health coverage and so on. Instead there are just "markets", in which everything is imagined to be reducible to numbers.

Economics shouldn't and doesn't have to be like this. Even more than physics, modern medicine, where the general practitioner shifts freely between knowledge narratives, exemplifies the approach economics needs. The germ theory of disease, along with psychosomatic, genetic and life-style explanations of disease, are each a family of approaches, and between which the competent doctor shifts freely back and forth in seeking a true and full explanation of his or her patient's complaint. These families of explanations have overlapping domains – for example, diet (not enough red wine and too much red meat) and stress (not enough leisure and too much aggro) contributing through bio-chemical processes to genetic susceptibility to heart disease. But there is no yearning nor pressure nor, indeed, tolerance in the community of medicine for a reduction of its many approaches to understanding human health to a master narrative. Instead the medical community understands that a multiplicity of viewpoints for understanding disease and its absence is needed to serve the complexity of medicine's empirical domain. Indeed, it is almost self-evident that the ill health and good health of the human organism are causally more complex than the fundamental properties of the physical universe, and, therefore, require a plurality of approaches. It should also be self-evident that this is even more true of the socio-economic realm.

If economics is to be a constructive part of the human conversation, rather than one that closes it down, it must be willing to adjust its conceptual vantage points both to fit changes in the topics of that conversation through time and to illuminate the many dimensions of its domain and the diverse perspectives of its participants. Above all, the conceit that because one is an economist one is blessed with a privileged or God's-eye view of the human world must cease to be indulged. This brings us to the fourth demand of the post-autistic economics movement.

4. Economics should be knowledge driven, not ideology driven

The fact that a conceptual system defines, at the exclusion of others, a point of view toward its object of enquiry has in the social sciences, in addition to its epistemological consequence, an ideological one. There are two reasons why this is so. First, the conceptual systems of social sciences can alter the objects of their enquiries by becoming part of the conceptual and belief systems through which humans conceive of themselves and of others and by which they make choices. In the daily functioning of societies this recursive dimension of the social sciences, economics especially, becomes increasingly significant as mass higher education becomes the norm, even more so when as in the United States there is a social science input into most undergraduate degrees. Second, the social sciences provide means by which governments preserve or reconstruct, sometimes fundamentally, the basic realities of societies. Different conceptual systems, such as institutional and neoclassical economics, present different sets of choices, real or imagined, to be chosen and acted upon by human populations at large.[3] It can never be the case that each of these sets of choices will equally favour every group in society, so that when a social science falls victim to anti-pluralism it becomes inescapably and profoundly ideological.[4] If only one conceptual framework is permitted, with the consequence that it alone is inculcated into the citizenry and its leaders, then the choices that in a democracy should be out in the open and belong to the people are hidden from view and the free discussion and debate upon which all democracy depends is silently eliminated. Peter Söderbaum explains it as follows:

> The "fact" that also ideology is present means that the "one-paradigm position" at departments of economics becomes untenable. Limiting economics to one paradigm means that one ideological orientation is emphasized at the expense of all others. This position is not compatible with normal ideas of democracy. Departments of economics should avoid the role of being political propaganda centres. With more than one paradigm as part of a pluralistic strategy, the ideological diversity in a democratic society will be better reflected. Furthermore, one specific paradigm, such as the neoclassical one, may perform well in relation to some fields of study while being more of a problem in relation to other fields. (Söderbaum, 2004, p. 159)

Economists of all varieties must, like physicists and biologists have done, learn to live without the belief that there is one right way of describing and explaining reality. Natural scientists have found it worthwhile to accept this existential burden purely for the purpose of advancing knowledge. For economists, if they are of a democratic persuasion, there is an additional reason, because economics as a discipline impacts on the object of its enquiry. Because each approach looks at the economic from a particular conceptual angle, different approaches will, *when presented to the public as if it were "THE economic truth"*, promote the interests of some groups in society over others, encourage and discourage different types of behaviour in individuals, illuminate or leave in the dark different problems and possibilities for humankind, and so on. In other words, when economic theories are handled in this way they function primarily not as sets of tools for human enlightenment, but, to the contrary, as *concealed ideologies*, which, when one wins out over the rest, smother real discussion, silence debate, blind the public to most of economic reality, and ultimately place the human project at risk.

The post-autistic economics movement is a broadly international response to the state of affairs described above. This book is a collection of 59 articles that have appeared in the *Post-Autistic Economics Review* and six documents related to the movement. The topics covered include:

- the strange story of how Neoclassical economics succeeded in cleansing non-believers from economics departments in most universities;
- the danger that the Neoclassical mainstream poses to the planet;
- the way that the economics profession is organized;
- the relation between psychological autism and the institutional autism found today in economics;
- the closed-system nature of Neoclassical economics and its lack of empirical grounding;
- the decline of economics in the student market;
- a section on the scandal surrounding what is incorrectly called the "Nobel Prize in Economics";
- nine articles about bringing realism back to economics;
- three articles on the pluralism versus monism issue;
- case history articles documenting how single-viewpoint economics has crippled various fields of economics, especially the economics of development;
- 14 pithy and interrelated articles about how microeconomics should be reformed;
- speculative articles on economics in relation to other concerns including dystopias, destructive power and thermodynamics;
- a section of articles on the relation of ethics to economics; and
- articles by students on their experience of studying economics.

All these articles are highly readable, succinct and accessible to the general reader. Many are engagingly written and most are provocative. The collection confronts unflinchingly a major public controversy of today and tomorrow. As Friedman, North, Leontief, Coase, Solow and Stiglitz have noted, economics is extremely sick. The discipline is so locked in its past that nearly all of its introductory textbooks are modelled on one that appeared in 1948. Economics cannot continue in its autistic state much longer. Humanity's fate cannot afford it. Pressure for economics to change fundamentally mounts daily from both inside and outside the profession. This book takes you to the heart of this fiery and many-faceted debate.

References

Bohm, David (1983), *Wholeness and the Implicate Order*, London: Routledge.

Coase, Ronald (1999), 'Interview with Ronald Coase', *Newsletter of the International Society for New Institutional Economics*, **2** (1) (Spring).

Friedman, Milton (1999), 'Conversation with Milton Friedman' in B Snowdon and H Vane (eds), *Conversations with Leading Economists: Interpreting Modern Macroeconomics*, pp. 124–44, Cheltenham: Edward Elgar.

Jevons, Willaim Stanley (1871, 1970), *The Theory of Political Economy*, Harmondsworth, England: Pelican.

Lawson, Tony (2004), "Modern Economics: the Problem and a Solution", in Edward Fullbrook, (ed.) *A Guide to What's Wrong with Economics*, pp. 21–32, London: Anthem Press.

Leontief, Wassily (1982), Letter in *Science*, 217, pp. 104–7.

North, Douglass (1977), "Markets and other allocation systems in history: the challenge of Karl Polanyi", *Journal of European Economic History*, **6**, 703–16.

Söderbaum, Peter (2004), "Economics as ideology and the need for pluralism", in Edward Fullbrook (ed.), *A Guide to What's Wrong With Economics*, London: Anthem, pp. 158–68.

Solow, Robert M (1997), "How did economics get that way and what way did it get?", *Daedalus*, **126**, pp 39–49.

Stiglitz, Joseph (2002), "There is no invisible hand", *The Guardian*, 20 December.

PART 1:

THE NATURE OF THE ENEMY

1.

THE RAND PORTCULLIS AND POST-AUTISTIC ECONOMICS

Edward Fullbrook

These days people like to call neoclassical economics 'mainstream economics' because most universities offer nothing else. The name also backhandedly stigmatises as oddball, flaky, deviant, disreputable, perhaps un-American, those economists who venture beyond the narrow confines of the neoclassical axioms. In an attempt to understand how this has happened, the first half of this section very roughly traces the strange history of economics from the 1870s through to the recent challenge to the neoclassical hegemony from the post-autistic economics movement, henceforth PAE. The second half surveys some of the substantive dimensions of PAE, a movement that began in Paris in the summer of 2000 and now involves thousands of economists worldwide in a long-term effort to free economics from its neoclassical straitjacket.

Physics envy

The origins of neoclassical economics are not what an outsider might think. Though today it cavorts with neoliberalism, it began as an honest intellectual and would-be scientific endeavour. Its patron saint was neither an ideologue nor a political philosopher, nor even an economist, but Sir Isaac Newton. The founding fathers of neoclassical economics hoped to achieve for the economic universe what Newton had achieved for the physical universe (and their descendants living today believe they have). Their aim was to fashion an economic model in the image of Newtonian mechanics – in which economic agents could be treated as if they were particles obeying mechanical laws. In principle it would be possible to describe the behaviour of such agents simultaneously, by a solvable system of equations. This narrative required the treatment of human desires as fundamental data: like the masses of physical bodies in classical mechanics, they would not be affected by the relations being modelled. It was to this end – not to the understanding of economic phenomena – that *homo economicus* or economic man and the hedonistic calculus were invented. Thorstein Veblen sums up the core metaphysic as follows:

> The human material with which the inquiry is concerned is conceived in hedonistic terms; that is to say, in terms of a passive and substantially inert and immutably given human nature … The hedonistic conception of man is that of a lightning calculator of pleasure and pains, who oscillates like a homogeneous globule of desire of happiness under the impulse of stimuli that shift him about the area, but leave him intact. He has neither antecedent nor consequent. He is an isolated definitive human datum …[1]

With this construct at its centre, the dream of a determinate model of the economic universe was realised in the 1870s by William Stanley Jevons and, especially, by Léon Walras, both of whom were in part physicists by training: it was called the model of general equilibrium. And this elaborate mechanistic metaphor, proudly devoid of empirical content, remains today the grand narrative of economic theory, for students and economists everywhere.

The model, which is invariably expressed in language so metaphorical that it would make a good poet blush, works by laying down *a priori*, like Euclidean geometry, a set of axioms:

- The economic universe is determinate.
- It exists in a void rather than in an ecosystem.
- All relations in an economy are self-regulating, in the sense that any disturbance 'sets in motion forces tending to restore the balance'.
- These 'forces' result exclusively from the behaviour of isolated individual agents.
- The behaviour of these agents conforms to certain mathematical properties. For example, consumer choice is characterised by transitivity (if X is preferred to Y and Y to Z, then X is always preferred to Z), completeness (out of the set of all possible bundles of goods, given a consumer's income, she will consider her preference between every pair

of them) and independence (consumers are not influenced by the choices of other consumers).

To their credit, few economists have tried to provide empirical support for these axioms. Instead this is a realm in which formalistic expediency rules. The entities of the model, and the relations between them, must be conceived in a way that makes them isomorphic to those of Newton's model of the physical universe. The exigencies of the grand metaphor rule even when the model is (as in the pedagogically popular Marshallian tradition) applied piecemeal and non-mathematically to individual markets. An example of such formalism is the elementary and ubiquitous notion of market demand for a product. Because a macro mass is *in fact* an additive function of its micro masses, neoclassical economics *defines* market demand as the additive function of the demands for product X of individual agents. But this assumes that everyone's demand for a product is independent of everyone else's demand for that product; for example, that one's choice of a disco is not influenced by whether it is crowded or dead empty. Without such an assumption of independence (that is, the absence of all inter-subjective effects) market demand as understood by mainstream economics does not exist. But as everyone knows – even neoclassical economists when they are off-duty – strong inter-subjective effects in markets are the rule rather than the exception in consumer societies. However, in spite of such obvious and widespread empirically observable difficulties, the metaphors of neoclassicalism have remained dominant.

Veblen and Keynes

At the very end of the nineteenth century, Thorstein Veblen launched a counter-revolution against the growing domination of the neoclassical approach in economics. Besides critiquing the neoclassical assumptions, he analysed institutions as well as isolated individuals, emphasized emergent social phenomena, argued that habit influenced economic choice more than rational calculation, rejected all forms of reductionism, and stressed the importance of knowledge in economic evolution. This approach steadily gained adherents in the years leading up to the first world war, and in 1917 one its leaders, John R Commons, was elected president of the American Economics Association (AEA). The following year this new school was christened 'institutional economics' at the AEA meetings, and was embraced by the association as a means of making economic theory capable of addressing the problems of economic development that would follow the conclusion of the war.[2] In the US in the 1920s the Institutionalists came to rival the Neoclassicals but in the 1930s their numbers declined. Like neoclassical economics, institutional economics had no explanation of, or solution to, the calamity that had befallen capitalist economies.

In stepped John Maynard Keynes. He offered a new theoretical interpretation of capitalist economies, which both explained their collapse and pointed to practical measures that would get them going again and keep them functioning smoothly without interfering with their general principles. Given the dire straits of capitalism and the growing fear of revolution, not even neoclassical economists dared for long to keep Keynes's theory from being given a try. When it was shown to work, that, at one level, ended the argument. Henceforth, in the basic management of the economy, all American presidents would be Keynesians. But at the theoretical level, which in the neoclassical tradition means theory that is axiom-led rather than empirically-led (otherwise their axioms would have been abandoned long ago), the argument had only just begun. In 1946 Keynes died and neoclassical economists began their counterinsurgency. This time they would not be satisfied until most economics departments in the world had been cleansed of economists who voiced non-neoclassical ideas.

The Pentagon

Keynes had trained at Cambridge University as a mathematician. In his mid-twenties he wrote *Treatise on Probability*, a book that was lauded by Whitehead and Russell ('it is impossible to praise too highly'), and launched what has become known as the 'logical–relationist' theory of probability. When he turned his attention to economics, he was shocked by the way mathematical economists abused mathematics, especially when they applied them in meaningless ways to unsuitable phenomena, and he made no secret of his professional contempt for their empty pretentiousness. But these economists were soon to have their revenge. Led by Paul Samuelson in the US and John Hicks in the UK, they set about mathematicising Keynes's theory – or, more accurately, a part of his theory. They left out all those bits that were inconsistent with the neoclassical axioms. Their end product was a formalized version of Keynes that is like a Henry Miller novel without sex and profanity. This bowdlerised version of Keynes, called 'Keynesianism', soon became standard fare in undergraduate courses. Even graduate students were discouraged from reading the primary text. With the real Keynes out of the way and Veblen and all the other free spirits forgotten, the road was now clear to establish a neoclassical tyranny.

Following the Second World War, the US increasingly came to determine (one might say dictate) the shape of economics worldwide, while within the US the sources of influence became concentrated and circumscribed to an absurd degree. This state of affairs, which persists to the present day, was engineered in significant part by the US Department of Defence, especially its Navy and Air Force.[3] Beginning in the 1950s it lavishly funded university research in mathematical economics. Military planners believed that game theory and linear programming had potential use for national defence. And, although it now seems ridiculous, they held out the same hope for mathematical solutions of 'general equilibrium', the theoretical core of neoclassical economics.

In 1954 Kenneth Arrow and Gerard Debreu achieved for this mathematical puzzle a solution of sorts, and it has been the central showpiece of academic economics ever since. Arrow's early research had been partly, in his words, 'carried on at the RAND Corporation, a project of the United States Air Force'.[4] In the 1960s, official publications of the Department of Defence praised the Arrow–Debreu project for its 'modelling of conflict and cooperation whether if be [for] combat or procurement contracts or exchange of information among dispersed decision nodes'. In 1965, RAND created a fellowship programme for economics graduate students at the Universities of California, Harvard, Stanford, Yale, Chicago, Columbia and Princeton, and in addition provided postdoctoral funds for those who best fitted the mould. These seven economics departments, along with that of MIT, an institution long regarded by many as a branch of the Pentagon, have subsequently come to dominate economics globally to an astonishing extent. Two examples will show what I mean.

The *American Economic Review* (*AER*), the *Quarterly Journal of Economics* (*QJE*), and the *Journal of Political Economy* (*JPE*) have long been regarded as the world's three most prestigious economics journals; being published in these journals adds the most value to an economist's CV, and does more than anything to help an economics department's ranking and research funding. A study has been made of the affiliation of the authors of full-length articles appearing in these journals from 1973 to 1978.[5] For the *QJE* it found that the eight departments with the most articles were the seven favoured through RAND by the US Department of Defence, and MIT, and that this Big Eight accounted for 77.3 per cent of the articles published. In the *JPE* all of the RAND Seven were in the top ten and, together with MIT, accounted for 63.1 per cent of the articles published. In the *AER* the top eight contributing departments were again the RAND Seven plus MIT, which together accounted for 59.3 per cent of the articles published. Even within this Big Eight there was an astonishing concentration of success. In the *QJE*, which is controlled by Harvard, 33.3 per cent of the articles were by Harvard-affiliated authors. In the *JPE*, controlled by Chicago, 20.7 per cent of the articles were by Chicago-affiliated authors. In the *AER*, nearly half of whose editorial board during these years was from, in rank order, Chicago, MIT and Harvard, 14.0, 10.7 and 7.1 per cent of the articles were by authors from these departments respectively. About 70 per cent of the board members were from the Big Eight, as were nearly 60 per cent of the members of the nominating committees for officers. As Canterbery and Burkhardt argue, it is unsurprising that these departments are seen as 'distinguished': 'The "best" departments are those who publish in their own journals, which are "best" since they publish the "best" departments.' As they comment, this academic incest would be considered genetically unsound if it involved biological reproduction (p. 28).

A glance through the 2003 edition of Penguin's *Dictionary of Economics* illustrates the accentuated continuation of this tiny all-powerful closed shop. The dictionary has entries for 29 living economists. Of these, 26 – 89.7 per cent – are from the US, or have spent all or the most important part of their careers there. Think about that: 26 for one country and three for the rest of world. And that is in a British publication by a team of three British authors. And what are the affiliations of the 26 US economists? All of them have either taught at or received their PhD from one of the Big Eight.

The post-autistic economics movement

In Paris in June 2000, a group of economics students wrote a short petition (see Appendix I) lambasting their curriculum and stating what they wanted instead. They passed their document among friends and posted it on the web. To everyone's amazement, especially the students, their little protest has turned out to be a tipping point of sorts. Like the late Soviet Union, mainstream economics is caught in a time warp, and when reality catches up with such worlds the events that follow nearly always take everybody by surprise.

There was a bit of conceptual genius at work in the French students' petition. For 40 years most critiques of economics had been filtered through sets of ideas such as Popperian falsification, Kuhnian paradigms, Lakatosian research programmes and related notions. The students' petition ignored all that. Instead it assailed mainstream economics for failing to illuminate most of economic reality (hence the term 'autistic'), and identified the causes as the establishment's commitment to viewing the world only through the narrow neoclassical point of view; its prohibition of critical thinking towards that system of belief; and its preoccupation with meaningless formalism. The solution was simple and realizable if given the political will: dump most of the maths, drop the prohibition on critical thinking and introduce 'a plurality of approaches adapted to the complexity of objects analysed'.

The students were making a major epistemological point – they may not have realised it but their mentor Bernard Guerrien must have done. They were breaking with the previous century's philosophy of science (which had included its application to economics), which had preoccupied itself with situations of transition – transition between theories that highlighted the same aspects of some corner of reality, but offered different conclusions and agendas. Thus Karl Popper's *The Logic of Scientific Discovery* argued for falsification as the ideal and operative criteria for change of theory allegiance; others, most notably Imre Lakatos and Thomas Kuhn, argued for other criteria. The epistemological concern of the French students is a fundamentally different one. They have identified a situation in which one theory illuminates a few facets of a domain, while its practitioners suppress other theories that illuminate some of the many facts that their theory leaves in the dark. In such a situation the solution is not abandonment of a theory or research programme, or a paradigm shift, but pluralism.

The history of economics is diverse, but the idea of pluralism is nevertheless anathema to economists. Beginning with the French Physiocrats in the mid eighteenth-century, economists of all varieties have been inclined to believe that their approach to economic phenomena reveals, if not the whole truth, at least all of it that is worth knowing. It is with these broad conceptualisations, which are called 'schools', rather than with subject areas, that economists form their primary professional identity. The assorted teachings and members of these schools are labelled orthodox or heterodox depending on whether their school is the dominant one or not. Until very recently economists of all varieties have been comfortable with this quasi-theological scheme of things.

The French students asked that their economics education be oriented primarily toward understanding the world's economic problems (globalization, inequalities, environment, technical progress, and so on). Any 'school's' teaching would be welcome to the extent that it threw light on the real world. Likewise, implicitly, a school's members would not be welcome if they did not place the pursuit of empirical understanding ahead of the inculcation of articles of faith. Furthermore, and this is extremely important, the inclusion of different 'schools', with their different conceptual viewpoints, would neutralise the ideological implications that every conceptual system, by design or accident, contains. No strong precedent existed for this demand, and its novelty, coupled with its self-evident reasonableness, came as a shock for economists, orthodox and heterodox alike.

Traditionally non-neoclassical schools of economics have quarrelled among themselves as much as with the neoclassical. But in the mid-1990s a peace movement began. Under the banner ICARE (Confederation of Associations for the Reform of Economics) (later changed to ICAPE, with 'pluralism' substituted for 'reform'), it sought 'to promote a new spirit of pluralism in economics, involving critical conversation and tolerant communication among different approaches'. ICAPE's pluralism in the mode of a council of churches was several giant steps away from what the French students were proposing, but it helped to decontaminate the p-word and breakdown blind acceptance of the simplistic Popperian and Kuhnian 'us-or-them' notions of science. So when the *Post-Autistic Economics Newsletter* (now *Review*) spread the ideas of the French students through the profession internationally, these ideas fell on partially prepared ground.

The speed with which the free electronic *PAE Newsletter/Review* picked up subscribers and became a focal point for the radical reform of economics surprised everyone, especially its editor. Nor does the momentum show signs of decreasing. The journal now has nearly 10,000 subscribers, mostly academics but also many economists employed in other capacities. Its website - www.paecon.net – receives 19,000 visitors a month.

Policy implications

The neoclassical monopoly in the classroom and its prohibition on critical thinking has meant that it has brainwashed successive generations of students into viewing economic reality exclusively through its concepts, which more often than not misrepresent or veil the world, especially today's world. Nearly all of these neoclassical notions have a bearing on judgements about social, cultural and economic policy. Consequently, if society were to learn to think about economic matters outside the neoclassical conceptual system, it would almost certainly choose different policies. One of PAE's projects has been to expose some of the many conceptual lunacies of today's mainstream, both in terms of the concepts it uses and the concepts it lacks. Drawing on recent essays by PAE economists in *A Guide to What's Wrong with Economics* (especially the chapters by Michael A. Bernstein, Geoffrey Hodgson, Peter Söderbaum, Hugh Stretton, Richard Wolff, Robert Costanza, Herman E Daly, Jean Gadrey and myself), I am briefly going to consider some of these concepts.[6]

Neoclassical economics regards *competition* as a state rather than as a process. It defines perfect competition as a market with a large number of firms with *identical* products, costs structures, production techniques and market information. But in real life, competition is a process by which firms continually seek to re-establish the conditions of their own profitability. To compete in a market requires firms to seek out and exploit differences between themselves and their competitors in production, technology, distribution, access to information and awareness of trends in consumption. These differences are the essential dimensions in which competition takes place. However, once the neoclassical conception of competition becomes embedded in the student's mind, appreciation of real-world competition, and hence the policies that might enhance it, becomes logically impossible.

Neoclassical economists love to talk about *freedom of choice*. But this is pure rhetoric, because they define rationality in a way that eliminates free choice from their conceptual space. By rationality they mean that an agent's choices are in conformity with an ordering or scale of preferences. The 'rational' agent chooses from among the alternatives available the one that is highest on his ranking. Rational behaviour simply means behaviour in accordance with some ordering of alternatives in terms of relative desirability. In order for this approach to have any predictive power, it must be assumed that the preferences do not change over some period of time. So the basic condition of neoclassical rationality is that individuals must *forego* choice in favour of some past reckoning, thereafter acting as automata. This conceptual elimination of freedom of choice, in both its everyday and philosophical meanings, gives neoclassical theory the hypothetical determinacy that its Newtonian inspired metaphysics requires. Without indeterminacy, there can be no choice. Without determinacy, there is no neoclassical model. This is far from just an academic matter, because society needs an economics that is able to address questions regarding freedom of choice.

No terms in neoclassical economics are more sacrosanct than *rational choice* and *rationality*. Everyone identifies with these words, because everyone wants to think of themselves as rational. But few people realise that economists give these words an ultra-eccentric meaning. Neoclassical economics begins with an *a priori* conception of markets and economies as determinate systems that, by the action of individual agents alone, tend towards an efficient and market-clearing equilibrium. This requires that the individual agents, like the bodies in Newton's system, behave in a prescribed manner. Neoclassicists have then gone on to deduce the particular pattern of behaviour that would make their imagined world logically possible, and named it 'rational choice' or 'rationality'; they have then declared that that is the way real people behave. But, thankfully, they don't. Everyday economic actors do many things that, in the neoclassical meaning of 'rational', are 'irrational'. Many common consumer behaviours are prohibited under the neoclassical notions of rational choice and rationality, including: looking to the choices of other consumers as guides to what one might buy; buying a stock because you believe other people will be buying it and so increasing its value; spending your money in a spirit of spontaneity rather than stopping to calculate the consequences and alternatives up to the limits of your cognitive powers; indulging a taste for change, that is, buying something that you did not previously prefer. All these actions are considered outside the scope of analysis of neoclassical economics.

These failings all connect with another. This is because neoclassical economics is by its own axioms incapable of offering a coherent conceptualisation of the *individual* or *economic agent*. It cannot explain the source of the preferences that supposedly dictate the individual's choice. The preferences cannot be explained through interpersonal relations, because if individual demands were interdependent they would not be additive, and thus the market demand function – neoclassicalism's key analytical tool – would be undefined. And they cannot come from society, because neoclassicalism's Newtonian atomism translates as methodological individualism, meaning that society is always to be explained in terms of individuals and never the other way around.

This leaves many things unexplained. For in the main, despite the neoclassical axioms, we all tend to categorise and classify according to prevailing cultural norms. Likewise our tastes and preferences for this and that reflect the social conventions and institutions with which we interact. Consequently individual choice is unavoidably and inextricably bound up with historically and geographically given social worlds. An economics that has nothing to say about the formation of economic tastes and preferences is silly and irresponsible, especially in an age of consumer societies, and in a world now threatened with climate change or worse.

For half a century, neoclassical economics has hidden its ideology behind the notion that it calls *positive economics*. This is the idea that it contains no value judgements because it mentions none. Of course such a notion belongs to an intellectually more naive age than today, but it nonetheless persists as an effective tool to indoctrinate undergraduates. The fact that neoclassical economics requires a highly restricted focus in order to maintain its atomist and determinist metaphysics compels it to make many extreme judgements about what is and is not economically important. There is not space here even to list them. But one key example is its notion of 'economic man': an acutely ideological term, as it emphasizes some roles and relationships and excludes others; by allowing only decisions based on utility maximization, it excludes other forms of ethics. As an economic agent, each individual acts in many roles, not just market ones, and is guided by his or her 'ideological orientation'. That orientation may be founded on utilitarianism, or it may not. It may, for example, be based on social and environmental ethics. PAE economists do not believe that economists have the right to select one form of ethics as the 'correct' one for framing economic analysis. Furthermore, the neoclassical insistence upon the utilitarian ideology legitimises a kind of 'market ideology' and 'consumerism' that increasingly appears dangerous to society, and sidelines the debate about sustainable development.

Like rationality, nearly everyone thinks *efficiency* is a good idea. Neoclassical economists adore using this word, especially when addressing the public. But the meaning of 'efficiency' always depends on what you choose to count. For example, suppose five firms all manage to lower by the same amounts the production cost and selling price of a standard product that they all produce. One does it by cutting its workers' pay, another by working them longer hours, another by getting materials at lower prices from a poorer country, another by replacing some of its workers with robots, and another by inventing machinery improvements that allow it to cut work hours with no loss of output, profit, jobs or pay. Are all of these changes equally efficient (or inefficient)? A neoclassical economist will answer yes, because the five firms all end up producing the same product at the same cost and selling it at the same price. For them, that is all that matters.

The prevailing mainstream also holds that in the realm of public affairs this concept of 'efficiency' can and should determine the net balance between the positives (total benefits) and negatives (total costs) that would result from an economic policy or act. In place of public debate, economists would substitute 'cost–benefit analysis'. But any such analysis depends on the consequences selected and the kinds of 'measurements' made. No efficiency claim is ever based on an identification of all the consequences, and quantitative guesstimates of the future inevitably have a crystal-ball dimension. In the final analysis, 'efficient', like 'beautiful', is little more than a way of expressing a positive opinion.

Mainstream economics, and in consequence most policy dialogue, also conflates two very different meanings of *economic growth* that are in common usage, with GNP mistakenly taken to be a measure of both. There is *quantitative growth*, meaning an increase in the quantity of production and consumption, and there is *qualitative growth*, meaning an improvement in well-being. For example, an epidemic may lead to growth of medical expenditure and hence increase GNP at the cost of well-being. Pollution and congestion lead to huge expenditures to escape them (e.g. commuting from the suburbs, double glazing, air filters, security measures), the creation of new industries and an ever-larger GNP, but they also decrease well-being. Quantitative growth that causes negative qualitative growth can also be called *uneconomic growth*. This is both a reality and a concept with which policy-makers must come to terms, the sooner the better.

Closely related to these new anti-neoclassical concepts is another one, *sustainable development*. This refers to the physical scale of the economy relative to the ecosystem. Ecological economists view the economy as an open subsystem of the larger ecosystem which is finite, non-growing and, except for solar energy, materially closed. This point of view compels asking questions regarding scale. How large is the economic subsystem relative to the earth's ecosystem? What is its maximum possible size? What is its most desirable size in terms of human welfare? These questions, around which policy decisions will and must increasingly be made, are not found in standard economics textbooks. Neoclassical economics cannot accommodate the concept of sustainable development, because, if it was adopted as a goal it would require that goods be valued in part by their contribution to that goal and not solely on their contribution to individual utility maximization.

The position of neoclassical economics is close to monopoly and thus incompatible with normal ideas of democracy. Economics has some of the qualities of a science, but because of the very nature of its subject matter, it is forever and fundamentally ideological. It is best not to deceive oneself and others about this. The preoccupation of economics with values and worldly acts means that in a democratic society it has a moral responsibility to promote the exploration of economic knowledge from more than one point of view, so as to make possible the informed and intelligent debate and discussion that democracy requires. But the hegemony of neoclassical economics means that departments of economics have become political propaganda centres. In 2002, Joseph Stiglitz, a recent winner of the Nobel Prize for Economics, wrote in *The Guardian* that economics as taught 'in America's graduate schools … bears testimony to a triumph of ideology over science'. Is this a legitimate use of public funds? What is certain is that it is a dangerous state of affairs, but one that is now being challenged. The PAE movement immodestly seeks over the next 10 years a revolution: the transformation of economics into a genuinely pluralistic enterprise wishing to contribute to, rather than subvert, democratic processes. The success of this movement depends in part on other disciplines and professions withdrawing their patronage from the neoclassical hegemony, in favour of the now thousands of economists working for the new order.

Notes

1. Thorstein Veblen, 'Why is economics not an evolutionary science?', *Quarterly Journal of Economics*, Vol. 12, 1898, p. 373.
2. Geoffrey M Hodgson, *How Economics Forgot History*, Routledge 2001, p. 155.
3. This paragraph draws heavily on Michael A Bernstein, 'Rethinking Economics in Twentieth-Century America', in Edward Fullbrook (ed.), *The Crisis in Economics*, Routledge 2003.
4. Kenneth Arrow, *Collected Papers of Kenneth J. Arrow: Volume 1: Social Choice and Justice*, Harvard University Press 1983, p. 1.
5. E Ray Canterbery and Robert J Burkhardt, 'What do we mean by asking whether economics is a science?', in Alfred S Eichner (ed.), *Why Economics Is Not Yet a Science*, Macmillan 1983.
6. Edward Fullbrook (ed.), *A Guide to What's Wrong with Economics*, Anthem Press 2004.

2.

THE SOCIAL AND INTELLECTUAL ORGANIZATION AND CONSTRUCTION OF ECONOMICS

Kyle Siler[1]

Many of the articles published in outlets friendly to heterodox approaches to economics focus on challenging and/or refuting mainstream economic theory[i]. This tacitly serves as a means of precipitating further thought about economics, and in most cases, also functions as a means of promoting change in the discipline and beyond. However, as evidenced by history, be it the notion that the Earth revolves around the Sun, the double-helix model of DNA (see Watson, 1969), or the hegemony of mainstream neoclassical economics today, merely having innovative or possibly better ideas does not necessarily equate with the ability to establish immediate scientific and societal acceptance of those ideas, or make widely accepted truth claims.

Stephen Cole (1992) bridges a long-standing fissure in science studies and the sociology of science between constructivists and non-constructivists by arguing that all sciences are comprised of both socially-constructed and scientific components. It follows that economics should be no different. Hence, understanding, harnessing or changing economics will be a social process, in addition to being a scientific one.

My account of the social and scientific construction of economics is largely derived from British sociologist Richard Whitley's (1984) seminal work, *The Social and Intellectual Organization of the Sciences*. The crux of Whitley's argument is that in addition to what they study empirically, scientific fields are shaped and affected by the degrees and types of *mutual dependence* and *task uncertainty* they possess. In other words, the things economists study and the tools they use to examine them influence the organization of the discipline, and vice versa. The next two sections will explain how these characteristics exist and function in mainstream neoclassical economics.

Mutual Dependence

Whitley (ibid, p. 88) broadly defined *mutual dependence* as "…the need to adhere to particular standards of competence and criteria of significance in order to reward important reputations for contributions." More specifically, mutual dependence is comprised of two analytically distinct agents: *functional* and *strategic* dependence. Economics has high *functional dependence*, as economists generally have to adhere to a dominant neoclassical strategic paradigm to be taken seriously in the mainstream of the discipline. Conversely, it also has low *strategic dependence*, as owing to this consensus, economists generally spend little time arguing over theoretical issues. Hence, many debates about the theoretical and philosophical underpinnings of economics occur outside mainstream economic forums (such as is the case with the *Post-Autistic Economics Review*).

Whitley (ibid, p. 31) also adds: "Intellectual fields must have distinctive work procedures if they are to function as reputational work organizations." These distinctive work procedures set the context for self-conscious and self-regulating colleague groups being based "on their power to validate the expertise, and thus mediate the careers of, members" (ibid, p. 20). The arcane and esoteric mathematical nature of neoclassical economics is a powerful context, contributing to a very strong, unified organizational discipline, thus influencing both the profession and "science" of economics. Mathematics is not only an effective means of creating scholarly hierarchies, but also makes economic work difficult to comment on (at least in the mainstream economists' domain and language) for those outside the discipline and economists with less mathematical and technical virtuosity.

Further, the many theoretical quirks and idiosyncratic uses of mathematics that characterize mainstream economics also render it difficult for other mathematically-inclined scientists to fully comprehend it. This places control over the discipline largely in the hands of the most advanced mathematical economists, while insulating and empowering the discipline as a whole. It is also the epitome of what Thomas Gieryn (1983) dubbed *boundary work* as a means of demarcating "science" from "non-science". Social and cultural norms which value abstractness, theoretical complexity, esoteric science and quantification also help make economics trusted, well-supported and respected. As Andrew Abbott noted (1988, p. 16),

> [P]rofessions often legitimate themselves by attaching their expertise to values with general cultural legitimacy – increasingly those of rationality, efficiency and science. Hence, having a theoretical and professional core characterized by esoteric abstractions allows mainstream economics to derive rents from employment, scientific and intellectual closure, in addition to benefits from espousing rhetorical and theoretical devices that are commonly seen as "legitimate" and tend to receive deference in modern societies.

As mutual dependence (which is the basis for much of economics' power and prestige) increases, local and individual circumstances tend to become irrelevant, and become the turf of less prestigious economists, academics and fields. Espeland and Stevens (1998) offer the concept of *commensuration* to describe this cognitive (and arguably, social) process. Commensuration is defined as the transformation of different qualities into a common metric. The mathematization of social phenomena is an archetypal example of this. Commensuration has the potential of integrating disparate interests groups and phenomena. Thus, it can be seen as a form of organization, even if it is only implicit and cognitive. However, it may also underpin critiques of economics (and often, science in general) that claim it ignores and marginalizes the experiences of certain groups and places in society. Class (as in Wolff and Resnick, 1987) and gender-based (as in Ferber and Nelson, 1993) perspectives are the most common sources of these critiques. Hence, it is not surprising that economics tends to privilege abstract thought, shunning context and historically dependent work.

There are a number of additional factors that are indicative of the high mutual dependence in economics. These include:

- The existence of a relatively small, concentrated, theoretical disciplinary core of economists.
- Inimicality and/or ignorance of cross-disciplinary, pluralistic and heterodox thought (see Klamer and Colander, 1990).
- Agreed hierarchies of competence and knowledge.
- Insulation from the lay public and most other academics.
- The existence of a Nobel Prize, which serves to galvanize the discipline, and confer significant prestige upon economics as a whole in the public perception, and upon the winning economists, who tend to further perpetuate the prevailing orthodoxy.

It is difficult to ascertain whether these characteristics are causes and/or effects of high mutual dependence (or each other). Regardless, this complex interweaving of social characteristics is a significant factor contributing to the power, scope, autonomy and legitimacy of neoclassical economics today.

Economics and Task Uncertainty

The social sciences are generally characterized by a greater degree of task uncertainty than most of the natural sciences. Laboratory controls and manipulation of research subjects are rarely viable options in social science research. Economists cannot manipulate the behaviour and social and historical contexts of governments, firms and actors in various contexts in order to test and re-test hypotheses about economies.[ii] Whitley (1984, p. 120) observes that "… the more paradigm-bound a field is, the more predictable, visible and replicable are research results, and the more limited is permissible novelty". Hence, the degree of task uncertainty in a field is influenced by a socially constructed component, via the social organization of a given discipline, as distinct from empirical, data-based, or so-called scientific considerations.

Whitley (ibid, Chapter 4) identifies three major contextual factors that influence task uncertainty.

Reputational Autonomy – Reputational autonomy alludes to the degree to which a given field can adjudicate standards of quality and worthiness without influences from other interests. As per Abbott (1988), the ability of a profession to monitor and control the content and membership of its intellectual turf is vital to its empowerment in the larger, overarching competitive system of professions. Mainstream economics is empowered with a very high degree of reputational autonomy. For example, while the government and the lay public are generally unwilling (or unable) to engage in dialogue with academic economists on their own terms, they are willing to be amateur sociologists on such issues as inequality and culture. In other words, economics receives a disproportionate amount of deference from within and inside academia. Further, while some social science departments are prone to being subsumed by topical or interdisciplinary studies in universities, economists are generally immune. In addition, when economists do participate in interdisciplinary work (e.g. for governments), they usually do so "on their terms", often as atheoretical data miners and crunchers with scarce quantitative skills, credentials and cultural legitimacy from their professional status. "Peripheral" economists enjoy these benefits, despite being divorced from the abstract core of the discipline.

Concentration over the means of intellectual production and dissemination − Economics has relatively high concentration in journals, paradigmatic thought, prestige and universities. This is in part results from (or contributes to) its aforementioned high reputational autonomy. As an example of the degree of concentration of intellectual production in the United States, Pieper and Willis (1999: p. 86) show that 54 per cent of economics faculty at doctoral universities, and more than two-thirds of the thesis supervisors at the 47 top-ranked programmes in the US, come from one of the "top ten" schools. These schools include Chicago, Harvard, Stanford, and MIT, which are of course among the strongest purveyors of highly mathematical neoclassical economics. As Devine (2001) observed, the more famous the university, journal or student, the more likely they are to adhere to the rigid positivism of neoclassical economics. The degree of control these schools have over economic education is well evidenced by a report done by the Commission on Graduate Education in Economics in the United States, which concluded: "The content and structure of graduate programmes is amazingly similar" (Hansen, 1991: p. 1085).

Audience Plurality and Diversity − Economics has relatively low audience plurality and diversity, largely due to the practice of conducting esoteric, mathematical research published in academic journals kept largely away from public scrutiny. Economists seldom write books, and if they are written in a publicly accessible fashion, they are often derided as "lacking rigour", or as "Galbraithism" (as a slight against the eminent Harvard economist who was (in)famous for often writing in a publicly accessible manner). Further, academic economics is also shielded by the fact that most public economic debate occurs outside the academic sphere, far removed from the behavioural assumptions and arcane analyses couched in powerful academic economics journals, and textbooks. This will shortly be discussed further.

All of the above factors, which are all social factors to some extent, serve to reduce the perceived task uncertainty. This is despite the fact that economics operates in the often complex, contextual realms of the human sciences. This apparent contradiction will be explored in the next section.

Economics as a Partitioned Bureaucracy

Economics is extremely unusual in academia in that it combines the high technical task uncertainty of the social sciences, with very low strategic task uncertainty. Whitley (1984, p. 181) states that this mix should be highly unstable *unless the central core of conceptual orthodoxy is partitioned away from empirical sources of uncertainty*. Hence, privileging theoretical data (informed by the central core), at the expense of empirical considerations is a necessary condition for maintaining strategic consensus in the discipline.

Mainstream economics does exactly that. As in many facets of economics, there is a clear hierarchy (made possible by high mutual dependence) of sub-fields in economics, with the more theoretical endeavours enjoying epistemological, and organizational superiority. This occurs both within and outside economics. Within economics, econometrics, labour, and health economics, and other relatively applied work remains subordinated to, and to a certain extent, derivative of the dominant paradigm, couched in the theoretical core of the discipline. This also appears to be indicative of Abbott's (1988) thesis that professional groups use abstraction as a means of protecting and amassing intellectual turf and power, in addition to professional prestige. Doing applied, or socially relevant work is acceptable to mainstream economists, provided one does not use their experiences in the applied realm to question the theoretical core. Accordingly, as would be expected in Whitley's partitioned bureaucracy, most "applied" economic work is atheoretical.

Outside economics, much applied or context-dependent work is actually done in lower status economics departments, in business/finance and social science departments in universities, and by businesses and governments outside academia. In the case of business and finance departments using economic theory, there appears to be somewhat of a symbiotic relationship, where applied economists (who may for example, work in professional schools, government agencies or business) use neoclassical economics for methodological and moral legitimacy. In return, the theoretical core of economics is insulated from empirical concerns, uncertainties and contingencies that could undermine their strategic consensus, or at least reveal anomalies that could call the dominant orthodoxy into question. This symbiotic relationship also may help contribute to maintaining (if not reinforcing) the "bourgeois" focus of mainstream economics (which may or may not be intentional), which tends to trumpet the virtues of capitalism more than it criticizes the economic, social and moral shortcomings it may possess.

Concluding Thoughts

John Kenneth Galbraith (1984: 3) remarked that the shortcomings of contemporary economics are not necessarily due to original error, but "uncorrected obsolescence". Given the intricate tapestry of social, empirical, and organizational factors buttressing mainstream economics today, it is little wonder that the neoclassical paradigm and the economics profession is not opening itself up to different viewpoints, philosophies or epistemologies.

Much of the work by heterodox economists and other critics of mainstream economics illustrates many of the excellent ideas and debates that at the very least, call into question the dominant economic paradigm both in theory and in practice. However, as Kuhn (1962) made clear, merely being right scientifically is not necessarily sufficient by itself to significantly modify a discipline, especially one as powerful and entrenched as economics. A cognizance of the interplay between the social and intellectual underpinnings of economics is valuable because it not only helps explain why mainstream economics is so powerful, but also how it can remain so in the face of often inconsistent empirical evidence from the "real world".

Although I cannot profess to know the best strategy for improving economics, knowledge of the social construction of science and economics should be a vital part of constructing any such strategy. As opposition to mainstream neoclassical economics burgeons, it should be kept in mind by such dissenting groups that scientific change is not entirely a scientific endeavour. This could aid the construction of strategies for social and scientific change, both in academic and lived realms, as they are all inexorably linked.

Note

i   The post-autistic economics movement appears to be an example of what Frickel and Gross (2005) dubbed Scientific/Intellectual Movements (SIMs).

ii   This limitation also characterizes the natural sciences to varying degrees, particularly biology.

References

Abbott, Andrew (1988), *The System of Professions: An Essay on the Division of Expert Labor*. Chicago: University of Chicago Press.

Cole, Stephen (1992), *Making Science: Between Nature and Society*, Cambridge: Harvard University Press.

Devine, James G (2002), 'Psychological Autism, Institutional Autism and Economics', *Post-Autistic Economics Review*, 16, 16 September, article 2 http://www.btinternet.com/~paenews/review/issue16.htm.

Espeland, Wendy N and Mitchell L Stevens (1998), 'Commensuration as a social process', *Annual Review of Sociology*, 24, 313–43.

Ferber, Marianne A and Julie A Nelson (eds) (1993), *Beyond Economic Man: Feminist Theory and Economics*, Chicago: University of Chicago Press.

Frickel, Scott and Neil Gross, 'A general theory of scientific/intellectual movements', *American Sociological Review*, 70, 204–32, 2005.

Galbraith, John Kenneth (1984), *The Affluent Society*, 4th edn, Boston: Houghton Mifflin.

Gieryn, Thomas F (1983), 'Boundary-work and the demarcation of science', *American Sociological Review*, 48, 781–95.

Hansen, W L (1991), 'The education and training of economics doctorates: major findings of the American Economics Association commission on graduate education in economics', *Journal of Economic Literature*, 31 (3), pp. 1054–87.

Klamer, Arjo and David Colander (1990), *The Making of an Economist*, Boulder, CO: Westview Press.

Kuhn, Thomas (1962), *The Structure of Scientific Revolutions*, Chicago: University of Chicago Press.

Pieper, Paul J and Willis, Rachel A (1999), 'The doctoral origins of economics faculty and the education of new economics doctorates', *Journal of Economic Education*, pp. 80–89, Winter.

Watson, James D, (1969) *The Double Helix: A Personal Account of the Discovery of the Structure of DNA*, New York: Atheneum.

Whitley, Richard (1984), *The Social and Intellectual Organization of the Sciences*, Oxford: Oxford University Press.

Wolff, Richard and Stephen A Resnick (1987), *Economics: Marxian versus Neoclassical*, Baltimore, MD: Johns Hopkins University Press.

3.

PSYCHOLOGICAL AUTISM, INSTITUTIONAL AUTISM AND ECONOMICS*

James G Devine

As an economist with a son having heavy autistic leanings, the discussion of the "autistic economics" quickly caught my attention. I had never thought of the economics profession or its neoclassical orthodoxy as "autistic." I think that this way of thinking can be useful, at least as a preliminary step, allowing the economics profession eventually to transcend autism. But as with all analogies, we must examine not only the similarities between autism and orthodox economics, but also the differences.

The autism spectrum

As a layperson interested in psychology, I have reached a preliminary understanding of autism, based on others' research and on discussions with other parents of autistic or semi-autistic children. "Autistic disorder" is a social communication disorder and a developmental delay, involving "restricted, repetitive, and stereotyped patterns of behaviour, interests, and activities."[1] I interpret this constellation of symptoms as being the result of an organically-based (neurobiological) sensory-processing problem which is much like the opposite of being deaf. Instead of hearing too little, a person with autism may hear *too much*, and be unable to filter out the noise or to prioritize the information received to make it intelligible. The external stimuli that most treat as normal seem to be a constant barrage of blackboard chalk scraping the wrong way. Not surprisingly, an autistic person slams hands over his or her ears, trying to shut out the meaningless cacophony. Alas, for that person, information overload occurs not simply with sound, but with the other commonly-known senses (sight, taste, smell, touch), along with proprioception (the sense of movement through space) and the vestibular sense (understanding one's own body's internal signals). So folks with autism tend to not only shut out external stimuli, but also to be extremely anxious and physically uncoordinated, and communicate poorly with others.

Just as with "neurotypical" individuals (that is, many or most of those reading this book),[2] each person with autism or autistic tendencies is unique. Different individuals with autistic problems have different combinations of these sensory-processing difficulties, so that one may be better than another at screening sounds than at prioritizing and understanding visual information – and so forth. Some, but far from all, compensate for processing problems in one sphere with genius in another, as with cinema's *Rainman*. There are also degrees to which the whole neurobiological package hits an individual – and the amount of emotional or intellectual resources she or he has to resist impairment. Thus, professionals write of the "autistic spectrum," the continuum from hard-core autism to high-functioning autism, to Asperger's syndrome or borderline autism (*AS*), to the loner mentality so common among professors, accountants, and computer specialists.[3]

In terms of behaviour, folks on the autism spectrum tend to be isolated from the world; have troubles with communication with others; engage in repetitive body movements; insist on sameness, repetition, and routine; and seem to treat others as objects.[4] Those with *AS* have been described as follows:

> Persons with *AS* show marked deficiencies in social skills, have difficulties with transitions or changes and prefer sameness. They often have obsessive routines and may be preoccupied with a particular subject of interest. They have a great deal of difficulty reading nonverbal cues (body language) and very often the individual with *AS* has difficulty determining proper body space. Often overly sensitive to sounds, tastes, smells, and sights, the person with *AS* may prefer soft clothing, certain foods, and be bothered by sounds or lights no one else seems to hear or see.[5]

This is just a partial list of symptoms, but the general idea is clear: people with autism have a hard time doing anything but to live inside their heads, no matter how friendly the social environment is.

It is not surprising, therefore, that one autistic mother that I know had to explain to her two autistic children that there was something "out there" called "society" which had norms and mores which they had to learn and obey. Those on the spectrum instinctively see Baroness Thatcher's dictum that there is no society, only individuals,[6] as self-evident.

Autism and economics

The orthodox economist's *a priori* agreement with Thatcher's assertion – its commitment to methodological individualism – suggests that the textbook *homo economicus* (*HE*) might be autistic. For example, as with *HE*, autistic individuals often have preferences that are little shaped by their social environments (or at least seem that way to frustrated parents or partners).[7] But there are major differences. First, unlike in the case of neurotypicals or *HE*, information-processing problems are extremely important to autism, as with Herbert Simon's "bounded rationality." Second, just as with neurotypicals but unlike *HE*, people with autism have consciences, are torn by inner mental and emotional conflicts, and often want to connect socially with other human beings, if they can.[8]

Instead of being autistic, *HE* is more robotic or cybernetic in nature. The use of this kind of one-dimensional "man" in theoretical work is appropriate to a profession suffering from "institutional autism" (see below). Someone with autism is likely to treat other human beings as if they were furniture or automatons. Put another way, like those with autism, the economics profession's dominant vision lacks a "theory of mind." This means that, like autistic individuals, those who employ *HE* as a theoretical concept "do not understand that other people have their own plans, thoughts, and points of view ... [and] have difficulty understanding other people's beliefs, attitudes, and emotions."[9]

Turn now, before any analysis of their etiology, to other specific "autistic" symptoms of the profession. The original statements by the rebellious French economics students[10] define autistic economics in terms of its one-sided and exclusionary interest in "imaginary worlds" (as opposed to empirical study), "uncontrolled use of mathematics" (as an end in itself rather than merely as a tool), and the absence of pluralism of approaches in economics (the monopoly of the neoclassical approach).

The first two of these characteristics seem at first to fit with the idea of autism. Indeed, they merge into one symptom in many cases, since mathematics almost always portrays an idealized and thus imaginary world.[11] However, there is a major difference from autism here: many folks with autism have difficulty with abstract thought, since they are overwhelmed by the concrete details of life. While the focus on an imaginary internal world is an obvious result of autism, the use of abstraction should be seen instead as a *defence mechanism* against the confusion arising from the blooming, buzzing, confusing concreteness of the empirical world.

The third characteristic – a tendency for a single paradigm to dominate – seems to fit well with an autistic person's rigidity and desire for sameness, expressed as a preference for clear simple answers rather than intellectual debate or critical thinking. However, it does not explain why neoclassical economics – which includes methodological individualism and the focus on *HE* – is the prevalent orthodoxy. Nor does this list of "symptoms" say anything about treatment. So the profession must be described.

An autistic profession?

It would be a mistake to apply the psychological description of autism to economics in an unvarnished way. Even though high-functioning autistic people are often attracted to academia, where they can lecture others without listening, engage in research alone, and develop beautiful mind pictures, it is hard to say that a majority – or even a large minority – of economists have autistic tendencies. Individuals on the autistic spectrum do not have to specialize in economics to succeed in academia since there are other outlets for expression of their proclivities besides economic theory.[12] Being able to "work well with others" helps one achieve success in academia, as in most spheres, so that those with autistic tendencies would need to be very smart or to work very hard to compensate for social skills deficits. In sum, self-selection can only be one part of the basis for autistic economics.

More profoundly, it would be a mistake to apply an autistic person's own highly individualistic perspective, i.e. seeing "economics" as a simple aggregation of isolated economists. Instead, the economics profession is an institution, spawning a collective product and should thus be analysed in a sociological or social-psychological (institutionalist) way. The profession trains people to accept autistic assumptions (and attracts those who do so already) and rewards them for doing so. Thus, the autistic aspect of the field involves more than the sum of its parts.

Again delaying a full discussion of the basis for this institutional autism, it must be stressed that the French students' summary does not apply exactly to the empirical world. As with psychological autism, there is a spectrum.

The hard-core autistic walling-off from the societal environment can be seen most strongly in the specific, highly abstract, axiomatic, or "Bourbakist," school that the students protested against.[13] Further down the spectrum toward "normal," the approach of only dealing with the world by lecturing or dictating to it (as with Asperger's syndrome) can be seen with the International Monetary Fund, which applies the same preconceived vision of the ideal market system (and the same neo-liberal set of policy imperatives) to every country it encounters. At the other end of the spectrum, there are all sorts of economists who work for government, business, foundations, and even labour unions: the fact that these real-world institutions are willing to pay for their contributions indicates that these economists' degree of social connectedness is adequate to the task. They may use abstract math or econometrics, but it would be libelous to apply the autistic tag to these economists.

The existence of a spectrum does not mean that the profession itself lacks institutional autism. The autistic economics of the Bourbakists and their Anglophone counterparts or the IMF and similar organizations define the most prestigious segment of the economics profession, the one that "smart young economists on the rise" wish to emulate. Thus, autistic economics tends to dominate the "big name" departments, along with most professional journals, departments, professional associations and textbooks.

Since much of the socio-institutional basis for the prevalence of autistic economics is shared with other academic fields, the nature of the subject matter must be considered. As a "soft science" dealing with the complexity of human social interaction as participant-observers, economists cannot approach the objectivity – or the ability to attain consensus – of the physical sciences. But economics deals with a much simpler subject matter than does, say, the sociology profession, and thus some hope of consensus arising exists, at least on key issues. That is, economics is in the middle of a spectrum between easily reaching consensus on many issues and being unable to form any consensus. In this context, economists seem to have an autistic drive for sameness – a "physics-envy" wish to imitate the natural sciences' ability to attain consensus. Unlike sociology, for example, they can do so partly by restricting the subject matter to easy topics such as markets and market-like processes, in this way restricting acceptable ways of thinking.

In order to explain physics envy and other autistic symptoms, the profession must be understood as an artificial societal institution, created by people, that has taken on a life of its own partly independent of individual preferences while feeding back to shape those preferences and perspectives. Having roots in medieval guilds, academic institutions such as the economics profession center on a hierarchy topped by "big name" professors, universities, professional associations and journals. Lacking a basis for true scientific objectivity, the identity of these "big names" cannot be decided in the course of academic debate, as in physics. Thus, the existing "big names" ("the insiders" or the "superstars"[14]) select the professors, universities, professional associations, and journals that are to be most influential. Thus, the dominant ideology of the past is perpetuated over time.

Despite the top-down organization of the profession, it would be a mistake to assume that either a monopoly or a conspiracy exists. Competition also plays a role, in which "success" is defined by rising in that hierarchy. In the pyramidal nature of such hierarchies, the rise of one individual toward the top excludes others from such success, so that competition encourages individuals to over-invest time and effort in order to succeed.[15] Departments, associations, journals and textbooks also compete to attain the pinnacle of prestige and power defined by the current in-group.

This system implies a dynamic that perpetuates autistic pathology over time: people at the bottom of the hierarchy are not only trained to think and practice the dominant ideology, but find it in their professional interest to do so whole-heartedly and sincerely. Otherwise, they do not get the desired publications, jobs, promotion, tenure, attention and fame. Those who accept the dominant world view most profoundly are most able to be creative in developing new applications and are seen as *wunderkinder* who can rise to the top. This result is reinforced by self-selection, as the deviants leave the profession or sink into professional backwaters. Of course, those who rise feel they must teach it to those further down the hierarchy (students), since they believe in it and want the students to succeed at the higher levels of a profession they value. Those textbooks (or their conceptions) produced by "big name" economists tend to dominate, while the "winner-take-all" nature of the textbook market limits the number of textbooks available.[16] Finally, the neoclassical approach of excluding critical thinking and intellectual debate makes the task of teaching easier.

The self-referential nature of this system encourages the focus on imaginary worlds, including that of mathematics. The latter also plays a major role because of its use in grading subordinates' success, a crucial part of any hierarchy. It has always been very difficult to judge how hard or well an academic actually works, while such decisions often threaten to become unpleasant political processes. Student course evaluations are almost always inadequate, as is the number or size of a professor's publications (along with the number of times they are cited). But most feel that the quality of her or his mathematical technique can readily be judged. Simultaneously, the ambitious scholar can bemuse the older professors whose mathematical techniques are rusty or out-dated by applying the newest and fanciest methods. Just as we see the prevalence of jargon or obscurantism in other fields, in economics the one-upmanship of academic competition encourages the over-use of mathematics and the embracing of physics envy.

However, the institutional autism of the profession exists in a societal context. The economics profession cannot be understood without stressing its separation from the other social sciences. During the last century or so, the economics profession has defined itself in comparison to other fields. This, along with its self-satisfied sense of mathematical virtue, has encouraged economists to sneer at other specializations (especially sociology), the way the hatters' guild mocked the labourers – or to try to conquer them, as Gary Becker and his school does. Either way, the main flow of information is from economics to other fields, rather than vice-versa. This Asperger-style elitism means that the profession eliminates whole sets of questions and parts of society from analysis, restricting the empirical and theoretical information that economists have to process, adding order to a complex and confusing reality. It allows the economists to maintain their beloved assumptions, however unrealistic.

Of course, the economists' guild exists in a modern capitalist environment, not a medieval one. It must sometimes prove its usefulness to business, government, and other societal institutions, which can threaten to de-fund academic programmes that are totally "irrelevant".[17] This, of course, explains why the dominant form of economics is *neoclassical* (studying idealized markets), just as a different style of economics (one emphasizing planning) prevailed in the old Soviet Union. This role for the societal environment implies that the profession cannot be entirely autistic, just as no individual can be so.

This point is reinforced if we define neoclassical economics. This approach can be seen as involving adherence to (1) mathematical method, with an emphasis on (2) utilitarianism and methodological individualism, (3) equilibrium, (4) naturalism and (5) positivism.[18] Last but hardly least, in the neoclassical ideal (6), all human activity is seen as exchange or as organized by markets, in reality or as an ideal.

In terms of the discussion above, all but one of these may be seen as reflecting the profession's autistic attitudes, at least in part. I have discussed the first two of these above. Moving down the list, the centrality of equilibrium seems a symptom of totally autistic thinking in a society such as capitalism in which endogenously-driven change – sometimes drastic, as with financial crises – is the norm.[19] Related is item (4), the view that human-made institutions such as markets can be reduced to "natural" forces such as individual preferences and technology, in which the complexity and artificiality of human institutions is abstracted from or forgotten. The profession's positivism – its view that value-free research is an achievable ideal, that the observer is unaffected by being a participant in the system, and that serious philosophical reflection is unnecessary – also fits with generally autistic attitudes.

However, the emphasis on markets and exchange – as opposed to other kinds of human institutions such as tradition, democratic cooperation, and hierarchy – clearly reflects the society in which economists live and learn. Though the neoclassical vision of exchange and markets may be unduly restricted, idealized, formalized, static and individualized – symptoms of autistic attitudes – the fact that it is actually engaged with a real-world problem gives us a glimmer of hope.

Cures?

Returning to the case of neurobiological autism, there is no cure at this point. That is, there is no known method (such as a pill) to definitively prevent or end this disorder. But autism represents a developmental delay, which opens the door for a long-term struggle to speed up that development, to improve an individual's functioning in society. Various methods (from behaviour modification, to making an active effort to engage a person socially in his activities,[20] to encouraging occupational therapy) can speed up an individual's ability to learn to cope with the shower of stimuli. Pills can help handle symptoms (such as anxiety), making it easier for therapists to apply other methods. All of these involve trying to break down the walls between the autistic individual and the empirical world.

What about "curing" the economics profession of its institutional autism? It should not surprise anyone that there is no quick fix. The persistence of autistic symptoms (as described by the French students) is based in the hierarchy and the competition to rise in those ranks. This autism encourages, and is in turn shored up by, a refusal to engage with other social scientists in a serious way, as peers. As well as efforts to get rid of unnecessary hierarchy and competition, outsiders and deviants may be able to push the profession up the developmental ladder to minimize solipsism. These efforts might be helped by the course of events, as when the shock treatment of the Great Depression pushed the profession away from classical economics and toward Keynes. In any event, the effort to force the profession to engage actively with reality must be central.

But such empirio-criticism is never enough. Just as autistic individuals need help making sense of reality, it takes a theory to trump a theory. In many cases, that means that we need to do better than the neoclassical economists, presenting improved theories to understand empirical reality. Such theories would be conscious of the limits of mathematical method, embrace the heterogeneity of empirical reality, take into account a deeper understanding of individual social psychology, treat economies as undergoing hard-to-reverse processes, involve institutionalist insights, eschew excessive pretensions of unjustified scientific objectivity and avoid reducing all activity to exchange, partly by learning from the other social sciences.[21] If enough people are willing to make the effort, perhaps the profession will move toward pluralism.

In terms of research, it would be a major mistake to reject totally the economics profession, or even its neoclassical elements. In my experience, many interesting insights can be drawn from the more sophisticated work of neoclassical economists, especially if treated sceptically with an eye to finding the valid aspects of their work rather than simply rejecting them. Despite its problems, it is better to know the state of the orthodoxy's knowledge than to be ignorant of it. Finally, there are reasons for hope. Magazines such as *The Journal of Economic Perspectives*, which center on presenting ideas without unnecessary formalism, along with such fields as experimental economics, which are empirical by necessity, show the possibility for improvement.

Notes

* Thanks to Edward Fullbrook, Barkley Rosser, and Lynn Kilroy for their input. Of course, the full weight of any blame for misleading, inaccurate, or ambiguous content is on my shoulders.

1. See the *Diagnostic and Statistical Manual* (DSM-IV), Washington, DC: American Psychiatric Association, 1994, 4th edn, category 299.00.

2. See http://isnt.autistics.org/ for an analysis of "neurotypical disorder," which affects 9,625 out of 10,000 individuals.

3. See, for example, Tony Attwood (1998), *Asperger's Syndrome: A Guide for Parents and Professionals* (London and Philadelphia: Jessica Kingsley Publishers).

4. A more complete list can be found in many places. Mine is based on a web page of by the Los Angeles-based United Autism Alliance (http://www.unitedautismalliance.org/knowledge/).

5. See "What is *AS*?" at http://www.udel.edu/bkirby/asperger/.

6. In reality, she said, "there is no such thing as society. There are individual men and women, and there are families." (See: http://www.cooperativeindividualism.org/thatcher_society_and_responsibility.html).

7. Contrary to this assertion, autistic children, like neurotypical children, can be very suggestible, absorbing all sorts of attitudes and preferences from popular culture.

8. Despite its lack of conscience, *HE* is also not sociopathic or psychopathic since a person with antisocial personality disorder (to use the up-to-date term) often exploits society's mores for his or her selfish aims. This shows that both *HE* and the autistic individual lack a clear understanding of society.

9. From Stephen M. Edelson of the Center for the Study of Autism, "Theory of mind," at http://www.autism.org/mind.html. The concept – also used in animal ethology – was first applied to autism by Uta Frith.

10. See the "Open letter from economics students to professors and others responsible for the teaching of this discipline," and "Petition for a debate on the teaching of economics" (from June and July 2000, both found at http://www.paecon.net/); Appendix I, this volume.

11. Of course, it is quite possible to describe an ideal world without math, as in utopian novels.

12. However, I doubt that very many autistic individuals study sociology or social psychology, which (as their names suggest) are inherently societal in their nature.

13. See, for example, Philip Mirowski and Roy Weintraub. "The pure and the applied: Boubakism comes to mathematical economics," *Science in Context* (Summer 1994), **7**, 245–72. A classic case of Boubakism is Gerard Debreu's *Theory of Value* (New York: Wiley. 1959).

14. On the former, see for example, Olivier J Blanchard and Lawrence H Summers, "Hysteresis and the European unemployment problem," *NBER Macroeconomics Annual*, 1986, pp. 15–78. On the latter, see Sumner Rosen, "The economics of superstars," *American Economic Review*, **71** (December 1981), 845–58.

15. For this vision of competition, see Robert H Frank and Philip J Cook, *The Winner-Take-All Society: Why So Few at the Top Get So Much More Than the Rest Of Us*, New York: Penguin, 1995.

16. Again, see Frank and Cook, 1995.

17. Critics of autistic economics should recognize the possibility of the rise of an economics that is totally subservient to these interest groups.

18. See Philip Mirowski, *Against Mechanism: Protecting Economics from Science*, Towota, NJ: Rowman and Littlefield, 1988, pp. 24–5.

19. This point should remembered by those who confuse the opposition to autistic economics with left-wing economics, since the generally conservative Austrian and Schumpeterian schools reject the static conceptions of the orthodox school.

20. By coincidence, Dr Stanley I Greenspan, the advocate of active social intervention ("floor time") is the brother of economist Alan Greenspan.

21. For one of my efforts on this front, see "The positive political economy of individualism and collectivism: Hobbes, Locke, and Rousseau," *Politics & Society*, **28** (2), June 2000, 265–304. A draft is available at http://bellarmine.lmu.edu/~jdevine/HLR.html.

4.

WHY NEOCLASSICAL ECONOMICS EXPLAINS NOTHING AT ALL[1]

Steve Fleetwood

Introduction

Critical realists (*c.f.* Lawson, 1998; Fleetwood, 1999a&b, 2001a&b) argue that neoclassical economics is rooted in the *deductivist method*.[2] Deductivism seeks to 'explain' something by deducing or predicting a statement about that something from a set of initial conditions, assumptions, axioms and a covering law and/or some other form of constant conjunction of events which drives the inferential machinery. These conjunctions, where for every event y there exists a set of events x_1, x_2 ... x_n such that y and x_1, x_2 ... x_n are regularly conjoined, only occur in, and are constitutive of *closed systems*. There are, however, very few spontaneously occurring closed systems in the natural world, and virtually no non-trivial ones in the socio-economic world. Using deductivism, therefore, means engineering artificially closed systems by means of *known* falsehoods, reducing neoclassical economics to what Hodgson (1999: 11) calls 'the economics of nowhere'. What is not always appreciated, however, is that *the presence of known falsehoods removes all explanatory power from neoclassical economics*. This chapter illustrates the point via a brief analysis of the theory of labour demand.

Closed system theorising: the example of the theory of labour demand

The law of labour demand, which states that the quantity of labour demanded varies indirectly with the (real) wage, is an example of one kind of constant conjunction of events – a Humean law. Incidentally, the significance of this apparently arcane law should not be underestimated: it underpins the entire neo-liberal project of making labour markets more flexible. This constant conjunction is artificially engineered via (at least) four assumptions known as the Marshall-Hicks conditions. Demand for labour is alleged to be more elastic if the following conditions apply:

1. *The elasticity of substitution between labour and capital is high.* The demand for labour will be more responsive to a change in wages the more easily labour can be substituted for capital;
2. *The elasticity of demand for the final product is low.* The demand for labour will be more responsive to a change in wages if the cost increases caused by wage increases can be passed directly to the consumer without a loss of revenue;
3. *The share of wages in the total cost of production is high.* The demand for labour will be more responsive to a change in wages if production is labour intensive because wages constitutes a relatively high proportion of overall costs;
4. *The elasticity of supply of other factors is high.* The demand for labour will be more responsive to a change in wages if, when capital is substituted for labour, the suppliers of this additional capital are able to increase their supply immediately and effortlessly.

The M-H conditions close the system: without them there would be no constant conjunctions between changes in labour demand and changes in the wage. Unfortunately, however, the M-H conditions also introduce *known* fictions into the theory. Let us consider the four M-H conditions as four *closure conditions*.

Intrinsic closure conditions (ICC)

To close the system, the *internal state* of individuals must be artificially engineered so that the individual (person, production system, firm or whatever) *always* responds in the same predictable way. The ICC is maintained, for example, by assuming ubiquitous substitution between labour and capital.[3] In cases where production involves a relatively fixed crew of workers operating a relatively fixed set of machinery it is often impossible to substitute a worker for a machine. Where production requires human emotion such as a helpful attitude, a machine cannot be substituted for a human. In some cases substitution of labour for capital is not feasible:

how does one substitute a machine for a nurse to carefully bath an elderly patient? Even where is it technically possible, substitution is often not socio-politically possible. If, however, the ubiquity of substitutability is *not* assumed, a change in relative factor prices cannot be said to cause the substitution of labour for capital, and the constant conjunctions of events that constitute the law of labour demand fail to emerge. Assuming ubiquitous substitution is a falsehood. Where non-substitutability *is* recognized it is treated as a special case. Knowingly false claims are, thereby, treated as the norm, and knowingly true claims (e.g. that firms may offset a legislated wage rise by introducing flexible working practices that raise efficiency and reduce costs) are relegated to an afterthought.

The extrinsic closure condition (ECC)

The ECC ensures that the system is completely isolated from any *external* influences that would violate closure. This occurs if we assume, for example, that (a) the suppliers of other factors of production can increase their supply immediately and effortlessly should need arise, (this is unrealistic, especially when the economy is running near to capacity); (b) the elasticity of demand for the final product is low so that firms can pass wage increases on to customers (this is a rather tenuous assumption in highly competitive global markets). Maintaining the ECC, then, often requires falsehoods.

The aggregational closure condition (ACC)

The ACC ensures that the response remains constant, irrespective of the level of aggregation. Hence, the need to assume that the share of wages is high no matter what the industry. If for example, the industry was, or became, highly capital intensive, an increase in wages might be lost in the overall costs and demand for labour might not fall following a wage increase. In capital-intensive industries, then, the ACC is a falsehood.

The reducibility closure (sub) condition (RCsC)

The RCsC requires the existence of assumptions whose *sole purpose* is to ensure mathematical tractability. These are merely technical assumptions used to ensure the relevant functions are well behaved, thereby preventing perverse outcomes. Even where substitution of capital for labour is possible, it is often not continuous or 'smooth' but 'lumpy'. Production functions would have 'lumps' in them and could not be differentiated.

If any of these four closure conditions are not met (and there are, of course, more ways of meeting them than mentioned here) constant conjunctions will not emerge. Incidentally, that there are four M-H and four closure conditions is merely coincidence. Moreover closure requires far more than the M-H conditions: the latter are merely those explicitly mentioned in the theory. Other assumptions lie buried within the *ceteris paribus* clause; are attached to sub-components of the theory, such as diminishing marginal returns; or are made by omission.

Neoclassical economists *know* perfectly well that they are using falsehoods (hence the reference to *known* falsehoods) but often ignore the *causes* and *consequences* of constraints on their freedom to choose the M-H conditions, or assumptions in general. They *cannot* choose assumptions on the grounds that they resemble the truth, because the need to maintain systemic closure often overrides these (and other) considerations – such as descriptive adequacy. Faced with a decision between adopting an assumption that is known to be false yet closes the system, and one that is known to be true yet violates closure, the known falsehood *must* be chosen or the constant conjunctions will not emerge.

Removal of explanatory power

A damaging consequence of adopting *known* falsehoods is that their presence removes explanatory power, for (at least) three reasons – for an explanation see Runde (1998).

Explanation is not merely efficient causality

Many critical realists share with Lipton (1993; 33) the thesis that to 'explain a phenomenon is to give information on the phenomenon's causal history'. The causal history of a phenomena is not merely (if at all) one couched in terms of the event(s) that precede the phenomena, but in terms of the underlying causal mechanisms. One does not, for example, adequately explain (the event of) a lamp becoming illuminated simply by pointing to the (event of) flicking of the switch that preceded it. One does not adequately explain an increase in the demand for labour by pointing to the fall in wages that (allegedly) preceded it. Yet this form of 'explanation' is all that deductivism offers. The overriding necessity of closure requires the removal (theoretically of course) of all causal mechanisms that might violate the closure conditions. So, for example, the theory of labour demand omits reference to trade unions, the introduction or abolition of labour laws and responses to them, government policy, political ideology, management systems, different working practices and so on, mechanisms that have had considerable causal impact on labour demand. But here is the rub: once removed from the theory these causal mechanisms cannot subsequently be recalled and offered as part of the causal explanation. Relevant causal mechanisms are either included in the theory, in which case they can contribute to the causal explanation, or they are excluded, in which case they cannot.

Explanation is not prediction

Prediction does not constitute explanation. The conflation of prediction and explanation is referred to as the 'symmetry thesis' whereby the only difference between explanation and prediction relates to the direction of time (Caldwell 1991; 54). Explanation entails the deduction of an event after it has (or is known to have) occurred. Prediction entails the deduction of an event prior to (knowledge of) its occurrence. One can, however, predict *without explaining anything at all*. One can predict the onset of measles following the emergence of Koplic spots, but the latter does not explain measles. Even supposing an econometric model successfully predicted an event (and the predictive power of neoclassical economics is arguably weak), the regression might be grounded in no economic theory whatsoever, or be grounded in a theory that contains known falsehoods. In this case, even a successful prediction would not constitute an explanation.

Explanation does not allow known falsehoods

If, as part of a causal account, one includes a *known* falsehood, or leaves out some important causal mechanism (falsehood by omission) then the 'explanation' can immediately be rejected as a *bona fide* explanation by pointing to this falsehood. Consider an analogy. In explaining how my rubbish bags get ripped during the night, I might hypothesise that it is the work of a fox or I might hypothesise that it is the work of a ghost. The explanation involving the fox is advanced because I believe it to be true. The 'explanation' involving the ghost is *known* to be false but is advanced for a pragmatic reason: I want to frighten my young nephew and stop him playing with the bin bags. Whilst the explanation involving the fox is valid (even if it turns out to be mistaken) the 'explanation' involving the ghost, pragmatically useful as it is, is invalid because it is *known* to be a falsehood. One only has to reflect upon this for a moment to see this conclusion is self-evidently correct: if known falsehoods are allowed to constitute 'explanations' imagine the bizarre explanations that could be advanced!

Counter arguments considered

Two counter-arguments are commonly deployed to legitimise the use of known falsehoods. The first runs as follows: 'all theory has to leave out the inessential, has to abstract from reality, has to make unrealistic assumptions, so all theory is inevitably false in the strict sense of the word'. Now whilst abstraction is legitimate, the process is complex and cannot be elaborated upon here (*c.f.* Sayer, 1998). I defend my claim with the following observation. Theories like that of labour demand are replete with such obvious falsehoods that to suggest they are really (legitimate) abstractions is merely a rhetorical ploy to avoid methodological discussion. In any case, as noted above most neoclassical economists admit to knowingly using falsehoods. The second counter-argument invokes the 'method of successive approximation' (Sweezy, 1968; 11) or the 'method of isolation' (Maki, 1992, but see Pratten, 1999), and runs as follows: 'The initial stages of theorisation use known falsehoods. Explanatory power is added in stages as realistic assumptions are successively substituted for false ones.' There are two objections to this.

1. The method of successive approximation or isolation *might* be appropriate when the successive analytical steps merely involve the *mechanical* addition of factors that were previously assumed away. This mechanical addition is, however, not appropriate for systems where the elements possess *emergent properties*. When, for example new technology is introduced to a workplace or a new management regime is installed, its behaviour often evolves, giving rise to properties that were not present before. Many theoretical propositions derived on the basis of pre-emergent properties provide no grounds for the analysis of post-emergent forms of behaviour.
2. Theory is still reliant on closed systems. All that has happened is that one closed system has been added to another (slightly larger) closed system. A succession of closed systems does not, however, add up to an open system. Consider the following example:
    *   closed $system_1$ assumes demand for labour is determined *solely* by wages;
    *   closed $system_1$ generates the deduction/$prediction_1$ that the introduction of a minimum wage will cause a fall in labour demand;
    *   closed $system_2$ now allows labour demand to be determined by

wages *and* (say) aggregate demand;

- system$_2$ is, however, still a closed system: it just contains more variables. Many of the previous (false) assumptions remain in place and, new (false) ones are added to ensure closure in this more complex system.

Falsehood is then piled upon falsehood – and the dream of one day removing all false assumptions evaporates.

The method of successive approximations, or successive closures might, therefore, be more accurately termed the 'method of successive falsehoods' or the 'method of successive closed systems'. In short, the counter-arguments do not evade the critical realist critique.

Conclusion

To the extent that neoclassical economic theory is rooted in the deductivist method, constant conjunctions of events, artificially closed systems and *known* falsehoods, it explains nothing at all.

Notes

1. I wish to thank Paul Lewis for his careful comments.
2. Deductivism is also found in some heterodox (Austrian, Institutionalist, Marxist and Post-Keynesian) economics whereupon these perspectives also become vulnerable to the following critique.
3. Neoclassical theorists do, of course, recognize that substitution between labour and capital is not ubiquitous and attempt to deal with it via non-convex isoquants. 'L' shaped isoquants imply only one production technique based upon one capital-labour combination and allow no substitution. Isoquants with n 'flat' sections imply $n-1$ production techniques and allow limited substitution. But, where tangency between the isocost curve and the isoquants is at a corner, factor prices could change without 'causing' substitution. Where tangency occurs along the face of one of the 'flat' sections of the isoquant, then the choice of technique becomes indeterminate.

References

Caldwell, B (1991), *Beyond Positivism: Economic Methodology in the Twentieth Century*, Unwin Hyman.

Fleetwood, S (1999a), 'The inadequacy of neoclassical theories of trade unions', *Labour*, 13 (2), 445–80.

Fleetwood, S (ed.) (1999b), *Critical Realism in Economics: Development and Debate*, Routledge.

Fleetwood, S (2001a), 'Causal laws, functional relations and tendencies', *Review of Political Economy*, 13 (2), 201–20, reprinted in P Downward (2002) *Applied Economics and the Critical Realist Critique*, Routledge.

Fleetwood, S (2001b), 'What kind of theory is Marx's *Labour Theory of Value?* A critical realist inquiry', *Capital & Class*, 73, 41–77.

Hodgson, G (1999), *Economics and Utopia: Why The Learning Society is Not the End of History*, Routledge.

Lawson, T. (1998), *Economics and Reality*, Routledge.

Lipton, P (1993), *Inference to the Best Explanation*, Routledge.

Maki, U (1992), 'On the method of isolation in economics', C Dilworth (ed.), *Intelligibility in Science IV*, Rodophi.

Pratten, S (1999) 'The "closure" assumption as a first step', in S Fleetwood (ed.) *Critical Realism in Economics; Development and Debate*, Routledge.

Runde, J (1998) 'Assessing causal economic explanations', *Oxford Economic Papers*, 50, pp 151–72.

Sayer, A. (1998) 'Abstraction: a realist interpretation', in M Archer, R Bhaskar, A Collier, T Lawson, A Norrie (eds), *Critical Realism: Essential Readings*, Routledge.

Sweezy, P (1968) *Theory Of Capitalist Development*, Modern Reader.

5.

A SCIENCE TOO HUMAN? ECONOMICS*

Bernard Guerrien

Economic science is far from being exact: the divisions between economists are notorious and their predictions are subject to disputes and revisions. Nor has there been any major discovery in economics in 2003 or in 2002 or in preceding years. One could even ask if there has ever been any; the annual awarding since 1968 by the Swedish Royal Academy of Sciences of a prize for economic science (commonly called the "Nobel prize for economics" although from this it does not follow that it is one) fails to convince.

Nevertheless, economic relations exist; they even constitute an important part of human activities, and a scientific mind can only try to understand them. Generations of economists, of whom the most famous have often had a solid scientific education, have tried; thus one cannot ignore their thought, and eventually the influence that they may have had on the evolution of societies. So doing an update on economic knowledge and on the theories of economists is consistent with a scientific approach – even if, in the end, the results are slight or subject to caution. Knowing that we don't know, or that we know little, is also part of scientific knowledge.

Economic science and science

The term "economic science" is usually used to designate a collection of economic theories. By "science" one generally means a body of knowledge or set of theories about which there is a broad consensus: they are considered to be true on the whole because they have been verified – or at least non falsified – by experience or observation. But in economics it is not uncommon to see different theories coexist for a long time, although they concern the same phenomena and give rise to divergent, maybe opposite, predictions. One can offer two reasons for this, which explain why the situation in economics is radically different from sciences in the strict sense.

1. Economic theories are concerned with relations between men, i.e. relations that are difficult to reduce to a few simple parameters (which all theories do); furthermore, these relations vary in space (they are not the same in all the regions of the world) and in time (societies and customs change, sometimes very fast).
2. The theoretician is not, even if he wants to be, a disinterested party to the societies he studies, because he inevitably has an opinion about them, and thus also an opinion on what is to be done to improve them. This is why economists rarely content themselves with observing what is (or what they believe is) and find it so difficult to refrain from saying what *should be* (what they think is good for the society). This frequency of the normative dimension in the discourse of economists is a source of much confusion. Among other things, it explains a certain reluctance to consider their approach as scientific. It is why it is essential to distinguish the normative from the positive in all presentations linked to the economy – which is as difficult to do, as it is to set aside one's opinions.

Economic theory and experimentation

Theories, whatever they may be, are in the beginning the fruit of imagination, of beliefs, or even sometimes of the opinions of those who formulate them. In order to sort them out, so as to retain only one concerning a given phenomenon, the ideal method is that of controlled experiment, where the studied phenomenon is isolated, by conserving only what is taken into account by the theory, apart from certain perturbations considered as trivial. But in economics such experiments are not possible. As John Stuart Mill noted in 1843:

> The instances requisite for the prosecution of a directly experimental inquiry into the formation of character would be a number of human beings to bring up and educate from infancy to mature age; and to perform any one of these experiments with scientific propriety, it would be necessary to know and record every sensation or impression derived by the young pupil long before it could speak. It is not only impossible to do this completely, but even to do so much of it as should constitute a tolerable approximation. One apparently trivial circumstance which

eluded our vigilance might let in a train of impressions and associations sufficient to vitiate the experiment as an authentic exhibition of the effects flowing from given causes. (*A system of Logic,* Book VI. Chapter 5, point 3) What is true on an individual level is even more true on the level of society, formed by a multitude of individuals and where the "apparently insignificant circumstances" are obviously much more numerous.

Yet for a long time some economists have, in spite of everything, undertaken "experiments". It was not, however, until 2003 that the profession took a little interest in this kind of approach (Nobel Prize awarded jointly to Daniel Kahneman and Vernon Smith). This reluctance is easily explained. On the one hand, the first type of experiment, concerning the behaviour of individuals (the subject of Kahneman's work), revealed that the subjects of the experiments (including students in economics) generally do not react as the theory assumes they do – the "apparently insignificant causes" (routine, a sense of injustice, for example) to which Mill refers, seem, on the contrary, very significant. On the other hand, the second type of experiment, like those conducted by Vernon Smith on the functioning of markets, does not attempt to reproduce what happens in reality because this is impossible; the aim is to test the reaction of individuals placed in particular frameworks, and to look for those that are the most efficient (the approach is *de facto* normative).

A student in economics can, however, go through his entire degree course without having heard of such "experiments" and, obviously, without ever having carried one out – a situation which would be inconceivable in physics, in chemistry, or even in biology.

Knowledge and laws in economics

Certainly astronomers, for example, do not carry out experiments. However they use results reached by sciences that do undertake them and, above all, give an essential place to observation. The regularity of physical phenomena, their repetition, their universal character (in time and space, at least on a certain scale), enable astronomy to explain a great number of phenomena and, even, to make highly accurate predictions.

The situation is very different in economics, where it is impossible to find situations which in the main are differentiated only by the action of one or a few well identified factors – the first step towards the establishment of causal relationships and therefore of laws.

This is why it is not possible in economics to find laws taking the form of precise relations, always verified, between two or more variables, other things remaining unchanged – this last condition being almost never verified, even approximately. Economists however create confusion by using the word "law" where it does not apply. This is the case, for example, of the "law of supply and demand", according to which the price of a good whose supply exceeds its demand tends to decrease – or to increase in the contrary case. As soon as one tries to give a more precise content to this so-called "law", one perceives that it is very vague: who makes the price vary? And how? Is this price unique? Can't it happen that the people who demand the product organise themselves and refuse to pay a higher price? Can they not purchase other goods instead? In fact, the use of the verb "tend" fits what economists can at the very most hope to achieve: to detect some tendencies in the phenomena studied.

Tendencies rather than laws

The word "tendency" suggests a direction, but not a certain result. The tendency is in itself the manifestation of a law, but this does not appear clearly because of the existence of disruptive non-negligible elements, which can be called "counter tendencies", whose effects it is not possible to isolate. Thus instead of talking of a "law" of the equalization of profit rates (widely evoked by David Ricardo, John Stuart Mill and even Karl Marx), we will say there is a "tendency", because this equalization can take time and also resources in collecting information and in comparing various profit rates and the risks with which they are associated.

A more controversial case is that of the tendency for the profit rate to decrease (set out by Karl Marx). The idea is simple: if one thinks that all value comes from labour, and that with time, the accumulated labour (in the form of machines, equipment, offices, etc.), or "dead labour", increases in comparison to the living labour; then the profit rate must diminish. But here there is only a "tendency", which can be blocked by an increase of the profit (the share of living labour appropriated by the capitalists), or by a reduction in the value of the "accumulated" labour (obsolescent or unused equipment). The problem faced by the theoretician, if the diminution of the profit rate is not evident, is to know whether this is due to the existence of counter tendencies or due to the erroneous nature of the theory, i.e. the tendency to diminution does not exist. Because it is not possible to perform a controlled experiment to settle the matter, both points of view can continue to coexist indefinitely.

Economic theory and self-realisation

There is another aspect of economics that distinguishes it fundamentally from the natural sciences; its theories can transform the world that it studies. This is what we call, not altogether correctly, self-realisation.

The discourse of economists, their predictions and their speculations often turn out to be erroneous. Even so economics influences the people at which it is aimed, and whose actions shape economic life and constitute its substance. People base their economic decisions on more than just "objective" factors such as tastes, available technology and the distribution of resources. They also base their decisions on their beliefs at the time of deciding, for example, beliefs regarding the "business climate" or future prospects. There is also the fact that the government, big firms and participants in stock exchanges act according to economics theories, which often take the form of mathematical models – whose form affects economic reality to a greater or lesser extent, even if this influence is not that assumed by these models. This action of the subjective (beliefs) on the real world is called, somewhat incorrectly, self-realisation, and concerns the very special case where what has been predicted is realised as a direct consequence of the prediction itself.

Where then is the "reality", the "real" world that the science intends to analyse and understand independently of the opinions and beliefs of the scientist? Two typical examples show why the answer to this question is not obvious. Assume that an upturn in the stock market, accompanied by a decrease in interest rates and an increase in household expenditure, has been followed, say four out of five times, by a revival of the economy. If these conditions (stock market upturn, low interest rates, increased spending) are observed at a given moment, and if the idea that they should entail a revival is widely held, then those who share it will, by their actions, make it happen. The revival is thus as much a consequence of shared beliefs concerning a causal relationship, as it is a consequence of the causal relationship itself (assuming that it really exists).

Another example concerns the stock market, where the beliefs of investors play a central role. Take the price of options, i.e. the premium that someone has to pay at a certain time for the right to buy a security or commodity at a future date at a given price (fixed in advance). This premium will depend in particular on the expectations held regarding future fluctuations of stock market prices, on their "volatility". It is thus that Fisher Black and Myron Scholes (Nobel Prizewinners) proposed a formula to calculate the price of options – assuming among other things that stock exchange prices follow a law of the type "random walk". If all actors in stock markets adopt this formula, attributing the same value to these parameters, then this formula will, very precisely, give the observed prices of the options. But is one to say that Black and Scholes's model perfectly explains reality, as if it were independent of the model? No, of course not. One can, at the most, note that there is consensus among the actors on the price of options – all agreeing on the price given by the formula of Black and Scholes, which plays the role of a convention. Here the conjunction of the subjective and the objective is at a maximum.

The beliefs of members of a society and the theories and models of the economists – resulting from *their* beliefs – are facts, data, which can play an important role in the economic life. Even if they are difficult to figure out and define, a scientific approach in economics must take them into account – even if this results in rendering vain or impossible purely mathematical formulations (something the profession has difficulty accepting).

Economy and Mathematics: a serious drift

The prominence that economics books and journals give to mathematics, sometimes very complex, is impressive. Together with physicists, economists are probably those who use advanced mathematics the most. There would appear to be a paradox here: mathematics being synonymous with rigour and precision, how is it that they can play such a role in a discipline where vagueness reigns? The answer probably lies in the roots of this vagueness: the economic and social world being particularly difficult to grasp schematically, to reduce to simple laws, the temptation is great to flee it and to take refuge in fictitious worlds, in models having little to do with what we can observe (especially concerning forms of social organization), but which lend themselves to endless mathematical developments.

It is symptomatic that among the journals of reputable disciplines, those of economics have, by far, the highest proportion of purely theoretical articles, with lots of mathematics but without any concrete data (this also happens in theoretical physics, but much less). Some economists – including famous ones who have sometimes built their reputation on their mathematical expertise – lament this state of affairs. These include the Nobel Prizewinners Wassily Leontief, John Hicks, Paul Samuelson, Robert Solow and Joseph Stiglitz. Nevertheless, the recruitment and selection processes for economics teachers and researchers continue to privilege those who demonstrate (particularly in their publications) their knowledge of mathematics, thereby perpetuating the situation and even making it worse. This approach that economics uses to give itself the image of having a scientific character can, however, have the opposite effect, by providing evidence that economists are charlatans and pedants, who try to impress others with their formulae, while the predictions that follow from them leave, at the very least, much to be desired.

Economy and Ideology

The desire to prove that economic science could be different from other human and social sciences, because it can be put into a mathematical form, also leads to aberrations. It was with this desire that the currently dominant theory of the formation of prices was originally proposed in the 1870s by Leon Walras, who sought above all to determine prices that would, according to him, be "fair", that is to say, such that the rights of each person would be respected. In order to do this, Walras conceived a form of social organization where prices are "called out" by an entity exterior to the traders, and where there is "tâtonnement" (without exchanges) until the "faire prices" are reached, (these prices happening to be those which equalise the global demands and supplies).

The mathematic form which was progressively adopted to represent this system happens to describe a very centralised economy, where the person who calls out the prices, and makes them vary, plays an essential role, especially by organizing the exchanges (they can only occur through him). However, this very special form of organization is necessary to demonstrate what is considered to be the principal result of economic theory: a system of prices that equalises, on the basis of these prices, supply and demand. The demonstration of this "existence theorem" – for which the Nobel Prize was awarded to those who conceived it, Kenneth Arrow and Gerard Debreu – is undoubtedly a piece of technical wizardry. But it also is the source of a great confusion, because it is systematically presented as proving "mathematically" that a market devoid of hindrances – "perfect" – always leads to a desired situation (where the choices of participants are compatible, and thus realizable). This is absurd, because the demonstration assumes a very centralised form of organization, the opposite of the idea one generally has of market systems. Only a central planner can possibly be interested by this "theorem". Yet what formal economic theory relies upon and pretends generally relates to markets.

Another example of this kind of absurdity is the "representative agent" models, very fashionable since the 1990s (one here thinks of another Nobel Prize winner, Robert Lucas). These models suppose that the observed "macroeconomic" evolution of some of the basic variables of an economy (such as GNP, consumption and investment, and employment and price levels) can be assimilated to the choice of a unique individual (obviously imaginary), who is both a consumer and producer, and who decides to divide his available time (present and future) between labour and leisure, and to divide what he produces between consumption and investment. Various mathematical techniques are then used – among others, the optimisation of non-linear programmes – to determine the share that enables this individual to maximize his (present and future) satisfaction. The result obtained is then compared to that of the economy as a whole (at it appears in statistical series, concerning employment, production, etc.), and theoreticians then try to give the parameters, which characterize the "representative agent", values that reproduce at best the observed evolutions.

Only ideology – here, the belief in the overwhelming power of mathematics joined to the virtues of the "market" – can explain why people who are otherwise very reasonable can dedicate their time and energy to these types of models.

Do we need economists and economic theories?

For a critical mind, the situation in economics is like this. On the one hand, it consists of an important accumulation of facts, data and statistical treatments, more or less elaborate, which try to bring out relations or tendencies by relying on relatively simple theories – but between which it is hardly possible to discriminate, because the elements which are not included in each theory are numerous and often non negligible. On the other hand, it consists of endless speculations, which use mathematics like Molière's doctors used Latin, trying to make us believe in the scientific character of the discourse, when on the contrary, it is the scientific approach that is sacrificed.

Many economists, however, both undertake sensible studies on specific points, using a certain number of simple ideas, yet participate in the speculations of "grand theory", when it has (almost) nothing in common with their empirical studies. The "simple ideas" that are the basis of these studies are generally old ideas, the fruit of observation and of the experiences of our societies. Thus, there is now a fashion for the "asymmetry of information" (a theme which led Joseph Stiglitz to his Nobel Prize in 2001). This term refers to the fact that in many transactions the parties involved do not have the same information regarding the object of the transactions. A typical example is that of the relation between insurer and insured, or between a banker and a borrower. Insurers and bankers have always known of the problem and tried to avoid it, but without talking about "asymmetry of information" or trying to put it in a mathematical form. Stiglitz, however, has earned his stripes (and the Nobel Prize) by "demonstrating" that the existence of asymmetries of information profoundly modifies the behaviours and the allocation of resources – a thing we have known for long time. But he also has led concrete studies, based on observations and available data, where he shows the importance of the asymmetry of information to many important questions of economic policy. To do so, he called upon a few simple ideas, accessible to all, far from the mathematical formulas of his academic publications. The conclusions he comes to, and the policies he recommends, are however far from being approved unanimously, as testifies the controversy – at the end of the 1990s – between the IMF and the World Bank (where Stiglitz was at the time the chief economist) on the way to tackle the crises that then affected certain developing or "in-transition" countries. It is clear that mathematics are not the element which will enable the settling of the controversy, and that behind it lie very different visions of the world and different arguments concerning especially the consequences of the intervention of the State.

It is obviously unsatisfactory not be able to settle such matters. But knowing what are the arguments advanced, and on the basis of what observations and from what data, is part of scientific knowledge. Given the importance of economics in the life of our societies, this knowledge is necessary, even though it is inevitably limited.

Note

* Translated by Emmanuelle Benicourt and Edward Fullbrook.

References

Israël, G (1996), 'La mathématisation du réel', Paris: Seuil.

Malinvaud, E (1996), 'Pourquoi les économistes ne font-ils pas de découvertes?', in *Revue d'économie politique*, 106.

Mill, J S (1866), 'Système de logique', Pierre Mardaga.

Quinet, E and B Walliser (1999), 'À quoi sert la science économique?', in *Revue d'économie politique*, 109.

6.

ECONOMICS: THE DISAPPEARING SCIENCE?

Alan Shipman

Economics can easily explain the demise of wheelwrights, weavers and wallpaper hangers. Technical progress dispelled the first group, globalization the second, changing preferences the third.

The 'dismal science' has more difficulty accounting for its own disappearance. But the downtrend in UK economics has now persisted too long to be dismissed as a mere correction after momentary excess.

Entry of home students to PhD courses has fallen to 'dangerously low levels' according to Royal Economic Society research published in 2000. Two of the country's most prestigious institutions (London School of Economics and Nuffield College, Oxford) had, that year, attracted no new UK doctoral students. Demand for national funds to support these had also slumped to the level of supply, while sociology and politics maintained their usual over-subscription.

The Royal Economic Society gives a predictably economic explanation for the flight from higher degrees. 'Relatively low pay and unattractive working conditions in academia' persuade high-flyers to seek higher returns on their instructional investment. Writing before stock markets stumbled, report authors Stephen Machin and Andrew Oswald noted that City economists could earn up to five times their academic counterparts, with senior management, consultancy and civil service jobs also catapulting more basically qualified economists above the professors who taught them. At Oswald's Warwick University, the proportion of first-class honours students staying on for further study dropped from 80 per cent in 1983–5 to 33 per cent by 1995–7.

But if this were the only explanation for decline, demand for more basic economic qualifications would have held up. In reality, the PhD numbers plunge is the culmination of a fall in interest all along the economist production line. Shrinking UK postgraduate entry results from steady decline in undergraduate and taught masters interest, now mirrored in the final pre-university years. Entries for economics A-level slid from over 32,000 in 1993/4 to less than 20,000 in 2000/1.

The American Economic Association has dug more deeply for explanations of its own declining undergraduate enrolments, which peaked in 1990. American Economics Association research suggests this is due not just to doubts on the economic rewards of staying the course, but disillusionment with the way it is structured and taught. From being a historical and literary subject, whose journals could still be understood by non-specialists into the 1960s, the subject's 'mainstream' research has become submerged in mathematical modelling and statistical analysis. A shift in assessment methods from essays to exercises and multiple choice tests further opens the subject to mathematicians who have never read the economics 'classics', while closing it to those who study nothing else.

By 'formalizing' past ideas into highly stylised models, economics has become a narrow problem-solving exercise, denying students the big picture they expect it to provide. With dialogue confined to a shrinking range of specialists familiar with the same formulae, the subject's past power to clarify everyday dilemmas has if anything been reversed. 'Many college seniors who have taken an economics course still show a lack of understanding of basic economics,' laments the latest American Economics Association survey of economic literacy by William Wallstad and Sam Allgood, echoing recent British results. Though adept at deducing a rational agent's optimum consumption bundle, new graduates are often baffled by practical questions – what happens when an exchange rate falls, who sets monetary policy, or what can be done to fend off a recession.

Detachment from reality is especially a deterrent for women and ethnic minorities, whose second-class status is confirmed in other Royal Economic Society surveys. In the UK women comprise one-third of PhD candidates and hold almost the same proportion of fixed-term lecturers in economics, but hold only 17 per cent of permanent lectureships, and 4 per cent of professorships. Although family-unfriendly faculties are part of the explanation, the earnings gap for unmarried women (14 per cent below male counterparts) is actually greater than that for married women ('only' 9 per cent). Similar discrimination was found in the case of ethnic minority economists, who on average earned 8 per cent less than white counterparts, even after adjusting for their relative youth and resultant shorter experience and publication records.

Reviewing these millennial results, Royal Economic Society president Partha Dasgupta and women's committee chair Carol Propper looked across the Atlantic for salvation, inferring from a strong PhD market that 'clearly US economics continues to generate innovation and intellectual excitement'. When, as end-century chair of the Cambridge economics faculty, Dasgupta led a radical redesign of its undergraduate course, he had little hesitation in swapping 'Cambridge Tradition' for the North American approach.

Cambridge's new course, whose final phasing-in this year will coincide with the hundredth anniversary of the original, downgrades Keynesian demand deficiencies, business cycles, capital debates and income distribution effects, in favour of more statistics and mathematical modelling. Supporters say the expanded technical toolkit will restore the subject's relevance to those who currently by-pass it for business studies or other social disciplines.

However, critics charge that narrower focus and procedural prescriptiveness are what have stifled interest, just when the spread of everyday economic problems – from widening world inequality to underfunded personal pensions – should be reviving it. A reductionist search for optimising 'microfoundations' neglects economies' 'emergent' properties, produced by individuals' interactions and not predictable from their actions. Economists build an unrealistic 'micro' picture, based on well-informed rational choices that even statistically trained subjects seem incapable of making. They thereby lose the macro picture, denying (or ascribing to state interference) such awkward phenomena as persistent unemployment and growth-rate differences, because the models point to 'equilibrium' and 'convergence'.

In *Reorienting Economics* (Lawson, 2003), Dasgupta's Cambridge nemesis and leading 'realist' Tony Lawson goes beyond the usual arguments about what to measure and how to model, tracing the economists' troubles to the way they view the world. He accuses the mainstream of twisting the economy to fit mathematical analysis by treating it as a 'closed' mechanical system, ignoring complexities due to reflection and reaction by its constituent parts, and their need for social institutions to steer through the complexity. Economists' search for surface 'event regularities', showing which policy levers to push, displaces concern for the more relevant underlying tendencies and structures, whose surface manifestations resist statistical disentanglement. Mainstreamers' mistake, Lawson argues, is to mimic (nineteenth-century) natural scientists in 'inducing' general principles from superficial observation, or 'deducing' them from axioms, when all they can realistically do is infer the deeper reality from surface effects.

Instead of arguing, in a classic example, whether sighting of a black swan negates the universality of white swans, realists want to re-focus on the mechanisms that generate and change swans' colour. Many alternative views are demanding attention from the mainstream. Evolutionists emphasize the path-dependent nature of technological and industrial change. Institutionalists deny the reducibility of all social structures to individual decision making and voting. 'Austrian' theorists point out how markets can coordinate choice by interdependent individuals with scattered and limited information, inverting the textbook depiction of fully informed and behaviourally independent individuals. 'Post-Keynesians' seek the return of aggregate demand to explanations of economies' short-run cycles, and of income distribution to accounts of their long-run growth.

Calls in the UK for a rethink have found strong resonance elsewhere in Europe, notably the 'post-autistic economics (PAE) movement' launched on the internet by disgruntled French students in 2001. As the PAE's *Crisis in Economics* manifesto hit the press in early April 2003 (Fullbrook, 2003), the plea for pluralism reached the 'other' Cambridge, with 700 Harvard students rallying behind Professor Stephen Marglin's campaign for a broader-spectrum introductory course. Colleagues' rejection of his eclecticism drove home the dissenters' point (see Harvard students' petition at Appendix VI).

Machin and Oswald speculate at the end of their 2000 study that shrinking supply will eventually cause a jump in economists' price, until their soaring pay brings financially savvy students flocking back onto their courses. But losing the initiative to more inclusive disciplines could thwart that recovery. Non-mainstream staff and students displaced from economics faculties have often found more fertile ground in business schools and other social science departments, where methodologies snubbed by peer review still prosper in the marketplace.

In an accompanying survey of minority representation, David Blackaby and Jeff Frank interpreted the high proportion of expatriate staff in higher-ranked UK economics departments as confirming the UK's entry into a global market for top economic talent. But if the commercial capture of home-grown high flyers is as widespread as the Royal Economic Society suggests, this import of labour to resolve local skill gaps owes more to the pattern of the UK's National Health Service than football's Premier League.

Economists used to joke that they had solved the unemployment problem

– for economists. For much of their subject's history, this could be done without any professional entry restriction. As chroniclers Keith Tribe and Alon Kadish have shown, pioneering courses at London and Cambridge faced a protracted struggle to attract sufficient students. Most continued to see classics, history, law or moral philosophy as firmer career foundations, or preferred to keep their elegant mathematics unsoiled by social concerns. A century on, that attitude seems to be returning. Economics that continues to sidestep reality could soon be down to economy size.

References

Fullbrook, Edward (ed.) (2003) *The Crisis in Economics*, London and New York: Routledge.
Lawson, Tony (2003) *Reorienting Economics*, London and New York: Routledge.

PART 2:

THE FAUX NOBEL PRIZE

7.

BEAUTIFUL MIND, NON-EXISTENT PRIZE: THE BANK OF SWEDEN PRIZE IN ECONOMICS SCIENCE[1]

Yves Gingras

Much has been said about the Oscar-winning movie *A Beautiful Mind* and its hero, the mathematician John Nash. Just as spring is the time for Oscars, a new crop of Nobel prizes has accompanied the fall of autumn leaves every October since 1901. As Daniel Kahneman and Vernon L Smith share an award this year, it's a good time to pose a question raised by a neglected aspect of the movie: exactly what prize did Nash really win?

The answer is not as obvious as it seems. When *A Beautiful Mind* hit our screens, one correspondent to an entertainment weekly pointed out that the 'Nobel Prize in Mathematics' he had read about did not actually exist. Many will recall the brief scene in the movie when the young Nash – suffering from lack of recognition of his true genius – remarks to his MIT colleagues that he has been robbed of the 'Fields Medal'. What is that? Ask any mathematician, and he will tell you: 'this is the equivalent of the Nobel prize for mathematicians'. Established in 1936, it is given once every four years to no more than four exceptional mathematicians under 40 years of age.

The incident confirms that John Nash, in coveting this most prestigious prize in the mathematics community, was at that point still rooted in reality. In contrast, though the story of a man from Stockholm waiting for Nash after his class to share the good news that he had won a prize is confirmed, it is doubtful that the prize itself was real. Or so I will claim.

The currency is prestige

Which 'Nobel prize' was the man from Stockholm talking about? Most journalists (and every economist) will of course answer, the 'Nobel Prize in Economics' – even though it is never specified in the movie. Against this taken-for-granted 'fact', I am arguing here that this prize does not exist: and moreover, that this so-called 'Nobel prize' is an extraordinary case study in the successful transformation of economic capital into symbolic capital, a transformation which greatly inflates the symbolic power of the discipline of economics in the public mind.

The confusion can be traced back to 1968 when the governor of the Central Bank of Sweden decided to mark the tercentenary of that institution by creating a new award. It could have been named after a well-known ancestral economist, such as Adam Smith, or more simply, though unimaginatively, the 'Bank of Sweden Prize in Economics'. After all, every discipline has its own 'prestigious' prize. Their number grows every year. However, the problem is that all these prizes, though well known within the microcosms of their discipline, have little public appeal. Only the Nobel prizes have a real public impact. But they are limited to five fields: physics, chemistry, physiology and medicine, literature and, finally, peace.

Moreover, the enormous symbolic capital of the very name 'Nobel prize' has been accumulated over the years by a careful selection of prizewinners. Like every new prize, by definition unknown, the Nobel faced the problem of what we can call (invoking Pierre Bourdieu's apt concept) the 'primitive accumulation of symbolic capital'. This obstacle was overcome by giving the prize early on to already renowned scientists who would bring the prize real credibility. The idea was that, over the years, this symbolic capital would surely accrue to such an extent that it could in turn bring recognition to the chosen winners.

The organisers, conscious of this conundrum and wishing to endow the discipline of economics with as much public credibility as possible, decided to call the prize: 'The Bank of Sweden Prize in Economic Sciences in Memory of Alfred Nobel'. Curiously then, it was the memory of Nobel, not that of an economist, that was being recalled. This mystery can be explained if we unpack the process crystallised in that bizarre and awkward name.

First, despite the scepticism of some scientists towards the 'scientificity' of economics, the Bank managed to convince the Royal Swedish Academy of Sciences and the Nobel Foundation to administer their prize. Secondly, identical procedures for the selection and nomination of the prize were chosen to those of the real Nobel prizes. Of course, the prize money would come from the Bank of Sweden, not the Nobel Foundation, but all the rest would be done exactly as if it was in fact a Nobel prize, up to and including the ceremony of 10 December.

Thus, the inclusion of the term 'in Honour of Alfred Nobel' in the title created the necessary bridge to the Nobel prize, and by exactly mimicking the process, the Bank created all the conditions enabling the association and even the identification of its prize with those established by Alfred Nobel at the turn of the century. Note that, for obvious reasons, it is much simpler to say 'Nobel Prize in Economics' than 'Bank of Sweden Prize in Economic Sciences in Honour of Alfred Nobel'! No surprise that, since 1969, all journalists and economists have commonly referred to the Bank of Sweden Prize as the 'Nobel Prize in Economics'. The strategy was a complete success.

The social alchemy of belief

Now that we understand why a bizarre name was chosen, transforming a peculiar social alchemy into a 'Nobel prize', let us look at the 'flow of capital' involved in the whole process. The Bank started with economic capital and 'invested' it in the Nobel Foundation to transform it into symbolic capital as fast as possible. Even a very large amount of cash is not sufficient in itself to assure the prestige of a prize. The key point was to effect a complete transfer of the already accumulated symbolic capital of the Nobel prizes to the new Economic Prize instituted by the Bank. Any other strategy would have been more risky given the difficulty, uncertainty and time lag attending any primitive accumulation of symbolic capital. In other words, this history makes visible the well-managed transformation of economic into symbolic capital, thus confirming Bourdieu's theory of the convertibility of the basic kinds of capital (economic, social, cultural and symbolic).

Of course, many will say: 'We all know it is the Bank of Sweden Prize, but it is much simpler to say "Nobel Prize".' In point of fact, the Nobel website is careful to make the distinction, thus habitually announcing the '2002 Nobel Prizes and the Prize in Economic Sciences in Memory of Alfred Nobel'. But this argument is either naive or disingenuous. For the success of the strategy of creating a 'Nobel by association' has obvious social consequences.

As anyone knows, the attribution of a Nobel prize gives instant world fame to the winners, who become oracles commenting on anything journalists can fathom: war, peace, philosophy, environment, irrespective of their particular fields of expertise. Interestingly, there is a strong correlation between the dates of attribution of a Nobel prize and the subsequent publication of memoirs or opinionated books by Nobel Laureates. This is a sociological consequence of the fact that the legitimacy bestowed by the Nobel prize is rapidly put to use in the public space to voice ideas that the winner would not have dared to submit were he or she a 'simple scientist'.

Whereas the 'spontaneous' philosophy or sociology of scientists can be considered relatively harmless, the situation is quite different in economics. By its annual offer of a public image of 'hard science' through its association with the Nobel prizes, the Bank of Sweden Prize in Economic Sciences gives the discipline and its laureates the 'scientific' aura it lacked to put forward authoritative but often simplistic theories about the economy (or, worse, the whole of society) conceived as a big 'market' where everything can be submitted to the so-called 'law of demand' – be it a house, a wedding, or even an idea.

What is even more fascinating is that the social alchemy which transmuted the Bank of Sweden prize into a Nobel prize, affected not only the general public (via its media coverage of course) but the members of the discipline and even the winners themselves, who are convinced they have won a real 'Nobel Prize in Economics'. Thus, James Buchanan (1986 prize) offers the readers his 'Notes on Nobelity'. Before him, Paul Samuelson (1970 winner) wrote about his 'Nobel coronation' – not his 'Bank of Sweden Coronation' – and filled his talk with references to Einstein (four times) Bohr (twice) and eight other winners of the (real) physics Nobel prize (not to mention, of course, Newton) plus a few other names as if he were part of this family. Curiously there is not a single economist named in this talk. A simple counterfactual *gedanken experiment* (as physicists like to call these thought experiments) makes it easy to understand that such a talk would have been impossible had the prize been called the 'Adam Smith Prize in Economics' and accompanied with a million dollar cheque.

As for the discipline – in a move typical of the pushy newcomer – it markets with ostentation its (false) membership in the Nobel club by publishing books, such as *Lives of the Laureates: Seven Nobel Economists* (1986 and carefully updated to 'ten' in 1990), which promote the discipline by associating it with the Nobel prize, a practice not observed in the scientific fields covered in the will of Alfred Nobel.

It would seem that engineers, frustrated not to have a Nobel of their own, have also approached the Nobel Foundation to create one, only to be told that, in order not to dilute the prestige of the Nobel prize, there should not be any more. Though the effect of scarcity applies to the value of economic as well as symbolic capital, the credibility of the Foundation may already be affected by association with the Bank of Sweden and the economists. Having played an important role in lobbying the Swedish Academy of Sciences to accept the Bank's offer and after having himself received the prize, Swedish economist Gunnar Myrdal changed his mind and became a fierce advocate of the abolition of the prize. More recently, a few days before the Nobel ceremony of the 2001 prizes, descendants of Alfred Nobel criticized the used of the term 'Nobel prize' applied to economics. Peter Nobel, a great-grandnephew of Nobel told journalists that his familly is 'asking for a clear distinction between the original Nobel prizes and this (prize)'. True to economic 'laws' (or maybe in a spirit of irony) he noted that the actual use of the name 'is like an intrusion in the trademark'! (See *Chronicle of Higher Education*, 7 December 2001).

Though this suggestion may be considered extreme by many (not including myself), it is clear that there are now many people coming to the conclusion that the institutions involved made a mistake in associating themselves with this symbolic coup d'État in the 'Republic of Science' – a move aimed at enforcing the dominant status of economics as a 'hard' science not only among the disciplines of the social sciences, but first and foremost in the mind of the public and its elected representatives.

In his classic book *How to Do Things with Words*, philosopher John Austin explained that words not only describe the world but create it through their performative aspect. Those of us who want to resist the symbolic violence inherent in the usurpation of the 'Nobel Prizes' by economists and do something against this annual propaganda can begin by calling the prize by its real name: the 'Bank of Sweden Prize in Economic Science'. They can also correct systematically those who still persist in talking about the 'Nobel prize in Economics'. Where the mere repetition of words has contributed to the 'reality' of that prize in the public mind, it is not impossible that a systematic counter-attack could deconstruct this chimera propagated by the media and idolized by economists.

8.

AN IGNOBEL SCANDAL

Alex Millmow

In his play *The Importance of Being Earnest* Oscar Wilde said of political economy that 'even these metallic problems have their melodramatic side'. That prophecy came true at this year's Academy awards. Apart from the Nobel Prize and the Oscar almost melting into one with the fanfare meted out to the film *A Beautiful Mind*, there was a whiff of scandal with Russell Crowe missing out on a best actor award for his portrayal of John Nash Jr, even though the production did well in all the other major award categories. Nash, who was in the audience, remarked that, like the Nobel Prize, there was an element of politics in the awards. Indeed there was, and not just because Nash himself was a bit lucky to win the Nobel Prize with the Prize-bestowing committee barely convinced about the wisdom of giving it to a schizophrenic mathematician. As Sylvia Nasar, author of *A Beautiful Mind* shows, the committee reluctantly came round to the chairman Assar Lindbeck's view that Nash should be given the award, as Russell Crowe, aka John Nash, put it in a southern drawl, for his 'one truly original idea'. It is often overlooked too that Nash actually shared the Nobel Prize in Economic Science with two mathematical economists, namely John Harsanyi and Reinhard Selten. The fact that the economics community bestowed the prize upon Nash tells us something about what that profession adores, namely, a mathematically driven formalism that basically reduces to second-guessing your rival's gameplan.

Ironically, Nash has openly stated that he is not really an economist. But there is, in all this, an even greater controversy in the Nobel Prize in Economics. It concerns the great English economist, Joan Robinson, who died in 1983. Apparently she died lamenting that she was never given the gong. This might come as a surprise because it is alleged that Robinson made clear to the committee that she did not want to be considered for the accolade. An alternative version is that she much preferred 'having a grievance' in not being awarded the prize. It was a mark of distinction not to be given the award. She would, moreover, have been horrified to be awarded the prize in company with someone with polar views to herself as had occurred in 1974 when the Nobel Prize for Economics was, in an ideological balancing act, shared by the Austrian economist, F A Hayek, and the Swedish institutional economist, Gunnar Myrdal. When Milton Friedman was awarded the 1976 Nobel Prize, Myrdal spat the dummy and embarrassed the committee for its overly political decision with a string of denunciations, not least about the merits of having a prize for economic science.

Robinson, the stormy petrel of Cambridge economics, spent most of her life trying to undermine the pillars of neoclassical thought and replacing it with a new critical economy. She failed in that endeavour, but as her *bête noire*, Paul Samuelson, conceded, Robinson was a pioneering theorist in so many fields that she deserved the gong. In 1975 there was immense speculation that Robinson was to be honoured. It was, after all, the International Year of the Woman and there was no more outstanding candidate than Robinson. The gossip in the economics profession was that Robinson was a shoo-in for the prize (McCarty, 2000) To everybody's surprise the Nobel Prize committee overlooked her and continued to do so right up to her death. To borrow a journalistic cliché, Joan Robinson became, at the stroke of a committee chairman's pen, the best Nobel Prize winner we never had. It is said that sunk costs do not matter, but that decision has cost the profession dear, since surely having not one female in the pantheon of economic laureates does little to inspire one half of the student population to do a major in economics.

How could she have been overlooked? Milton Friedman felt she was 'blackballed' because of espousal of Keynesianism and that it had nothing to do with gender (Feldman, 2000). Arguably it could have been due to her works, which were mostly destructive of conventional economic theory and therefore, in the committee's eyes, nothing really to build on. Nor was her methodology of the ilk befitting a true deterministic science.

It seems however that Lindbeck, the powerful chairman of the Nobel economics committee was more concerned that the cantankerous Robinson would use the prize to attack mainstream economics or, even worse, publicly refuse it, especially, if awarded for her earlier work, *The Theory of Imperfect Competition* which she had disowned. Unlike many other prizewinners,

Robinson had more than just 'one big thing' to hang her fame on. The consensus was that Robinson would, either way, be too risky. For a while perhaps it helped her cause to establish a more heterodox economics. However, the award of the Nobel prize to a self-confessed left-wing Keynesian would have given the post-Keynesian movement weight as a viable alternative to the mainstream.

In the case of Nash, the Nobel Prize committee sent someone to check to make sure he was no longer receiving messages from extraterrestrials. If the same courtesy had been extended to Robinson in 1982, they would have found her amenable to the idea of getting the award. According to Juliet Schor, a professor of sociology at Boston University who looked after Robinson while she did a semester of guest teaching at Williams in 1982, the *grandedame* of economics was 'terribly disappointed' not to have won that year's Nobel economics prize. Adding insult to injury it went to another Chicago economist and arch polemicist, George Stigler, for his work on deregulation. Robinson apparently desperately wanted to win not so much for the recognition but for the million dollars that came with it. She intended to donate it to the peace movement. One could, therefore, liken Robinson's experience to all those great films and superb acting performances that missed out on an Oscar. However even mainstream economists agree that even in Robinson's time all the titans of the profession have been deservedly rewarded bar her. Whatever the truth behind the failure of Joan Robinson to be honoured by the committee it remains the most mystifying incident in the history of the awards. Mark Blaug, a conservative historian of economic thought, has no doubt that Robinson's omission from the list of Nobel laureates is 'one of the most extraordinary acts of academic vindictiveness ... in recorded intellectual history' (1985). And, like the Oscars, the Nobel Prize cannot be given posthumously to repair the damage.

References

Blaug, M (1985), *Great Economists since Keynes*, Cheltenham: Edward Elgar.

Feldman, B (2000), *The Nobel Prize*, New York: Arcade Publishing.

McCarty, M H (2001), *The Nobel Laureates*, McGraw-Hill: New York.

Nasar, S. (2002), *A Beautiful Mind*, Faber and Faber email :amillmow @csu.edu.au.

9.

THE NOBEL PRIZE IN ECONOMICS – A BARRIER TO NEW THINKING

Peter Söderbaum

The Nobel Prizes in physics, chemistry and medicine are not uncontested but have become reasonably respected. Lately, the Bank of Sweden's economists' award in memory of Alfred Nobel has been added and instituted. It has been argued that economics is an established discipline comparable to physics and chemistry and with similar ideas of good science and scientific progress.

Economists can refer to a distinct paradigm – that is, a clear theoretical perspective. The tendency is to stick to this perspective, and today neoclassical economics holds a monopoly position in almost all university economics departments. Its theories are useful for some purposes, for instance, as a way of understanding financial and monetary policy.

Confronted with the present challenges related to sustainable development, the neoclassical paradigm has limitations. Viewing humans as consumers maximizing their self-interest is not very constructive if you wish to discuss the issues of environment and survival. Focusing on profit maximization in business will not make it easy to understand the present debate about corporate social responsibility, environmental certification of organizations and similar phenomena. Interpreting economic phenomena and relationships in terms of markets and prices and monetary indicators is not always a good strategy.

Neoclassical economists can of course continue to refer to their conceptual framework and turn their arguments in the best possible way. But a problem that they cannot get away from is that economics, just as other social sciences, is both science and ideology. As an example, focusing on the role of consumer and her self interest is not neutral in value terms.

One of the scholars who received the Bank of Sweden's Award in Economics in memory of Alfred Nobel, Gunnar Myrdal, repeatedly argued that 'values are always with us' in our research. This being the case, it becomes problematic from a democratic point of view to stick to one and only one paradigm at a university economics department. The ideological features and character of this paradigm mean that the department plays a role of political propaganda centre; 'human beings are consumers, forget about other roles as citizen, professional …' ;'anything connected with business can be reduced to a matter of maximum monetary profits', and so on.

The solution to this is a pluralistic attitude, that is, open-mindedness to different possible theoretical perspectives compatible with different valuational or ideological points of view. Just as economists otherwise celebrate competition, this should also be applied to their own discipline. The Bank of Sweden's Prize in Economic Sciences in memory of Alfred Nobel unfortunately has become an obstacle for new thinking.

Even prizewinners who present and support theories that could be connected with a criticism of neoclassical theory, for example Douglas North and Amartya Sen, tend – for tactical reasons, it seems – to profess themselves adherents to orthodoxy. Gunnar Myrdal is the exception among prizewinners, with his outspoken criticism of the mainstream and clear declaration in favour of institutional theory.

Today much is happening internationally in developing institutional theory, social economics, feminist economics, ecological economics and so on. Ecological economics can be described as 'business management and economics for sustainable development', and in this field neoclassical theory holds a minority position.

Adhering to neoclassical theory with its focus on economic growth in GDP terms is perceived by an increasing number of people as 'unsustainable'. For several years this has been a focus of the *Post-Autistic Economics Review*, which also stresses the limitations of mathematics as a language for economics. Books are now being published, with contributors from many countries, which caution new students in economics about the narrow-mindedness of the textbooks to which they are exposed.

The problem is that these textbooks legitimise simplistic thinking about economic growth and markets in a situation where instead a multidimensional and ethically open analysis is needed. Systematically propagating this simplistic economics to countries such as Russia and China is irresponsible.

Against this background, one possible way of acting is to withdraw the prize in economics in memory of Alfred Nobel. The alternative is to admit that economics much like other social sciences has a specific ideological content and therefore belongs to the same category as the Peace Prize. This would make it natural to return to the term 'political economy', the language used in the nineteenth century. It would also make it clear that the project to develop a 'pure' economics has been a failure.

With this change, the idea becomes one of identifying potential winners of the prize who, through their research and other actions, have contributed something to humanity. Choosing people who claim to have developed models useful for predicting shareholder values would then become more difficult.

I am sure that there are those who see markets of different kinds as the salvation of the world, but there are also many citizens who are less enthusiastic about market solutions.

PART 3:

REALISM VERSUS ILLUSION

10.

SEVEN THESES FOR A THEORY OF REALIST ECONOMICS*

Jacques Sapir[1]

The issue of realism has been central to the PAE movement from its beginning. As I have previously stated in *Post-Autistic Economics Review* and elsewhere, realism is not a clash between a 'factual' world and a 'theoretical' one, between reality and abstraction. Rather realism is both a methodological stance and the definition of a theoretical research programme.

Realism however can give rise to different interpretations. Uskali Mäki has made an important distinction between world realism and truth realism.[2] This distinction nevertheless raises the issue of what we understand as being the 'real world', and there is here a kind of fast lane to positivism.

I agree with Tony Lawson's distinction between events and processes.[3] A 'process' is a notion central to the works of Marx and Keynes,[4] and here we understand it not as a sequence of events but as '... the genesis, reproduction and decline of some structural mechanism or thing, the formation, reformation and decay of some entity in time'.[5] This realism is completely different from empirical realism, which takes for granted the notion that any human agent can have a direct, non-mediated access to reality.

'Realism' as I use the word is both procedural and subjectivist. Subjectivism does not mean that human subjectivity is the only possible reality, a fallacy commonly found in some post-modern authors, but that subjective views of reality, insofar as they shape human decisions, are part of reality. Realism will then define methodological constraints for economists. That does not mean that economics must have a specific methodology, which is the position of mainstream economists defending Friedman's instrumentalism, but rather that the methodological requirements for social science can have distinct applications for economics, with specific methodological rules for conducting enquiries or for story-telling.[6] Elsewhere I have described what such applications in the methodology of economics could be.[7] Realist economics does not bear kindly theoretical tinkering or *ad hoc* arguments. There are limits to pluralism, as I have explained in *Post-Autistic Economics Review*.[8]

A coherent research programme needs to be developed for a realistic economics. To this end I offer the following seven theoretical theses.

Thesis 1: The central issue in economics is the co-ordination of decisions and interactions generated by decentralised, heterogeneous and interdependent agents whose decision-making abilities are constrained by limited cognitive capacities.

In the real world, in its theoretical sense, decision-making is done in a decentralised way. Not to acknowledge this fact is to reduce human agents to the status of mere parts of a giant machine, the issue then being who is the power behind such a machine – God Almighty, the market auctioneer (pace Walras), the Party general secretary or the mainstream economist himself.

But human agents are not only decentralised, they also are heterogeneous. Not to acknowledge heterogeneity, as when one assumes identical decision-making patterns and initial positions or a single commonly shared rationality principle, transforms 'the community of human agents' into a world of clones. If this were really the case there would be no sense in talking about decentralisation even in a politically free society.

The decentralisation principle is then largely grounded on refuting the possibility of a single rationality principle that could be shared by all agents, everywhere, always and under every possible condition. Daniel Kahneman and his colleagues, the late Amos Tversky especially but also Richard Thaler, Paul Slovic and Sarah Lichtenstein to name just a few, have made this refutation.[9] The reluctance of mainstream economists to acknowledge these scientific results – a paradoxical position for a group professing fondness for the Popperian legacy – betrays their unwillingness to accept true decentralisation, whatever they may say about possible different initial human and material resources allocations to individuals. Heterogeneity is a necessary concept for understanding decentralisation. Ultimately heterogeneity means more than just that situations can be different and thus also the social positions from where decisions are made. This is heterogeneity in its descriptive sense. In a more analytical sense heterogeneity derives from the fact that patterns of decision-making, models of rationality – here to be understood as the simple fact of having a reason for doing something – are different. Heterogeneity is not exogenous to the decision-making process, something that a dedicated policy could eradicate, but instead something at the very heart of this process.

The interdependency of decentralised and heterogeneous agents must be understood. The standard economics theoretical tradition emphasizes the Robinson Crusoe metaphor, negating the interdependency issue, and envisions the social process from the point of view of a completely isolated individual. Against this tradition, realist economists conscientiously put the issue of possible unintended effects of individual decisions on other agents at the very centre of economic activity and as part of social life. Here they reclaim both Hayek's legacy, at least the one coming from *The Constitution of Liberty*,[10] and the Durkheimian one with its concept of *social density*.[11] This last, that the web of intentional and unintentional relations and the perceptions related to them is the real place where decisions are made, was developed by Emile Durkheim in his seminal work on the social impact of the division of labour.[12]

Jointly to acknowledge decentralisation and interdependency implies a switch from the allocation paradigm to the co-ordination one. Co-ordination can be achieved through intentional processes (networks and hierarchies) as well as through unintentional ones (markets). But whatever the process one thinks fits best at a given time and for a given problem, decentralisation is the central issue.

Anti-realism as a methodological strategy supported by mainstream economists does not stop with rejection of heterogeneity and/or interdependency. Perfect information, as in the initial Walrasian model or the rational expectations theory, is part of such a strategy. Refutation of the perfect information assumption can be epistemic. Simon and de Groot have shown that even if a perfect information structure could exist, our cognitive capacities preclude us from computing in enough time for this structure to be of actual use in our decision-making process.[13] But refuting the perfect information assumption can also be ontological. Perfect information could be an unreachable goal because the real world is too complex to be understood – the classical Hayekian understanding of uncertainty – or because our own attempts to gather more information generate endogenous modifications of the information structure (Stiglitz, Akerlof). Uncertainty is then not an exogenous addition but is endogenously generated. This understanding of uncertainty puts the asymmetrical information school on the right side of the methodological realism border when compared to the information search school (Stigler).

One has to add that if we agree with the fact that there cannot be a single and common rationality principle then the rational expectations theory is devoid of any logical basis. Whatever the reason for endogenous uncertainty, this assumption is another defining characteristic of mainstream or non-realist economics. It is so as to deny uncertainty that neo-classical economics pretends to give to profit and price a natural law dimension.[14]

Denial of the relevance of time and money is a common attribute of varieties of non-realist economics, whether because they refuse to acknowledge heterogeneity or interdependency or endogenous uncertainty, is their Realist economics, on the other hand, stresses time and money relevance. Time is relevant as a causal factor,[15] something that was understood quite early by Gunnar Myrdal who pointed to the relevance of the ex-ante/ex-post divide in the perceptions of economic agents,[16] and by the classical institutionalist school with its first mover/second mover paradigm.[17] Time is also relevant as a delay between decision and effects or between a demand and a supply response, as clearly understood by Mordecai Ezeckiel a long time ago.[18]

Money is a necessary institution for co-ordination. It generates the illusion of homogeneity that agents need to make complex decisions on the basis of their limited cognitive capabilities and because, by allowing for the separation between income formation and income utilisation, money makes possible a better use of time.

Thesis 2: If money is a necessity in an uncertain world, money also introduces a specific form of uncertainty, casting doubts on the market's ability to process information efficiently.

In a world devoid of uncertainty money would not matter. But money gives to every agent in an uncertain world the ability to shelter himself in liquidity. Liquidity in turn allows every agent to defect from the long and continuous chain of interdependencies generated by the division of labour. This very possibility of defection introduces a new strategic uncertainty that is at the heart of economic decision-making in money-based economic systems. Actually there is a deep interaction between uncertainty and the flight to liquidity, which in turn generates this strategic uncertainty. This was perfectly described years ago by G L S Shackle:

When knowledge seems especially elusive, we desire money rather than specialised, vulnerable assets. We sell the assets, their prices fall and it becomes no longer worthwhile to produce them, no longer worthwhile to invest, to give employment. Had Keynes attended to Cantillon, he could have freed himself from the proposition that an employer will always offer a wage equal to marginal product of value of his body of employed people. For since he must employ people first and sell their product later, he cannot know for sure what their marginal product is going to be.[19]

Hyman Minsky has shown how financial innovation, has burgeoned during the second half of the twentieth century, could be deeply destabilising.[20] From Marx to Keynes, realist economists have analysed how the flight to liquidity should put crisis – not equilibrium – at the centre of economic thinking. Crisis is the permanent horizon of a capitalist economy because either liquidity is too much in demand or is not wanted at all. The specific uncertainty generated by liquidity pushes economic systems toward under-investment and under-employment. This uncertainty cannot be managed by economic computation and can be called radical uncertainty.

Here we are facing the first paradox of money. As an institution money pretends to solve the heterogeneity problem by setting monetary prices as a common norm for decision-making, something that makes the deepening of the division of labour possible. However by doing so money generates the radical uncertainty that constrains the expansion of the division of labour.

A second paradox of money is that as an institution it would seem to unify time through interest rates and its function as a reserve of value. But money, through its liquidity function, contributes greatly to making the future even more uncertain.

The twin paradoxes of money stress the fact that if monetary prices are a necessary fiction, from the realist economics point of view, they nonetheless are a fiction. That was precisely what Max Weber tried to show when explaining that monetary prices are necessary in a decentralised economy but are not the result of demand and supply equilibrium – as capitalist spontaneous collective thinking pretends. Monetary prices actually reflect the balance of power between social or individual forces and interests.[21] Keynes, in one of his first works, wrote something very similar. He explained that inflation and deflation translated into the monetary world social conflicts opposing large, structured social groups.[22]

However if monetary prices are a necessary fiction they also are an uncompleted one.[23] They are unable to carry the whole range of information needed for decision-making. Because we need information that cannot be conveyed through monetary prices and that belong then to different information spaces, our decisions are situated and embedded in multidimensional worlds. One consequence is that the transitivity of individual preferences is broken in a systematic way.[24] Then the Allais Paradox holds true,[25] and we can forget the subjective expected utility theory and every device invented by mainstream economics to transform the static Walrasian world into a dynamic one and to cope with uncertainty (even in a Bayesian form). A second consequence, as demonstrated by Grossman and Stiglitz, is that in such a situation, where prices do not convey all needed information, competitive markets are not informational efficient.[26]

Thesis 3: Time and money are at the very heart of the interchange between the individual and collective levels.

Time matters, inter alia, because of the time constraint: the more we wait before making a decision the more we lose even if our decision is the perfect one. However the time constraint has not the same meaning for individuals and groups. Our decision tempo is largely shaped by our more or less deep insertion into collective groups, from the family to the enterprise, including social and political organizations. In turn, the way collective groups are institutionalised also shapes their impact on our individual use of time and our sensibility to the time constraint.

The power that money gives, particularly as liquidity, is not used in a vacuum of representations. Kahneman and his colleagues have demonstrated that our individual preferences are shaped, or more precisely 'framed' by collective contexts.[27] But the way I use my liquidity power could affect decisively some collective groups to which I belong, even if I have no idea of this fact. A run on the bank, even if induced by misguided collective representations, is a movement of thousands of individuals who try to protect their savings but by doing so, usually destroy most of the economic context supporting collective groups (enterprises) from where their income is generated.

Any serious attempt to make time and money relevant, from a theoretical point of view, amounts to repudiating methodological individualism. But because time and money relevance comes from interdependency and from social density, we also have to repudiate the idea of a single dominating collective context. If realist economics embraces methodological holism it is a non-deterministic holism.

Thesis 4: Any attempt to negate the theoretical status of time and money leads to non-scientific assumptions and transforms the economist himself into a producer of ideology.

Being serious about time and money places economics in the very middle of the social sciences. If statistical regularities and stabilities are to be found, they are not the products of intemporal laws but of social systems of institutions. The stability of these systems is itself a local and temporary phenomenon. On the other hand if one wants to ground economics on laws similar to ones found in natural sciences, in physics or mechanics, one has to negate time and money relevance. Such a strategy is logically coherent if and only if one negates either decentralisation or interdependency. Both are radical retreats from realism.

Here we have one of the most fanciful paradoxes of mainstream economics. To reject realism for axiomatics, mainstream thinkers have to invoke ergodicity.[28] But to pretend that economic processes could be in any sense a kind of ergodic process, one has to demonstrate that they are subject to a determination which is non-human (thereby violating the initial assumption of decentralised decision-making) and non-social. Obviously the standard theory of individual preferences and its conclusion, the closed and universal model of rationality, fit nicely here.

Traditional assumptions about individual preferences (transitivity, continuity, reflexivity, independence and time monotony) are then not just ad hoc assumptions but the logical core for any instrumentalist methodology grounded on preference utilitarianism.[29] They provide the stable, non-social, reference point needed to pretend that observable local economic stabilities are like the exposed tips of yet unknown 'natural' laws of economics.

It happens to be the case, however, that all these axioms can be tested and found to be invalid.[30] Facing such results, most mainstream thinkers pretend they are irrelevant. They dismiss the very idea of confronting an economic theory with real life experiments.[31] By doing so they fail to understand that they can claim legitimacy for the axiomatic approach if and only if they can find empirical grounds for their ergodic assumption. What psychology has done is no less than to destroy the only substantial argument for ergodicity, that is, the universality and stability of the neoclassical model of rationality.

A willingness to integrate into economic theory the findings of applied psychology, versus a refusal to do so, is the true borderline between economics as a scientific activity and economics as production of ideology. The defence of axiomatism clearly no longer belongs to any kind of scientific approach to economic phenomenon but instead is a form of religious thinking.

In contrast to the we-do-not-want-to-know approach, George Akerlof has succeeded in integrating recent psychology results to a theory of inflation, which is clearly Keynesian.[32] Akerlof's writings are living proof that Kahneman and Tversky works can be solid ground for Keynesian assumptions, particularly when it comes to money and time.[33]

Thesis 5: To regard money as the one central institution in a market economy fails to break free from the neo-classical framework. Emphasizing only money could be as theoretically misleading as ignoring money.

It is clear that understanding money's relevance is a cornerstone of economic theory. Yet this position can evolve into a mistaken one no less dangerous than the neo-classical denial of money's relevance: monetary essentialism. It is the path taken by two French authors with whom otherwise I generally agree, Michel Aglietta and André Orléan, the latter a well-known and long-standing PAE contributor. Because they claim to have developed a workable alternative to the money denial strategy favoured by neo-classical and some Marxist authors alike[34] (which gives monetary policy and Central Bank independence a strong legitimacy), monetary essentialism is worth serious investigation. As a matter of fact, if one could demonstrate that money is as pivotal as monetary essentialism pretends it is, one would have a pretty good argument for asserting the superiority of monetary authorities over political ones.

Monetary essentialism moves beyond acknowledging money relevance against the neo-classical cum-monetarist tradition to the point of proclaiming money the central, pivotal, market economy institution.[35] It acknowledges the fact that there is a deeply entrenched violence in monetary relations that cannot be reduced to an allocative process. Monetary essentialism is innovative in its aim of linking economics to anthropology and it is grounded on what Aglietta and Orléan call the Fundamental Girardian Theorem from the French Catholic philosopher and anthropologist René Girard.[36]

Years ago Girard developed an anthropological theory of violence that he opposes to one emphasising the social roots of conflicts. His theory is grounded on the genesis of violence erupting from an undifferentiated mob driven by a demand for wealth. This word resonates in the economist's ears. However in Girard's works wealth is an all-encompassing notion running from material goods and money to social status and parental love. Because it is such a global, all-encompassing notion, it is possible to conceive of a universe of one-dimensional choices where 'wealth' is the measure of everything. This conception resembles the neoclassical concept of price that is supposed to carry all necessary information. In a Girardian world an economist would be, to paraphrase Oscar Wilde, a cynic who knows the wealth of everything and the value of nothing. In this universe of one-dimensional choices, individual preference transitivity could then be logically demonstrated and the neoclassical theory of preference and rationality given a new rationale. One could then forget that in the real world, and specifically when money is at stake, it has been demonstrated that violations of transitivity are systematic.[37]

It is, however, perfectly clear that the Girardian genesis of violence is no less unrealistic and anti-social than the Robinson Crusoe metaphor that Austrian marginalists were so fond of. All the perfumes of Girardian wealth could not sweeten the neo-classical price. Aglietta and Orléan run into a serious contradiction. Admirably they profess their willingness to break with the neo-classical logic. However although they claim to reject the view of a fully determined world – a position I completely share with them – they fall into another fallacy: that of pretending that there are no central rules but money. To do this they have to stick with violence as understood by René Girard.[38] Then they have to pretend that there are no stable social relations between agents, that they are un-socialised social actors.[39] This is one dimension of the neoclassical fallacy. The so-called Fundamental Girardian Theorem is supposed to say that unanimity could be the result of a spontaneous convergence, hence the undifferentiated demand for wealth could give birth to a global social agreement. However Orléan remarks with some ingenuity that if we introduce one differentiation level in the primitive wealth-driven population then unanimity is no longer a spontaneous result.[40] Substitute unanimity for equilibrium and you would have an exact restatement of the Grossman–Stiglitz paradox.[41] The Girardian Theorem's sensitiveness to heterogeneity is another proof that it is next-of-kin to the neo-classical equilibrium and Girardian wealth to Walrasian price. Anyone cruel enough to introduce the endowment effect and the framing effect into the picture would lead the Girardian Theorem to its self-destruction and monetary essentialism to its methodological collapse.

What is problematical with monetary essentialism is not its emphasis on violence or its attempt to link economics to anthropology. The problem lies with the anti-social anthropology that it mobilises, a theory leading not to a definitive break with neo-classical orthodoxy but to the reverse, a return toward typical neoclassical simplifications and methodological unrealism.

Thesis 6: The idea that there is one pivotal institution in a market economy is devoid of meaning. Institutions cannot be assessed in isolation. What matter are institutional systems or precisely defined hierarchical clusters of institutions

If money cannot be seen as the central institution of a market economy, then maybe property rights could be seen as an alternative[42]. After all, without property rights it is difficult to understand market transactions. However when one discusses property rights it is frequently private property that is at stake. But, as explained years ago by Richard Nelson, private property does not work as an operational concept enabling us to delineate differences between forms of social organization.[43] To oppose private to collective ownership is to run quickly into an interesting, if frequently forgotten, paradox.

If property rights are to be defined inside a society, then we have more than one economic agent to think about. Hence, what agent (a) is doing could affect in an unintentional way the wealth and position of agent (b). The latter could sue the former who then would think twice before doing anything if the penalty were significant by comparison to the expected result of his own action. This is nothing more than a restatement of the Shackle Paradox, explaining that decentralised decision-making gives birth to uncertainty and that uncertainty could prevent decentralised agents from making decisions.[44] To prevent unintended effects from paralysing the whole of social life, every society has developed a different set of rules to constrain our individual freedom to use and abuse our properties. Rules, without which no individual action is possible in a society, are nothing less than collective property rights. Hence, individual property rights cannot exist without collective ones. And if to avoid this problem we attempt to define individual property rights from the Robinson Crusoe metaphor, then we define something that does not exist. Before the landing of Friday, Robinson, alone on his island, owns everything and yet nothing. Property rights here have no meaning.

Private and collective property rights cannot be opposed and are actually closely integrated. But, if we have to think about collective ownership to understand private ownership then it is mandatory to think about the way human collectives are organized. Political issues (how legitimacy and legality interact) matter then as much as property rights. They cannot be substituted for money as the pivotal market economy institution, and I hope that this discussion had made a case against the whole idea of defining any 'pivotal' institution.

Let us now return to the problem of money. We have to reckon with the fact that barter trade can exist simultaneously with money, meaning that there is more to be considered than just the fact that money is a more effective and rational transaction medium than barter.[45] The development of barter trade in Russia from 1993 to 1998, a period when inflation was actually decelerating (barter was at its highest point early 1998 when inflation was down to 12 per cent a year), raises an important theoretical issue. The use of money receded not because the value of money was disappearing as happens during a hyperinflation crisis (remember the Weimar Republic and the wheelbarrows full of banknotes) but because institutions, without which money cannot be used, were missing.[46] The development of barter trade in Russia was the result of a lack of financial institutions, the result of the liberal monetary policy implemented from October 1993 onwards.[47] It was also the result of a lack of trust[48] resulting from the weakening of State institutions through the particular privatization process then implemented by Anatolyi Chubays and his US crony advisers.[49] Money, as an institution, needs both technical institutions (mostly in the finance sector) and political ones to support it and make it effective. In turn, after the August 1998 crash, barter receded not because of any hard monetary policy (actually inflation rose) but because Primakov's government worked hard to rebuild state legitimacy and institutions.[50]

Money can be relevant when two specific freedoms or rights can be found in any transaction: the freedom to engage in a transaction with whom one wants and the freedom to engage when one wants. Both these freedoms do not exist for every possible transaction. Sometimes technical constraints drastically reduce the first one, so that vertical integration, that is the substitution of a hierarchy for a market, is then the logical evolution. And social constraints can reduce both the first and the second freedoms. In any case, these freedoms or rights imply a whole set of institutions which, in turn, defines the place and form money can take at a given time in a given market economy.

The central issue is then not the functionality of a single institution but how institutions in a given set can be mutually supportive. In the end it is the coherence level achieved by the institutional system that is the analytical key of statistical stabilities and medium-term trends. When money is at stake, it is the coherence (or the lack of it) between managing institutions (central bank, financial markets, banking system, international financial institutions) and related ones (public regulations, labour–management relations, balance of property rights between individual and collective ownership, institutional forms of the social protection system, regulation of human, material and financial trans-border flows) that really matters. The coherence issue, be it static or dynamic, is then the central one for realist economics.

Thesis 7: The embeddedness of any institutional system in a given territory, itself a social and historical construction, is an omission from mainstream economics that is hidden behind the denial of time and money relevance.

Time and money have led us to institutions. Not just the usual discussion about institution functionality but to the understanding that an institution cannot be considered in isolation. Institutional systems, coherent and hierarchal sets of institutions, are the main issue. Rejecting the functionalist fallacy about institutions means also rejecting any functionalist understanding of the birth of institutions.[51] The Hayekian view of spontaneous selection raises many methodological and theoretical problems. Among them the two most vexing are:

(a) the Hayekian selection process introduces a methodological holism dimension into an otherwise individualist theory (institutions are selected through groups) and

(b) that without assuming temporal monotony of individual preferences it is impossible to prove that selection has not been accidental unless one assumes a stationary universe.

Up to now the only realist theory of institution generation has been that of François Guizot. Social conflicts of opposing human groups have been the historical process of institutional development and selection.[52] The dynamic of these conflicts develops in the space of sovereignty, which is then shaped by the development of conflicts. Such a process makes the distinction between rules and the principles on which rules are founded a pervasive necessity.

Social density implies the necessity of rules, as individual agents are unable to forecast all possible unintentional effects of their own actions. This makes them unable to write complete and perfect contracts. Contract incompleteness and imperfection make rules a necessity. Institutions generate rules but individual institutions are incomplete as shown above. To make institutional systems work in a coherent way, rules of a greater magnitude are needed. They are laws as produced by political institutions. But the human agent's inability to write complete and perfect contracts applies here too. It is then to be expected that laws will be contested even if the process under which they have been produced has respected its own rules. Hence, the rule of law is not enough unless we can prove that the concerned human community is perfectly homogeneous and composed only of people driven by the best set of sentiments possible.[53] The emphasis put on the rule of law, as in the British and American mainstream tradition, reveals a deep negation of the heterogeneity principle.[54]

The legality of the process does not confer on a law the legitimacy it needs. Legitimacy proceeds from the principles that characterise political communities which, historically, are territorially defined. In turn one can see how the neo-classical view of a world with perfect information is congruent to an understanding of institutions reduced to their functionality and to the negation of the legitimacy principle for the sake of making the rule of law the one and only benchmark.[55]

If we agree that economics is not a natural science, that on the contrary economic processes are embedded in social and historical construction, then the institution building process is as much political as economic. It cannot be divorced from links between a given territory and a political community. Even in the globalization age, the nation state matters. It matters both when it functions and when, weakened by decades of neoliberal policies, it is no more able to play its part. The the way Malaysia rode the financial storm in 1998 which sank Indonesia shows not just a difference between a wise and an unwise economic policy. The Malaysian state was still functional whereas the Indonesian one had been dramatically weakened. Malaysian economic and political elites were then in a position to resist IMF policy and implement effective decisions (like currency control) when Indonesian elites were so fragmented and deprived of legitimacy that they had to abide by IMF prescriptions with their usually catastrophic results.[56]

If institutional systems can only be understood in a dynamic way by including the shaping of space by centuries of social and political processes and conflicts, it follows that economics has meaning only as a study of the political economy. This political economy needs to seriously address the nationstate issue as well as the fact that no nation state is fully homogeneous and that institutional differentiation can be found within any state. Institutional differentiation inside a given nation state can explain why regional competitiveness is frequently not uniform and why some regions develop faster than others do at a given time. In turn this can be understood only on the basis of acknowledging the social dimension of any institution, including given sets of markets. The development of an effective market economy ('effective' and not 'efficient' because outside the neo-classical theoretical framework this word is devoid of meaning) is always the result of a given social process. Markets are socially constructed systems.[57] The development of regional studies is then a logical and necessary addition to a comprehensive research programme for realist economics.[58]

Notes

*   This chapter is a translation and adaptation of one that appeared in the French journal *Alternatives Économiques* (**57**, 2003, hors série, pp. 54–6, see also www.alternatives-economiques.fr) and is published here with authorisation of the journal's editorial board. The initial aim was to review assumptions developed in an earlier book, *Les trous noirs de la science économique* (Albin Michel, Paris, 2000) and to specify some details that could be of use for the PAE readership.

    This book was published in the very middle of the battle following the French students' appeal for more realism in the teaching of economics (Spring 2000) and sold quickly, being re-printed twice before its pocket edition in September 2003. This coincidental publishing was a pure stroke of luck. The book was written between 1995 and 1998 when I was teaching at the *Vyshaya Shkola Ekonomiki* (Higher School in Economics, Moscow). From lectures delivered in Moscow I wrote first a basic book for Russian students (*K Ekonomicheskoy teorii neodnorodnykh sistem opyt issledovaniya –decentralizovannoy ekonomiki* (Economic theory of heterogeneous systems; an essay on decentralised economies)) which was published by Vyshaya Shkola Ekonomiki Press, Moscow, in 2001. At the same time I re-focused and expanded part of its content to write *Les trous noirs*, this time not as a basic book but as a critical essay on mainstream economics. This second book is not then the translation of the Russian one, although they are closely related.

    I have adapted and developed here the arguments of the *Alternatives Économiques* paper for the sake of an English language readership not necessarily aware of debates currently raging in Paris.

1. Professor of economics, EHESS-Paris, director CEMI-EHESS.
2. U Mäki, 'How to combine rhetoric and realism in the methodology of economics', in *Economics and Philosophy*, 4, April 1988, pp. 353–73.
3. T Lawson, 'Realism and instrumentalism in the development of econometrics, in *Oxford Economic Papers*, 41, January 1989, pp. 236–58.
4. For the latter, A M Carabelli, *On Keynes's Method*, Macmillan, London, 1988.
5. T Lawson, *Economics and Reality*, Routledge, London & New York, 1997, p. 34.
6. C Lloyd, *Explanations in Social History*, Basil Blackwell, Oxford, 1986.
7. J Sapir, 'Calculer, comparer, discuter: apologie pour une méthodologie ouverte en économie, in *Économies et Sociétés*, série F, 36, January 1998, pp. 77–89.
8. J Sapir, 'Realism vs. Axiomatics' in Edward Fullbrook (ed.), *The Crisis in Economics*, Routledge, London & New York, 2003, pp. 58–61.

9. For a now quite old review of this literature see J Sapir, 'Théorie de la régulation, conventions, institutions et approches hétérodoxes de l'interdépendance des niveaux de décision', in A Vinokur (ed.), *Décisions économiques*, Économica, Paris, 1998, pp. 169–215. Also: A Tversky, 'Rational theory and constructive choice', in K J Arrow, E Colombatto, M Perlman and C Schmidt (eds), *The Rational Foundations of Economic Behaviour*, Macmillan and St. Martin's Press, Basingstoke and New York, 1996, pp. 185–97.

10. F Hayek, *The Constitution of Liberty*, University of Chicago Press, Chicago, 1960.

11. E Durkheim, *Les règles de la méthode sociologique*, PUF, coll. Quadriges, Paris, 1999 (1937).

12. E Durkheim, *De la division du travail social*, PUF, coll. Quadriges, Paris, 1991 (1893).

13. A de Groot, *Thought and Choice in Chess*, Mouton, La Haye, 1965. De Groot's work has been much used by Herbert Simon. See H A Simon, 'Theories of bounded rationality', in C B Radner and R Radner (eds), *Decision and Organization*, North Holland, Amsterdam, 1972, pp. 161–76.

14. G L S Shackle, 'The origination of choice', in I M Kirzner (ed.), *Subjectivism, Intelligibility and Economic Understanding*, Macmillan, London, 1986, pp. 281–7.

15. M Capek, *The Philosophical Impact of Contemporary Physics*, Van Nostrand, Princeton, 1961, G P O'Driscoll Jr and M J Rizzo, *Economics of Time and Ignorance*, Basil Blackwell, Oxford, 1985, pp. 60–61.

16. G Myrdal, *Monetary Equilibrium*, W Hodge, London, 1939, pp. 43–4.

17. W M Dugger, 'Transaction cost economics and the state', in C Pitelis, (ed.), *Transaction Costs, Markets and Hierarchies*, Basil Blackwell, Oxford, 1993, pp. 188–216.

18. M Ezekiel, The cobweb theorem', in *Quarterly Journal of Economics*, 52 (1), 1937–8.

19. G L S Shackle, *Business, Time and Thought. Selected Papers of G L S Shackle*, New York University Press, New York, 1988, p. 43.

20. H P Minsky, *Stabilizing an Unstable Economy*, Yale University Press, New Haven, CT, 1986.

21. M Weber, *Economy and Society: An Outline of Interpretative Sociology*, University of California Press, Berkeley, 1948, p.108. See also about the nature of money in Chapter 2 in the first part of *Wirtschaft und Gesellschaft*, translated as M Weber, *The Theory of Social and Economic Organization*, Free Press, New York, 1964.

22. J M Keynes, 'A tract on monetary reform', reprinted in J M Keynes, *Essays in Persuasion*, Rupert Hart-Davis, London, 1931.

23. C Deutschmann, 'Money as a social construction: on the actuality of Marx and Simmel', in *Thesis Eleven*, 47, November 1996, pp. 1–19.

24. This is clearly a consequence of the 'endowment effect'. See D Kahneman, J Knetsch and R Thaler, 'The endowment effect, loss aversion and status quo bias', in *Journal of Economic Perspectives*, 5 (1), 1991, pp. 193–206.

25. M Allais, 'Le comportement de l'homme rationnel devant le risque. Critique des postulats de l'école américaine', in *Econométrica*, 21, 1953, 503–46. Also M Allais and O Hagen (eds) *Expected Utility Hypotheses and the Allais Paradox*, Reidel, Dordrecht, 1979.

26. S J Grossman and J Stiglitz, iInformation and competitive price systems, *American Economic Review*, 66 (3), May 1976, Papers and Proceedings of the Annual Meeting of the American Economic Association.

27. The framing effect is well described in D Kahneman, 'New challenges to the rationality assumption', in K J. Arrow, E Colombatto, M Perlman and C Schmidt

(eds), *The Rational Foundations of Economic Behaviour*, St. Martin's Press, New York, 1996, pp. 203–19.

28. For an enlightening analysis about how not to use the ergodicity concept see P Mirowski, *More Heat than Light*, Cambridge University Press, London and New York, 1989. See also B Ingrao and G.Israel, 'General equilibrium theory: a history of ineffectual paradigm shifts', in *Fundamenta Scientiae*, 6, 1985, pp. 1–45 and 89–125; P Mirowski, 'Energy and energetics in economy theory', in *Journal of Economic Issues*, **22**, 1984, pp. 811–30.

29. C Harsanyi, 'Morality and the theory of rational behaviour', in A Sen and B Williams, *Utilitarianism and Beyond*, Cambridge University Press and Éditions de la Maison des Sciences de l'Homme, Cambridge and Paris, 1982, pp. 39–62.

30. D Kahneman, 'New challenges to the rationality assumption', in K J Arrow, E Colombatto, M Perlman and C Schmidt (eds), *The Rational Foundations of Economic Behaviour*, St. Martin's Press, New York, 1996, pp. 203–19.

31. For a good example of such an argument, see M Friedman, 'The methodology of positive economics', in M Friedman, *Essays in Positive Economics*, Chicago University Press, 1953, pp. 30–31.

32. G A Akerlof, W T Dickens, G L Perry, (1996), 'The macroeconomics of low inflation', in *Brookings Papers on Economic Activity*, pp. 1–76 ; Andersen T M, (2001) 'Can inflation be too low?', in *Kyklos*, 54 (4), pp. 591–602.

33. G.A. Akerlof, 'Behavioral macroeconomics and macroeconomic behavior', in *American Economic Review*, 92 (3), June 2002, pp. 411–33, p. 424; the source quoted here is D Kahneman and A Tversky, 'Prospect theory: an analysis of decision under risk', in *Econometrica*, 47 (2), March 1979, pp. 263–92.

34. M Aglietta and A Orléan, *La Violence de la monnaie*, PUF, Paris, 1982; Idem, *La Monnaie entre violence et confiance*, Odile Jacob, Paris, 2002. Both authors explicitly state that their theory is not just a refutation of neo-classical assumptions but also of the Marxian Theory of Value.

35. M Aglietta and A Orléan, *La Monnaie entre violence et confiance*, op cit, p. 81.

36. A.Orléan, 'Monnaie et spéculation mimétique', in P Dumouchel (ed.), *Violence et vérité autour de René Girard*, Paris, Grasset, 1978, pp. 147–58.

37. L Ausubel, 'The failure of competition in the credit-card market', in *American Economic Review*, 81 (1), 1991, pp. 50–81.

38. M Aglietta, 'L'institution de base des sociétés marchandes,' in *Alternatives Économiques*, **57**, 2003, p. 32.

39. A Orléan, 'Monnaie et spéculation mimétique', op cit, p. 148.

40. Ibid, pp.151 and 152.

41. S J Grossman and J E Stiglitz, 'On the impossibility of informationally efficient markets', op cit.

42. O Hart and J Moore, 'Property rights and the theory of the firm', in *Journal of Political Economy*, 98 (6), 1990; E G Furobtn and S Pejovich, 'Property rights and economic theory: a survey of recent literature', in *Journal of Economic Literature*, 10 (4) 1972.

43. R R Nelson, 'Assessing private enterprise: an exegesis of tangled doctrine', in *Bell Journal of Economics*, 12 (1), 1981, Spring, pp. 93–111.

44. G L S Shackle, *Decision, Order and Time in Human Affairs*, Cambridge University Press, Cambridge, 1969.

45. This opinion has been developed in A Alchian, 'Why money?', in *Journal of Money*,

Credit and Banking, 9 (1), 1977, pp. 133–40. For the opposite view and a discussion of the simultaneous presence of both money and barter, J Sapir, 'Le troc et le paradoxe de la monnaie', in *Journal des Anthropologues*, 90–91, December 2002, pp. 283–304.

46. D Woodruff, *Money Unmade: Barter and the Fate of Russian Capitalism*, Cornell University Press, Cornell, 1999.

47. J Sapir, 'À l'épreuve des faits ... Bilan des politiques macroéconomiques mises en oeuvre en Russie', in *Revue d'études comparatives est-ouest*, 30 (2–3), 1999, pp 153–213.

48. D Marin, 'Trust vs. illusion: what is driving demonetization in Russia?', discussion paper series, no. 2570, CEPR, London, September 2000.

49. J. Sapir, 'La crise financière russe comme révélateur des carences de la transition libérale', in *Diogène*, 194, April–June 2001, pp. 119–32.

50. J Sapir, 'Russian crash of August 1998: Diagnosis and prescriptions', *Post-Soviet Affairs* (ex-*Soviet Economy*), 15 (1), 2000, pp. 1–36.

51. On the functionalist fallacy, see Stiglitz's Nobel Lecture, J E Stiglitz, 'Information and the change in the paradigm in economics', in *American Economic Review*, 92 (3), June 2002, pp. 460–501.

52. F Guizot, *Histoire de la civilisation en France depuis la chute de l'Empire Romain*, Didier, Paris, 1869, 7th lesson, 1828.

53. This argument has been well demonstrated by Carl Schmitt. Although one may reject his conclusion and be disgusted by his political positions between 1920 and 1945, he is certainly a founding father for a realist understanding of paradoxes of a democratic society. See C Schmitt, *Legalität und Legitimität*, Duncker & Humblot, Berlin 1932 (there is one French translation of this book as *Légalité et Légitimité* but, to the best of my knowledge, none in English). Idem, *The Crisis of Parliamentary Democracy*, MIT Press, Cambridge, MA, 1985 (1926).

54. See C Mouffe, 'Carl Schmitt and the paradox of liberal democracy', in C Mouffe (ed.), *The Challenge of Carl Schmitt*, Verso, London & New York, 1999, pp. 38–53.

55. J Sapir, *Les économistes contre la démocratie*, Albin Michel, Paris, 2002.

56. For a good discussion about the Asian crisis and different responses put by different governments, R Wade, 'The coming fight over capital controls', in *Foreign Policy*, 113, Winter 1998–9, pp. 41–54; R S Rajan, 'Sands in the wheels of international finance: revisiting the debate in light of the East Asian mayem', Institute of Policy Studies working paper, Singapore, April 1999; and B J Cohen, 'Contrôle des capitaux: pourquoi les gouvernements hésitent-ils?, in *Revue économique*, 52 (2), March 2001, pp. 207–32.

57. A Bagnasco and C Trigilia, *La construzione sociale del mercato. Studi sullo sviluppo di picola imprese in Italia*, Il Mulino, Bologna, 1988.

58. G Benko and M Dunford, (eds), *Industrial Change and Regional Development*, Pinter/Belhaven Press, London, 1991; G Benko and U Strohmayer (eds), *Space and Social Theory*, Blackwell, Oxford, 1997; G Benko, *La Science Régionale*, PUF, Paris, 1998.

11.

HOW REALITY ATE ITSELF: ORTHODOXY, ECONOMY AND TRUST

Jamie Morgan

Quis custodiet ipsos custodies? (Who guards the guards?)

An economic theory that cannot sustain its own viability is a poor one but can also be a powerful one. A market economy may valorise the symbolism of the invisible hand but it is as equally beholden to the symbolism of the tacit handshake. The handshake is a metonym for a relationship and a market economy is a set of relationships inscribed in rules, tacit or otherwise. First among equals are trust and the means by which trust is enacted and maintained. Without trust nothing else functions and social reality would be impossible.

The philosopher J L Austin was one of the first to recognize the importance of this.[1] There are at least two dynamics to talking about social reality. First, description, where we designate things true or false by reference to them as objects or past events – the hat is black, yesterday was Wednesday and we had lunch. Second, performance, where current conduct and dialogue constitute a new conceptual element to social reality with material repercussions for future relations – the meeting of hands and 'it's a deal', or the negotiation and witnessed signing of a contract. In the immediate sense, performance is neither strictly true nor false since it is not initially a description, but a doing or making. The doing is in this first instance appropriate or inappropriate, sincere or insincere, successful or a failure. That it is done is in the second instance true or false – the contract as negotiated by two parties with the legal authority to engage in those negotiations was signed by each and entered into in good faith. The glue in this transition is the trust that binds the particular rules of appropriate interaction. The interaction may fail for a variety of reasons that cause immediate problems – an earthquake may prevent the delivery of a consignment required for a just-in-time production process. But these reasons are not devastating to the social institution in which they occur – the sustainability of business agreements perpetuating economic activity. However, when practices are designed to confound basic principles of transparent dealing, when rules are insincerely observed, when a promise ceases to be something you intend to keep, trust dissolves and markets cease to look quite so 'spontaneously' vibrant.

The orthodox Cheshire cat

As has often been argued, the timeless, ahistorical, institution-free fundamentals of orthodox method cannot be easily reconciled to the problems of markets as rule systems. But does it mean that trust and the rules that constitute market systems are not a central problem for orthodox economics? Orthodoxy is about the spontaneous optimality that emerges from the removal of impediments. Since the very idea of rules tends to be conflated with regulation there's nowhere left to hang the structuring of markets. This of course forgets that deregulation is itself a (demonstrably inefficient) form of regulating rule. Its inefficiency and contradiction is that this form of regulation tends to create the conditions for abuse that undermine the trust on which the free economic activity of markets is based. The radical individualism inscribed in it provides for the belief that 'freedom to' massively predominates over 'freedom from'. 'Freedom from', our collective protection from the abuses that undermine the very possibility of individual action, is pushed aside. This deep ideological commitment can be heard in the words of Milton Friedman:

> What's interfering with the recovery is all this fuss about corporate governance, which, in my opinion, is being carried too far. In all these cases – Enron. Global Crossing, WorldCom – it was the collapse in the market that brought attention to them. What's happening now is that the hullabaloo, which in effect is saying that to be a CEO is to be a member of a criminal class, is very adverse for enterprise and risk.[2]

But the collapse of the market is not some natural event, it is the dynamic consequence of complex interactions, many of them unanticipated or unintended. One aspect of this is how the practices that constitute markets can undermine the trust that markets require to function. Criminalising CEOs *is* adverse for enterprise and risk but would not occur if their practices did not contribute to crises that can no longer be disguised or ignored. Economists tend to forget about power, but all human systems have power asymmetries. Holding the powerful to account indicates deep concerns. That orthodoxy cannot recognize this, still less contribute to its analysis in terms of its own theoretical tenets, indicates that it has little that is constructive to say concerning the analysis of an important cause of economic crisis.

In any case, one rarely sees far when the view is from the top, however clear the view may potentially be. In a recent speech Federal Reserve Chairman Alan Greenspan argued that both the eight-trillion-dollar loss of share value on the DOW at the start of the new century and the problems incurred as a result of Enron, etc indicated that the general health of the financial system was good.[3] The basis of his argument was that technology had produced new opportunities for financial 'risk dispersion' and that 'a more flexible world economy' was spreading costs and absorbing shocks more readily. The proof? 'No major US financial institution was driven to default.' In adopting this position, Greenspan reveals himself as something of a stoic, believing that whatever doesn't kill us makes us stronger. Still, the US financial institutions are scarcely the whole body of economy. Default has a quite different meaning for those impoverished by collapsing share values and 'financial irregularities'. Risk dispersion is a hollow term for those unable to pay their mortgages or with no jobs to go to (US unemployment is 6 per cent and rising). If we call the financial head healthy we must still ask ourselves how it is treating its economic body – as a temple or a trash can? And need we call it healthy? The year 2001 broke records in fraud class actions (488 of them) against firms in the US.[4] The majority of actions were against state pension funds and union pension schemes. Around 8,000 to 10,000 individual cases are being filed each year at the National Association of Securities Dealers (NASD). And all of this despite a change in the law to make it more difficult to sue firms for compensation for irregularity: the 1995 Private Securities Litigation Act means that 'aiders and abetters' of wrongdoing in a fraud case cannot be held liable.

Practices that undermine trust

The context of the problem of trust is a finance system dedicated to the unrelenting pursuit of the nearest profitable firm and the next growth sector. Consistent growth provides the basis of a profitable firm and a profitable bull market for the financial industry. When a firm meets its revenue forecasts it can mean a large increase in its share valuation. Analysts categorise firms as 'market out-performers' (MOs), 'market performers' (MPs) and 'market under-performers' (MUs). Whether a stock is rated as a 'buy' a 'neutral' or a 'sell' is, in principle, related to which direction it is tending to in terms of these categories. Conventionally, our perception of shares is based on their price–earnings ratio or P/E.[5] The lower the ratio the greater the earnings of the stock as a proportion of its price and thus the faster one recoups the initial investment. P/E therefore provides a measure of the attractiveness of stock as equity. But how reliable are the price of the share and the earnings of the firms as indicators of the decision to invest? What lurks beneath the numbers? Here, knowledge is power:

- The power to construct the firm's reported revenue stream is subject to strong pressures to place it in the best possible light. In terms of trust, one confronts the question of how far the relationship between the accountants and the firm can stretch. When does creative accounting become aggressive accounting, that in turn becomes collusion in fraud?
- The power to manipulate stock prices through complex financial arrangements on the basis of information that others do not have. Here, the problem of trust comes up against the question, at what point does expertise becomes self-interest to the detriment of the system from which it feeds?

This is not just an issue of legality since trust is more than a question of 'were any laws broken?' Part of the constitution of trust are the ethics that inform how law is made and how it is adhered to – in its spirit or in its letter? The grounds of trust are extremely difficult to define, but easily lost. Losing sight of the importance of trust is the downfall of the system. Its dysfunction becomes ravenous and reality begins to eats itself. Its clearest expression is a debilitating scepticism. Its immediate, though by no means final, consequence is a downward spiral of corporate valuation.

Cannibalising reality?

The past five or six years have seen numerous financial scandals. Since economy is an open system one tends to find a complex interaction of some or all of the above practices within those scandals. The dot.com bubble provided a great deal of scope for spinning (the preferential allocation of stock to favoured clients) and laddering (having investors promise to buy more stock at progressively higher prices once trading begins).

Though cases of spinning are alleged on the London markets, New York has been the focus of investigation.[6] New York Attorney-General Eliot Spitzer has been engaged in protracted investigation of 12 of the major financial institutions for forms of spinning. Most of the evidence is based on private e-mails and documents that contradict the public statements of investment analysts. Henry Blodget, a Merrill Lynch analyst, for example, publicly rated Infospace stock as a buy whilst privately noting, 'This stock is a powder keg … given the bad smell comments that so many institutions are bringing up.'[7] Breach of Chinese walls is also alleged against Citigroup's investment banking arm Salomon Smith Barney, which consistently rated Qwest Communications as a 'buy' up to the point of its price collapse. At the same time, Philip Anschutz, Qwest's founder, was selling Qwest shares amassing a $1.45 billion profit. Anschutz also received 57 allocations for various share issues at a personal profit of around $5 million from Salomon whilst Qwest had generated $37 million in revenue for Salomon from its transactions.[8] Fines imposed by the Securities and Exchange Commission (SEC) on the banks currently stand at $1.4 billion, $900 million of which constitutes compensation for investors, $450 million funding for independent research (to maintain Chinese walls) and $85 million for 'investor education'.[9] Four hundred million dollars of the total will come from Citigroup (who have also set aside $1.5 billion to meet the costs of compensation for further investor litigation).[10]

The dot.com firms themselves and also the new telecommunications companies were highly prone to creative accounting based on capacity swaps and barter in order to massage their revenue figures during the early phase of set-up. This, and talk of new business models making money in completely new ways with extremely low long-run fixed costs, sucked in masses of venture capital (over $40 billion of which is now lost).[11] At the same time, as a high-growth sector, dot.coms provided one of the initial areas of high risk that proved extremely attractive to split capital trust (SCT) managers (along with various high-growth sectors of overseas markets). The fact that some of these issues were spun, of course, meant that the estimation of risk by those managers was baseless and their vulnerability far greater than even they could imagine. Any other shock to the system, such as 9/11, could only exacerbate their vulnerability. The collapse of Aberdeen Asset Management's SCTs contributed to the £10 billion lost by more than 50,000 private investors in this sector.[12]

The possibility that even apparently low-risk investments are not what they seem also emerged. The misuse of 'special purpose vehicles' and 'off-balance sheet obligations' (OSOs) prevents investors relying on firms' accounts with any degree of confidence. WorldCom used OSOs to keep $4 billion off the balance sheet. In 2000 Enron was seventh in the *Fortune* top 500 with reported revenue in excess of $100 billion (a 150 per cent increase on the previous year).[13] Its shares traded at over $60. Its chief financial officer, Andrew Fastow, orchestrated several SPVs set up in the name of his children and his wife, from which he allegedly earned $30 million in fees and siphoned assets. The decline of the DOW over the turn of the millennium made the use of Enron stock to finance continued debt restructuring more difficult and on 16 October 2001 Enron posted a bombshell $1.01 billion loss. The vulnerability inherent in its revenue enhancements then kicked in in earnest. On 17 October the *Wall Street Journal* publicized Fastow's SPV connections. On 29 October, Moody's Investor Service down-rated Enron's credit rating, increasing the servicing costs of its newly revealed debt.

By December 2001 the firm had filed for bankruptcy and it was all over. Its share price had collapsed to less than a cent. Numerous small investors who had relied on its stock for their pensions and large pension funds themselves were hit hard. State pension funds in New York, Georgia and Ohio lost over $350 million. By February 2002 the Bank of America had $231m in Enron-related losses. One hundred Merrill Lynch executives lost $16 million of their own money that had been invested Enron partnerships.[14]

Ordinary Enron employees received no severance pay. In November 2001, however, senior staff had awarded themselves $55 million in 'retention bonuses' from the dregs of its coffers. Just prior to the loss statement of 16 October, 29 senior executives sold stock, over a dozen reaping in excess of $10 million. A class action suit has now been brought against them for insider trading whilst Fastow, and a number of collaborating London bankers, have been indicted for fraud.[15] Meanwhile, Enron's accountant, Arthur Andersen, was indicted for obstruction of justice. Its other clients bailed out to the remaining 'big four' accountancy firms and Arthur Andersen, previously the fifth largest professional services firm in the world, was liquidated. The nature of Andersen's relation to Enron is suggested by the following statement from an anonymous former executive of the firm:

> Everyone makes the mistake of thinking Andersen and Enron are separate companies. There are hundreds of ex-Andersen people inside Enron, a bunch of young kids just out of college. Give those new

Andersen kids a downtown loft, a new Lexus and show each one the golden path to becoming a partner. Hey, learn to do things the Enron way.[16]

The initial fallout from Enron was the re-auditing of accounts previously held by Andersen. Deloitte & Touche, for example, took over the audit of MyTravel from Arthur Andersen, and its re-audit took £15m off the profitability of the firm. Share prices subsequently fell by 36 per cent.[17] With revelations concerning SPVs reported as major news items, corporations moved quickly to distance themselves from any hint of scandal. Blue-chip firms, such as Xerox, have been publicly realigning their former accounts and future forecasts. But according to the IMF, 'questions regarding the quality of reported corporate profits in the aftermath of Enron's failure continue to have an adverse impact on international and corporate bond markets'. As Mathew Wickens of ABN Amro says, part of the problem are the figures firms are posting because 'we don't really know what they mean'.[18] Presswatch ranks accountancy as the top service sector for column inches of negative publicity. People are sceptical about stock markets. In a survey by the investor group Pro-Share more than half the 450 investors questioned felt less confident in the accuracy of company accounts. 'One in three believes auditors are not independent of the companies they audit.'[19] The collapse of trust, therefore, places Friedman and Greenspan's rather blithe accounts of the $8 trillion fall in the DOW in a rather different light.

The effects of the collapse have been widespread. California, the richest state in the union with an economy of $1.3 trillion, faces a $21 billion budget shortfall in 2002.[20] Some of this is due to general recession to which the collapse of the stock market has contributed. Some if it is directly attributable to that collapse. In 2000, California received $17 billion in taxes on stock market profits, mainly from dot.coms – in 2002 that figure fell to $5 billion. Cuts in state spending of $10 billion have subsequently been announced including state worker redundancies, pay freezes and also reduced healthcare expenditure for the poorest in society.

Californians were also direct victims of Enron. It has been alleged that Enron traders triggered widespread blackouts by buying huge blocks of power capacity in the state's electricity market to increase artificially the price of their own supply.[21]

What secrecy reveals

Sophisticated capitalism allows for a variety of primitive abuses. This is not simply an issue of lies and deceit. To argue this way is to reduce the problem to the agent, to the bad apple, rather than the conditions of enablement within the orchard. Analytically, this does not move one far enough away from orthodoxy and radical individualism. Deceit is the tip of the structural iceberg. The full nature of the rules of the structure and the way in which they are held needs to be considered. The US Sarbanes–Oxley Act, which now requires finance directors and CEOs of listed companies to attest to the accuracy of their accounts or risk jail, is a step forward in giving teeth to corporate governance, but it is not in itself corporate governance. Nor does it restore trust, since once rules are codified firms will seek to exploit them. What is also needed are ethics of appropriate action that mitigate the desire for such exploitation. How one might maintain them under the pressures of competitive capitalism is an open question, but it is not one that should be conflated with lying *per se*.

There can be an ethical good in being economical with the truth. In macro policy it makes no sense to confirm a run on a currency, or some policy that relies on surprise for its effectiveness but has been leaked (such as currency devaluation). Equally, rules cannot be overly general across an economy – there are good reasons why the police don't work on commission. What is certain is that orthodoxy adds nothing constructive to the debate on markets as rule systems. It does not lie, but it is false. A lie in social science, like honesty in politics, is usually found out and punished. But false knowledge has a life of its own. Ironically, one wonders, therefore, if Keynes is entirely correct in his sentiment when he argues, 'you can't convict your opponent, you can only convince him'.

Notes

* Thanks to Vicky Chick for reminding me of the quote from Keynes used in the conclusion.
1. J L Austin, *How To Do Things With Words*, Oxford: Oxford University Press, 1962, pp. 45–52.
2. D Smith, 'Feisty at 90 – Friedman speaks out', *The Times Business*, 8 September 2002.
3. Text reproduced in full *The Times Business*, 27 September 2002.
4. J Doran, 'After the bust, a boom in fraud suits for Wall Street's lawyers', *The Times Business*, 30 November 2002.
5. PE = p–g/(1 + e–g)p; R Marris, 'Have the markets reached bottom?' *The Times Business*, 7 November 2002. R. Cole, 'P/E ratios indicate good value,' *The Times Business*, 20 July 2002.

6. In the UK see, Insight team, 'Revealed: the cosy deals that taint Goldman Sachs,' *The Sunday Times Business*, 24 November 2002.

7. See A Rayner, 'Spitzer poised to reveal fresh evidence against 12 banks,' *The Times Business*, 2 November 2002.

8. R Lambert, 'Are Wall Street's ethics dead?', *The Times*, 8 October 2002.

9. D Rushe, 'War is over (on Wall Street at least)', *The Sunday Times Business*, 22 December 2002.

10. J Doran, 'Citigroup plans $1.5bn fund for compensation', *The Times Business*, 24 December 2002. A Rayner, 'US banks to settle with regulators', *The Times*, 9 December 2002.

11. N Hopkins and T Bawden, 'Spectre of high-tech bubble lingers on', *The Times Business*, 8 November 2002.

12. P Durman and L Armistead, 'Dotty, the champion of split caps', *The Sunday Times Business*, 27 October 2002.

13. See B Cruver, *Anatomy of Greed*, London: Hutchinson, 2002.

14. D Rushe, 'Enron watch'. *The Sunday Times*, 3 February 2002.

15. Seventy-eight charges have been filed at the time of writing. 'Former Enron chief to face more charges', *The Times Business*, 27 December 2002.

16. B Cruver, 'I had a lucrative career… but it cost me my soul', *The Times Business*, 2 October 2002.

17. J Ashworth, 'Unearthing the Arthur Andersen time bombs', *The Times Business*, 10 October 2002.

18. L Paterson and G Duncan, 'IMF fears more shares misery', *The Times Business*, 13 June 2002.

19. D Wild, 'A horrible year, but at least now accountancy is sexy', *The Times Business*, 19 December 2002.

20. C Ayres, 'Economic woes take lustre off Golden State,' *The Times*, 11 December 2002.

21. J O'Donnell, 'Enron's tricks plunged California into darkness', *The Sunday Times Business*, 6 October 2002.

12.

TOWARDS A REALISTIC EPISTEMOLOGY FOR ECONOMICS

Claude Mouchot

If there is one point on which all economists would agree, it is that they will never agree. And of course these disagreements have always existed. There was a time when we attributed them to the 'youthfulness' of our discipline, but today we are forced to admit that economics will remain eternally 'youthful'. It therefore seems critical that we abandon this 'youth' fable, as well as stop aiming for the unification of our discourse; a fable and an aim that arise from comparing economics to physics. That a century after Walras some of us still hold to the same epistemological position as he did is, at the very least, surprising.

I wish to propose here a realistic epistemology for the 'science of economics' that hopefully will enable us to explain our perpetual disagreements and thus the reasons why economics is pluralist. In order to avoid the temptation to state the argument in terms of physics, let us begin by considering in the context of economics the following key sentence from Thomas Kuhn:

> Normal science ... is predicated on the assumption that the scientific community knows what the world is like. (1970, p. 5)

One needs only to re-read this sentence carefully to realize that it will never be applicable to the world of economics nor to the social world in general. Economists will never agree on what the economic world is like, and partly because of what such an agreement would signify. It would mean that the ideological oppositions that have always run through the conceptions of man and society, the great visions of the world – individualism/holism, liberalism/socialism, etc – would have disappeared. Now each of us is aware that repression of these oppositions is possible only by totalitarian means, and, moreover, the worst of their kind; a totalitarianism that, with no form of explicit violence, would prohibit even the very thought of the term 'opposite', given that the very notion of opposition would be nonexistent!

Therefore, since these oppositions are a part of society, it follows that economics will never be a 'normal science' in T S Kuhn's sense of the words. The unification of economic theories will never be achieved, at least not in a democratic society. Hence it is necessary to abandon all reference to physics and to make a new effort to work out the epistemological status of our discipline.

Economics is a 'Totalité'

Let us begin by considering two 'classical' definitions of economics:

1. Economics is the study of humanity in the ordinary affairs of everyday life. (A Marshall)
2. Economics is the science that studies human behaviour in relation to ends and scarce resources having alternative uses. (L Robbins)

It is clear that both definitions define not just economics but also the entire social setting. The first definition includes, friendship, fatigue, pain, power, prestige and so on, and for many people even war. The second definition is no less general as it pertains to all finalized action, (Godelier, pp. 19–20), and, moreover, is at the very foundation of the totalitarianism mentioned above.

But if on the other had one tries to narrow these definitions by in Marshall's substituting 'economic' for 'ordinary' and in Robbins's substituting 'economic ends' for 'ends', then the definitions dissolve in obvious circularity.

The impossibility of separating the economic from the social, and the circularity of the definitions, (economics is economics) which result when this impossibility is ignored, illustrate the unfeasibility of defining economics. This fact can be summed up by one word: economics is a *Totalité*. Defining an object, involves distinguishing it from other aspects of reality, and one cannot distinguish an aspect of reality, if not from within the whole of which it is a part. The whole, on the other hand, cannot be distinguished except to say that is the whole! Let us insist on the lack of a definition for the word 'whole'. We have said that it sums up the problems posed by the proposed definitions for economics, but it does not resolve them. It only illustrates the impossibility of definition in this case.

Here we have more or less reached a cul-de-sac: economics is economics, and not much can be added to that. But of course it does not end here, as the existence of numerous economic theories proves.

Constructing Scientific Domains

A science sets out to adequately delimit the problems likely to define a field of research and on which a consensus can be reached … (Piaget 1970, p 41)

This simple sentence supports our proposition that 'economics is not a science', and explains it further: given that economics remains undefined, it cannot, as a whole, be considered and accepted as a science. How then, should we go about effectively delimiting these problems so as to constitute a domain that can be studied scientifically? My answer takes the form of identifying a necessary and sufficient condition: in order to develop a scientific discourse in economics, it is necessary and sufficient to privilege certain aspects of this *Totalité*, to distinguish the aspects that we wish to study, in other words, to define the object of study.

This condition is sufficient. For example, if I define my object as the study of how an individual allocates his income among different expenditure alternatives, I end up with the marginalist's consumer equilibrium theory. Or if I define it as the study of the conditions under which the division of income between wages and profits is made in a capitalist economy, I end up with a production cost theory, either neo-Ricardien or Marxist, depending on what further hypotheses are made.

This condition is also necessary. It follows from the demonstrated nature of *Totalité*. Economics is economics, and nothing more can be said about it without specifying the discourse, that is, without prioritizing certain aspects of this whole. *All positive economic discourse is simply the expression of a certain point of view on economic reality, a point of view that consists of defining an object within a whole and constructing for this object a scientific theory.*

All the major approaches to economics involve the construction of a scientific object focused on a particular aspect of the whole. Therefore, classical, neoclassical, Marxist and Keynesian theories are sciences highlighting certain aspects of economic reality, while equally neglecting others. We may say that each of these sciences 'cuts out' its object within the whole of the social and economic reality. This can be represented diagrammatically as follows:

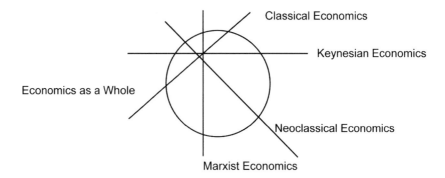

Each theory neglects certain aspects of reality:

- The Keynesian theory has no means of explaining value.
- Classical and Marxist theories fail to account for market prices (apart from what can be explained from simple common sense according to which market prices depend on the interaction between supply and demand).
- 'This theory [neoclassical] lacks a simple answer to the question: Why are salaries and profits what they are? This is an interesting issue when we are considering the allocation of revenue amongst social classes, and these social classes are not variables that can be explained by the neoclassical theory.' (Hahn 1972)
- The phenomenon of power – more or less taken into account by Keynes (real demand is the actual power held by entrepreneurs to reach an equilibrium characterised by underemployment.) and by Marx (the struggle of classes) – does not exist in classical theory and is explicitly rejected by the neoclassical theory (all agents are equal).

Finally, one should note that each of these theories prioritizes certain aspects of reality at the expense of others, constituting *ipso facto* an ideological characteristic: partisans of these theories did not choose them for 'objective' reasons in the 'natural sciences' meaning of this word, rather they chose them because they reflected the political values that they themselves favoured.

You will have noticed that in the preceding diagram, all the theories intersect at the same point, this being the economic situation under consideration. Furthermore, it is my contention that these theories have one characteristic in common: although they privilege different logics, each describes an aspect of every economic situation. For example, all the theories have elements that explain the current unemployment condition in France. Is it not E Malinvaud who thinks this unemployment is partly classical and partly Keynesian?

To accept this is also to accept that the logic of a theory ends where that of another begins. Consequently, if we prioritize one kind of logic over another and insist on pushing it to its limits, we end up with absurdities, in theory as well as in practice. For example:

- It is impossible to reject the consumer's utility maximization hypothesis because in a market economy the consumer's equilibrium clearly represents an aspect of his/her behaviour. But when pushed to its theoretical limits it logically leads to a general equilibrium that can never exist in economic reality. And if pushed to its practical limits, it gives rise paranoid financial markets.
- It is impossible to reject J M Keynes's logic on effective demand. But if pushed to its limits it would give rise to a constant increase in inflation rates, as well as to the return of hyper-liberalism.
- It is impossible to reject the Marxist logic according to which the structure of the system of production, the relations of production that determine 'the places and functions in which the individuals are but only the occupants'. The French production system has a shortage of over two million places and functions. But pushed to the limit, this logic theoretically gives rise to an eternal structure and to what in practice would amount to communism.

Thus, each theory illuminates only one aspect of reality, and each theory should allow a place for other theories to succeed which will illuminate other aspects of reality. The challenge then becomes the harmonization of these numerous theories.

Finding a common structure for these discourses

The impossibility of a logical harmonization

Talking about the logical harmonization of two or more theories, means synthesising them into one main theory that encompasses them all. Within this main theory, the constituent theories would be considered as special cases, arising for instance within certain specified parameters. However, such harmonization is not possible.

This impossibility has been historically proven: the multiplicity of economic theories is itself a form of concrete proof. If their logical harmonization were possible, we would at least expect that some of the theories would have been unified. This impossibility is also inscribed within the very idea that we are proposing, i.e. that of economics being a 'whole' within which each theory constructs its very own scientific object. The results obtained will no doubt depend on the constructed object, and there is no reason whatsoever why they should hold true for the objects of other theories.

The possibility of having contradictory results is, indeed, very high. A good example is that of excess supply in the market. Before the Keynesian period, economists claimed that lowering prices was all it took to attain market equilibrium, be it the market of a particular good or the global market. But although true in the former case (micro), it sometimes proved false in the latter case (macro), even if each producer behaved 'rationally' by lowering the price. This is an example of how sometimes decisions taken by a group of rational individuals can lead to global irrationality.

Diverging scientific objects, disjointed theories, partial discourses, disharmonious and at times contradictory logic – despite all these, we still have to continue. And so to explain and understand the economic reality as well as act on it, it is necessary for us to harmonize the different discourses in question. Given that logical harmonization is impossible, we need to find other means of harmonizing these theories.

A reasonable harmonization

Given that we already have access to an abundant literature on the current economic reality, as well as the desire to act on it, how then can we harmonize the numerous different theories in the absence of all other forms of unification?

All economic policy seeks to modify reality and, in principle, to modify it in a precise direction with a view to realizing the particular values – solidarity, justice, equality, etc – that each individual regards as 'good reasons' for acting. Of course it goes without saying that wanting something and the ability to have it are two different things. Therefore, we still need to find mechanisms that will enable us to create a 'better' reality (with respect to the values we hold); hence the necessity of a coherent analysis of the situation to be modified.

It is precisely at this point that the multiplicity of theories poses a problem: faced with different explanations, it is evident that one explanation and only one has to be chosen over the rest. If not, the actions taken may prove totally ineffective, like accelerating and breaking simultaneously. So what should be the criteria for this choice?

Let us review what was said earlier. In principle what we are saying is that whatever the concrete economic problem under consideration (unemployment for instance), it can be explained within a number of different logical structures, belonging to different theories. Consequently, the choice of criteria although easy in the abstract may be difficult to implement in reality. The politician considers and attempts to understand today's dominant logic as it pertains to the real world situation under consideration, so as to decide according to that logic the measures to be undertaken. But the currently dominant theory may not fit the current situation. For example, the current talk in favour of supply-side oriented policies aimed at increasing investment makes no sense today in France where both personal savings and the self-financing of business enterprises are very high.

Good reasons, careful consideration, decision making, choice of policy, temporary conclusions (because today's conclusions will be revised tomorrow, as the dominant logic will not be the same); this set of elements defines what 'reason' means, way beyond and above simple rationality, and takes into full account individual freedom which, though limited, is part of the reality that enables man to confront reality.

I have tried to clarify the reasons as to why economists perpetually differ in opinion. I have noted that each economist chooses the theory that supports the values that (s)he holds. It therefore follows that these differences of opinion among economists are only the reflections of the underlying political dispute. Our discipline, being far removed from the scientific status of the natural sciences and whose limits have been revealed, ought to be re-named 'political economics'.

References

Hahn, Frank (1972), *The Shares of Wages in National Income: an Inquiry into the Theory of Distribution*, London, Weidenfeld and Nicolson.

Kuhn, Thomas (1970), *The Structure of Scientific Revolutions*. Chicago: University of Chicago Press.

Mouchot, Claude (1996), *Méthodologie économique*, Paris, Hachette.

Piaget, J (1970), *Épistémologie des sciences de l'homme*, Paris, Gallimard.

13.

NEUTRALITY IS OVERRATED

Juan Pablo Pardo-Guerra

In past issues of the *Post-Autistic Economics Review*, I have encountered some interesting statements on the things that must change in order to build a post-autistic economic theory. Being a citizen of the South, I subscribe to most of them and greatly welcome the discussions. However, of the sea of comments and proposals, the ones that most caught my attention were those which used specific terms that conceal, in one way or another, the idea of 'good' and 'bad' science, and in general hinting at the notion that existing economics falls into the second category and should be moved onto the first. So let me start by saying that science, in any of its forms and in any time and place, cannot be measured within the uncomfortable parameters of 'goodness' or 'badness'. Doing so is a wild goose chase and one of the impasses that a post-autistic economic theory should try to avoid. Therefore, as I will explain, talking of a more scientific economic theory is a dead-end road.

In particular, there have been two *PAER* articles in which economics is either directly or indirectly related to science by means of the construction of either a new discourse or of a new methodology. The first and most comprehensive of these is the paper by James Galbraith, in which he mentions the necessity of building a 'theory of human behaviour based on the principles of social interaction', which privileges empirical work while being free from 'interest-group politics'.[1] On the other side of the spectrum, Claude Mouchot presents ideas on how to develop a 'scientific discourse in economics' from a purely philosophical, realist perspective.[2]

The problem with these two and many other discussions on the topic lies in the attempt to make economics a more scientific discipline, as if its level of *scientificity* were to assure success of any kind. Pursuing a scientific discourse for economics is perpetuating the age-old idea that science is better, that science is good and that science leads us to the truth and to an improved description of our universe and our future.

But science is, just as economics, a particular discourse, a tradition connected to the ideals of rationality and of progress that are rooted in a culture-specific, western perspective.[3] We say that science works and that science is good because, to a considerable degree, we have defined 'efficiency' and 'goodness' on the basis of what science can achieve. Science is not a miracle-worker nor is it a tool with unlimited reach. Science has boundaries, and is human, flawed and biased. Any economic theory consistent with the prevailing scientific discourse is bound to inherit all the flaws and quirks of the discourse it was built upon.

Furthermore, the idea that a scientific economic theory – whatever this may come to mean – is neutral, cannot be further from the truth. The neutrality of science is a construct and, in general terms, grossly overrated. And in a world where billions of people live under the line of extreme poverty, where macro-policies have left myriad micro-disasters, and where conflicts for resources as vital as water are imminent in the short run, neutrality is our worst term of reference. What we need is not to pursue the ghost of neutrality and *scientificity*, but rather to build economic theories for the new political agenda, confronting the issues of cultural diversity, resource sustainability and overall human security.

A central component in many of the discussions on the steps we need to follow in order to achieve a more scientific corpus for economic theories is the idea of assembling a dogma-free, politically sterile discipline. Many of the complaints about the current way economics is being handled are that it hides vested interests, conceals political agendas and sequesters propaganda, thus being a sort of ill-constructed doctrine freely imposed throughout the world. Some believe that by ridding the discipline of its unscientific nature, all this will fade away.

To some extent the first ideas about the biased nature of economics are correct. For the specific case of the neo-classical theory we can find a great number of suppositions and hypotheses that are unlikely to be the object of generalization. A peasant in rural Oaxaca is not likely to embody the utility-maximizing rational agent portrayed throughout mainstream economic textbooks. Neoclassical economic theory provides the prototype that is (was) needed for economic survival and expansion in the West, but that does not necessarily have to work elsewhere. However, the problem here is not with the theory itself, but rather with the way it is being implemented. Theory is simply not the same as application. They work at different levels and thus have to be clearly delimited. But by trying to link economics to scientific discourse, this application is immediately shielded from criticism and hard to break down, since it no longer is the prescription of a fragile discipline but rather the product of hard science.

In this sense, it is imperative to recognize that economics has a manifest dual nature: on one hand it can serve as a reinforcement for a set of normative structures by generating instructions about how things *ought to be* on the other hand, it can be a descriptive set of statements on how the world will react given a very specific collection of conditions and hypotheses. If we are careful enough to segregate these two faces of the discipline in both classrooms and textbooks and remember constantly that application is not the same as theory, many problems can be prevented, specifically the unmeasured use of economic theory as a form of the scientific discourse. Economics is not physics (even physics may not be physics), so we should cut this risky idea at the root.

Closing the gap between the hard sciences and economics could be counterproductive in domains other than the applied. Instead of expanding our knowledge, pursuing this may leave us with less than what we started with. Science, specifically physics, is the art of simplification, a body of approximated facts about our surroundings (as one of my teachers once said, 'physicists live in a world of point masses, coherent states and spherical cows'). The economic world is far more complex than what physics, biology or chemistry can depict. In fact, even the physical world is far more complex than what physics can depict. And though the last couple of decades have seen the birth of a new type of physics – namely, complex systems analysis – dedicated precisely to studying processes which normal, old-school physics has trouble approaching. This area is still in diapers and is a long way from obtaining important, tangible achievements. Until there is a scientific theory of complex systems, binding economics and science is one of the worst things we can do.

So what can we do with science in connection to economics? Is searching for a connection useful at all? My answer to the last question is a robust yes. Other sciences may not provide us with the blueprint for a post-autistic economic theory, but they do give us an impressive toolbox for the analysis of real economic systems. Computer simulations, the dynamics of phase transitions, non-equilibrium thermodynamics, genetic algorithms and evolutionary theory are just some of the specific areas that might prove to be useful for the study of economic processes since they are, in many ways, the first theories of complex, real-world behaviours.

However, this does not mean that we should be constrained only to what physics and other disciplines may offer. If we are to succeed in the creation of a stronger and less autistic economic theory, we need to develop our own toolbox – perhaps inspired by the one provided by other disciplines – applicable to the behaviours of individuals, groups and societies with different historical and cultural backgrounds and without relying on specific behavioural hypotheses.

But tools are only tools, and we should not forget that they do not constitute the main body of a theory. Economics should be more than mere analysis. If we are to build a theory that escapes the current autistic cycle, we must become more sensitive to the possibility of change, something that cannot come from analysis alone. We need to innovate, not to copy what others have done or at least attempted to do. The world we live in, with its mountain of problems and needs, requires fresh solutions, not old ones dressed in post-modern clothes.

Notes

1. James K. Galbraith, 'Can we please move on? A note on the Guerrien debate', *post-autistic economics review*, 15, 4 September 2002, article 2.
2. Claude Mouchot, 'Towards a realist epistemology for economics', *post-autistic economics review*, 15, 4 September 2002, article 4.
3. Jurgen Habermas, *Ciencia y tecnica como 'ideologia' Tecnos*: Madrid, 1997.

14.

ECONOMIC HISTORY AND THE REBIRTH OF RESPECTABLE CHARACTERS

Stephen T Ziliak

How long can irony and cynicism sustain the economics profession? When will we see the rebirth of the Intellectual, the Social Activist, and the Teacher as respectable characters in the world of economics? (Arjo Klamer, 1990)

I have been asked to name some contributions that economic history can make to the Post-Autistic Economics Movement. The occasion made me think of the questions Arjo Klamer asked in Klamer and Colander (1990: 185), a study of graduate students at the universities of Chicago, Columbia, Harvard, MIT, Stanford and Yale.

I thought of Klamer's question – how long till the rebirth? – because in America, the study of economic history was killed off along with the intellectual, the social activist and the teacher. The timing was ironic. I am not referring to the literal killings in Paris, Budapest or Mississippi (though the connection is worth exploring).

The irony is that when Harvard cut a full year of history from the core of its graduate programme in the 1960s (a fashion that was completed at most schools, including Chicago, by the mid-1970s), economic history was simultaneously and radically transforming.[1] Historians at Harvard and Purdue were its prime movers. It was a fantastic re-invention of the field, and brought – as such things go in the human sciences – a new methodology, a change of guard at the journals, and a large increase in output, prestige and resources. In 1994 two inventors of 'the new economic history', Robert Fogel and Douglass North, were awarded the Nobel Prize for Economics. Tragically, many economists could not say why.

Economic history, then, is in one story a victim and a failure. As Deirdre McCloskey put it, the new economic historians had spent most of their energy explaining to departments of history the 'wonderful usefulness' of economics.[2] But they forgot to sell their wares to their own hiring and curriculum committees – in economics. (McCloskey's article was published in 1976 in the *Journal of Economic Literature*. She tried to stop George Stigler from taking history out of Chicago's curriculum.) Economic historians continue to speak in the wonderfully useful language of statistics and constrained maximization. But to the Samuelsonians of the 1970s who crafted the curriculum of micro-macro-and-metrics while fetching money to mathematize economics, the numerate historians' talk of politics, religion, institutions, open fields, lacks of freedom, legacies of slavery, narrative voice, contested meanings, census manuscripts, personal diaries and plantation account books was, to use a technical term from the sociology of science, 'humanities crap'. A real economist was a 'problem solver', a calculus wonk.

Economic history, then, like foreign languages and the history of thought, was killed when the problem solvers killed the intellectual, the activist, and the teacher – 'the respectable characters'. It's difficult to imagine a re-valuation and legitimization of these social roles – so central to post-autistic economics – without a simultaneous revival of historical inquiry.

Now it's true that some people, loyal to the new Chicago School, have called the ahistorical problem solver, Robert Lucas, an intellectual. If you begin with standard Samuelsonian assumptions, then yes, Lucas is an intellectual. If an intellectual is someone fastened to the belief that there is one way of doing 'operational' economics 'consistent with' real 'science', if an intellectual (in published work) has read mainly in some corners of engineering mathematics and rational choice, free market economics; if an intellectual is a person who does not value social or cultural history as a mode of economic understanding; if an intellectual is someone unwilling to argue in his own seminar his privileging of a simple utilitarian social welfare function (for example, in Iowa City, Iowa, in 1994), then yes, Lucas is definitely an intellectual. Similarly, under Samuelsonian assumptions, Robert Barro is a teacher, George W Bush is an orator, and Gary Becker is a social activist (in Tantric healing).

In other words, one contribution of history to post-autistic economics is this: valuing economic history for the serious economics it is (while retaining what it is now perceived to be: serious history) will hasten to economics the return of the lost and wandering tribes of respectable characters. (One example of the potential gain can be found in Nicholas's Dawidoff's *The Fly Swatter* (New York: Random House, 2002). the amazing and sad story of the great economic historian, Alexander Gerschenkron, who was twice forced to wander.) A group of French students in the post-autistic movement have suggested a new curriculum, setting theirs against present-day Chicago (*PAE Review* **4**, 29 January 2000; Appendix I). They propose to put economic history back into the core curriculum.

Why should a post-autistic economist study history? McCloskey's rubrics from 1976 provide some of the answers:

History has more facts.   When today's economists begin a paper on America's Welfare Reform Act of 1996 they naturally introduce the subject historically. But because they do not collect facts from history they get the facts wrong. The Institute for Research on Poverty (IRP), is unfortunately a good example. The IRP believes that poverty and the collective strategies to eradicate it began with President Johnson's War on Poverty. (To be fair, some of its activists will refer to the Great Depression. But their data sets still begin in the 1960s.) America has had poverty and public assistance since the Elizabethan Poor Law of 1601.[3] In the late nineteenth century the largest cities abolished 'public outdoor relief' – tax-financed subsidies in cash and in kind. Abolition was part of the charity organization movement, a British import that attempted to privatize, moralize, scienize, localize, and personalize poverty and charity. It is an open secret that the nineteenth-century experiment inspired today's Republicans to abolish entitlements. Data on the failed movement are voluminous and contain evidence relevant to the Act of 1996.[4]

History has better facts.   Economic historians – for example, Simon Kuznets, Eli Heckscher, John R Commons, Lance Davis, Stanley Engerman, Jeffrey Williamson, Susan Carter, Richard Sutch, Roger Ransom, William Sundstrom, Gavin Wright, Warren Whatley, Claudia Goldin, Robert Margo, Emily Mechner, Elyce Rotella, Lee Craig, Ann Carlos, Dora Costa, Fernand Braudel, Joel Mokyr, Yasukichi Yasuba, Jean-Laurent Rosenthal, Pierre Bourdieu, Paul Baran, Paul Sweezy, Nancy Folbre, Kyle Kaufmann, Thomas Weiss, Sam Williamson, Jeremy Atack, Rick Steckel, John Murray, Joerg Baten, William Collins, George Selgin, Robert Higgs, Price Fishback, Shawn Kantor, Hugh Rockhoff, Peter Lindert, Avner Greif, Joan Hannon, Robert Humphreys, George Boyer, Mary MacKinnon, Timothy Hatton, Cormac O'Grada, Richard Easterlin, Gus Giebelhaus, Metin Cosgel, Mary

Beth Combs and Santhi Hejeebu – collect their own facts. You can see that it's the industry standard. Labouring in the archives yields an intimate knowledge of the scope and limitations of facts collected. Downloading a *.gif file from www.economagic.com does not. In our second look at significance testing in the *American Economic Reviewi* (this time we examined the 1990s) McCloskey and I found that among all the subfields of economics, the historians and labour economists pay most attention to the economic significance of their estimates.

History yields better theory. What caused the Great Depression? A problem solver in the mid-1990s put to paper one answer, and gave it to me: 'a technology shock in a real business cycle model'. There is in truth little consensus. But Milton Friedman, Anna J. Schwartz, John Kenneth Galbraith, Peter Temin, Charles P. Kindleberger, Barry Eichengreen and many other historians have advanced the theoretical conversation by insisting their theory connect with actual world events.

History makes better policy. The history of welfare is a case in point: 'time limits' do not produce self-sufficient wages. But then, most economic policy is a case in point. 'The competitive supply of professional services in the nineteenth century, it is said, grievously injured consumers, justifying official cartels of doctors and undertakers.' So midwifery and home birth have been virtually outlawed in the United States. 'If marijuana were legally and competitively supplied there would be a huge increase in demand for it.' Hey, I mean, look at that Robitussin go! 'The United States will not lift the embargo on Cuba,' President Bush told a crowd in Miami in Spring 2002, 'because that would make Castro rich and therefore more difficult to remove.' *I just got here*, you can almost hear him dreaming, *C'mon, America, give embargoes a chance.*

The rhetoric of problem solving needs revising. What is the point of emphasizing the size of the *t*-test, or formalizing the set of pooling equilibria, if history shows that you are solving the wrong problem? A non-experimental science ought to look at real world experiments when nature coughs them up. For example, economists have much to learn about policy from East and West Germany by looking at them when they were together, then separate, then together again. Similar lessons can be learned from South Africa and Palestine. The labour economists David Card and Alan Krueger were not the first to see 'natural experiments' in the adoption of minimum wage legislation: the method is old and historically sound. Still, the laboratory of history is strangely under-utilized by the problem solver.

History makes better economists. Arjo Klamer and David Colander asked their sample of graduate students to name the 'most respected economists' (p. 42). At every school except Chicago, at least half the heroes listed (there are no women on the lists) did their significant work in historical economics: they are Smith, Marx, Veblen, Keynes, Hicks (part-time), Schumpeter, Myrdal, Polanyi, John Kenneth Galbraith, and Friedman. And still others on the list, such as Boulding, Sen, and Stigler, were deeply historical in the way they conceived of economic problems. Economic history is apparently a major field of inquiry for the world's most respected economists.

Economic history is their major field because hstory offers more facts, better facts, better theory and better policy. But the reasons for reintroducing history exceed those that McCloskey raised against Stigler. Since that time a small but growing band of economists and historians have allowed discourse, feminism, postmodernism and classical rhetoric to affect their work. Like feminist economics and economic methodology, the conversations of economic history are now more open and pluralistic. (Easy does it, Clio: it's not like trade theory but we have a long way to go.) History provides the alternative stories that give meaning to timeless models and 'obvious' nulls. History exposes the contested meanings of utility, labour, freedom and justice. History keeps us honest in our assumptions. History connects teachers of economics to the concerns of the humanities. History connects teachers to the concerns of minority and international students, and it connects students to the assumptions and the graphs. For example, when I introduce undergraduate students to externalities with Upton Sinclair's *The Jungle* (1905), or to comparative advantage with Steinbeck's *The Grapes of Wrath* (1939), or to labour economics with *The Philadelphia Negro* (1899), by W E B Du Bois, it is no surprise that women and students of colour become differently engaged.

How can we bring history back in? First: realize that Chicago and Columbia do not set world prices for economic education. But when others think they do, distortion – autistic economics – emerges. In fact, in another story, economic history is not dead; it's already back in. Today's core curriculum at Harvard, MIT, Stanford, Berkeley and Northwestern University requires from PhD students a satisfactory grade in a course on economic history during the first or second year of study. It's not like Gerschenkron's Harvard – a full-year of history – and it's a lot of micro, macro and metrics; but clearly, in many of America's elite programmes, economic history is still inside the core. What can we do? History stays out of the curriculum when the problem solvers say, 'that's not what MIT does'. Show the problem solvers that they are wrong. Let it be known, moreover, that economic historians are the department chairs at Harvard (Jeffrey Williamson, 1997–2000), Stanford (Gavin Wright, currently, and for a second time), MIT (Peter Temin, 1994–7), Northwestern (Joel Mokyr, 1999–2002), Arizona (Price Fishback, currently), and elsewhere. These Department Chairs are on your side.

Second. I say we call out the Chicago, Columbia, Harvard, MIT, Stanford and Yale PhDs who, as students, had spoken honestly with Klamer and Colander and are now writing and teaching as junior or tenured professors. It's time they speak up and say who they are.

Of the 212 respondents to Klamer's and Colander's survey in the late 1980s, 98 per cent said that a study of history was at least 'moderately important' and 68 per cent said that history was of highest importance (Klamer and Colander, 1990, Table 2.1, p. 16). Let me make a plausible out-of-sample observation. Not long ago knowledge of history was ranked by today's professors of economics as being of highest importance to the skills of a good economist, second in importance only to mathematics. (Seventy-three percent said that mathematics was of highest importance: ibid, p. 16.) If the respondents have changed their minds, if knowledge of what Gerschenkron called 'economic backwardness in historical perspective' is not useful, if they believe that a knowledge of the railroads, the Poor Laws, the Beveridge Plan, the gold standard, slavery, Jim Crow, the East India Company, women's suffrage, public education, world war, free immigration or markets before central banking is no longer important, they will of course agree to defend their change of mind at next year's ASSA meetings. These are nameable professors who could help to rescue the young from the autism of the middle-aged and to repopulate the world of economics with respectable characters. These professors are acquiring the power to change the demand curve. They can refuse to vote for the pseudo-mathematician, famous for formalizing nothing of consequence. They can hire economists who care about the world and its many ways of knowing, and who show it in their teaching and their scholarship. They can fill the pages of economics with the image they had of themselves when they were happy.

But I am sorry to say with Nike that an important way to bring history back in lies solely within you – the obligation to just do it. There is a simple proposition that clarifies my point. If you are going to change the conversation, you have to change the conversation. Inspired by the critical pedagogy of Paulo Freire, the African American writer and English professor, bell hooks, has made a similar point in *Teaching to Transgress: Education as the Practice of Freedom* (1994). On the second day of classes I discuss with my students her Chapter 10, 'Building a teaching community', which is a dialogue with a white male philosopher on the history and style of power and knowledge in the classroom and how to change them. Students find the dialogue an inspiration (if an unnerving one) for claiming their own power, finding their own voice, in my classroom. Students who support a post-autistic economics could take 'education as the practice of freedom' as a second motto, a kind of just-do-it.

Education as the practice of freedom means taking graduate courses in history and other historical sciences, such as philosophy, biology, anthropology or communication studies, and then putting your questions to your teacher, your dissertation, and your seminar speaker. It is simply not true what department chairs say, and repeat, with liturgical command, 'that there is no time for those courses'. Insisting to the young that 'there is no time' is at best an example of blackboard economics (but the costs are of course higher than that). Ask, what did Alex do? Your courage to forge your own path will inspire others to do the same. Conventional teachers will be angered and embarrassed by their ignorance and by the fragility of their top-down and consumerist metaphors of power and knowledge. Who cares? Science is criticism. They should learn to take it. Your teacher of labour economics may bark you off the podium when you reveal to your classmates the private fantasies and the racist histories of black people and public assistance that you found in *The Bell Curve*. Big deal. How long should irony and cynicism rule the economics profession?

Notes

1. I thank Deirdre McCloskey and Jeffrey G Williamson for helping me to put the economic history requirement in historical perspective. Errors are my own.
2. Deirdre N McCloskey, "Does the past have a useful economics?", *Journal of Economic Literature* (June 1976), 434–61. Reprinted in R Whaples and D C Betts (eds), *Historical Perspectives on the American Economy*, Cambridge University Press, 1995, Chapter 1, p. 31.
3. S T Ziliak and Joan Underhill Hannon, "Public assistance: colonial times to the 1920s", Forthcoming in S Carter et al. (eds), *Historical Statistics of the United States: Colonial Times to the Present*, Cambridge University Press and US Bureau of the Census.
4. S T Ziliak: "The end of welfare and the contradiction of compassion", *The Independent Review* (Spring 1996); "Some tendencies of social welfare and the problem of interpretation", *Cato Journal* (Winter 2002); "Pauper fiction in economic science: 'Paupers in Almshouses' and the odd fit of *Oliver Twist*", *Review of Social Economy* (June 2002).

15.

REVISITING *The Crisis of Vision in Modern Economic Thought*

Robert Heilbroner and William Milberg

In the six years since our book, *The Crisis of Vision in Modern Economic Thought*, was published in English, there are hints of some important methodological developments within (and outside) the mainstream of economic thought. While these developments may temporarily obscure the role of vision in economics because of the sense of consensus they create, over the longer run the issue of vision will likely come to the forefront of economic debate. But before we try to predict the future of economic ideas, let's take a step back to look at their recent history.

Over the past five to ten years we have observed a distinct empiricist turn in economic research. Appeals to empirical observation rather than theoretical (i.e. mathematical) knowledge are a reaction against the "new economics" that developed in the late 1970s – what we describe in *The Crisis of Vision in Modern Economic Thought* (Chapter 5) as an "inward turn". New economics was itself a reaction to the era of general equilibrium, in which economic knowledge was understood to progress through mathematical proofs of the existence, stability and uniqueness of a general equilibrium set of prices and quantities – with appeal to successively weaker sets of assumptions. New economics was a response to the widely perceived irrelevance of the general equilibrium approach. It reversed the hypothesis generation process from a strict hypothetico-deductive formula to a "creeping inductivism", in which casually observed phenomena were explained within models of individual rational choice by the addition of such deviations from the competitive ideal as imperfect competition, increasing returns to scale technology and strategic behaviour by firms and states. The "results" generated by the new economics models were (by intent) more relevant. But they were less robust. Robustness had been the main measure of the progress of economic theory in the general equilibrium era. In new economics, robustness was considerably less important – highly stylised, unrobust results became acceptable as long as the results were deemed (usually *a priori*) interesting or relevant for policy making.

But the lack of robustness was a problem for those interested in drawing policy conclusions from the models. Equally important was the growing sentiment that the models were *ad hoc* and could be used to model *any* pre-determined outcome. Cynicism towards theory of any sort set in, and a quiet backlash has ensued.

The response to the weaknesses of the new economics in the late 1990s was an empirical turn, something that we did not predict as we wrote *The Crisis of Vision in Modern Economic Thought* just six years ago. In this era, hypotheses are often rooted in simple economic logic, intuition, or even in casual response to current events, and emphasis is placed instead on the sophistication of the measurement of variables and correlations among them. While new economics was concerned with the ex post construction of rational individual choice theoretical foundations, much of the recent mainstream work makes no appeal to a formal mathematical model but moves quickly into sophisticated measurement and statistical analysis.

The new empiricism has a double edge. On one side, it constitutes a welcome appeal to relevance and could be considered "pragmatist" in the longstanding American philosophical tradition of Pierce and Dewey with its emphasis on inductive and contingent knowledge. David Colander has lauded the arrival of a more pragmatic economics, going so far as to describe it as "the death of neo-classical economics".

On the other side, the methodological development constitutes a rejection of theory, along the same lines that Koopmans so vehemently criticized Burns and Mitchell in his 1947 review article "Measurement without theory".

Curiously, the tendency to pragmatism in mainstream economics comes at a time when a number of other schools of thought also claim pragmatism as their philosophical foundation. Some groups, including Friedmanian monetarists and American institutionalists have a long tradition and a longstanding claim as representatives of pragmatist thought applied to the field of economics. Others, including feminist economists and complexity theorists, are relative newcomers on the scene. Given their common philosophical moorings, there may be the making of a new consensus in economics. Such a consensus would no doubt be tenuous, but if it could hold together, the possibilities for exciting new research and debate and policy would be certain progress. Economics would be more pluralist than it has been in the past.

Does the recent methodological consensus imply the end to the crisis of vision in modern economics? Whatever methodological consensus may arise, the retreat from theory ultimately leaves unresolved the crisis of vision that we describe in *The Crisis of Vision in Modern Economic Thought*. If anything, as widely different tendencies in economics vie for the mantle of pragmatism, it is likely that the question of vision will rise to the surface instead of looming in the background of economic discourse. This is an optimistic prediction for the quality and depth of future debate among economists. The history of the crisis – revealed in our book – indicates that other, less rosy, outcomes are also possible.

Authors' note

This short essay is being published in Japanese as the preface to the forthcoming Japanese edition of our book *The Crisis in Vision in Modern Economic Thought*, Cambridge University Press, 1996. We are grateful to the Japanese publisher for granting permission to publish it in English in the *Post-Autistic Economics Review*.

16.

MODERNIST AND PRE-MODERNIST EXPLANATION IN ECONOMICS

Kevin Quinn

Science likes to imagine that it has vanquished religious approaches to the world, but it remains vulnerable to religious criticism precisely because it remains religious in important respects. The idea that truth is singular, rather than potentially plural, that it is non-arbitrary, and that it is meaningful – all of these dogmas amount to a survival, in the heart of science, of an essentially religious, pre-modern, approach to the world. The silly, post-modern-inspired argument that science, as one more interpretation of the world, stands on equal footing with religious interpretations, can thus gain a foothold (for different reasons than it imagines: the pre-modernism that clings to science is *anti*-science, not its essence). To avoid confusion with religion, science needs to shed its vestigial religiosity and achieve its modernist potential. As Shakespeare knew, reality is "a tale told by an idiot, signifying nothing", divine or otherwise: it is not an allegory for God – pre-modern science gets that right – but neither is it an allegory for nature, reason, progress, for fitness or complexity or anything else.

Pre-modern science: Smith and Coase on Smith

Smith's concept of the "invisible hand", many have argued, has roots in theology. And in general it is easy to find passages in Smith that seem to rely on the notion of a divinely-ordained harmony in the world. In his essay, "Adam Smith's view of man",[1] Ronald Coase argues, contra Jacob Viner, that Smith's views on psychology in *The Theory of Moral Sentiments* do not, despite appearances, have theological underpinnings. Smith, says Coase, in showing "that particular characteristics of human beings which were in various ways disagreeable were accompanied by offsetting social benefits",[2] did not typically appeal to a divine harmony as an explanation. I think he makes a persuasive case in this regard. Smith appeals not to God but to Nature as the well-designing author of our harmonious-despite-appearances psychology. Coase goes on to say that, in this respect, Smith was essentially an evolutionist before his time: "In all these cases nature, as Adam Smith would say, or *natural selection, as we would say, has made sure that man possesses those properties which would secure the propagation of the species*" (emphasis added).[3]

Examine this astonishing statement. To vindicate Smith's scientific credentials, Coase compares patent providentialism to modern science! What is the difference between an evolutionary providentialism and a divine one? And yet, of course, to this day evolutionary theory is marred by such providentialism – a thoroughly anti-scientific excrescence. The idea that evolution promotes the good of the species is more or less gone, thankfully – though it had a long run. But the idea that evolution promotes the good of the organism is alive and kicking. The fact that Darwin himself, in his theory of sexual selection, rejected this more subtle species of providentialism, has not prevented its remaining intact in biology until fairly recently. But we still have prominent evolutionists trying to explain the human brain, human art and science, human morality, by appeal to the survival value of these innovations – and rejecting more or less out of hand explanations that fail to identify such survival value.

The history of the reception of the theory of sexual selection in biology, recently well recounted by Geoffrey Miller in his book, *The Mating Mind*,[4] is a case study in the struggle of the pre-modern and the modern in science, and can serve as a preliminary to a more general discussion of the elements of what I am calling modernist explanation. This will be followed by an account of the struggles of modernism in that most pre-modern of sciences, economics, culminating in a claim that the real scandal that Keynes's work represented for the discipline was its modernism.

Sexual selection, especially the idea of runaway sexual selection developed by H A Fisher in 1930,[5] makes clear in a startling way that adaptive traits may hinder the organism's chances of survival. The peacock's tail, famously, reduces the peacock's chances of survival but increases the chances that its genes will spread by making it more attractive to mates. A providentialist may still take solace in the thought that the female preference for long tails remains unexplained, but here is where, in its runaway version, sexual selection becomes strikingly modern, in my terms: the female preference for long tails, so the theory goes, can be self-justifying. If enough females have a bias toward longer tails in mates, the preference for longer tails will be adaptive, by leading to offspring with longer tails who will be preferred as mates!

Certain conceptions of science, those I am calling pre-modern, find this sort of theory *prima facie* absurd. It opens the door, patently, to arbitrariness and indeterminacy and unpredictability: why not short tales? The ground starts to slip out from under the explanation: how can a "scientific" explanation make something, in effect, its own cause? And providentialism is obviously shaken to its roots by this sort of thinking, Miller summarizes the reaction to Fisher of the famous biologist Julian Huxley: "He defined evolutionary progress as 'improvement in efficiency of living' and increased control over and independence of the environment." Since sexual ornaments had high costs that undermined survival chances and did not help an animal cope with a hostile environment, Huxley viewed them as anti-progressive, degenerate indulgences.[6] Huxley was not unique: sexual selection, which Darwin regarded as equally as important as natural selection, did not enter the mainstream of biological thinking until more than 100 years after Darwin wrote – namely the 1980s.

The modern

The modernism I want to discuss finds its proper antonym not in the post-modern but in the pre-modern or traditional. The sense I intend to describe is most adequately delineated in Marshall Berman's *All That Is Solid Melts Into Air: The Experience of Modernity*,[7] an enormous and *sui generis* piece of scholarship. The hallmarks of modernism I want to focus on are, first, the subsuming of ends by means, and, second, closely related, the ubiquity of self-reference. An example will clarify. How does modern art differ from pre-modern art? One important way, surely is that for a good deal of the former, art is not the transparent means to an end outside itself, mimesis or representation, but instead becomes its own subject – art about art, art for its own sake, etc. So art, traditionally the means of representing the world, now seeks to represent its own activity – the end has been subsumed by the means in some sense – and self-reference, with its associated paradoxes, invariably moves center stage. An associated idea is that of bootstrap phenomena. Bootstraps, as in "pulling oneself up by one's own", are self-generated or self-caused phenomena. Modern thinking spurns foundations: think of Sartre's notion that man's essence is to have no essence, to be condemned to be free and forced to create his own meaning, willy-nilly. The absence of external foundations, theological or otherwise, makes modernity both exhilarating and terrifying. It would fill reams and reams of paper to do justice to all the ways in which the theme of means becoming ends, and the associated themes of self-reference and bootstrapping, are played out in area after area of modern thought and thought about the modern.

I don't intend these three elements to capture the richness of Berman's argument, but I believe they are central to modernism in the sense in which he uses it, although in no way exhaustive of that sense. Summing up his argument, he writes:

> To be modern … is to experience personal and social life as a maelstrom, to find one's world and oneself in perpetual disintegration and renewal.

Examples of "modernist" explanation

How and where do we see modernism in this sense in scientific explanation? What follows surveys the ground with a collection of examples, some of which will be further elaborated in later sections.

1. *Asset Bubbles*: Why does an asset have a high price today? Because it is expected to have an even higher price tomorrow. Alternatively, why does an asset have a low price today? Because it is expected to have an even lower price tomorrow. (See Keynes's famous Chapter 12 in the *General Theory*,[8] on the stock market as beauty pageant.)
2. *Increasing Returns*: Suppose that there is a positive externality associated with investment, so that the greater the level of aggregate investment, the higher the average level of return on investment. (Investment in knowledge may have this characteristic.) Then we can ask, why is the level of investment so high? Because the rate of return on investment is high. But why is the rate of return on investment high? Because the level of investment is high. Alternatively – in the same economy, same fundamentals – why is the level of investment so low? Because the rate of return on investment is low. And why is that? Because the level of investment is low. (See Phillipe Weill, "Animal spirits and increasing returns"[9]).
3. *Conventions*: Why do you, an American, drive on the right side of the road? Because you expect others to do the same. Why do others do so? Because they expect you and others to do so as well. Collectively, then, we drive on the right side of the road because we drive on the right side

on the road. Alternatively, why do you, an Englishman, drive on the left side of the road. Because you expect other English people to do the same, etc.

4. *Money*: Why do you give up real goods and services for worthless pieces of paper? Because you expect others to give you (different) real goods and services for the paper in turn tomorrow. Alternatively – same fundamentals – why do you refuse to give up real goods for worthless pieces of paper? Because you expect others to refuse as well.[10]

5. *Co-evolution* Why does animal A have such long, sharp teeth? Because animal B, its prey, has such a hard carapace. Why does animal B have such a hard carapace? Because animal A, its predator, has such sharp teeth. Alternatively – same fundamentals – why does animal A have such short, dull teeth. Because animal B, its prey, is so soft and mushy. Why is animal B so soft and mushy? Because animal A, its predator, has such short, dull teeth. (See Sigmund, *Games of Life*, on co-evolution.[11])

6. *Runaway Redux:* Why is the peacock's tail so long. Because long tails are preferred by females, so the low survival value is offset by the increased chance of mating. But why do females prefer long tails? Because, *given a substantial group of females in the population who prefer long tails*, a female with a gene for preferring long tails will also carry the gene for long tails. Its offspring will thus do better reproductively.

7. *Leijonhufvud's Keynes:* Imagine saving and investment curves as functions of the interest rate. Saving is saving out of full employment income. The intersection determines the Wicksellian natural rate of interest. The investment curve shifts back. The natural rate of interest falls. But bear speculators with inelastic expectations sell bonds to prevent the adjustment. They expect the rate of interest to remain at the old level. Their action leads to a positive gap between full employment saving and investment, a shifted-in saving function due to falling income, and an equilibrium rate of interest higher than the new natural rate which will now prevail even without speculation. The bears are proved correct. Their expectations that the interest rate would not fall have been confirmed, for the nonce. This is Keynes as interpreted by Axel Leijonhufvud in *On Keynesian Economics and the Economics of Keynes*.[12] Why is the rate of interest so high? Because it was expected to be high.

8. *Nineteenth-century capitalism*: How can the level of investment be so high while the level of consumption is so low? Means of production are being produced today to be used to produce means of production tomorrow, etc – the means have become ends. Alternatively, a low level of investment might make sense despite robust consumption if the level of

investment will be low tomorrow – the means of production needed for the consumption goods industry is high, but the means of production needed to produce means of production are low.

So, *modernist* explanations, I shall stipulate, are characterized by:

a   The ubiquity of self-reference: X because, ultimately, X.
b   No appeal to fundamentals: God, providence, reason, efficiency, fitness.
c   The reversal of means/end relationships. Means become ends in themselves.
d   Bootstrapping phenomena, as in "pulling yourself up by your own". As a consequence, arbitrariness, and multiple equilibria.

Modernism on the fringe: Marx

In economics, the locus classicus of modernism, indeed its source, is the work of Karl Marx: definitely far outside the mainstream. [– in the *Manifesto* – of the phrase Berman uses as the title of his book] Marx, throughout his writing, returns again and again to the essential difference between a pre-modern economy of small producers where, in his well-known terminology, exchange proceeds according to the transparent schema C-M-C' (a commodity of one type, C, is exchanged for money, M, which is in turn used to purchase a different commodity C'), on the one hand; and the modern capitalist economy, whose dynamism springs from its obedience to a diametrically opposed schema: M-C-M', on the other. Here, money purchases commodities (labour and raw materials), which are fashioned into goods to be sold for still more money, so that the process can begin again.

Unlike the first, this second process has no natural stopping point, and no foundation or rationale outside of itself, in some pre-existing human needs, the need to satisfy which begins and the satisfaction of which ends the exchange process in the first schema. The mere means in the first schema, money, has become the end in the second. And what is the money for? To create more money. Thinking about the second schema, we experience the same dizziness, the same hall-of-mirrors effect that I would argue characterizes the modernist turn in all areas of life and culture. (I think of this modernist experience as the Land O' Lakes effect, after the butter box of my youth, which pictures an Indian woman holding a box of butter, on which is pictured an Indian woman holding a box of butter, on which is pictured …) Marx's most succinct definition of capital captures this modernist theme beautifully. He calls capital "self-expanding value". Again we have a self-referring infinity in which means has become end: value creating value creating value … Our pre-modern, traditionalist, religious inclination is to ask "to what end?" and to feel frustrated by our inability to get an answer.

Marx argued that to represent the modern capitalist economy as, underneath the trappings of a sophisticated financial system and a highly complex division of labour, nothing but a barter economy operating according to C-M-C', a giant means to satisfy the end of human consumption, was a huge mistake. He raged against the "Robinsonades" of the classical economists – their attempts to explain the workings of a modern capitalist economy by telling stories about Robinson Crusoe solving his economic problem (*the* economic problem) all alone on his desert island. The idea that capital, the dynamic process of self-expanding value whose revolutionary consequences Marx documented, could be understood by analogy with the fishing net that Robinson sacrificed some potential fish consumption today to construct, in order transparently to increase his fish consumption tomorrow – Marx found absurd and laughable. On the contrary, the capitalism he saw and described was just as capable of producing means of production today to increase the capacity for producing means of production tomorrow, which in turn would make possible further means of production *ad infinitum* – to produce for production's sake, as it were. The economic world he described, in other words, was a modern economy, not the pre-modern and traditional economy of a Robinson Crusoe. To miss this distinction, Marx would have said, is to miss, in effect, everything.

Thoroughly Modern Maynard

Prior to Keynes, however, the mainstream of the profession *did* miss this distinction, and, despite Keynes, still in large part does. What are the "representative agent" models so beloved of modern macroeconomists, real business cyclists and others, if not hi-tech Robinsonades?

I believe Keynes's modernism was pervasive. Its most obvious manifestations, however, can seem at first sight fairly isolated in his work, and have been so treated by his interpreters. The Keynesian who believes Keynes's message to have been well captured in the Hicksian ISLM apparatus has very little use, it would seem, for Keynes's brilliant Chapter 12 in *The General Theory*, "The state of long-term expectation".[13] Here is Keynes's oft-cited discussion of the stock market, of infinitely-lived asset valuation in general. The modernism of this chapter is hard to miss. Here we are asked to contemplate the bootstrap character of the valuation of an open-ended asset whose price today depends on dividends it is expected to pay, to be sure, but also on the price it is expected to fetch tomorrow, which latter price will depend on the price it is expected to have further on in the future, and so on ad infinitum. Keynes asks us to take seriously the notion that the asset's price may very well lose any connection with the "solid" fundamentals and become an airy bubble of self-fulfilling expectations. It is important to see, too, that such an essentially modernist phenomenon Keynes regards not as temporary and bound to disappear just as soon as professionals – investors knowledgeable about the fundamentals – appear on the scene, but as comparatively long-lasting and immune to arbitrage:

> This battle of wits to anticipate the basis of conventional valuation a few months hence, rather than the prospective yield of an investment over a long term of years, does not even require gulls among the public to feed the maws of the professionals; – it can be played by professionals among themselves.
>
> Nor is it necessary that anyone should keep his simple faith in the conventional basis of valuation having any genuine long-term validity. For it is so to speak a game of Snap, of Old Maid, of Musical Chairs – a pastime in which he is victor who says Snap neither too soon nor too late, who passes the Old Maid to his neighbour before the game is over, who secures a chair for himself before the music stops. These games can be played with zest and enjoyment, though all the players know that it is the Old Maid which is circulating, or that when the music stops some of the players will find themselves unseated.[14]

In contemporary terms, Keynes is talking in this passage about "rational bubbles".[15] They are rational because there is no assumption of stupidity on the part of purchasers of the bubbled asset that a canny professional might profit from – and by doing so burst the bubble. The bubbled asset provides a normal return in expectation, with the bubble itself growing at the rate of return, and therefore passes a no-arbitrage or efficient markets test, no matter how wildly divergent from fundamentals its price becomes, and is destined increasingly to become.

Only an infinitely-lived agent could undo, via arbitrage, a bubble on an infinitely-lived asset, which fact puts Keynes's reminder that "in the long run we're all dead" in a whole new light! It is somewhat ironic that the development of rational expectations, a development that in its early stages was used as a battering ram against Keynesian economics, enables us to understand the bootstraps and bubbles of Chapter-12-Keynes with much greater depth and clarity than we could before. The determination of the present not by the past but by the unknown future – via expectations – can never be grasped, with all its dramatically modernist implications for our economic lives, as long as we reduce expectations about the future, by means of an adaptive expectations scheme, to some determinate function of the past. Rational expectations – honestly deployed – can be a potent generator of modernist outcomes: unfortunately, this is usually noted, if at all, in the footnotes, where one finds the specious arguments for ignoring all but the fundamental solutions covered in the main text.

It is important to see that Keynes, despite twinges of pre-modern revulsion which lead him to propose at one point, half-seriously, that we marry the asset to the asset-holder for life, to defeat speculation and thus the melting of all that is solid into air – ultimately felt that bubbles could not be disposed of so easily: "This is the *inevitable* result of investment markets organized with a view to so-called liquidity."[16]

Contemporary thinkers who have carried on and developed Keynes's modernist views of asset bubbles find the profession scarcely more receptive than it was and is to Chapter 12. The pre-modernism of the profession lies very deep: Look, for one example, at the vehemence of the reaction to Robert Shiller's 1981 article on stock market volatility, work directly in the tradition of Chapter 12.[17] In a symposium on bubbles in the *Journal of Economic Perspectives* a few years back, we find one participant arguing quite seriously that the Great Tulip Mania in seventeenth-century Amsterdam – what Saddam Hussein might have called the "mother of all bubbles", on previous accounts – can be parsimoniously explained as a response to changes in fundamentals![18]

But I have argued that modernism is pervasive in Keynes, not a phenomenon confined to a chapter here or there. Here, I want to suggest that we broaden our minds about the Keynesian message and remember, above all that his work stands in two traditions simultaneously, both the mainstream, and the underground, heretical tradition of under-consumption theorists, numbering among its members thinkers such as Marx, Hobson, Major Douglas and Malthus[19] – some of whom Keynes explicitly acknowledges as progenitors in his appendices to the *General Theory*. The common vision of this latter tradition is the one I have identified in Marx, of a modern capitalist economy subject to stagnation because its ability to produce outruns its ability to consume: the modernist possibility of production for production's sake is here taken very seriously indeed.

Moderns and Pre-Moderns: Keynes, Robertson, and Our Grandchildren

The modernist impulse in Keynes can be observed in the reaction it provoked in his anti-modernist contemporaries. A small but symptomatic incident provides an illustration. Keynes's theory of liquidity preference contained the modernist idea that what determines the interest rate today is speculator's expectations of what it will be tomorrow. This couldn't be the end of the story, insisted D H Robertson[20] and others (famously Leontief): Where were the fundamentals of the process? Robertson's reaction was vehemently anti-modernist:

> Thus the rate of interest is what it is because it is expected to become other than it is; if it is not expected to become other than it is, there is nothing left to tell us why it is what it is. The organ which secretes it has been amputated, and yet it somehow still exists − a grin without a cat.[21]

Robertson is not alone among economists in thinking that to establish the bootstrap, foundationless character a theory attributes to an economic phenomenon is *ipso facto* to refute that theory. Alice in Wonderland is one thing; *reality* cannot have this airy character. If your theory tells you it does, it must need work. As with under-consumption, I cite this aspect of Keynes as an instance of his attraction to modernist explanations. I don't mean to condition my argument on an acceptance of the speculative demand for money any more than on the acceptance of, say, Alvin Hansen's Keynesian stagnationism. There are contemporary theories of the interest rate that inherit from Keynes the modernist form without the particular content he filled it with.

Keynes himself, like many another great modernist, combines his modernist description with a deep anti-modernist revulsion at the *prima facie* absurdity of the phenomena he is transcribing and, in his weaker moments, with what amounts to a pious hope for an overcoming of modernism and a return to a pre-modern golden age where means have been put back in their place a vehicle to independent ends to which they are transparently related, where bubbles have burst and social life, as it were, makes sense again. (Berman, by the way finds some of these same tendencies in the arch-modernist Marx, who seems sometimes to hold up a vision of socialism as a rest from the ceaseless flux, an overcoming, indeed, of history, a putting-paid to the ceaseless, permanent revolution of modern life.)

This modernist/anti-modernist dialectic in Keynes is most apparent in his

1930 essay, "Economic possibilities for our grandchildren",[22] where he contrasts the "purposiveness" of contemporary economic life with its potential overcoming in the lives of our grandchildren. The former idea represents still another ringing in Keynes's work of the by now familiar modernist changes. The purposive man, he says:

> … is always trying to secure a spurious and delusive immortality for his acts by pushing his interest in them forward in time. He does not love his cat, but his cat's kittens; nor, in truth, the kittens but only the kittens' kittens; and so on forward forever to the end of cat-dom. To him jam is not jam unless it is a case of jam tomorrow and never jam today.[23]

But after describing and dissecting this modernist purposiveness – interestingly named since it seems almost paradigmatically anti-purposive to pre-modern eyes – Keynes sounds an almost religious anti-modernism. The purposive era will end one day ("when science and the power of compound interest" have solved the economic problem!). And in this future made possible precisely by virtue of the abundance obtained through centuries of purposiveness:

> … We shall once more value ends above means and prefer the good to the useful. We shall honour those who teach us to pluck the day virtuously and well, the delightful people who are capable of taking direct enjoyment in things, the lilies of the field, who toil not, neither do they spin.[24]

But Keynes, unlike the great majority of the economics profession in his day and our own, did not allow his anti-modern hopes and values – delusive or not – to interfere with his ability to limn the modernist reality in which we live and breathe. The modernist present is highlighted and set off by the stark contrast with the imagined anti-modernist future.

Keynes's modernism is, I believe, the most deeply interesting and at the same time has proven so far the least assimilable dimension of his legacy to the economics profession.

L'Envoi

Taking the contra-positive formulation of Nietzsche's famous declaration, if everything is not permitted, then God is not dead. A determinist science, science that recoils from arbitrariness and meaninglessness, that doesn't permit, in principle, *everything*, that only counts as explanations the pre-modernist subset – keeps God alive, and its adherents children.

Notes

1. Ronald Coase, 1994, *Essays on Economics and Economists*. University of Chicago Press, Chicago: 95–118.
2. Ibid: 107.
3. Ibid: 109.
4. Geoffrey Miller, 2000, *The Mating Mind*, Doubleday, New York.
5. Karl Sigmund, 1993, *Games of Life* Oxford University Press, New York: 128–31.
6. Miller, op cit, 58.
7. Marshall Berman, 1982, *All That Is Solid Melts Into Air*, Penguin Books, New York.
8. J M Keynes, 1965, *The General Theory*, Harbinger, New York.
9. Philippe Weill, 1989, "Animal spirits and increasing returns", *American Economic Review*, September.
10. See Neil Wallace, 1980, "Overlapping generations models of Fiat money" in *Models of Monetary Economies*, Federal Reserve Bank of Minneapolis.
11. Sigmund, op cit, 148 ff, on co-evolution.
12. Axel Leijonhufvud, 1968, *On Keynesian Economics and The Economics of Keynes*, Oxford University Press, London.
13. J M Keynes, 1965, *The General Theory*, Harbinger, New York: 147–64.
14. Ibid, 155.
15. See Blanchard, Olivier and Stanley Fischer (1989), *Lectures on Macroeconomics*, MIT Press, Cambridge MA, Chapter 5, for a good discussion of this literature. Chapter 5 is titled "Multiple equilibria, bubbles and stability", and it sits uncomfortably in the text, an apparent swerving away from the main track (which of course it is). The last sentence of the chapter states " …though we find the phenomena analysed in this chapter both interesting and disturbing, we are willing to proceed on the working assumption that the conditions need to generate stable multiplicities of equilibria are not met in practice". So it's goodbye to bubble solutions from then on. I wonder how many syllabi in courses that use the text leave this chapter out?
16. Ibid, emphasis added.
17. Robert Shiller, 1989, *Market Volatility*, MIT Press, Cambridge MA, contains the original article along with Shiller's responses to the veritable cottage industry of critics that grew in its wake. The article is "Do stock prices move too much to be justified by subsequent changes in dividends?", *American Economic Review*, **71**, 1981, 421–35, and appears as Chapter 5 of *Market Volatility*.
18. Peter Garber, 1990, "Famous first bubbles", *Journal of Economic Perspectives*, **4**, 35–54.
19. See Michael Bleaney, 1976, *Underconsumption Theories*, (1976), International Publishers, New York, for an excellent overview of this tradition.
20. D H Robertson, 1940, "Mr Keynes and the rate of interest", in *Essays in Monetary Theory*, Staples Press, London, 1–38.
21. Ibid, 25.
22. In Keynes, 1963, *Essays in Persuasion*, Norton, New York: 358–73.
23. Ibid, 370.
24. Ibid, 372.

17.

GAME THEORY: A REFINEMENT OR AN ALTERNATIVE TO NEO-CLASSICAL ECONOMICS?

Matthew McCartney

This chapter[iii] is not intended to say much that is new; rather it takes issue with the traditional manner in which economics has presented game theory. In particular this paper emphasizes that game theory has some quite radical implications; these are however smothered by a heavy emphasis in textbooks and in teaching on what is neo-classical about game theory rather than presenting game theory as a very different way of modelling economic life. As in a previous paper[iv] I take for my texts three books that form the core of many masters programmes in microeconomics.

Neo-classical economics, Game Theory and General Equilibrium

The intellectual centrepiece of neo-classical economics is general equilibrium:

> The view of the economy central to microeconomics is that it is an interrelated system of markets through which one particular resource allocation is achieved out of infinitely many which are possible. Until now[v] we have been considering the constituent elements of this system: households, firms, goods markets, and factor markets. We now have to synthesise all these elements into a model of the equilibrium of the economy as a whole. (Gravelle and Rees, 1992, p. 438)

There is nothing inherently neo-classical about general equilibrium. For example Keynesians postulate that an economy may become stuck in an underemployed equilibrium. An equilibrium in game theory may be equivalent to one in general equilibrium. In the example (Figure 1) below (Up, Left) represents a Nash equilibrium, a dominant strategy equilibrium and, we could suggest, a general equilibrium of a simple two-person economy.

Figure 1

		Player 2	
		Left	**Right**
Player 1	Up	(3,3)	(0,0)
	Down	(0,0)	(0,0)

The key assumption that distinguishes a game theory world from a neo-classical economy is that of interdependence. In game theory the payoffs or utilities of any strategy depend on the strategy of the other player(s), or even the expectations of the strategy of the other player. In the above example the possibility of Player 1 getting a payoff of 3 from choosing Up is contingent on the choice of Left by Player 2.

There are a variety of assumptions in the neo-classical version of general equilibrium necessary to prove the *existence*, the *uniqueness* and *stability* of equilibrium. Important among those assumptions is independence. For the *stability* of equilibrium, if all goods in the economy are gross substitutes, then the time path of prices, p(t), determined by the tâtonnement adjustment process ... converges to an equilibrium' (Gravelle and Rees, 1992, p. 450). An equilibrium may not exist in the case of goods that are complements. If there is excess demand for a particular good such as CDs the price in a Walrasian type economy will rise. This will have the undesirable (from the perspective of equilibrium) effect of reducing the demand for CD players. Such complications from interdependent markets may prevent the economy converging to a stable equilibrium. For *uniqueness* the neo-classical version of general equilibrium likewise demands that choices be independent. What happens otherwise can be best illustrated by another example of a game.

Figure 2

		Player 2	
		Left	**Right**
Player 1	Up	(3,3)	(0,0)
	Down	(0,0)	(3,3)

In this example (Figure 2) there are multiple equilibria.[vi] Once the utility from a strategy or choice by one individual depends on the strategy or choice of another individual, any presumption of uniqueness of equilibrium breaks down. This then is the crucial difference. Game theory drops the assumption of independence. The implications of this are profound: they open the door for a completely different way of analysing the stability and efficiency of an economy, the role of the state, expectations, and the role of conflict in economic exchange. I will return to this later. First I will try to make the case that so completely has game theory been colonized and smothered by neo-classical economics that these implications may escape us.

Is Game Theory a Theory?

I would argue that game theory is perfectly entitled to stand alone as a theory of how economies behave in a situation of interdependence in decision-making. However, game theory is commonly presented as an appendage.

> Game theory *by itself* is not meant to improve anyone's understanding of economic phenomena. Game theory (in this book) is a tool of economic analysis, and the proper test is whether economic analyses that uses the concepts and language of game theory have improved our understanding' (Kreps, 1990b, p. 6). Kreps (ibid.) further argues that game theory comprises 'formal mathematical models that are examined deductively' (p. 6), and 'a taxonomy for economic contexts and situations' (p. 37), to 'ask questions about the dynamics of competitive interactions' (p. 87).

Game Theory and Methodological Individualism

Despite game theory being a 'representation of a situation in which a number of individuals interact in a setting of strategic interdependence' (Mas-Colell et al., 1995, p. 219), there is still a heavy bias towards the methodological individualism of neo-classical economics:

> Thus it is easy to portray game theory as an extension of a theory of rational decisions involving calculated risks to one involving calculations of strategies to be used against rational opponents, competitors or enemies; that is, actors who are also performing strategic calculations with the aim of pursuing their goals and, typically, attempting to frustrate ours. (Rapaport, 1970, p. 45).

Formalism, Rationality, Equilibrium and Game Theory

Game theory has been subjected to the same formalism as much of neo-classical economics, in fact 'game theory (as developed by people who have come to be recognised as game theorists) is properly a branch of mathematics' (Rapaport, 1970, p. 49). Like neo-classical economics, game theory has been heavily saturated by the concept of rationality: it is 'the branch of mathematics concerned with the formal aspect of rational decision' (Rapaport, 1966, p. 16). Likewise, any reading of a basic game theory text reveals the central, almost defining, importance of equilibrium. With this it clearly shares with neo-classical economics a 'slavish devotion to the concept' (Keen, 2001, p. 164).

Glancing through Mas-Colell et al. (1995), Chapters 7 to 9 reveal the exclusive emphasis of its exposition of game theory on formalism, rationality and equilibrium. The basic elements of game theory are outlined with relevant definitions, proofs and corollaries (formalism). The exposition runs through dominant strategies, rationalisable strategies, sequential rationality, backward induction, reasonable beliefs and forward induction (rationality)[vii]. These rationality assumptions are extreme. The combination of consistent alignment of beliefs and common knowledge of rationality implies that instrumentally rational individuals with the same information sets must converge in their expectations. The remainder is concerned with Nash equilibrium, Bayesian Nash equilibrium and subgame perfection (equilibrium). The notion of equilibrium refinement is an important avenue in game theory (see for example Kreps, 1990b, pp. 108–28). In the narrow world of neo-classical game theory this trinity contrasts with the other in general equilibrium, the sacred truths of existence, uniqueness and stability.

Gravelle and Rees (1992) do not deal explicitly with game theory, but use it to model the behaviour of oligopolies (Chapter 12). Their treatment is a specific example of all of these general points. They seek a 'precise prediction of the market equilibrium' (p. 298); it is certainly mathematical and formal. 'Each firm is assumed rationally to think through the consequences of its choices, in the knowledge that the other firm knows the situation and is also thinking things through' (p. 302). Happily for the non-mathematical reader, 'the general issues of existence, uniqueness and stability of equilibria are not dealt with.' (p. 300).[viii]

Like neo-classical economics, game theory as it exists places an immense and rarely questioned burden of information on individuals. 'A central concept of game theory is the notion of a player's strategy. A strategy is a *complete contingent plan*, or *decision rule*, that specifies how a player will act in *every possible distinguishable circumstance* in which she might be called upon to move' (Mas-Colell et al., 1995, p. 228). The information requirements become even more burdensome when we consider ideas such as iteration of dominated strategies or rationalisable strategies. These require that we 'assume that all players are rational and that this fact and the players' payoffs are common knowledge (so everybody knows that everybody knows that ... everybody is rational)' (Mas-Colell et al., 1995, p. 239).

The Developmental State, Efficiency and Expectations and the Radical Implications of Game Theory

Game theory cleanly and simply models a number of situations very different from neo-classical economics and its corollary general equilibrium. Those that are discussed here include the developmental role of the state in both its 'market failure' and 'political conflict' guises and also the role of expectations and multiple equilibrium.

The Developmental State

Fine and Stoneman (1996) suggest there have been two broad approaches to the developmental state – the economic and political schools[ix]. The first focuses on the role of the state as correcting market failures, such as externalities, economies of scale, infant industries, asymmetric information, etc. The second examines the political capacity of the state to identify and implement growth-promoting interventions. Game theory can help present these two approaches in a very straightforward manner and capture key points of both arguments. The two relevant generic approaches are co-ordination games (the economic role of the developmental state) and chicken games (the political role of the developmental state)[x].

a. Co-ordination Games

A very interesting implication of a game theory economy is that of multiple equilibria. Only if we share such a narrow neo-classical view of the world can we accept Kreps (1990b, pp. 95–105) that the presence of multiple equilibria in game theory is a problem. With multiple equilibria we can have no presumptions of efficiency in a market economy. In Figure 3 below there are two (pure strategy) mixed equilibria, (Not Invest, Not Invest) and (Invest, Invest). While the latter is Pareto optimal there is no necessary reason why an economy stuck in the inferior equilibrium should move there. This is an example of a strategic complementarity (Cooper and John, 1988); there are Pareto-ranked multiple equilibria. In a decentralised system there is no incentive for a single firm to increase production because it will take the actions of other firms as given. The externality is generated by demand linkages that firms do not internalise.

In terms of a practical example from development (Figure 3) we could consider Firm 1 to be a steel industry and Firm 2 to be a ship-building industry. The steel industry supplies inputs for the ship-building industry. The two firms are only jointly profitable in the case of simultaneous investment. Investing alone will create excess capacity for the steel producer and losses of (–5), while lonely investment for the shipbuilder will create a shortage of steel inputs, driving up their price and leading to losses of (–5). This is an example of a co-ordination failure.

Figure 3

		Firm 2	
		Not Invest	**Invest**
Firm 1	Not Invest	(1,1)	(0,–5)
	Invest	(–5,0)	(3,3)

The problem was theorised by Rosenstein-Rodan, and Scitivsky in the 1940s and 1950s as the 'big push' approach to economic development. With interdependence change (industrialization) would not be automatic. Only simultaneous investment across a wide range of industries would be viable. It might be possible for investors in a complementary project to agree to a contract though this will be costly to draw up and monitor (Chang, 1999). Such transactions cost considerations would be particularly relevant in the case of a large upstream industry supplying inputs to a large number of firms. This could be the case with a railway system that would then be used by a host of small firms, (Murphy et al., 1989). The takeover mechanism could provide a solution but profound capital market imperfections during the early stages of development are likely, (Bardhan, 1999).

Foreign investment in crucial sectors may be seen as an unacceptable loss of domestic economic sovereignty. In East Asia the state played an important role in resolving this kind of co-ordination failure. Such interventions can be simply modelled using game theory. Intervention in the capital market to subsidise credit, changes the payoffs in the game to make (Invest, Invest) more likely.[xi] The organization of Chaebols in South Korea can be thought of in a stylised manner as a merger of the two firms in this game. The choice for the single firm would be straightforward Invest for a profit of 6 or not invest for a profit of 2.[xii] The state itself may undertake the investment, as in Taiwan, which largely retained crucial large-scale upstream industries in the state sector. Indicative planning exercises may provide a focal point for private sector co-ordination between such complementary investment projects. (Chang, 1999).[xiii]

b. Chicken Games

A 'chicken game' is represented in Figure 4. Individuals can be aggressive or concede. The two positions that optimise the social surplus (Concede, Aggressive) and (Aggressive, Concede) require that one player concede. The worst outcome is mutual aggression, which leads to a negative outcome for both players. There is an inherent conflict because outcomes are unequal; for both to gain, one player must resign himself to an inferior position.

Figure 4

		B	
		Aggressive	**Concede**
A	Concede	(2,5)	(0,0)
	Aggressive	(–2,–2)	(5,2)

The chicken game can illustrate an aspect of the second issue facing the developmental state noted by Fine and Stoneman (1996). The political capacity of the state to identify and implement policies, specifically that conflict over income distribution can prevent reforms or perpetuate inefficient institutions over time.

This game captures nicely the notion that development is an inherently conflictual process. Chang (1999) notes that development is the process of shifting resources from low to high productivity areas. Less mobile assets are likely to become obsolete, leading to unemployment and income inequality. Those with a vested interest in the status quo will resist such changes. The diffusion of technology may be blocked in order to protect economic rents. This need not occur solely through opposition from those likely to be displaced[xiv], but because new technology and economic change may simultaneously affect the distribution of political power. Acemoglu and Robinson (1999) propose a 'political losers' hypothesis – groups may resist technological change that would otherwise erode their political power (rather than economic rents). The market failure is the lack of any credible commitment to compensate political losers after economic changes have occurred. In the game above there is no mechanism to allow a credible commitment to compensate the player who concedes. In a dynamic political economy context, the resulting income inequalities may be perpetuated over time. The wealthier player may be able to institutionalise influence on the state and bias future changes to his own benefit.

This approach has been followed by Knight (1992), who explains the development of institutions not in terms of responses to collective goals or benefits but rather as a product of distributional gains. The main goal of institutional development is to gain a strategic advantage over other actors. This view of institutions introduces the concept of power. There are numerous practical examples of this in the development literature. Sokoloff and Engerman (2000) argue initial inequalities in Latin America and the Caribbean in the early years of colonization were perpetuated over time, resulting in the slow spread of the voting franchise, literacy and education. Harriss (2002) gives an example of agrarian institutions in Eastern India as inefficient institutions that have persisted over time. Usury and speculative trading in food grains were privately profitable for a small class of landowners to the extent that there was little incentive to make productive investments in agriculture. These inefficient institutions supported and were supported by the power of the landowning oligarchy with a strong vested interest in the reproduction.

The chicken game can also help explain the paradox of land reform (Bardhan, 1999). Without significant scale economies in farm production and problems of monitoring hired labour, the family farm is the most efficient institution for production. Land reform has been fiercely resisted by landowners despite possible efficiency gains. Landowners have tended not to lease or sell land to family farmers to secure the surplus from expanded production. There are problems of monitoring, insecurity of tenure and fear that the tenant will gain occupancy rights. Imperfect credit markets and insecure property rights mean small farmers are frequently unable to afford a market price. More generally we could consider the game as representing the overall process of industrialization. This requires the allocation of property rights to form a class of capitalists, and either player A or B must concede and become a worker. Industrialization will lead to an improvement in aggregate income (2,5) or (5,2) but also to increased levels of inequality. Political opposition to increasing inequality, especially if it is structured on regional or ethnic lines, may lead to conflict and an outcome of (−2,−2) instead.

c. *Expectations and Self-fulfilling Crisis*

Game theory can easily model how expectations can have a fundamental impact on the real economy and any efficiency properties of the market economy disappear. Keynes assigned an important role to expectations as an autonomous causal factor. Woodford (1991) shows that changes in beliefs become important in generating fluctuations in circumstances in which they tend to become self-fulfilling. Much of the literature emphasizes particular economic structures that enable revisions of expectations to become self-fulfilling.

Figure 5

		B	
		Hold	**Sell**
A	Hold	(5,5)	(−2,2)
	Sell	(2,−2)	(1,1)

Figure 5 shows a situation in which the optimal social position is for both players to hold (retain possession of a share, currency or other financial asset). If either player has any expectation that the other is likely to sell the best thing to do is to sell, avoid a loss and settle for a positive if lower payoff. Negative expectations can become self-fulfilling without any change in the underlying economic fundamentals. Much literature about the 1997 Asian Crisis is framed in just these terms. Herd-like behaviour can be important; fund mangers would be faulted for not getting out when others do but not for making losses when everyone else does. The effect will be compounded by imperfect information, when entry or exit by one actor is interpreted as his having access to superior information. As Krugman says:

> The lesson for the real world is that your vulnerability to the business cycle may have little or nothing to do with your more fundamental economic strengths and weaknesses: bad things can happen to good economies. (1999, p. 10)

The problem of multiple equilibria is not a fault of game theory but a justifiable reflection of how a real economy works. The particular structure outlined above was created by financial liberalisation in East and South-East Asia in the early 1990s. Inexperienced domestic banks were able to take out large dollar denominated loans from foreign lenders. Deregulation of the domestic economy allowed these loans to be lent on for construction and real estate investment and speculation. The inflow of short-term capital created a game-like scenario in which investors had to consider the decisions of other investors. The reintroduction of capital controls by Malaysia in 1998 effectively removed the sell option. Wade (1998a, b) criticizes the IMF for pushing for bank closure in countries without full deposit insurance – in effect, for raising the cost of being caught holding when the other player sells. The IMF stand-by credits and loans would, it was hoped, mitigate this effect by reducing the cost of not selling early.

Conclusion

Game theory can and should be a theory that stands on its own to model economic processes that occur in a situation of interdependence. It offers a radical alternative to neo-classical economics. Game theory illustrates just how non-robust are the efficiency properties of neo-classical economic theory, it provides a neat framework in which to model and justify a developmental role for the state and can neatly illustrate how expectations can, contrary to neo-classical economic theory, have an important impact on the real economy. Game theory deserves better than to be emasculated by the obsessions of neo-classical economics, its formalism, rationality and its slavish devotion to equilibrium. Perhaps there is a case to be made for a heterodox Microeconomics text-book that begins with game theory as the standard case and introduces general equilibria as a special case?

Notes

1. The author thanks Neil McLaughlin for feedback and suggestions regarding this paper. Earlier versions of this article appeared in the *Post-Autistic Economics Review* (issue 22, November 2003) and *Kurswechsel* (Vol. 4, 2005; German translation by Beat Weber). This article was supported by a Social Sciences and Humanities Research Council of Canada Doctoral Fellowship. Contact: 323 Uris Hall; Ithaca, NY; 14853. E-mail: kss46@cornell.edu.
2. The post-autistic economics movement appears to be an example of what Frickel and Gross (2005) dubbed Scientific/Intellectual Movements (SIMs).
3. The post-autistic economics movement appears to be an example of what Frickel and Gross (2005) dubbed Scientific/Intellectual Movements (SIMs).
4. This limitation also characterizes the natural sciences to varying degrees, particularly biology.
5. Many thanks to Alan for invaluable editorial assistance.
6. Matthew McCartney, 'Dynamic versus static efficiency: the case of textile exports from Bangladesh and the developmental state', *post-autistic economics review*, issue no. 26, 2 August 2004, article 4, http://www.btinternet.com/~pae_news/review/issue26.htm.
7. This is chapter 16.

8. More precisely three, two pure strategy and one mixed strategy equilibria. The latter are not considered here.

9. Kreps (1990a) is little different but does have several pages dealing with 'irrationality' (pp. 480–9). Such value-laden terms in supposedly positive economics is evident. If players do not play the way the equilibrium of the game says they should they are 'irrational'. The theory is correct by its by its own definition.

10. The 'interested reader is directed to the more specialised references at the end of the chapter for a fuller treatment' (p. 300).

11. See also Fine (1999).

12. Grabowski (1994) attempts a synthesis of these two approaches using game theory, Fine and Stoneman (1996) are not particularly complementary about his efforts.

13. Gerschenkron (1962) emphasized the importance of state supported development banks among late industrialisers in Europe.

14. The combined profits of the two independent firms.

15. An otherwise sterile analysis of 'focal point equilibria' can be found in Kreps (1990a, p554).

16. Most famously the Luddites, skilled weavers who attempted to block the introduction of new machines.

iii   Many thanks to Alan for invaluable editorial assistance.

iv   Matthew McCartney, 'Dynamic versus static efficiency: the case of textile exports from Bangladesh and the developmental state', *post-autistic economics review*, issue no. 26, 2 August 2004, article 4, http://www.btinternet.com/~pae_news/review/issue26.htm.

v   This is Chapter 16.

vi   More precisely three, two pure strategy and one mixed strategy equilibria. The latter are not considered here.

vii   Kreps (1990a) is little different but does have several pages dealing with 'irrationality' (p480–9). Such value-laden terms in supposedly positive economics is evident. If players do not play the way the equilibrium of the game says they should they are 'irrational'. The theory is correct by its by its own definition.

viii The 'interested reader is directed to the more specialised references at the end of the chapter for a fuller treatment' (p300).

ix   See also Fine (1999).

x   Grabowski (1994) attempts a synthesis of these two approaches using game theory, Fine and Stoneman (1996) are not particularly complementary about his efforts.

xi   Gerschenkron (1962) emphasized the importance of state supported development banks among late industrialisers in Europe.

xii   The combined profits of the two independent firms.

xiii An otherwise sterile analysis of 'focal point equilibria' can be found in Kreps (1990a, p554).

xiv   Most famously the Luddites, skilled weavers who attempted to block the introduction of new machines.

References

Acemoglu, D and J A Robinson (1999), 'Political losers as a barrier to economic development', September, mimeo.

Bardhan, P (1999), 'Distributive conflicts, collective action, and institutional economics', University of California at Berkeley, March, mimeo.

Chang, H-J (1999), 'The economic theory of the developmental state', in Woo-Cumings *The Developmental State*, Ed M. New York, Cornell University Press.

Cooper, R and A John (1988), 'Coordinating coordination failures in Keynesian models', *Quarterly Journal of Economics*, 103, August.

Fine, B (1999), 'The developmental state is dead – long live social capital', *Development and Change*, 30, pp 1–19.

Fine B and C Stoneman (1996), 'Introduction: state and development', *Journal of Southern African Studies*, 22 (1).

Gerschenkron, A (1962), 'Economic backwardness in historical perpective', Cambridge, Harvard University Press.

Grabowski, R (1994), 'The successful developmental state: where does it come from?', *World Development*, 22 (3).

Gravelle H and R Rees (1992), *Microeconomics*, 2nd edn, London, Longman.

Harriss, J (2002), 'Institutions, politics and culture: a case for "old" institutionalism in the study of historical change', LSE, DESTIN working paper 02.

Keen, S (2001), *Debunking Economics: The Naked Emperor of the Social Sciences*, Annandale, Pluto Press.

Kreps, D M (1990a), *A Course in Microeconomic Theory*, London, Harvest Wheatsheaf.

Kreps, D M (1990b), *Game Theory and Economic Modelling*, Oxford, Clarendon Press.

Krugman, P (1999), *The Return of Depression Economics*, New York, W W Norton.

Mas-Colell, A, M D Whinston and J R Green (1995), *Microeconomic Theory*, London, Oxford University Press.

Murphy, K M, A Shleifer and R M Vishny (1989), 'Industrialisation and the big push', *Journal of Political Economy*, 97 (4).

Rapoport, A (1966), *Two-Person Game Theory*, New York, Dover Publications.

Rapoport, A (1970), *N-Person Game Theory: Concepts and Applications*, New York, Dover Publications.

Wade, R (1998a), 'The gathering world slump and the battle over capital controls', *New Left Review*, 23, September/October.

Wade, R (1998b), 'The Asian debt-and-development crisis of 1997–?: causes and consequences', *World Development*, 26 (8).

Woodford, M (1991), 'Self-fulfilling expectations and fluctuations in aggregate demand', In N G Mankiw and D Romer (eds), *New Keynesian Economics, Volume 2, Coordination Failures and Real Rigidities*, Cambridge, MA, MIT Press.

18.

TOWARDS A POST-AUTISTIC MANAGERIAL ECONOMICS

Sashi Sivramkrishna

A course in economics finds a place in almost every management education programme. This course, usually called managerial economics, is intended to help students to solve decision-making problems that they will encounter as managers. Most students find the course quite fascinating and the economic models *seem* to provide them with tools to solve important problems they are likely to face as managers. The MC = MR rule, in particular, tells a manager what she needs to know most, namely the price of the product and quantity to be produced for maximum profit!

I had a student who came up to me at the end of the managerial economics course and asked me to be a consultant for a project to dispense a popular Indian food through vending machines. He wanted my help in finding $p*$ and $Q*$. I had to tell him that a local restaurant manager would be of greater help to him than an economist. Quite irritated, he asked me of what use then was a microeconomics course to managers. This led me to think about why economics may have so little to offer managers and entrepreneurs in their actual decision-making problems.

The essential problem with the term managerial economics is its vague meaning: is it economics *for* managers or is it the economics *of* management? If managerial economics means economics *for* managers then this course can be considered supportive in nature, providing awareness, insights and a general understanding of the market system – important ingredients for managerial decision-making – but not meant to provide tools to solve managerial decision-making problems *per se*. In other words, the course is not intended to teach managers MC = MR type rules that they can "apply" in business.

> Conventional price theory was never intended to serve as a conceptual framework for the study of pricing of the individual firm ... price theory has been primarily developed for use in the analysis of broad economic changes and the evaluation of social controls ... therefore, it would be unfruitful (and erroneous) to use conventional price theory as a unified framework to guide the theoretical and empirical study of price determination within real-world firms. (Diamantopoulos & Mathews)

Such a managerial economics course, however, becomes essentially an economics course; there is nothing managerial about it. In this case it is also not necessary to take just a neoclassical approach – economic history, political economy, institutional economics and even Marxist theory could all provide invaluable insights into the working of a capitalist economy to managers. And what is being discussed in the *Post-Autistic Economics Review* is of utmost relevance to managerial economics courses.

I usually begin my managerial economics course with a reading of Heilbroner's *Worldly Philosophers*. Students must understand that economists, not just the neoclassical ones, try to unravel the mystery of the market system, how it works, when and why it fails, where government intervention may be useful and what are the effects of intervention on societal welfare. Managerial economics must be seen in this light – putting the market system in perspective – the efficiency of the market system in a perfectly competitive structure, the deadweight loss from tariffs and quotas, the inefficiency of monopolies, the need for regulation of natural monopolies, excess capacity in monopolistically competitive markets, price and output of firms in oligopolistic markets, market failure under information asymmetry or externalities like pollution and so on and so forth.

The problem I find with most managerial economics textbooks is that they are written as economics *for* managers, not in the way discussed above, but as economics providing tools *for* the manager. In other words, we can go about using MC = MR kind of rules. Consider a popular text, "Managerial economics: economic tools *for* today's decision makers" (italics my own) authored by Keat and Young. This text propagates "managerial economics as the use of economic analysis to make business decisions involving the best use of an organization's scarce resources". The many "applications" (usually in boxes) and numerical examples are intended to make the student feel and reinforce the hope that their economics tools will one day be "used" by them. However, when encountered with a problem like the one my student faced, they realize that such a managerial economics course is autistic. Why?

When advocating economics as a bag of tools to managers, the economist must realize that managerial economics suffers from a case of asymmetric information – what the economist works with is different from what a manager has to work with. The result: economics fails to give any answers to, even to articulate, the problems of managers. If managerial economics were to be used as a set of tools for managers, we need to begin with the economics of management, articulating problems confronting the manager from a manager's perspective, taking into account the constraints they actually face, which must then be related to their decision-making problems.

What is this information that an economist assumes but a manager does not have? Recall Part I of your managerial economics course: the *actual* demand curve. If you browse through an economics or managerial economics text, you will notice that the demand curve derived from consumer choice models is taken as the actual demand curve with a known slope and location – giving information on what consumers are willing to buy, and at what price. If the *ceteris paribus* assumption is relaxed, the economist also knows how much the demand curve will shift. The economist then freely uses this demand curve when she studies firm behaviour, whatever the market structure. She knows precisely what quantity of output the firm must produce and at what price it must be sold in order to realize its objectives.

The conventional managerial economics text "cheats" the student by introducing a chapter on demand curve estimation: a brief chapter on how to estimate demand curves. Even if you are told not to attempt this exercise yourself, given the dangers of estimating a wrong demand curve, the student feels that "it can be done nonetheless". Students can then go about the rest of the course feeling assured about the usefulness of the course. Interestingly, this chapter on demand estimation is missing in many (pure) economics texts.

As a manager or entrepreneur, are you in the economist's privileged position? Do you have the actual or estimated demand curve for your product on your table or computer screen? Obviously not. If only we think about all those cases that Jack Trout talks about in his book, *Big Brands Big Trouble* (Trout, the failure of New Coke, A1 Poultry Sauce, Xerox computers, Firestone tires). If these companies, with access to the best resources, could have estimated the demand curves for their products, would they have ended in failure?

The manager does not know or can never know with certainty where the *actual* demand curve lies. In fact, if she knows the actual demand curve for the firm's product, there really isn't much of a management problem. With the actual demand curve, all one has to do is to apply the profit-maximizing rule (MR = MC) or any other rule meeting the firm's objective, and the firm's balance sheet could be prepared, not just for the current year, but maybe even for the next year. A manager may still have to motivate employees or obtain raw materials from the cheapest source, but those are not usually the problems with which a manager goes to the economist.

It is useful for the economist to delve into the world of managers and entrepreneurs. Al Ries and Jack Trout provide some useful tips for the economist trying to understand the economics *of* management:

- You can't predict the future. So don't plan on it.
- The fatal flaw in many marketing plans is a strategy based on "predicting the future".
- Seldom are the predictions obvious. Usually, they are so buried in assumptions that you need a degree in rhetoric to ferret them out.
- Remember Peter's Law: "The unexpected always happens".

There is something more that an economist needs to learn about management before theorizing about it and that is, that management is not about "predicting" the future, but about "creating" the future (Ries & Trout). It is not enough that top management "sees" the demand curve for their product; they also must create it. In other words, they must not only know what people want but also make them want it – through advertising, building brands, tactics or whatever. Management decision-making is not only about setting p^* and Q^* given the demand curve but also shifting the demand curve to meet the company's objectives. In his book on entrepreneurship, *In the Company of Heroes*, David Hall comments that "entrepreneurs do not find high profit opportunities, they create them".

We must, however, be fair to the economist. The idea that the actual demand curve is unknown to a manager is not a novel one in economics. Diamantopoulos & Mathews (1995) quote several economists on this point:

> The most challenging problems occur in attempting to estimate the firm's demand schedule, for typically the pricing executive only knows one point in its demand curve – the number of units being sold for the existing price. (Alpert)
> From the standpoint of decision-making, the relevant demand curve is the one on which management basis its pricing and production decisions. This need not be the actual demand curve. From the decision-making standpoint, it suffices that management behaves *as if* it

were the demand curve. (Horowitz)

The demand curve whose image spurs entrepreneurial action will be referred to indiscriminately as the subjective, or imagined, or anticipated demand curve. It may even be called the ex ante demand curve. (Weintraub)

McKenzie and Lee also point out the problem in knowing the actual demand curve:

Saying that the firm must choose the "right" price is easier than actually choosing it … Managers can never be completely sure what the demand for their company's product is.

The average-cost pricing model in economics recognizes the impossibility of a determinate demand curve:

Tastes in the market change continuously and the reaction of the competitors is impossible to predict. Thus firms cannot estimate their future demand. Past experience does not help much in reducing uncertainty, because extrapolation of past conditions in the future is hap hazardous given the dynamic changes in the economic structure. Given this uncertainty average-cost pricing theorists reject the demand schedule as a tool of analysis, thus abandoning half the apparatus of the traditional theory of the firm. (Koutsoyiannis, 1994)

But outright rejection of the demand curve really "reduces" the manager to an accountant. All she must do is to compute average cost and add required mark-up, leaving it to the market to determine sales. Do managers then sit back and do nothing? Don't they engage with the market? Try to influence demand for their products? A post-autistic (neoclassical) managerial economics course needs to consider these facts to become less autistic and more useful to managers.

Chamberlin also talks about an actual demand curve and an expected demand curve, the latter being more elastic than the former. This notion of an expected demand curve assumes a manager to be a naïve individual, always repeating the same mistake of not considering the actions of rivals. Once again this approach may be acceptable if managerial economics is about telling managers what economists think of them. But the real world is not this way. Otherwise most companies would have economists as their CEOs.

To conclude, teaching managerial economics needs to take a clear stance:

is it economics *for* managers based on an economics *of* management? If not, there is no need to restrict course contents to neoclassical theory and one should include a wider understanding of economies and economics. If one were to look at managerial economics as the economics *of* management, then a neoclassical approach could be useful but is currently inadequate for direct application to business management. We need a theory based on an unknown or uncertain demand curve. The present approach of masquerading neoclassical economics with determinate demand curves as economics *for* managers is certainly autistic.

References

Chamberlin, Edward H, 1969, *The Theory of Monopolistic Competition: A Re-orientation of the Theory of Value*, Harvard University Press, Cambridge, MA.

Diamantopoulos, Adamantios & Brian Mathews, 1995, *Making Pricing Decisions: A Study of Managerial Practice*, Chapman & Hall, London. Hall, David, 1999, *In the Company of Heroes: An Insider's Guide to Entrepreneurs at Work*, Kogan Page, London.

Heilbroner, Robert L, 1980, *The Worldly Philosophers: The lives, times, and ideas of the great economic thinkers*, 5th edn, Simon and Schuster, NY.

Keat, Paul G & Philip K Y Young, 2000, *Managerial Economics: Economic Tools for Today's Decision Maker*, 3rd edn; Koutsoyiannis, A, 1994, *Modern Microeconomics*, ELBS, 2nd edn.

McKenzie, Richard & Dwight Lee, *Microeconomics for MBAs*, http://www.gsm.uci.edu/~mckenzie/onlinebooks.htm.

Ries, Al & Jack Trout, 1998, *Bottom-up Marketing*, McGraw-Hill Company.

Trout, Jack, *Big Brands Big Trouble: Lessons Learnt the Hard Way*, East West Books (Madras), Chennai.

PART 4:

PLURALISM VERSUS MONISM

19.

THREE ARGUMENTS FOR PLURALISM IN ECONOMICS[1]

J E King[2]

Is there a single correct alternative to neoclassical economics? The purpose of this short chapter is to suggest that there is not, and to show that this is increasingly recognized by eminent practitioners of several varieties of heterodox economic theory.

For most mainstream economists, of course, there is only one way to do economics. It requires the construction of a model, the collection of relevant data and subsequent testing. The model itself must be consistent with the fundamental principle of methodological individualism: that is to say, it must be based on the assumption of optimising behaviour by rational agents. The tests must employ the most advanced econometric techniques rather than – or at least in addition to – descriptive statistics. For the defenders of mainstream economics these simple rules are what make it a science, which is envied and increasingly imitated by the practitioners of less favoured disciplines in the areas of management and social studies (Lazear, 2000).

This is a seductive story, and it is widely believed, inside and outside economics (Fine, 2000). When applied to the more disreputable branches of business, there is probably something to be said for it. If, however, it is taken as mandating the liquidation of sociology, political theory, social psychology and anthropology as autonomous bodies of scholarly knowledge it is obvious nonsense. As a methodological prescription for economics it is, to say the least, very questionable. In what follows I examine three counter-arguments, each making a different case for pluralism in economic thought. Two of the authors I cite are followers of the Cambridge economist Piero Sraffa, one is an institutionalist, and two are post-Keynesians

Apart from Pierangelo Garegnani, Heinz Kurz and Neri Salvadori are the two most prominent and tenacious defenders of modern-day 'classical' economics, by which they mean the study of the laws governing the pace of accumulation and the way in which output is distributed between the social classes, by means of a rigorous long-period analysis of a competitive capitalist economy. In a recent collection of essays they turn, rather surprisingly, to the defence of pluralism. Economic reality, they note, is widely believed to be very complicated. The questions that economists ask are therefore inherently difficult, and it is unlikely that they have simple answers. Since no theory can consider all relevant factors in any particular economic context, there is a strong *prima facie* case for theoretical pluralism. Different theories will often be complementary rather than alternative, so that 'to seek dominance for one theory over all the others with the possible result that all the rival theories are extinguished amounts to advocating scientific regress. To paraphrase Voltaire: in a subject as difficult as economics a state of doubt may not be very comfortable, but a state of certainty would be ridiculous (Kurz and Salvadori, 2000: 237). Even classical theory has its limits. Kurz, in particular, has long acknowledged that it must be married to Keynesian macroeconomics if a comprehensive understanding of capitalist society is to be attained (Kurz, 1990).

In his latest book the well-known institutionalist Geoff Hodgson argues that the notion of a single 'general' theory applicable to human behaviour in all societies, at all points in time, is a dangerous delusion that has led astray not only neoclassical economists but also many heterodox theorists. Failure to appreciate the need for historical specificity in economic theorising has not only blighted the work of several generations of general equilibrium theorists, but also reduced the analytical achievements of some of their most vocal opponents, including Clarence Ayres, John Maynard Keynes and Joan Robinson. One does not have to agree with all the names on Hodgson's charge sheet (see King, 2002) to accept the truth of his contention that 'there are several problems with general theorising in the social sciences. One is of analytical and computational intractability. Facing such computational limits, general theorists typically simplify their models, thus abandoning the generality of the theory. Another related problem with a general theory is that we are confined to broad principles governing all possible structures within the domain of analysis. In practice, a manageable theory has to confine itself to a relatively tiny subset of all possible structures. Furthermore, the cost of excessive generality is to miss out on key features common to a subset of phenomena' (Hodgson, 2001: 16). Hodgson's own proposal for the reconstruction of economic theory, putting history back into it, is innately and profoundly pluralistic (ibid, Chapters 18–23).

The post-Keynesians Victoria Chick and Sheila Dow make an equally powerful, if largely implicit, case for pluralism in their penetrating analysis of what is implied by mathematical modelling in economics. Formalizing an argument is not, they suggest, an unambiguous improvement, as neoclassicals believe. On the contrary, it is a matter of costs and benefits. Formalism entails a particular view of the world, namely that it displays event regularities strong enough for it to approximate to a closed system. It also requires that the meaning of economic terms be fixed rather than context-specific, and that these terms are separable rather than internally related. If these assumptions are rejected, classical or formal logic is inapplicable and Keynes's 'ordinary logic' may be needed in its place. Ordinary common-sense or human logic 'generates knowledge which is imperfect, partial or vague', and provides 'reasoned grounds for belief which are nevertheless not conclusively demonstrable' (Chick and Dow, 2001: 711, 714). Economic statements may therefore be true in some historical and institutional circumstances, but false in others. Here Chick and Dow share common ground with Hodgson, since their argument casts doubt on:

> ... the possibility of finding immutable laws applicable to, say, feudalism and capitalism alike, or even to capitalism in various stages of its development. From this perspective, a theory can be 'right' at one time and become 'wrong' (more accurately, outdated) at another. The notion of imbuing a closed theoretical system with meaning is thus not an objective procedure; it requires the exercise of judgement. (Ibid, 709).

In this way their critique of formalism leads them to pluralism, not just in substantive theory but also in method, since Keynes's ordinary logic 'supports a methodology which encompasses a range of methods in order to build up knowledge' (ibid, 719; c.f. Dow, 1997).

Note that Chick and Dow do not completely deny the legitimacy of formalism in economics, in all circumstances, for all purposes. On the contrary: some problems lend themselves to closed-system thinking and cry out for precise, formal solutions. They argue only that it is a serious mistake to suppose that all economic problems are of this type. They would certainly disagree with Kurz and Salvadori on the size of the contribution that can be expected from formal reasoning. The two Sraffians, Kurz and Salvadori, follow Garegnani in placing great emphasis on the so-called 'core' of

classical economic theory, which consists of propositions that can be
established with certainty about the relationships between inputs, outputs,
prices and distributional variables in a closed economic system where the
same rate of profit is paid in all industries (Kurz and Salvadori, 1995). The
two post-Keynesians, Chick and Dow, see very little point in exercises of this
type, while Hodgson, the proponent of institutional economics, seems to
deny their validity altogether. Certainly he shows no sympathy for those self-
proclaimed institutionalists who use prey–predator models, chaos theory
and similar sophisticated mathematical tools derived from the biological
sciences.

If pluralism does not (quite) rule out formalism, what does it exclude?
Unqualified relativism, for one thing; logical incoherence, for another.
Hodgson is the most outspoken in denying that 'anything goes', and the
most sternly critical of postmodernist claims in this regard. 'An acceptable
policy of pluralism', he suggests,

> … concerns the policy of institutions towards the funding and
> nurturing of science. Such a policy involves 'pluralism in the academy'.
> But it would not extend to the individual practices of science itself. This
> confusion, between encouraging contradictory ideas in the academy
> and encouraging them in our own heads, is widespread in post-
> modernism … There is much to be said for tolerance of many and
> even antagonistic scientific research programmes within an academic
> discipline or university. But we should not tolerate the existence of
> inconsistent ideas within our own heads. The policy towards science
> must be pluralistic and tolerant, but science itself must be intolerant of
> what it regards as falsehood … Any failure of social science to erect an
> adequate and coherent general theory is not rectified by applauding
> incoherence. (Hodgson, 2001: 35)

Horses for courses, as Geoff Harcourt has always put it (see Comim, 1999),
but they must each have four legs and a jockey and proceed anti-clockwise
around the course.

Sheila Dow has also defended the principle of consistency against its
postmodernist and constructivist opponents. Thus she proposes that a clear
distinction be drawn between 'pure' and 'modified' pluralism. To be a pure
pluralist entails 'a refusal to appraise methodologies and thus also [a refusal]
to advocate one method rather than a plurality'. This, she maintains, offers
'no scope for scientific (or indeed any) discourse'. According to modified
pluralism, however,

> ... no one system of knowledge can claim to have captured reality; each is partial, reflecting one vision of reality. Each school can support its approach to knowledge with reason while recognizing the legitimacy of alternative approaches ... World-view and theory of knowledge cannot be eradicated; yet recognition of differences at this level allows for more reasoned debate over appraisal criteria and analysis of different methodologies (Dow, 1996: 45–6).

Kurz and Salvadori also insist on the need for logical consistency in economic theorising. For them this criterion is enough to rule neoclassical analysis out of the race, since its conception of capital is fundamentally flawed. If the 'principle of substitution' is central to mainstream theory, they argue, it should be applied in a logically consistent manner. In the long period, this means that an increase in the price of one input induces a decrease in the quantity of that input per unit of output. 'All propositions of the theory can be traced back to this basic idea. If it is not true in general, the theory appears to be in trouble' (Kurz and Salvadori, 2000: 238). But it has been known since the mid-1960s that it is, in general, false when applied to the collection of heterogeneous commodities known as 'capital'. From a quite different perspective the post-Keynesian Paul Davidson has criticized what he terms the 'babel' of New Keynesian economics, in which market imperfections that prevent downward price and wage flexibility are denounced as the fundamental cause of involuntary unemployment while in the same breath a falling price level ('deflation') is decried as a serious macroeconomic evil (Davidson, 1999; compare Solow, 1997 and Taylor, 1997 for graphic examples of this incoherence). Horses for courses, once again, but all four legs must be pointing in the same direction.

No single case for pluralism in economics emerges from this brief discussion, and indeed it would be a cause for concern if one did. Similarly, there is no single version of 'unscientific' heterodox economics to stand in opposition to mainstream economic 'science'. Sraffians, institutionalists and post-Keynesians do quite different things, often in radically different ways – as do Marxists, social economists, feminists, greens and other schools of political economy. As Abbie Hoffman is supposed to have said, in the course of the 1968 Chicago conspiracy trial: 'Conspire? We couldn't agree on lunch'. But they did agree to keep on talking, which in the last resort is what pluralism is all about.

Notes

1. This article previously appeared in the *Journal of Australian Political Economy*, no. 50, December 2002, a special issue on post-autistic economics and the state of Political Economy. See the JAPE website at www.JAPE.org.
2. I am grateful to Sheila Dow, Heinz Kurz and Frank Stilwell for comments on an earlier draft.

References

Chick, V and S C Dow (2001), 'Formalism, logic and reality: a Keynesian analysis', *Cambridge Journal of Economics*, 25 (6), November, pp. 705–21.

Comim, F (2000), 'Forms of life and "horses for courses": introductory remarks', *Economic Issues*, 4 (1), March, pp. 21–37.

Davidson, P (1999), 'Keynes' principle of effective demand versus the bedlam of the New Keynesians', *Journal of Post Keynesian Economics* 21 (4), Summer, pp. 571–88.

Dow, S C (1996), *The Methodology of Macroeconomic Thought: A Conceptual Analysis of Schools of Thought in Economics*. Cheltenham, UK and Northampton, MA: Edward Elgar.

Dow, S C (1997), 'Methodological pluralism and pluralism of method', in A Salanti and E Screpanti (eds), *Pluralism in Economics: New Perspectives in History and Methodology*. Cheltenham, UK and Northampton, MA.: Edward Elgar, pp. 89–99.

Fine, B (2001), 'Economics imperialism and intellectual progress: the present as history of economic thought', *History of Economics Review* 32, Summer, pp. 10–36.

Hodgson, G M (2001), *How Economics Forgot History: The Problem of Historical Specificity in Social Science*. London and New York: Routledge.

King, J E (2002), review of Hodgson (2001), *Australian Economic History Review*.

Kurz, H D (1990), *Capital, Distribution and Effective Demand: Studies in the 'Classical' Approach to Economic Theory*. Cambridge: Polity.

Kurz, H D and N Salvadori (1995), *Theory of Production: A Long-Period Analysis*. Cambridge: Cambridge University Press.

Kurz, H D and N Salvadori (2000), 'On critics and protective belts', in Kurz and Salvadori (eds), *Understanding 'Classical' Economics: Studies in Long-Period Theory*. London and New York: Routledge, pp. 235–58.

Lazear, E (2000), 'Economic imperialism', *Quarterly Journal of Economics* 115 (1), February, pp. 99–146.

Solow, R M (1997), 'Is there a core of usable macroeconomics we should all believe in?', *American Economic Review* 87 (2), papers and proceedings, May, pp. 230–32.

Taylor, J B (1997), 'A core of practical macroeconomics', *American Economic Review* 87 (2), papers and proceedings, May, pp. 233–5.

20.

PLEAS FOR PLURALISM

Esther-Mirjam Sent

Pleas

The first stage of the movement that led to the establishment the Post-Autistic Economics Network involved a group of economics students in France publishing a petition in June 2000 under the banner "autisme-économie" (Appendix I).[1] Their plea was supported by an appeal from some economics teachers in France (Appendix II). The second stage was launched in September 2000 by the appearance of the first issue of an email newsletter (Appendix III). By its second issue, the *Post-Autistic Economics Newsletter* had subscribers from 36 countries, and it currently has over 5,000 subscribers from over 100 countries. In November 2000 http://www.paecon.net went live, ushering in further international interest. In 2001, 27 economics PhD students at Cambridge University in England who have come to be known as the "Cambridge 27" issued a petition entitled "Opening up economics" (Appendix IV). The third stage is where we are now: this contribution carefully considers pleas for pluralism that have featured prominently during the previous two stages, as well as before the establishment of the Post-Autistic Economics Network. As Wade Hands (1997, 194) observes: "The plea for pluralism in economics has been a frequent refrain throughout the history of modern economic thought. This refrain has usually been voiced by those who were outside, or critical of, the mainstream in modern economics."

Eight years before the first stage mentioned in the previous paragraph, in 1992, a group of economists issued a "Plea for a pluralistic and rigorous economics" in an advertisement in the *American Economic Review*, calling for "a new spirit of pluralism in economics, involving critical conversation and tolerant communication between different approaches. Such pluralism should not undermine the standards of rigour; an economics that requires itself to face all the arguments will be a more, not a less, rigorous science."[2] The announcement had been organized by Geoffrey Hodgson, Uskali Mäki, and D McCloskey, and signed by 44 illustrious names amongst which were Nobel laureates Franco Modigliani, Paul Samuelson, Herbert Simon and Jan Tinbergen.

In 1993, the International Confederation of Associations for Pluralism in Economics (ICAPE) was founded as a "consortium of over 30 groups in economics" that "seeks to foster intellectual pluralism and a sense of collective purpose and strength."[3] Its 1997 resource list contained 30 professional associations, 32 academic and policy journals, 11 publishers, 16 departments, 16 centers, and nine special projects, not all of which were formally affiliated with ICAPE. The consortium's statement of purpose suggests: "There is a need for greater diversity in theory and method in economic science. A new spirit of pluralism will foster a more critical and constructive conversation among practitioners of different approaches. Such pluralism will strengthen standards of scientific inquiry in the crucible of competitive exchange." ICAPE's first conference on "The Future of Heterodox Economics" was held during Summer 2003.

The "autisme-économie" petition mentioned before, published in 2000, favoured a diversity of approaches in economics.[4] The French students wrote: "We want a pluralism of approaches, adapted to the complexity of the objects and to the uncertainty surrounding most of the big questions in economics …" The petition of the economics teachers in France (Appendix II) also stressed the need for pluralism, focusing mostly on theories.[5] They concluded:

> Pluralism must be part of the basic culture of the economist. People in their research should be free to develop the type and direction of thinking to which their convictions and field of interest lead them. In a rapidly evolving and evermore complex world, it is impossible to avoid and dangerous to discourage alternative representations.

The proposal for reforming economics entitled "Opening up economics" issued by the "Cambridge 27" in 2001, ends as follows:

> "We are not arguing against mainstream methods, but believe in a pluralism of methods and approaches justified by debate. Pluralism as a default implies that alternative economic work is not simply tolerated,

but that the material and social conditions for its flourishing are met, to the same extent as is currently the case for mainstream economics. That is what we mean when we refer to an 'opening up' of economics."[6]

Implicit in all these appeals is the observation that economics lacks pluralism. The pleas are defended by means of an assortment of arguments, such as discussions of the complexity of the economy, evaluations of the restrictions inherent in modelling, and assessments of the cognitive limitations on the part of economists. The advertisement in the *American Economic Review* also employs a reflexive strategy: "Economists today enforce a monopoly of method or core assumptions, often defended on no better ground than it constitutes the 'mainstream'. Economists will advocate free competition, but will not practice it in the marketplace of ideas."[7] The remainder of this contribution highlights some problems with the pleas for pluralism, in an effort to open up ways for strengthening them further.

Pluralism?

Since pluralism itself is a reflexive doctrine – there can be more than one kind of pluralism – problems occur in using pluralism as an organizing principle. First, the nature of pluralism in the various pleas differs. A distinction needs to be made among theories, methods, methodologies, approaches, perspectives, models, explanations and so on (see Salanti and Screpanti, 1997). Whereas the French students stress approaches, their teachers focus more on theories, and British students emphasize methods and approaches. Somewhat troublingly, ICAPE's statement of purpose appears to confuse methods and methodologies, for instance when it notes: "One conspicuous consequence of the homogenization of economics has been a loss of methodological pluralism." Now, pluralism about methodologies involves adopting a pluralistic position towards one's own understanding of the multifaceted enterprise of economics, borrowing from a wide variety of "shelves," including history, literary criticism, philosophy and sociology (see Hands, 2001). This is not what ICAPE's reference to methodological pluralism intends to address. Instead, it is concerned with pluralism about methods, which involves types of models, reasoning, and so on upon which economics relies (see Dow, 1997, 2002).

Second, the source of pluralism varies. It could be ontological, epistemological, pragmatic, historical, sociological, heuristical, political, and so on (see Salanti and Screpanti, 1997). Whereas the French students focus on complexity and uncertainty, their teachers emphasize a wide range of contextual matters, and the British students are not explicit about the source of pluralism. Let us take a closer look at the mechanisms outlined by the teachers:

> "Pluralism is not just a matter of ideology, that is of different prejudices or visions to which one is committed to expressing. Instead the existence of different theories is also explained by the nature of the assumed hypotheses, by the questions asked, by the choice of a temporal spectrum, by the boundaries of problems studied, and, not least, by the institutional and historical context."

The argument that theories vary across different scientific contexts (domains, times, interests, etc) raises the question whether for every phenomenon, question, and so on there would be a single, best account. If so, then this view seems to reduce to monism, which foreshadows the arguments of the subsequent sections. Before moving there, we will make one more observation concerning pluralism.

Third, not much thought seems to have been given as to the classification of pluralism. The various objects of pluralism could be translatable or not and might be compatible or not. Reflexivity concerns should keep one from casting the classification in terms of complements and substitutes (see Mäki, 1999). The French students, their teachers and the British students all seem to view heterodox and neoclassical economics as neither translatable nor compatible. This, again, introduces the possibility of a reduction to monism, as elaborated in the following sections.

Monism!

Most importantly, despite these apparent appeals to pluralism, upon closer scrutiny, the pleas seem to be inspired my monism about theories. This motivation is evidenced, for example by the observation that the first conference of the International Confederation of Associations for Pluralism in Economics (ICAPE) is on the future of heterodox economics, while orthodox economics is considered to be "vapid, exclusionist, and detached from its social and political milieu." The French students write about neoclassical economics: "We no longer want to have this autistic science imposed on us." And their teachers concur: "Neoclassicalism's fiction of a 'rational' representative agent, its reliance on the notion of equilibrium, and its insistence that prices constitute the main (if not unique) determinant of market behaviour are at odds with our own beliefs."

Using a label introduced by Ronald Giere (forthcoming), the appeals to pluralism on the part of heterodox economics may be seen as an instance of strategic pluralism. Though advocacy of pluralism by the French students, their teachers, and the British students may be couched in metaphysical or epistemological terms, could be primarily inspired by efforts to achieve professional power and dominance. John Davis (1997, 209; original emphasis), therefore, concludes that the motivation of heterodox economists "is not that their own theoretical approaches are *also* correct – a theoretical pluralist view – but rather that neoclassical economics is mistaken and misguided in its most basic assumptions, and that their own approaches remedy the deficiencies of neoclassicism – a theoretical monist view."

Also against the spirit of pluralism, heterodox economists appear to be offering a rather monist reading of the mainstream. The French students "oppose the uncontrolled use of mathematics," their teachers "denounce the naive and abusive conflation that is often made between scientificity and the use of mathematics," and the British students dispute the "commitment to formal modes of reasoning that must be employed for research to be considered valid." Which mathematical formalism do they oppose (see Hands and Mirowski 1998; Mirowski and Hands 1998)? Is it that of Chicago University Economics Department (in particular Milton Friedman and George Stigler), of the Cowles Commission at the University of Chicago (especially Kenneth Arrow and Gerard Debreu), or of the Massachusetts Institute of Technology (most notably Paul Samuelson)? Or is it the mathematical formalism of the game theoretic approach of John von Neumann and Oscar Morgenstern, or of John Nash? And how about efforts to incorporate bounded rationality approaches, behavioural insights, chaos theory, complexity approaches, and experimental methods? As Sheila Dow (2002, 7) suggests: "[M]ainstream economics gives the appearance of a moderate form of pluralism." By monistically equating orthodox economics with mathematical formalism, therefore, heterodox economists ignore the fragmentation of the mainstream and manoeuvre themselves into a vulnerable position.

Concluding Comments

If heterodox economists are serious about their advocacy of pluralism, as we hope they are, they need to consider carefully the nature, source and classification of pluralism.[8] And they need to confront the charge that pluralism inevitably leads to an "anything goes" view. They also need to beware of sliding into monism. For instance, an ontological perspective that stresses the patchiness of the world runs the risk of being reduced to monism because it might be consistent with the idea that for every phenomenon there is a single, best account. An epistemological view that involves the hedging of bets may reduce to monism if the long-term goal is a single comprehensive account. An epistemological view that relies on the cognitive limitations of economists may reduce to monism if the limitations are merely delaying the development of a single, complete, and correct theory. If heterodox economists desire pluralism, they need to honour its spirit when offering interpretations of the mainstream. If heterodox economists employ appeals to pluralism strategically in an effort to achieve monism, they leave themselves vulnerable to criticism. Finally, they need to ensure, as stressed by the British students, that the material and social conditions for the flourishing of pluralism are met.

Notes

1. A brief history of the Post-Autistic Economics Network is available at http://www.paecon.net/.
2. The advertisement appeared in *American Economic Review*, 82 (2): xxv.
3. Information on ICAPE can be found at http://www.econ.tcu.edu/econ/icare/main.html.
4. The text of the French students' petition is available at Appendix I, this volume, and http://www.btinternet.com/~pae_news/texts/a-e-petition.htm.
5. The text of the professors' petition circulated in France can be found at Appendix II, this volume, and http://www.btinternet.com/~pae_news/texts/Fr-t-petition.htm.
6. The open letter of the 27 PhD students at Cambridge University may be accessed at Appendix IV, this volume, and http://www.btinternet.com/~pae_news/Camproposal.htm.
7. One of the organizers of the plea, Uskali Mäki (1999), clarifies that some economists who are supporters of free market (object-) economics refused to sign, whereas some economists who are less enthusiastic about free market (object-) economics did sign. He conjectures that "when economists talk about the 'free market' of ideas, they do not use the expression in the sense in which it appears in their theories of the goods market" (504). This enables consistency, but eliminates full self-referentiality.
8. Some of these observations draw on a very insightful list of questions about scientific pluralism that was drawn up by Stephen Kellert, Helen Longino and Kenneth Waters in preparation for a workshop on scientific pluralism. The list is available at http://www.mcps.umn.edu/pluralism/outstanding_questions.html.

References

Davis, John B (1997), "Comment", in Salanti and Screpanti, 1997, 207–11.
Dow, Sheila C (1997), "Methodological pluralism and pluralism of method", in Salanti

and Screpanti, 1997, 89–99.

Dow, Sheila C (2002), "Pluralism in economics", paper presented at the Annual Conference of the Association of Institutional and Political Economics, 29 November 2002.

Giere, Ronald N (forthcoming), "Perspectival pluralism", in Stephen Kellert, Helen Longino, and C Kenneth Waters (eds), *Scientific Pluralism*, Minnesota Studies in the Philosophy of Science.

Hands, D Wade (1997), "Frank Knight's pluralism", in Salanti and Screpanti, 1997, 194–206.

Hands, D Wade (2001), *Reflection Without Rules: Economic Methodology and Contemporary Science Theory* Cambridge: Cambridge University Press.

Hands, D Wade and Philip Mirowski (1998), "Harold Hotelling and the neoclassical dream" in Roger Backhouse, Daniel Hausman, Uskali Mäki, and Andrea Salanti (eds), *Economics and Methodology: Crossing Boundaries*, London: Macmillan, 322–97.

Mäki, Uskali (1999), "Science as a free market: a reflexivity test in an economics of economics", *Perspectives on Science* **7** (4): 486–509.

Mirowski, Philip and D Wade Hands (1998), "A paradox of budgets: the postwar stabilization of American neoclassical demand theory", in Morgan and Rutherford 1998, 260–92.

Morgan, Mary S and Malcolm Rutherford (eds) (1998), *From Interwar Pluralism to Postwar Neoclassicism*, annual supplement to Volume 30, *History of Political Economy*, Durham: Duke University Press.

Salanti, Andrea, and Ernesto Screpanti (eds) (1997), *Pluralism in Economics: New Perspectives in History and Methodology*, Cheltenham, UK: Edward Elgar.

21.

'EFFICIENCY': WHOSE EFFICIENCY?

Richard Wolff

The concept of "efficiency" common to most contemporary economic theories holds that analysis can and should determine the net balance between positive and negative effects of any economic act, event or institution. Sometimes, in practical economic applications, this same notion of efficiency refers to "cost–benefit" analysis. A quantitative measure of all the positive and negative effects of an economic act, event or institution is undertaken to determine whether, on balance, the positives (benefits added up) outweigh the negatives (costs added up). If so, it is judged to be "efficient" and should be undertaken; if not, the reverse holds.

Such a definition and use of the term "efficiency" prevails at both the micro and macro levels of social and economic analysis. The building of a factory extension may or may not be *micro*-efficient. An interest rate increase may or may not be *macro*-efficient. At the level of society as a whole, the institution of a "free market" may or may not be efficient. This same efficiency concept serves in comparative economics. Two or more alternative acts, events or institutions are compared as to their efficiencies. Then, the one that has the greatest quantitative net balance of positive over negative aspects is designated the "more/most efficient."

Such a concept of efficiency requires and presupposes, in all its usages, a rigidly and simplistically determinist view of the world. That is, it presumes that analysis can and does regularly (1) identify all the effects of an economic act, event, or institution, and (2) measure the positivity/negativity of each effect.[1] In sharp contrast, an overdeterminist view of the world renders that concept of efficiency absurd.[2] In this view, any one act, event, or institution has an infinity of effects now and into the future. There is no way to identify, let alone to measure, all these consequences. No efficiency measure – in any comprehensive, total, or absolute sense – is possible. Thus, none of the efficiency "results" ever announced, however fervently believed and relied upon for policy decisions, possessed any comprehensive, total or absolute validity.

Over-determinism undermines the efficiency calculus and the absolutist claims made in its name in yet another way. When considering the "effects" of any particular economic act, event, or institution, an over-determinist standpoint presumes that each of such effects actually had an infinity of causative influences. The "effects" can thus never be conceived as resulting from *only* the one act, event or institution chosen for the efficiency analysis. What efficiency analyses deem to be "effects" of a particular act, event or institution are never reducible to being solely *its* effects. Hence, such "effects" cannot and do not measure the "efficiency" of any particular act, event, or institution. This too renders the usual efficiency calculus and the efficiency concept null and void.[3]

It follows logically that all efficiency analyses and results are relative, not absolute. They are relative to (dependent upon) a determinist view of the world, a determinist ontology that presumes unique causes and "their" effects. Efficiency as a comprehensive, total, and absolute concept-cum-policy standard has no validity in and for analysis that presumes an over-determinist rather than a determinist ontology.

To say that all efficiency analyses are relative to a determinist ontology opens the way to a further critique of them. Given their notion of cause and effects, they all necessarily *select* a few among the many effects they attach to any particular act, event or institution whose efficiency they choose to determine. No efficiency calculus could ever identify and measure all such effects. What distinguishes one efficiency analysis from another are the different principles of selectivity informing each.[4] Usually, one principle of selectivity reigns hegemonic: one set of selected effects is deemed "important" and worth counting while others are marginalized or ignored altogether. These days, economics textbooks teach their readers which effects are to be considered in "applied economic analysis."

This has often provoked criticism. Feminist economists have shown how the hegemonic efficiency calculus has usually ignored the effects that pertain to women, households, reproduction, children and so on. Likewise, environmentalist economists have shown how the hegemonic efficiency calculus has ignored ecological effects, and so on. All too rarely have such critical economists gone beyond the demand that formerly ignored effects be henceforth added to those selected for inclusion in the hegemonic efficiency calculus. That is, their critique of the hegemonic principle of selectivity has focused chiefly on getting their preferred effects included within the hegemonic set. The same applies to much Marxist work. It seeks to challenge the hegemonic efficiency calculus by showing especially how it ignores all sorts of class effects of economic acts, events and institutions.

Yet all such critics could deepen and strengthen their arguments if they took the next step to challenge the hegemonic efficiency calculus per se on conceptual grounds. The relativism of all efficiency arguments and claims creates vulnerability for them and critical opportunity for those who challenge them. From an over-determinist perspective, the economy is an object of struggle among historically conditioned social groups. As such groups emerge within the circumstances of their time and place, they develop particular understandings of their problems and devise different programmes for their solution. In so doing, they inevitably concentrate on some problems rather than others (and the causes associated with them), conceive and decide among some solutions rather than others, attribute some (rather than others) effects to such solutions, and so on.

When formalized into "efficiency calculi," the different social groups perform them differently: they operate different principles of selectivity in identifying their problems and solutions, their causes and their effects.

These groups often clash. Struggles emerge that usually include conflicts over which principles of selectivity will govern the analysis of problems and solutions, which principles of selectivity will be hegemonic in their society and hence in their efficiency calculi. Each group tries to impose its particular principles of selectivity, its particular efficiency calculus, by transforming it into the *absolute* set of principles of selectivity for all efficiency calculi for all members of the society. In place of contending efficiency calculi there is to be one calculus to which all social conflict is to be subordinated: social conflict is to be resolved by determining what is *the* efficient policy or programme to follow. Advancing their own particular efficiency calculus as if it were the absolute notion of efficiency is thus one form taken by the social struggle for hegemony among contending groups. In today's world, the hegemony of social groups favouring capitalism is expressed and sustained by their heavily promoted presumption of an absolutist concept of efficiency and by policy decisions legitimated thereby. Not surprisingly, that absolute concept turns out to be their particular principle of selectivity.

An over-determinist critique of efficiency focuses on deconstructing the claim that any one efficiency calculus – one subset of the countless effects attributed to any act, event, or institution – has some absolute or socially neutral validity. There is no single standard of efficiency. Society always displays different, alternative understandings of and solutions for society's problems. Different social groups struggle for their alternative social programmes utilizing an arsenal of weapons that includes, for many, their respective efficiency calculi. When and where an absolute efficiency calculus is believed to exist, their particular efficiency calculus and particular group (or set of groups) have established its hegemony over others. Success in the struggle by those others to undo that hegemony requires undermining its absolutism as a key component of that struggle. An absolutized efficiency calculus will be used by the social groups that support it as a weapon to suppress contending social groups, their social analyses, and their programmes for social change.

Notes

1. The discursive ploy of retreating to the notion that efficiency analysis identifies and counts only the "most important" or "relevant" effects do not escape the problem. This ploy presumes, once again, that an analyst can know which of the effects are "the most important" or "relevant." To know that requires knowing all the effects, i.e. knowing that *all the other* effects are unimportant or irrelevant.

2. For a definition and discussion of over-determinism as used here, see S Resnick and R Wolff, *Knowledge and Class: A Marxian Critique of Political Economy*, Chicago and London: University of Chicago Press, 1987.

3. This applies to Pareto "optimality" as well. One can never know *all* the consequences of an economic situation so as to determine whether one person is better off and no one is worse off. Likewise, one cannot know, let alone measure, *all* the utility losses to determine whether they might even hypothetically be compensated by all the gains.

4. Thus, efficiency calculi are relative also in a second way: they are relative to the particular subset of attributed effects that they select to consider.

PART 5:

SAVING THE PLANET FROM NEOCLASSICAL ECONOMICS

22.

THE 'ILLTH' OF NATIONS AND THE FECKLESSNESS OF POLICY: AN ECOLOGICAL ECONOMIST'S PERSPECTIVE

Herman E Daly

Our traditional economic problems (poverty, overpopulation, unemployment, unjust distribution) have all been thought to have a common solution, namely an increase in wealth. All problems are easier if we are richer. The way to get richer has been thought to be by economic growth, usually as measured by GDP. I do not here question the first proposition that richer is better than poorer, other things equal. But I do question whether what we persuasively label "economic growth" is any longer making us richer. I suggest that physical throughput growth is at the present margin and in the aggregate increasing "illth" faster than wealth, thus making us poorer rather than richer. Consequently our traditional economic problems become more difficult with further growth. The correlation between throughput growth and GDP growth is sufficiently strong historically so that in the absence of countervailing policies even GDP growth frequently increases illth faster than wealth.

What we conventionally call "economic growth" in the sense of "growth of the economy" has ironically become "uneconomic growth" in the literal sense of growth that increases costs by more than it increases benefits. I am thinking here of the North rather than the South, because in many poor countries where the majority lives close to subsistence the benefits of production growth, even if badly distributed, justify incurring large costs. But since the South is striving with encouragement from the IMF and

World Bank to become like the North, I am not really neglecting the South by focusing on the North.

One will surely ask how do I know that growth has become uneconomic for many Northern countries? Some empirical evidence is referenced below.[1] But more convincing to me is the simple argument that as the scale of the human subsystem (the economy) expands relative to the fixed dimensions of the containing and sustaining ecosystem, we necessarily encroach upon that system and must pay the opportunity cost of lost ecosystem services as we enjoy the extra benefit of increased human scale. As rational beings we presumably satisfy our most pressing wants first, so that each increase in scale yields a diminishing marginal benefit. Likewise, we presumably would sequence our takeovers of the ecosystem so as to sacrifice first the least important natural services. Obviously we have not yet begun to do this because we are just now recognizing that natural services are scarce. But let me credit us with capacity to learn. Even so, that means that increasing marginal costs and decreasing marginal benefits of expanded human scale will accompany increasing human scale. The optimum scale, from the human perspective, occurs when marginal cost equals marginal benefit. Beyond that point growth becomes uneconomic in the literal sense of costing more than it is worth.

It is interesting to know empirically if we have reached that point (I think we have in many countries), but even if we have not, it is obvious that continued growth of a dependent subsystem relative to a finite sustaining total system will inevitably reach such an optimal scale. If we add to the limit of finitude of the total system the additional limits of entropy and complexity of ecological interdependence, then it is clear that the optimal scale will be encountered sooner rather than later. Additionally, if we expand our anthropocentric view of the optimum scale to a more biocentric view, by which I mean one that attributes not only instrumental but also intrinsic value to other species, then it is clear that the scale of the human presence will be further limited by the duty to reserve a place in the sun for other species, even beyond what they "pay for" in terms of their instrumental value to us. And of course the whole idea of "sustainability" is that the optimal scale should exist for a very long time, not just a few generations. Clearly a sustainable scale will be smaller than an unsustainable scale. For all these reasons I think that for policy purposes we do not need exact empirical measures of the optimal scale. If one jumps from an airplane it may be nice to have an altimeter, but what one really needs is a parachute.

So what policies constitute a parachute? Briefly, they are policies that limit aggregate throughput, the metabolic flow beginning with depletion and ending with pollution, by which we and our economy live. Although the market cannot itself set that aggregate limit, it can allocate the limited throughput – assuming the market is competitive and confined to some limited degree of inequality in the distribution of wealth and income. Such policy instruments are evolving now, e.g. cap-and-trade systems for extraction rights, pollution emission rights, fishing rights, etc. Also ecological tax reform limits throughput by making it more expensive. It shifts the tax base from value added (something we want more of) on to "that to which value is added", namely the throughput (something we want less of). In differing ways each of the above "parachutes" would limit throughput and expansion of the scale of the economy into the ecosystem, and also provide public revenue. I will not discuss their relative merits, having to do with price versus quantity interventions in the market, but rather emphasize the advantage that both have over the currently favoured strategy. The currently favoured strategy might be called "efficiency first" in distinction to the "frugality first" principle embodied in both of the throughput-limiting mechanisms mentioned above.[2]

"Efficiency first" sounds good, especially when referred to as "win–win" strategies or more picturesquely as "picking the low-hanging fruit". But the problem of "efficiency first" is with what comes second. An improvement in efficiency by itself is equivalent to having a larger supply of the factor whose efficiency increased. The price of that factor will decline. More uses for the now cheaper factor will be found. We will end up consuming more of the resource than before, albeit more efficiently. Scale continues to grow. This is sometimes called the "Jevons effect". A policy of "frugality first", however, induces efficiency as a secondary consequence; "efficiency first" does not induce frugality – it makes frugality less necessary, and fails to give rise to a scarcity rent that can be captured and redistributed.

So far I have briefly outlined what I take to be the problem of the "illth of nations" (apologies to both Adam Smith and John Ruskin), and indicated some policy guidelines for avoiding the uneconomic growth that increases illth faster than wealth. I probably do not need to tell readers of post-autistic economics that these views do not find favour with mainstream neoclassical economists. The concepts of throughput, of entropy, and even of optimal scale of the macro economy are foreign to them. The last is especially odd since in microeconomics the concept of the optimal scale of each micro activity is central. Yet the sum of all micro activities, the macro economy, is not thought to have an optimal scale relative to its sustaining ecosystem. Probably this is because macroeconomists think of the macro economy as the "whole," not as a "part" of some larger "whole." For them nature is not a containing envelope, but just a sector of the macro economy – mines, wells, croplands, pastures and fisheries. When the "whole" grows it expands into the "void," encroaching on nothing and incurring no opportunity cost. But of course the real economy is a "part" and it grows not into the "void," but into the rest of the ecosystem, and really does incur opportunity costs. I have long considered this "whole" versus "part" difference to reflect different pre-analytic visions (Schumpeter) or different paradigms (Khun). Different pre-analytic visions cannot, of course, be reconciled by further analysis. I still believe this is fundamental.

Recently, however, my experiences of teaching in a policy school and of dealing with ecologists and biologists as well as economists, has led me to see an additional problem at the level of policy in general. In other words, even if we could agree on the right pre-analytic vision of the basic way the world works, would we then be able to enact and follow effective policies, such as the "parachutes" briefly discussed? So far, our capacity to enact policies of "frugality first" seems very weak. Indeed, even "efficiency first" policies are not easy to enact. So let us turn our attention to the question of policy in general, and policy fecklessness in particular.

What are the presuppositions we must make before we can reasonably and seriously discuss policy – policy of any kind? There are two that I can see.

First we must believe that there are real alternatives among which to choose. If there are no alternatives, if everything is determined, then it hardly makes sense to discuss policy – what will be will be. No options, no responsibility, no need to think.

Second, even if there were real alternatives, policy dialogue would still make no sense unless there was a real criterion of value by which to choose from among the alternatives. Unless we can distinguish better from worse states of the world then it makes no sense to try to achieve one state of the world rather than another. No value criterion, no responsibility, no need to think.

In sum, serious policy must presuppose: (1) non-determinism – that the world is not totally determined, that there is an element of freedom which offers us real alternatives; and (2) non-nihilism – that there is a real criterion of value to guide our choices, however vaguely we may perceive it.

To be sure, not every conceivable alternative is a real alternative. Many things really are impossible. But the number of viable possibilities permitted by physical law and past history is seldom reduced to only one. Through our choices, value and purpose lure the physical world in one direction rather than the other. Purpose is independently causative in the world.

This seems pretty obvious to common sense – so what is the point of stating the obvious? The point is that many members of the intelligentsia deny one or both presuppositions, and yet want to engage in a policy dialogue. I don't mean that we disagree on exactly what our alternatives are in a particular instance, or about just what our value criterion implies for a concrete case. That is part of the reasonable policy dialogue. I mean that determinists who deny the effective existence of alternatives, and nihilists or relativists who deny the existence of value beyond the level of subjective personal tastes, have no right to engage in policy dialogue – and yet they do! This is my cordial invitation to them to remember, and to reflect deeply upon their option of remaining silent – at least about policy.

Who are these people? In the sciences I am thinking about the hard-line neo-Darwinists and socio-biologists; in the humanities, the post-modern deconstructionists; and in the social sciences, the evolutionary psychologists, and those economists who reduce value to subjective individual tastes any one of which is as good as another.

In practice, no one can live by the creed of determinism or nihilism. In this sense no one takes them seriously, so we tend to discount any effect on policy of these doctrines. We tend to dismiss them as academic posturing. However, we halfway suspect that the many learned people who publicly proclaim these views might be right – and that is enough to enfeeble policy. For example, many people tell me that globalization is inevitable; any attempt to counter global economic integration is futile. If I manage to convince them that it might not be inevitable, the next line of defence is, how do we know that globalization will be any worse than the alternative? We cannot tell, we don't really know that it won't be good for us (because we don't know what is good in the first place), so there is no point in opposing it. Either it is inevitable, or if not then we can have no reason to believe that any alternative would be better. Forget policy, go back to sleep.

Perhaps I can clarify my point by distinguishing four categories based on acceptance or non-acceptance of each of the two presuppositions identified:

(1) perennial wisdom (e.g. Judeo–Christianity in the West) – there exist real alternatives from which to choose by reference to objective criteria of value;

(2) criterionless choice – alternatives are real options, but there is no objective criterion for choosing among them (existentialist angst);

(3) providential determinism – there are no real options, but there is an objective criterion of value by which to choose, if only we had a choice. Fortunately providence has chosen for us according to the objective

criterion, which we would not be wise or good enough to have followed on our own (theological predestination; technological providentialism);

(4) criterionless determinism – there are no real alternatives to choose from, and even if there were, there is no objective criterion of value by which to choose. All is mechanism – random variation and natural selection, as claimed by the hard-line neo-Darwinists.

People engaged in policy, yet holding to positions (2), (3), or (4), are in the grip of a severe and debilitating inconsistency. Their participation in policy dialogue should be subject to the injunction of "estoppel" – a legal restraint to prevent witnesses from contradicting their own testimony.[3] It should be applied in academia as well as in the courtroom!

To summarize: avoiding the uneconomic growth that is increasing the illth of nations will require clear and forceful policy. All policy, especially such a radical one, requires a belief in both objective value and real alternatives. The fact that many people engaged in discussing and making policy reject one or both of these presuppositions is, in Alfred North Whitehead's term, "the lurking inconsistency," a contradiction at the basis of the modern worldview which enfeebles thought and renders action feckless. If we even halfway believe that purpose is an illusion foisted on us by our genes to somehow make us more efficient at procreation, or that one state of the world is, for all we can tell, as good as another, then it is hard to get serious about real issues. Whitehead noted, "Scientists animated by the purpose of proving that they are purposeless constitute an interesting subject for study." He went on to say that, "it is not popular to dwell on the absolute contradiction here involved."

I think, 75 years later, that it is high time we dwelt on this absolute contradiction. We pay a price for ignoring contradictions – in this case the price is feebleness of purpose and half-heartedness in policy. Citizens really must affirm that the world offers more than one possibility to choose from, and that some choices really are better than others. Determinists and nihilists have a right to exist, but an obligation to remain silent on policy. If hard-line, neo-Darwinist, deterministic materialists refuse to be silent, then they should be invited to explain why the survival value of such neo-Darwinism is not negative for the species that really believes it!

Notes

1.   For critical discussion and the latest revision of the ISEW, see, Clifford W Cobb and John B Cobb, Jr et al., *The Green National Product*, University Press of America, New York, 1994. For a presentation of the ISEW see appendix of *For the Common Good*, H

Daly and J Cobb, Boston: Beacon Press, 1989; 2nd edn, 1994. See also Clifford W Cobb, et al., "If the GDP is up, why is America down?", *Atlantic Monthly*, October, 1995. See also Manfred Max-Neef, "Economic growth and quality of life: a threshold hypothesis", *Ecological Economics*, 15, (1995), pp. 115–18. See also Clive Hamilton, *Growth Fetish*, Allen and Unwin, NSW, Australia. 2003.

2.   By "frugality" I mean "non-wasteful sufficiency," rather than "meager scantiness."

3.   "Estoppel" is a bar or impediment preventing a party from asserting a fact or claim inconsistent with a position that the party previously took, either by conduct or words, especially where a representation has been relied or acted upon by others. (Random House *Dictionary of the English Language*)

23.

ECOLOGICAL ECONOMICS IS POST-AUTISTIC

Robert Costanza

Autism: A psychiatric disorder of childhood characterized by marked deficits in communication and social interaction, preoccupation with fantasy, language impairment, and abnormal behaviour, such as repetitive acts and excessive attachment to certain objects. It is usually associated with intellectual impairment. (American Heritage® *Dictionary of the English Language*, 4th edn, 2000)

The post-autistic economics movement has correctly identified many of the failings of mainstream economics. With reference to the definition above, mainstream economics is "autistic" in its deficits in communication and social interaction with other disciplines, preoccupation with mathematical fantasy, language impairment in its limited and specialized vocabulary, and excessive attachment to certain objects (assumptions and models). This intellectual impairment has led to its inability to address many important real world problems.

Ecological economics has moved well beyond the autism of the mainstream and represents a viable post-autistic alternative. This chapter describes briefly what ecological economics is, how it developed, and why it is "post-autistic."

Ecological economics is a trans-disciplinary effort to link the natural and social sciences broadly, and especially ecology and economics (Costanza, 1991). The goal is to develop a deeper scientific understanding of the complex linkages between human and natural systems, and to use that understanding to develop effective policies that will lead to a world which is ecologically sustainable, with a fair distribution of resources (both between groups and generations of humans and between humans and other species), and which allocates scarce resources efficiently, including "natural" and "social" capital. This requires new approaches that are comprehensive, adaptive, integrative, multi-scale, pluralistic and evolutionary, and that acknowledge the huge uncertainties involved.

For example, if one's goals include ecological sustainability then one cannot rely on the principle of "consumer sovereignty" on which most conventional economic solutions are based, but must allow for co-evolving preferences, technology, and ecosystems (Norton et al., 1998). One of the basic organizing principles of ecological economics is thus a focus on this complex interrelationship between ecological sustainability (including system carrying capacity and resilience), social sustainability (including distribution of wealth and rights, social capital and co-evolving preferences) and economic sustainability (including allocative efficiency in the presence of highly incomplete and imperfect markets). A major implication of this is that our ability to predict the consequences of economic behaviour is limited by our ability to predict the evolution of the biosphere. The complexity of the many interacting systems that make up the biosphere means that this involves a very high level of uncertainty. Indeed, uncertainty is a fundamental characteristic of all complex systems involving irreversible processes and ecological economics is particularly concerned with problems of uncertainty. More particularly, it is concerned with the problem of assuring sustainability under uncertainty. Instead of locking ourselves into development paths that may ultimately lead to ecological collapse, we need to maintain the resilience of ecological and socioeconomic systems by conserving and investing in natural and social assets.

Ecological economics has historical roots as long and deep as any field in economics or the natural sciences, going back to at least the seventeenth century (Costanza et al., 1997). Nevertheless, its immediate roots lie in work done in the 1960s and 1970s. Kenneth Boulding's classic "The economics of the coming spaceship Earth" (Boulding, 1966) set the stage for ecological economics with its description of the transition from the "frontier economics" of the past, where growth in human welfare implied growth in material consumption, to the "spaceship economics" of the future, where growth in welfare can no longer be fueled by growth in material consumption. Daly (1968) further elaborated this fundamental difference in vision and worldview by recasting economics as a life science – akin to biology and especially ecology, rather than a physical science like chemistry or physics. The importance of this shift in "pre-analytic vision" cannot be overemphasized. It implies a fundamental change in the perception of the problems of resource allocation and how they should be addressed. More particularly, it implies that the focus of analysis should be shifted from marketed resources in the economic system to the biophysical basis of interdependent ecological and economic systems and their co-evolution over time.

Ecological economics is not, however, a single new paradigm based in shared assumptions and theory. It is instead a *metaparadigm*. Rather than espousing and defending a single discipline or paradigm, it seeks to allow a broad, pluralistic range of viewpoints and models to be represented, compared, and ultimately synthesized into a richer understanding of the inherently complex systems it deals with. It represents a commitment among economists, ecologists and other academics and practitioners to learn from each other, to explore new patterns of thinking together, and to facilitate the derivation and implementation of effective economic and environmental policies. Ecological economics is deliberately and consciously pluralistic in its conceptual underpinnings. Within this pluralistic metaparadigm, traditional disciplinary perspectives are perfectly valid *as part of the mix*. Ecological economics therefore includes some aspects of neoclassical environmental economics, traditional ecology and ecological impact studies, and several other disciplinary perspectives as components, but it also encourages completely new, more integrated, ways to think about the linkages between ecological and economic systems.

Ecological economics has also developed a solid institutional base. After numerous experiments with joint meetings between economists and ecologists, the International Society for Ecological Economics (ISEE) was formed in 1988 and currently has over 2,000 members worldwide (http://www.ecologicaleconomics.org/). The journal of the society, *Ecological Economics*, published its first issue in February 1989 and is currently publishing 12 issues per year, with an impact factor ranking it in the top fifth of all economics journals (http://www.elsevier.com/inca/publications/store/5/0/3/3/0/5/). Major international conferences have been held since 1990 (http://www.ecologicaleconomics.org/conf/conf.htm) with attendance as high as 1,500. Several ecological economic institutes have been formed around the world, a significant number of books have appeared with the term ecological economics in their titles (e.g. Martinez-Alier, 1987; Costanza, 1991; Peet, 1992; Jansson et al., 1994; Barbier et al., 1994; Krishnan et al., 1995; Costanza et al., 1997), and a fair number of university courses, certificate programmes (e.g. http://www.uvm.edu/giee/giee_certif.html), and graduate degree programmes (e.g. http://www.rpi.edu/dept/catalogue/97-98/ Interdisciplinary/ecological.html) have also developed.

So, is ecological economics post-autistic? The Kansas City Proposal (2001) lists seven changes needed to move to post-autism: (1) a broader conception of human behaviour; (2) recognition of culture; (3) consideration of history; (4) a new theory of knowledge (beyond the positive–normative dichotomy); (5) empirical grounding; (6) expanded methods; and (7) interdisciplinary dialogue. Ecological economics certainly has all of these characteristics. Its explicit links with the natural sciences result in a more scientific approach, which is inherently more pluralistic (Fullbrook, 2001) and empirically grounded. It places humans and human behaviour in a broader historical, evolutionary, and ecological context (Costanza et al., 1993). Humans are seen as a part of the natural world, not abstractions in isolation from nature and each other. It is problem-based, not tool-based, and its methods include any that are applicable to the problems at hand. These include everything from participatory processes (Campbell et al., 2000) to envisioning alternative futures (Costanza, 2000; Farley and Costanza, 2002) to complex systems simulation modelling (Costanza et al., 1993, 2002: Boumans et al., 2002). It recognizes the importance of envisioning and the limits of the positive-normative dichotomy (Costanza, 2001). It goes well beyond interdisciplinary dialogue. It aspires to be a truly transdisciplinary science.

One question is: given that ecological economics has been around since 1990 and seems to "fit the bill" for post-autistic economics, why has it not been recognized as such by the post-autistic economics movement which began around 2000? I can only conclude that this is just one more symptom of the autism of mainstream economics, which has been so hermetically sealed from the real world that it has not noticed (or more likely aggressively ignored) these developments and has not made its students aware of them. Now that the veil of that autism is finally being lifted, we can join forces and move together to create a transdisciplinary, pluralistic science that can help solve the pressing problems the world faces today and help create a sustainable and desirable world for the future.

References

Barbier, E B, J C Burgess and C Folke, 1994, "Paradise lost? the ecological economics of biodiversity", Earthscan, London.

Boulding, K E, 1966 "The economics of the coming spaceship Earth", in H Jarrett (ed.) *Environmental Quality in a Growing Economy*, Baltimore:Resources for the Future/Johns Hopkins University Press, Baltimore, MD, pp. 3–14.

Boumans, R, R Costanza, J Farley, M A Wilson, R Portela, J Rotmans, F Villa and M Grasso, 2002, "Modelling the dynamics of the integrated earth system and the value of global ecosystem services using the GUMBO model", *Ecological Economics* 41: 529–60.

Campbell, B M, R Costanza, and M van den Belt (eds), 2000, "Land Use Options in Dry Tropical Woodland Ecosystems in Zimbabwe", in special section of *Ecological Economics*, 33 (3), pp. 341–438.

Costanza, R (ed.), 1991, *Ecological Economics: The Science and Management of Sustainability*, New York: Columbia University Press.

Costanza, R, 2000, "Visions of alternative (unpredictable) futures and their use in policy analysis", *Conservation Ecology* 4 (1), 5, [online] URL: http://www.consecol.org/vol4/iss1/art5.

Costanza, R, 2001, "Visions, values, valuation and the need for an ecological economics", *BioScience* 51, 459–68.

Costanza, R, L Wainger, C Folke and K-G Mäler, 1993, "Modelling complex ecological economic systems: toward an evolutionary, dynamic understanding of people and nature", *BioScience* 43, 545–55.

Costanza, R, J C Cumberland, H E Daly, R Goodland and R Norgaard, 1997, *An Introduction to Ecological Economics*. Boca Raton: St. Lucie Press.

Costanza, R, A Voinov, R Boumans, T Maxwell, F Villa, L Wainger and H Voinov, 2002, "Integrated ecological economic modelling of the Patuxent River watershed, Maryland", *Ecological Monographs* 72, 203–31.

Daly, H E, 1968, "On economics as a life science", *Journal of Political Economy* 76, 392–406.

Farley, J and R Costanza, 2002, "Envisioning shared goals for humanity: a detailed shared vision of a sustainable and desirable USA in 2100", *Ecological Economics* 43, 245–59.

Fullbrook, E, 2001, "Real science is pluralist", *Post-Autistic Economics Newsletter*, issue 5, article 6, at http://www.btinternet.com/~pae_news/review/issue5.htm.

Jansson, A M, M Hammer, C Folke and R Costanza (eds), 1994, *Investing in Natural Capital: The Ecological Economics Approach to Sustainability*. Washington, DC: Island Press.

Kansas City Proposal, 2001, "An international open letter to all economics departments", *Post-Autistic Economics Newsletter*. issue 8, article 1, at http://www.btinternet.com/~pae_news/KC.htm.

Krishnan, R, J M Harris and N Goodwin (eds). 1995, *A Survey of Ecological Economics*, Washington, DC: Island Press.

Martinez-Alier, J, 1987, *Ecological Economics: Energy, Environment, and Society*, Oxford: Blackwell.

Norton, B, R Costanza and R Bishop, 1998, "The evolution of preferences: why 'sovereign' preferences may not lead to sustainable policies and what to do about it", *Ecological Economics* 24, 193–211.,

24.

PRICELESS BENEFITS, COSTLY MISTAKES: WHAT'S WRONG WITH COST–BENEFIT ANALYSIS?[1]

Frank Ackerman

The critique of economic theory is not just a theoretical problem. In the hands of conservatives such as the Bush administration, simplistic and misleading economic abstractions are incorporated into structures of political power. Ill-founded economic theories provide a seemingly scientific rationale for doing the wrong thing, time after time.

Consider the current abuse of cost–benefit analysis, which is now said to be essential for evaluating health and environmental protection. John Graham, formerly head of the Harvard Center for Risk Analysis, is the Bush administration's "regulatory czar," charged with evaluating regulations proposed by federal agencies to be sure that the costs do not exceed the benefits. Graham has frequently sent regulations back for revision or for additional analysis, when he concludes that the proposed rules would fail a cost–benefit test. Unsurprisingly, the end result has been a slowing and weakening of environmental protection.

The concept of cost–benefit analysis has a soothingly reasonable sound to it: why shouldn't we check that the benefits exceed the costs before adopting a new regulation? But move beyond comfortable rhetoric to rigorous theory, and the case for cost–benefit analysis of regulations fails on at least three grounds.

Failure #1: Incremental movement toward an unattainable theoretical ideal may not be desirable. Cost–benefit analysis of health and environmental measures requires monetizing non-monetary benefits, a process that is the source of most of the difficulties in the analysis (as described below). It might appear that monetizing and internalizing environmental externalities is bringing the economy closer to the welfare optimum described by the Arrow–Debreu "fundamental theorems of welfare economics." Yet that optimum depends on a host of unrealistic assumptions, including perfect competition among small, powerless firms in every industry, perfect information for all market participants, universal adherence to an implausible and unattractive model of consumer behaviour, and perfect internalization of *all* externalities (not just the few that environmental economists have studied and politicians have accepted).

Even if all these assumptions are granted, economic theorists have known for 30 years that the market equilibrium may be neither unique nor dynamically stable.[2] Perhaps most damning of all, the "theory of the second best," known to economists since the 1950s, shows that if any aspects of the free-market ideal are fundamentally unattainable (as is of course the case), then incremental movement toward that ideal is not necessarily a welfare improvement.[3] This point is not limited to environmental policy: the theory of the second best is a powerful argument against incremental market-based or market-oriented policy measures of any type. Such measures may or may not be desirable on other grounds, but they cannot logically be defended as small steps on the road to an idealized competitive market, since that ideal is clearly unattainable.

Failure #2: There is no crisis of excessive regulatory costs that needs to be addressed. The argument for cost–benefit analysis of public policy often involves the suggestion that we can't afford to do (regulate) everything, so we should be sure we're getting the most bang for the buck. This claim fails for two distinct reasons. First, there is no single budget, no lump sum of resources that is being allocated to one regulation or another by cost–benefit analysis. Most of the costs of environmental compliance are borne by the private sector, typically by the firms that cause pollution. Cost–benefit analysis of cleaning up the Hudson River in New York involves costs that might be imposed on the industrial corporations that pollute the river. Cost–benefit analysis of the use of harmful pesticides in Californian agriculture involves costs that might be imposed on agribusiness, in a different industry from the Hudson polluters and thousands of miles away from New York. If one of these measures passes a cost–benefit test and the other does not, no funds are transferred from one industry to the other; one industry just ends up with less regulation, more freedom to pollute, and more profits.

In some ultimate sense, it is true that overall resources are limited and we can't afford to spend everything we've got on environmental protection. However, no society has ever approached this limit; no significant policy proposal has ever advocated anything of the sort. The limit on aggregate resources is so far from being a binding constraint on environmental policy that it can be ignored in practice, just as our inability to exceed the speed of light can be ignored in the process of automobile design.

Second, the most common evidence for the crisis of regulatory costs is simply erroneous. The tables showing widely differing costs per life saved by different regulations are so consistent with the worldview of mainstream economics that they have been repeatedly reprinted with little or no critical scrutiny. As my co-author Lisa Heinzerling has demonstrated, these tables and their claims of regulatory inefficiency rest on just a few widely cited studies, which commit a series of empirical errors in their haste to establish their desired conclusion.[4] For example, many of the expensive-looking regulations in the familiar tables of regulatory costs are actually proposals that were never adopted, whereas the more cost-effective rules, such as removal of lead from gasoline, have often been completed and cannot be repeated for additional savings. There are no lives or money to be saved by moving imaginary resources from expensive proposals that were never adopted to cheaper regulations that have already been completed.

Failure #3: Compensation tests and "potential Pareto improvement" do not justify cost–benefit analysis. One of the underlying assumptions of cost–benefit analysis is that distribution can be ignored: costs and benefits to all economic agents are indiscriminately added together in calculating the bottom-line evaluation for society. This disinterest in distribution is justified by the Kaldor–Hicks compensation tests: if the winners from a policy could compensate the losers, leaving everyone as well or better off, then the policy is a potential Pareto improvement. There is no requirement that the winners actually pay compensation, and all too often, they choose not to do so; the Pareto improvement normally remains purely potential. As Amartya Sen has insisted, this potential improvement may not in fact be desirable. A policy that makes the rich much richer and the poor a little poorer is a potential Pareto improvement, but with enough of such improvements, the poor will starve. (If compensation is paid to the losers, then the policy becomes an actual, not just a potential, Pareto improvement.)

This and other problems with the Kaldor–Hicks compensation tests have long been known to theorists. Yet the practice of cost–benefit analysis continues to be justified in terms of the theory of compensation tests, along with the supposed crisis of regulatory costs and the general desirability of moving toward a competitive optimum. An old joke describes economists as seeing something working in practice, and asking whether it is possible in theory. In this case the joke is being told in reverse: having established that cost–benefit analysis of environmental protection is impossible in theory, its advocates have set out to see if it works in practice.[5]

Why benefits are priceless

In practice, cost–benefit analysis of health and environmental protection rests on an implausible process of monetization of priceless benefits. Human life, health, the natural world, and the well-being of future generations are priceless – not infinite in value, but fundamentally incommensurable with money. Here I will only summarize some of the arguments that Lisa Heinzerling and I have made at greater length elsewhere:[6]

It is not meaningful to put a dollar value on human life. The benefits of many environmental regulations include avoided human deaths; the attempt to monetize benefits and compare them to costs requires a dollar value for life and death. Under the Clinton administration, US Environmental Protection Agency (EPA) felt the answer was $6.1 million, based on a literature review of a number of empirical studies. Most of the studies looked at the risk premium in wages for jobs that had differing risks of death, holding everything else constant. If the average male blue-collar worker gets a risk premium of about 30 cents per hour over equivalent risk-free work, that is arithmetically equivalent to $6 million per life.

The Bush administration, leaving no methodology unturned in its quest for lower benefits and weakened environmental protection, decided that it preferred the results of studies in which people are asked to assign monetary values to small hypothetical risks of death; this yields numbers as low as $3.7 million per head, or, in a particularly controversial version, only $2.6 million for those over 70. These numbers do not offer a reasonable description of society's obligation to control and eliminate life-threatening health and environmental hazards. Indeed, there is no reason to think that society should spend the same amount of money on avoiding every type of preventable death, ignoring the many differences in context that determine the meaning of and responsibility for these deaths.

Valuation of non-fatal health hazards is conceptually and technically flawed. An enormous number of diseases and health conditions are affected by environmental policy measures; there is little hope of valuing them all. Health economists' attempts to measure QALYs

(Quality Adjusted Life Years) have led to paradoxes and inconsistencies, and have not been widely accepted. Willingness-to-pay measures favoured by environmental economists have foundered on the impossibly large data requirements, as well as underlying conceptual flaws. In EPA's cost–benefit analysis of removing arsenic from drinking water, the analysts could not find a value for avoiding a non–fatal case of bladder cancer, and (as usual) did not have sufficient time or budget to do a new empirical study. So they simply used a value that had been developed for chronic bronchitis more than a decade earlier – based on a shopping mall survey in which respondents were asked whether they preferred their current neighbourhood, or a similar one with a lower cost of living and a higher rate of bronchitis.

Borrowing of values estimated for other externalities is called "benefits transfer" by practitioners. If, in elementary or high school, you copied someone else's homework when you didn't have time to do your own, you were engaged in "homework transfer." As the practitioners discover at times, homework transfer can lead to grief if you do it carelessly and copy the answer to the wrong question. Despite its proclivity for similar mistakes, benefits transfer is ubiquitous in cost–benefit analysis, since in practice there is never enough time or funding to do a new, full-blown contingent valuation study for each relevant externality.

The natural world has a very large but non-quantifiable value to many people. In valuing impacts on nature, economists distinguish between use values and non-use values, such as the value placed on the existence of a species or wilderness. Use values are sometimes well-defined, but often small. Non-use values are often large, but poorly defined. In the case of the Exxon Valdez oil spill in Alaska, the losses to people who worked and lived in the affected area were estimated at $300 million, while the existence value of the area to the US population – the amount that American households were reportedly willing to pay to prevent a similar oil spill in a similar area – was $9 billion, or 30 times as large. If protection against oil spills is judged by a cost–benefit test, the existence value of the affected region justifies 30 times as much environmental protection as the use value.

But precise numerical existence values are conceptually problematical, as demonstrated by a brief digression on whales. The "use value" of whales is reflected in the amounts that people pay to go on whale-watching trips. This is an established tourist industry, with annual revenues of $160 million in the US. On the other hand, the existence of just one species, humpback whales, is, according to one study, worth $18 billion to the US population – more than 100 times the total revenues of whale-watching trips.

Suppose that you have bought the last ticket on a whale-watching trip, and someone offers to buy your ticket from you for twice the price you paid for it. You may or may not accept, but the offer is not offensive. Now suppose that someone offers $36 billion for the right to hunt and kill all the humpback whales in the ocean. Although this offer is twice the existence value, it would strike most people as offensive. The differing reactions reveal that the two types of "prices" are not comparable. The use value of whales is a real number; a seat on a whale-watching trip is a commodity with a meaningful market price. The existence of whales is enormously valuable to many people, but the $18 billion figure contains no quantitative information; it is not the price of a commodity that can be bought or sold. Existence values are real, but they are not really numbers. Some other way must be found to reflect those values in public policy.

Discounting distorts and trivializes future health and environmental outcomes. The process of discounting future costs and benefits is essential for short- and medium-term financial calculations. But the same mathematical techniques yield nonsensical results when applied to the far future, and to non-monetary values. There are two distinct problems that result from inappropriate discounting of the environment.

First, discounting is often used to suggest that events a century or two in the future don't matter today. Discounting at any positive interest rate makes serious intergenerational harms such as the future impact of climate change look relatively small in present value terms. The conceptual error here stems from forgetting the rationale behind discounting: the calculation assumes that a *single observer* compares (usually) costs now and benefits later, coming to his/her own conclusion about whether to accept the trade-off. But there is no individual who will have personal experience of both the costs of climate change mitigation today and the benefits that will be enjoyed 100 years from now. Another method is needed for decision-making about future generations.

Second, in the analysis of exposure to toxic chemicals, it has become common to discount diseases such as cancer over their latency period. Since cancers often show up 20 years or more after the exposure that causes them, discounting has the effect of sharply reducing the "present value" of the health benefits from controlling carcinogens. Advocates of risk analysis and cost–benefit analysis argue that the benefits should be interpreted as the reduction of risk of death for large numbers of people, not the reduction of actual deaths for a much smaller number. While this argument is itself problematical (it ignores the different experience of the people who will actually die), it implies that health benefits should not be discounted over the latency period. Risk is reduced at the time when exposure to carcinogens is reduced, typically soon after a policy change – not decades later when there is a reduction in the appearance of cancers.

Theoretical critiques and practical alternatives

Criticism of cost–benefit analysis inevitably leads to questions about the alternatives. If monetization of externalities, in the style favoured by most environmental economists, is not a reliable basis for public policy, then how should decisions be made? One answer is that there is no need for a new decision-making system, since the old one works so well. The environmental laws and regulations of the last thirty-odd years have been extremely successful, reducing pollution and protecting health and nature; although adopted, for the most part, without complex economic calculations, none of these protective measures have bankrupted us or proved unaffordable.

While this simple response has considerable merit, there is more that can be said about right and wrong ways to make policy decisions. Three strands of theoretical critique of the cost–benefit methodology point toward desirable features of an alternative.

Values of risks and damages depend on context; they cannot be measured in general. Underlying cost–benefit analysis, and the related field of risk analysis, is the assumption that equal damages should be valued equally in every context. If a death is worth X dollars, then 10 deaths are always worth $10X$, regardless of how and why they occur. It turns out that people do not think this way: 20 times as many Americans died from diabetes in 2001 as from terrorism on September 11, yet there is no doubt which of these categories of deaths mattered more to public life and policy. To cite another example, the risk of death in the US is almost identical from working in the construction industry and from downhill skiing (about one death per two million person-days), but there is a much greater public responsibility to protect construction workers on the job than skiers on the slopes.

The implication of this critique is that there is no hope of creating a purely quantitative, context-independent system of decision-making. Context is everything in evaluating health and environmental damages; externalities have to be valued and addressed "in the field," in the context in which they actually occur, not collected for later study in the laboratory. A political, not an economic, process is required to make the intrinsically context-dependent policy decisions.

Disaggregation of benefits makes the comparison of costs and benefits more opaque. There is a tautological sense in which everyone does "cost–benefit analysis" all the time – not monetizing benefits, but implicitly comparing costs and benefits of possible actions, perhaps according to rules of thumb or inarticulated personal standards. In this broad sense, every democratic decision can be said to have passed a cost–benefit test: policies are only adopted if the voters prefer the benefits of the policies to the costs.

The formal application of cost–benefit analysis to public policy employs a much narrower and more controversial methodology, assuming that the best way to compare costs and benefits is to disaggregate benefits into "elementary particles" of value – numbers of deaths and serious diseases avoided, hectares of wetlands preserved, and so on. Then the analysts supposedly can monetize each particle of value, and finally reassemble them into complex molecules of benefits, to be weighed against the costs.

This disaggregated methodology has failed in practice. It does not yield transparent or objective evaluations of benefits; rather, it renders the discussion of benefits obscurely technical, excluding all but specialists from participation. At the same time, political debate continues behind the veil of technicalities, as rival experts battle over esoteric valuation problems.

Rather than engaging in the hopeless effort to refine the disaggregated benefit estimates, we could ask people to judge costs and benefits on a more aggregated or holistic basis. Consider a policy proposal, debated in 2002–03, that would have increased the costs of many US power plants, in order to reduce the huge number of fish killed by their cooling water intake systems. One could, as EPA did, spend several person-years of effort in modelling the wide variety of fish populations and aquatic ecosystems, and in exploring intricately indirect ways to assign precise monetary values to the many affected categories of fish (most of which are not sold in markets). This led, in practice, only to more debate and disagreement about the minutiae of fish valuation. Or one could present the information on the costs of protecting fish, and the expected effect on electric bills, along with a description of the millions of fish that could be saved annually. Then voters, or their representatives, could decide whether the benefits as a whole – not monetized, but described in their natural units – justified the costs as a whole.

Precise estimates of future environmental impacts are frequently unavailable. Cost–benefit calculations rest on the best available estimates of health and environmental impacts. Much of the effort in cost–benefit analysis is required to develop these estimates; important effects are often omitted for lack of sufficiently precise data. EPA's analysis of arsenic in drinking water recognized that at least a dozen serious diseases are linked to arsenic, but found sufficient data to estimate the numerical incidence of only two diseases, bladder and lung cancer. For lack of data, the other ten diseases were implicitly valued at zero.

An apparently common-sense, intuitively Bayesian approach to statistics can be seen here: why not use whatever information we have to develop the best possible estimates of impacts? But the focus on precise point estimates distracts attention from the tremendous uncertainty that surrounds many important impacts. Public health and environmental policy have always been matters of decision-making under uncertainty. The more uncertain we are, the more important it becomes to plan for the credible worst-case outcome. People act this way in daily life, in buying insurance against low-probability but high-cost outcomes like house fires or car crashes. (It's possible in theory, too: just assume that people are liquidity constrained and risk averse, and the math works out perfectly.) Even such ordinary steps as arriving early at the airport or for an important appointment reflect precautionary approaches, based on planning for the worst, not playing the averages.

Cost–benefit analysis typically asks, what is the absolutely most likely outcome? But recognizing the pervasive uncertainty in our estimates and forecasts, we should instead be asking, what is the worst outcome that is at least as likely as risks that people normally pay to insure themselves against? Environmental activists are increasingly discussing the "precautionary principle" as a basis for decision-making; they might make more headway referring to it as the insurance principle.

Finally, in addition to these new directions, it is important to remember that the environmental decision-making of recent decades has been a remarkable success, without help from sophisticated new decision-making techniques. It may be a novel experience for critics of established economic theory to find themselves in the classically conservative role of defending history and tradition. (I've hardly been able to adjust to it myself.) But in the arena of US environmental policy, the radicals who want a sweeping, fundamental break with past practice are to be found in the White House and the halls of Congress, not outside in the street. The Clean Air Act, the Clean Water Act, and all the rest have, at entirely affordable cost, made you and your family much healthier. Don't leave home without them.

Notes

1. This chapter draws extensively on a book I have recently co-authored: Frank Ackerman and Lisa Heinzerling, *Priceless: On Knowing the Price of Everything and the Value of Nothing* (New Press, 2004).

2. Frank Ackerman, "Still dead after all these years: interpreting the failure of general equilibrium theory", *Journal of Economic Methodology*, 9 (2), (June 2002), reprinted in Frank Ackerman and Alejandro Nadal, *The Flawed Foundations of General Equilibrium: Critical Essays on Economics* (Routledge, 2004).

3. R G Lipsey and K Lancaster, "The general theory of the second best", *Review of Economic Studies* 24 (1956), 11–32.

4. Lisa Heinzerling, "Regulatory costs of mythic proportions", *Yale Law Journal*, 107, (1998); Lisa Heinzerling and Frank Ackerman, "The humbugs of the anti-regulatory movement", *Cornell Law Review*, 87, 648–70 (2002); Lisa Heinzerling, "Five-hundred life-saving interventions and their misuse in the debate over regulatory reform", *Risk: Health, Safety & Environment*, 13,151 (Spring 2002). For a summary of this work, see *Priceless*, Chapter 3 (c.f. note 1 above).

5. This point was made, in almost these words (though not as a joke), by Eric Posner, a legal scholar and leading advocate of cost–benefit analysis, in a recent debate on the subject at the University of Chicago. After acknowledging the theoretical weakness of the case for cost–benefit analysis, Posner maintained that it was nonetheless important to use it in practice.

6. The points made in this section are elaborated and documented in *Priceless*.

25.

IS GDP A GOOD MEASURE OF ECONOMIC PROGRESS?

Olivier Vaury

Every year, or even every quarter, economic growth figures are anticipated and scrutinized to assess the economic health of a country. In spite of abundant commentary in the media by politicians and economists, the very notion of economic growth remains elusive: who really knows what it really measures ? Yet the level of GDP (or GDP growth) is probably the most widely used indicator for piloting economic policies around the world and for making international comparisons.

When one says that "GDP growth reached 3 per cent in 2002", what does that mean ? Broadly speaking, GDP measures the amount of goods and services produced in a given place (a country, a region, etc), in a given period of time (a year, a quarter, etc). All goods and services? Well, that's where the whole issue lies!

Our point is that GDP includes goods and services that do not increase a country's economic wealth, and, furthermore, excludes goods and services that do. Thus, the use of GDP as an indicator of economic progress is flawed and results in biases in international comparisons.

What GDP forgets

"Marry your cleaning person, and you will make GDP drop!". This weird remark, made by the famous French economist Alfred Sauvy, points to the fact that GDP excludes (or significantly underestimates) goods and services produced outside the official market economy. The bits forgotten by GDP can be divided into three categories:

- Household production: marrying the cleaning person means transforming a standard marketed activity (house cleaning, paid at a given rate) into domestic work, not accounted for in GDP as there is no way to measure the value added by this service (no price paid). A priori, this change does not alter the level of service enjoyed by the newly married consumer (the house cleaning is still done by the same person; this example is used to point out the insufficiencies of GDP, not to advocate more domestic work). Is that a problem? Yes, as by any measure domestic production represents a large part of goods and services. For instance, one estimates that people spend 17 per cent more time in household production (cleaning, cooking, childcare) than in paid activities. According to various studies carried out in France, domestic production could represent as much as 75 per cent of standard GDP.

- Voluntary work: a bicycle repaired by a friend makes GDP fall if the work used to be done by a (paid) professional. Thus, a society where voluntary work is widespread will enjoy a higher level of economic well-being but a lower GDP.

- Public administration: in public accounting rules, GDP is the sum of values added by all economic entities, i.e. the difference between the value of production and consumed inputs (energy costs, raw materials, etc). Thus, value added is in fact constituted by two main parts: wages and profits. But for public administration, no value of production is available as public services are generally not bought by anyone on a market (think of public gardens maintenance or tax collection). To include them in GDP, accountants decided to measure value added as wage costs (we exclude capital depreciation from our analysis). As a result, the contribution of public services to GDP is always underestimated. By the same token, a free service resulting from a past public investment (a road, a fountain, a public park or a public sport facility) will not appear in GDP, contrary to its private equivalent (priced road, private sports facility, etc).

What GDP should forget

"Burn Paris and you will make GDP grow!". Another weird remark, another problem with GDP: GDP only includes positive values: if something is destroyed, then rebuilt by a private company, GDP goes up while economic well-being is unchanged. Those who use GDP as a good measure of economic progress forget that production is closely linked to destruction in two ways:

- Production as measured by GDP is often just compensation for a previous destruction (think of booming activity after a cyclone or of most legal and medical activities). If lawyers prosper because there are more crimes and more offences, does that mean the country is richer?

- Production is, by definition, destruction: destruction of human and natural capital. What about two countries achieving the same level of standard GDP, one of them by the exhaustion of its natural and human resources? It reminds us of those companies who report profits only by under-reporting depreciation of assets. The case is not just theoretical: Britain and France have roughly the same GDP but British workers work 25 per cent more than French ones.

The obesity connection

The remarks made above can be illustrated by the example of obesity. Obesity is not just a pathology, it is also a formidable way to create standard economic wealth without increasing well-being (figures below can be found at www.rprogress.org, the website of an American think tank, Redefining Progress):

- In the US alone, food companies spend around $20bn in advertising to convince consumers to eat more.

- Unfortunately their efforts prove successful, as each day, one in every four Americans eats in a fast-food restaurant, for a total expenditure of $110bn a year. Consequently, Americans are increasingly obese (over the past 30 years, the number of Americans not able to use a standard airplane seat – due to overweight, not to financial difficulties – has risen by 350 per cent).

- Obese people (and others) spend around $30–50bn a year in weight-losing products, gym facilities and so on, but most do not manage to lose the weight "gained" from fast foods, which feeds medical expenditure linked to obesity (obesity often leads to diabetes, increases the likelihood of heart attacks, etc), at around $50bn per year.

These expenditures boost GDP, but their contribution to economic well being is at best questionable. As asked by one of Redefining Progress's leaders: "if GDP is up, why is America down?".

Flawed international comparisons

The arguments presented above cast doubt on the usefulness of GDP as the main "pilot" of economic policy. If the thermometer is wrong, then the policy based on it should be wrong too. The use of GDP produces biases in favour of a particular set of political choices, consisting in marketisation of economic activity. This also means that international comparisons based on GDP are fundamentally flawed in two ways, related to the two problems associated with GDP:

- Two countries with different levels of "marketisation" cannot be compared on the basis of GDP, as GDP will not include the same activities in the two countries (part of economic activity will be excluded from the comparison).
- Two countries with different levels of destruction cannot be compared on the basis of GDP as these very destructions are not taken into account. Peaceful societies, characterised by a lower level of crime (and consequently legal activities, private prisons, etc) are penalised in terms of GDP! As are countries with a healthy way of life!

And all this is without even taking into account the technical difficulties: how to compare GDPs measured in different currencies? If we use simple exchange rates, we run the risk to have very volatile results (the euro lost 30 per cent of its value against the dollar between January 1999 and October 2000, but it would have been stupid to conclude that GDP dropped by the same proportion). The purchasing power parity method, used by economists to take into account the fact that currencies do not buy the same amount of goods and services, has problems too. Is it relevant to compare the price of the same basket of goods and services in different countries (to derive purchasing powers) when the structures of the studied economies differ. Finally, statistical methods used to measure outputs and prices differ significantly across the world. Thus, cross-country comparisons create many more difficulties than the already problematic national GDP calculation.

Paradoxically, it is mostly for poor countries that alternatives to standard GDP have been developed, though they are badly needed for rich countries too. For instance, the United Nations Development Programme (UNDP) calculates a Human Development Index (HDI), which includes GDP per capita, but also the literacy rate, life expectancy at birth and school enrolment ratios. A report to the French ministry for social economy (abolished by the current government) suggested that the human development report (now limited to poor regions) be extended to cover

Europe. Others have tried to build more relevant measures of GDP, by removing from standard GDP values added that do not increase well-being or contribute to the destruction of natural resources, and by adding domestic and voluntary work. One such example is the Genuine Progress Indicator, calculated by the US NGO Redefining Progress (see above) for the US, which has been stagnating since the early 1980s (while standard GDP almost doubled over the same period).

Yet these interesting experiments are not without drawbacks: besides numerous technical difficulties, similar to those identified for the measure of standard GDP, the choice to include or exclude economic activities from the new index can easily be arbitrary. For instance, should we exclude health care linked to avoidable diseases on the ground that it merely reflects a fundamentally unhealthy way of life (the counterpart of other parts of GDP such as fast food activities, or tobacco, so as not to be counted twice). Or should we include it because it enables people to live healthier lives, *everything else being equal*? Should we exclude legal activities linked to divorces because divorce is a sad thing that reflects the disintegration of families in contemporary society, or include them as they allow women to enjoy more independence?

In my opinion, we should give up trying to compete in terms of GDP (an aggregated indicator). Economic development is always something with many dimensions. Therefore, an economic system should be judged on its ability to provide individuals with what they need to achieve well-being: food, health, leisure, clean air, a high life expectancy, means of communication, etc. For each of these sub-categories, it is possible to build indicators that reflect the extent to which the population enjoys access to these resources. To demonstrate using not an average indicator but one that takes inequality into account: if two people have a phone each, that is better than one person with two phones and one without any. Thus, we would be to compare two countries by comparing their ability to provide these essential goods to the largest possible part of their population (in fact we already are, but these figures are never publicized). We would certainly have some surprises, such as that the World Health Organization ranks the US health system as thirty-seventh in the world, while France ranks first and Portugal twelfth, two countries with a much lower GDP per capita.

26.

LIVING IN AN AFFLUENT SOCIETY: IT IS SO 'MORE-ISH'

Shaun Hargreaves Heap

Introduction

Who do you know with recent publications in top rated journals, who teaches at one of the best economics departments and who has just written a best seller on the peculiar difficulties of living in an affluent society?

I suspect the answer is nobody; and I doubt that the reply would have been different had I enquired in a similar way during any of the last 40 years. However, had I asked the question in the late 1950s, there was someone: John K Galbraith.

Of course, there have been other well-known economists who have written for a popular audience, but none can match Galbraith's style or his canvass. He is probably the only economist during the post-war period who comes close to Keynes in these respects. I was reminded of this the other day when I came across a Readers' Union copy of *The Affluent Society*, while I was browsing in a second-hand bookshop. I bought and re-read it; and it is a gem. Here is why.

The Affluent Society: the main argument

> 'Among the many models of the good society no one has urged the squirrel wheel.'

So Galbraith remarks, yet living in affluent societies closely resembles a life on the squirrel wheel. This is the first aspect of the problem confronting those who live in a comparatively rich society. It arises because our aspirations get focussed on increasing income just as we have more of it than our parents or grandparents could ever have dreamt of. No sooner do we have more, than we want more .... and so the wheel turns one more time, we re-adjust our beady eyes and begin to ascend the ladder again .... with predictable effect.

This thought hardly needs introducing as it has achieved a certain acceptability in the mainstream now. The growing weight of the evidence, that we seem little, if any, happier than our parents or grandparents despite being much richer, has spawned a whole literature on how to account for the apparent absence of a relationship over time between the level of income and happiness. Galbraith deserves recognition for being one of the first to see this aspect of the peculiar problem of affluence and to have anticipated some of the contemporary explanations of this seeming paradox. For instance, his analysis of this problem centres on two, now well understood mechanisms that promote the expansion of 'wants' as income grows. One is the logic of relative comparison whereby one's happiness is based in part on how we are doing relative to others. So when everyone's income rises, no one feels better off. The other relates to the growth of industries, like advertising, which are concerned precisely to populate our dreams with hitherto unimaginable, yet now plainly desirable, objects.

The second aspect of the problem experienced by affluent societies is what Galbraith calls 'social imbalance'. This is his early version of what he referred to later in a more revealing way as 'private affluence and public squalor'. Our public services lag inexorably behind our private consumption. This is primarily, on his account, because there is no mechanism akin to the market that signals and generates the response of, for instance, more roads when we buy another car. The extra steel for this car gets produced, as does the material for the seats and the upholstery, because the increase in demand makes it profitable for these manufacturers to expand their output. But there is nothing like this with respect to roads or clean air. Yet just as surely, we will need more of these public goods as well as the steel and other privately produced materials when we buy and drive our new cars. This is a political failure and, although Galbraith's analysis and conclusions are different, he is recognising the failure that later distinguished the Public Choice School. So, again credit is due to Galbraith for anticipating something that is now well recognized.

His primary solution to both dimensions of the problem of affluence is to mandate growth in expenditure on public services financed by a sales tax. In particular, there has to be much bigger expenditure on education. In part this is because the obsession with income growth is encouraging both parents to work, so that the need for childcare is growing particularly fast. It is also necessary because the educational system supplies the one countervailing influence to the contemporary obsession with money. In other words, if we are to really enjoy being rich, then we have to build up our public services in ways that help sustain a more varied set of aspirations than just getting richer.

Although, this is a commendably Smithian view of the role of education in an affluent society, I suspect that Galbraith's particular remedies do not stand close inspection. This is largely because in the Public Choice School we have come to worry over what goes on in the public sector and our only remedy has the effect of recreating the mentality that only money matters within the public sector itself. I will say more on this below. I want to turn first to some of the supporting or subsidiary arguments in the book.

Some supporting arguments

There is a wonderful set of elaborations to the arguments that I have just sketched, but there are also a further group that Galbraith deploys in his analysis of our obsession with output and income. They are worth setting out because they signal something more about his contribution. It is perhaps most easy to bring out how these arguments come together and why they are interesting if I list the points made and comment on their contemporary resonance.

1) The ideas that we use to interpret events almost always relate to a different historical epoch.

On the one hand, this looks back because it is a version of Keynes's famous observation about politicians at the end of *The General Theory*, but it also looks forward because the same arresting conclusion, albeit drawn for different reasons, is one of the hallmarks of evolutionary psychology. It is important in Galbraith's argument as most of human history has known only the problem of getting enough to meet the strict necessaries of life. Indeed in most affluent countries, it is only during the twentieth century that real wages started to rise much above subsistence. As a result, our ideas regarding the economy have and continue to be dominated by concerns with raising output. What insulates this obsession from the reality of affluence is a combination of points 2) and 3) below.

2) 'Conventional wisdom' reigns.

> Because economic and social phenomena are so forbidding, or at least seem so, and because they yield few hard tests of what exists and what does not, they afford the individual a luxury not given by physical phenomena. Within a considerable range he is permitted to believe what he pleases. He may hold whatever view of this world he finds most agreeable or otherwise to his taste.
>
> As a consequence, in the interpretation of all social life there is a persistent and never ending competition between what is relevant and what is merely acceptable. In this competition, while a strategic advantage lies with what exists, all tactical advantage is with the acceptable. Audiences of all kinds most applaud what they like best. And in social comment the test of audience approval, far more than the test of truth, comes to influence comment. (p. 5)
>
> Ideas are inherently conservative. They yield not to the attack of other ideas but to the massive onslaught of circumstance with which they cannot contend. (p. 15)

Galbraith sets out in this way a view of what Kuhn later called 'normal science': in particular, its dependence on convention in the scientific community and its insulation from awkward facts. Sociologists of science have since made this idea commonplace, and it helps explain how we still fixate on output growth despite the experience of affluence, once it is also understood why output growth proves so agreeable to us as 'audience' – cue the third element in this group of arguments.

3) Output growth eases the tensions that come from inequality and makes for security.

This is why we applaud output growth. Inequality is always a potential source of tension in society, but this is mitigated by the growth in incomes because the numbers of people in absolute poverty falls. Likewise, the growth of output is fuelled by maintaining full employment and the most significant source of insecurity in society is the prospect of unemployment. Thus Galbraith is one of the early commentators to make the connections between growth and social harmony which have been central to social democratic politics in the post-war period; and when combined with the earlier two points we have a further explanation of how our expectations have become so narrowed on stuff, stuff and more stuff, please!

Does the analysis still apply?

There can be few who are not puzzled by the appetite of the affluent. The absence of any measurable effect of income growth on happiness is only one part of what is strange here. The failure to take measures that will address the global warming that has been and continues to be generated by output growth increasingly appears like some form of death wish. There are also more local pathologies. The highest earners in the UK and the US actually work longer hours than their counterparts 20 years ago. So the pursuit of more stuff is seemingly ornamental because the getting of it is now cutting into the time that we have left to play with it. To put the issue bluntly, if we could for one moment step outside the squirrel wheel, surely we would conclude that we are interested in output growth to an extent which casts doubt on whether we actually know where our interests lie any more. For these reasons, the subject of Galbraith's book is even more timely now than it was in the late 1950s.

How relevant, though, is Galbraith's analysis of the dynamics of the squirrel wheel for the contemporary world?

I have two criticisms here. The first is perhaps best summarized as a failure to anticipate the problem of identity. I believe that this holds the key to understanding why consumption is so central to our lives. There are two parts to this observation. One is that while one kind of insecurity does disappear with full employment, the collapse of traditional bonds of one kind or another in the modern world has made personal identity more fluid and with this fluidity comes another kind of insecurity. It is no coincidence that people talk now of identity politics. The term reflects the way in which identity has become problematic. So Galbraith was wrong to assume that full employment pushes insecurity into the background.

At the same time, consumer goods have more clearly come to form a language system. This is the important insight that anthropology gives economics. We use consumer goods to say things about ourselves and as our identity has become less well fixed through traditional bonds of one kind or another, we have had increasing recourse to the world of goods to do it for us. (Incidentally, this means that advertising is not so much a conspiracy, as Galbraith seems to hint: it actually works with the grain of human nature. And while making parenthetic remarks, it is perhaps worth adding that it is not just the advertising industry which plays such a crucial role, it is the whole set of mass media industries.)

The other part of the observation about identity relates to the intrinsic nature of relative comparison in general. Too often in economics, this has been treated pejoratively as a desire for status, something invidious, when it is actually more deeply rooted in a general sense in human nature. This is in part a lesson that Wittgenstein teaches us and it would be well for economists to take the point more seriously.

These are shorthand comments which sum to the thought that the impetus towards consumption is in some respects perfectly natural, if not ineluctable. We need to fix our identities, and consumption has been a key arena in which this is done. Since our concern with identity is not going to disappear, this means that if we are not happy with the part played by consumption in this, then we have to think about how identity can come to be more closely associated with non-consumption activities. This directly feeds into my next critical comment because Galbraith, following Smith, was surely right to see that the education system is a potential source of some other value system. It is not the only source, however, and nor is it an easy solution. This is the source of my second critical reflection.

There is a fundamental difficulty that has arisen with the public service solution to the problems of a market society. We apparently no longer trust public servants to do the job, and so require that they are accountable, and often minutely so, for their actions. But in making them accountable through performance indicators and all the other penumbra of the audit economy, we have re-encountered the old problems of control found in Soviet style economies. It is actually worse than this. It is not just that close observation fails to produce the desired results because it can never be quite close enough, it is that the professional value systems that used to thrive no longer have any space beside the discretion given to public servants. This is unfortunate because these professional value systems involve the subordination of strict individual self interest to some other standard that typically trades in concepts like 'honour', 'trust', 'justice', 'the good', etc. These are the natural vocabulary of all alternative value systems and so their dwindling currency among all parts of the public sector is a source of some regret in this context.

Of course, this is not to be taken as an argument against accountability. Rather it is a complaint that our ideas regarding accountability are often terribly impoverished. What we need are mechanisms of accountability that work with the grain of professional judgement rather than the reverse, which is what we increasingly have now. The point is in a sense trivial, but one cannot sensibly expect public institutions to act as founts for critical reflection if the organization of those institutions increasingly works with the very value system that one would like to see appraised.

I suppose that my two criticisms of Galbraith can be brought together in a single thought. It is that economics needs a better understanding of individual agency if the problem of the squirrel wheel is ever to be seriously addressed. This is, of course, happening in odd nooks and crannies and the point of writing this piece is not to dwell on these criticisms, it is to say that re-reading Galbraith is a marvellous encouragement to the enterprise.

PART 6:

CASE HISTORIES

27.

KICKING AWAY THE LADDER: HOW THE ECONOMIC AND INTELLECTUAL HISTORIES OF CAPITALISM HAVE BEEN RE-WRITTEN TO JUSTIFY NEO-LIBERAL CAPITALISM

Ha-Joon Chang

There is currently great pressure on developing countries to adopt a set of 'good policies' and 'good institutions' – such as liberalisation of trade and investment and strong patent law – to foster their economic development. When some developing countries show reluctance in adopting them, the proponents of this recipe often find it difficult to understand these countries' stupidity in not accepting such a tried and tested recipe for development. After all, they argue, these are the policies and the institutions that the developed countries had used in the past in order to become rich. Their belief in their own recommendation is so absolute that in their view it has to be imposed on the developing countries through strong bilateral and multilateral external pressures, even when these countries don't want them.

Naturally, there have been heated debates on whether these recommended policies and institutions are appropriate for developing countries. However, curiously, even many of those who are sceptical of the applicability of these policies and institutions to the developing countries take it for granted that these were the policies and the institutions that were used by the developed countries when they themselves were developing countries.

Contrary to the conventional wisdom, the historical fact is that the rich countries did not develop on the basis of the policies and the institutions that they now recommend to, and often force upon, the developing countries. Unfortunately, this fact is little known these days because the 'official historians' of capitalism have been very successful in re-writing its history.

Almost all today's rich countries used tariff protection and subsidies to develop their industries. Interestingly, Britain and the USA, the two countries that are supposed to have reached the summit of the world economy through their free-market, free-trade policy, are actually the ones that most aggressively used protection and subsidies.

Contrary to popular myth, Britain had been an aggressive user, and in certain areas a pioneer, of activist policies intended to promote its industries. Such policies, although limited in scope, date back from the fourteenth century (Edward III) and the fifteenth century (Henry VII) in relation to woollen manufacturing, the leading industry of the time. England then was an exporter of raw wool to the Low Countries, and Henry VII for example tried to change this by taxing raw wool exports and poaching skilled workers from the Low Countries.

Between the trade policy reform of her first Prime Minister Robert Walpole in 1721 and her adoption of free trade around 1860 in particular, Britain used very *dirigiste* trade and industrial policies, involving measures very similar to what countries like Japan and Korea later used in order to develop their industries. During this period, it protected its industries much more heavily than did France, the supposed *dirigiste* counterpoint to its free-trade, free-market system. Given this history, argued Friedrich List (the leading German economist of the mid-nineteenth century) Britain preaching free trade to less advanced countries like Germany and the USA was like someone trying to 'kick away the ladder' after he had climbed to the top.

List was not alone in seeing the matter in this light. Many American thinkers shared this view. Indeed, it was American thinkers like Alexander Hamilton, the first Treasury Secretary of the USA, and the (now-forgotten) economist Daniel Raymond, who first systematically developed the infant industry argument. Indeed, List, who is commonly known as the father of the infant industry argument, in fact started out as a free-trader (he was an ardent supporter of German customs union – *Zollverein*) – and learned about this argument during his exile in the US during the 1820s.

Little known today, the intellectual interaction between the USA and Germany during the nineteenth century did not end there. The German Historical School – represented by people like Wilhelm Roscher, Bruno Hildebrand, Karl Knies, Gustav Schmoller, and Werner Sombart – attracted many American economists in the late nineteeth century. The patron saint of American Neoclassical economics, John Bates Clark, in whose name the most prestigious award for young (under-40) American economists is given today, went to Germany in 1873 and studied the German Historical School under Roscher and Knies, although he gradually drifted away from it. Richard Ely, one of the leading American economists of the time, also studied under Knies and influenced the American Institutionalist School through his disciple, John Commons. Ely was one of the founding fathers of the American Economic Association; to this day, the biggest public lecture at the Association's annual meeting is given in Ely's name, although few of the present AEA members would know who he was.

Between the Civil War and the Second World War, the USA was literally the most heavily protected economy in the world. In this context, it is important to note that the American Civil War was fought on the issue of tariff as much as, if not more, on the issue of slavery. Of the two major issues that divided the North and the South, the South had actually more to fear on the tariff front than on the slavery front. Abraham Lincoln was a well-known protectionist who cut his political teeth under the charismatic politician Henry Clay in the Whig Party, which advocated the 'American System' based on infrastructural development and protectionism (thus named on recognition that free trade is for the British interest). One of Lincoln's top economic advisors was the famous protectionist economist, Henry Carey, who once was described as 'the only American economist of importance' by Marx and Engels in the early 1850s but has now been almost completely air-brushed out of the history of American economic thought. (On the other hand, Lincoln thought that African Americans were racially inferior and that slave emancipation was an idealistic proposal with no prospect of immediate implementation – he is said to have emancipated the slaves in 1862 as a strategic move to win the War rather than out of some moral conviction.)

In protecting their industries, the Americans were going against the advice of such prominent economists as Adam Smith and Jean Baptiste Say, who saw the country's future in agriculture. However, the Americans knew exactly what the game was. They knew that Britain reached the top through protection and subsidies, and therefore that they would need to do the same if they were going to get anywhere. Criticising the British preaching of free trade to his country, Ulysses Grant, the Civil War hero and the US President between 1868–76, retorted that 'within 200 years, when America has gotten out of protection all that it can offer, it too will adopt free trade'. When his country later reached the top after the Second World War, it too started 'kicking away the ladder' by preaching to and forcing free trade on the less developed countries.

The UK and the US may be the more dramatic examples, but almost all the rest of the developed world today used tariffs, subsidies and other means to promote their industries in the earlier stages of their development. Cases like Germany, Japan and Korea are well known in this respect. But even Sweden, which later came to represent the 'small open economy' to many economists, also strategically used tariffs, subsidies, cartels and state support for R&D to develop key industries, especially textiles, steel and engineering.

There were some exceptions like the Netherlands and Switzerland that have maintained free trade since the late eighteenth century. However, these were countries that were already on the frontier of technological development by the eighteenth century and therefore did not need much protection. Also, it should be noted that the Netherlands deployed an impressive range of interventionist measures up till the seventeenth century in order to build up its maritime and commercial supremacy. Moreover, Switzerland did not have a patent law until 1907, flying directly against the emphasis that today's orthodoxy puts on the protection of intellectual property rights (see below). More interestingly, the Netherlands abolished its 1817 patent law in 1869 on the ground that patents are politically-created monopolies inconsistent with its free-market principles – a position that seems to elude most of today's free-market economists – and did not introduce another patent law until 1912.

The story is similar in relation to institutional development. In the earlier stages of their development, today's developed countries did not even have such 'basic' institutions as professional civil service, central bank or patent law. It was only after the Pendleton Act in 1883 that the US federal government started recruiting its employees through a competitive process. The central bank, an institution dear to the heart of today's free-market economists, did not exist in most of today's rich countries until the early twentieth century – not least because the free-market economists of the day condemned it as a mechanism for unjustly bailing out imprudent borrowers. The US central bank (the Federal Reserve Board) was set up only in 1913 and the Italian central bank did not even have a note issue monopoly until 1926. Many countries allowed patenting of foreign invention until the late nineteenth century. As I mentioned above, Switzerland and the Netherlands refused to introduce a patent law despite international pressure until 1907 and 1912 respectively, thus freely 'stole' technologies from abroad. The examples can go on.

One important conclusion that emerges from the history of institutional development is that it took the developed countries a long time to develop institutions in their earlier days of development. Institutions typically took decades, and sometimes generations, to develop. Just to give one example, the need for central banking was perceived at least in some circles from at least the seventeenth century, but the first 'real' central bank, the Bank of England, was instituted only in 1844, some two centuries later.

Another important point that emerges is that the levels of institutional development in today's developed countries in the earlier period were much lower than those in today's developing countries. For example, measured by the (admittedly highly imperfect) income level, in 1820, the UK was at a somewhat higher level of development than that of India today, but it did not even have many of the most 'basic' institutions that India has today. It did not have universal suffrage (or even universal *male* suffrage), a central bank, income tax, generalised limited liability, a generalised bankruptcy law, a professional bureaucracy, meaningful securities regulations or even minimal labour regulations (except for a couple of minimal and barely-enforced regulations on child labour).

If the policies and institutions that the rich countries are recommending to the poor countries are not the ones that they themselves used when they were developing, what is going on? We can only conclude that the rich countries are trying to kick away the ladder that allowed them to climb where they are. It is no coincidence that economic development has become more difficult during the last two decades when the developed countries started turning on the pressure on the developing countries to adopt the so-called 'global standard' policies and institutions.

During this period, the average annual per capita income growth rate for the developing countries has been halved from 3 per cent in the previous two decades (1960–80) to 1.5 per cent. In particular, Latin America virtually stopped growing, while Sub-Saharan Africa and most ex-Communist countries have experienced a fall in absolute income. Economic instability has increased markedly, as manifested in the dozens of financial crises we have witnessed over the last decade alone. Income inequality has been growing in many developing countries and poverty has increased, rather than decreased, in a significant number of them.

What can be done to change this?

First, the historical facts about the historical experiences of the developed countries should be more widely publicized. This is not just a matter of 'getting history right', but also of allowing the developing countries to make more informed choices.

Second, the conditions attached to bilateral and multilateral financial assistance to developing countries should be radically changed. It should be accepted that the orthodox recipe is not working, and also that there can be no 'best practice' policies that everyone should use.

Third, the WTO rules should be re-written so that the developing countries can more actively use tariffs and subsidies for industrial development. They should also be allowed to have less stringent patent laws and other intellectual property rights laws.

Fourth, improvements in institutions should be encouraged, but this should not be equated with imposing a fixed set of (today's – not even yesterday's – Anglo–American) institutions on all countries. Special care has to be taken in order not to demand excessively rapid upgrading of institutions by the developing countries, especially given that they already have quite developed institutions when compared to today's developed countries at comparable stages of development, and given that establishing and running new institutions is costly.

By being allowed to adopt policies and institutions that are more suitable to their conditions, the developing countries will be able to develop faster. This will also benefit the developed countries in the long run, as it will increase their trade and investment opportunities. That the developed countries cannot see this is the tragedy of our time.

28.

JAPAN, REFUTATION OF NEOLIBERALISM

Robert Locke

No-one wants to talk about Japan these days. The conventional wisdom is that the bloom went off Japan's economic rose around 1990 and that the utter superiority of neoliberal capitalism was vindicated by the strong performance of the American economy during the 1990s. Furthermore, everyone is now convinced that China – whose economy is one-eighth the size of Japan's – is the rising economic power and therefore the appropriate object of attention.

But Japan is, despite everything, still one of the master keys to understanding the future of the world economy, because Japan is the clearest case study of why neoliberalism is false. Simply put, Japan has done almost everything wrong by neoliberal standards and yet is indisputably the second-richest nation in the world.

This doesn't mean that neoliberalism is wholly without merit as an economic theory or as a development strategy, but it does mean that its claim to be the *only* path to prosperity has been empirically falsified. Japan's economy is highly regulated, planned centrally by the state and often contemptuous of free markets. But it has thrived.

What follows is for space reasons necessarily a sketch and exceptions, subtleties, and refinements have been left out. Facts have been homogenized and caricatured to make structural fundamentals clear. But a reader who bears this in mind will not be misled, as detailed analyses are available elsewhere.

Are we lied to about Japan?

Contrary to popular opinion, Japan has been doing very well lately, despite the interests that wish to depict her as an economic mess.

Globalists and other neoliberals have used the illusion of Japan's failure by to discourage Westerners, particularly Americans, from even caring about Japan's economic policies, let alone learning from them. The Japanese government has encouraged it as a way to get foreigners to stop pressing for changes in its neo-mercantilist trade policies. Corporate interests who gain from free-trade extremism with respect to Japan have propagated it. And ideologues committed to the delusion that only a *laissez-faire* economy can prosper have promoted it.

This is a formidable set of potential liars, equipped with money, technical expertise, transnational reach and state power. The Japanese government is centralized, elitist, and quite capable of fudging statistics if it wants, particularly since there are few Westerners who understand Japanese accounting. National accounting is notoriously susceptible to creative accounting anyway, as the world learned at the time of the Asian Crisis of 1998. So the assumption that the standard published figures about Japan's economy are true is dubious at best.

Japanese culture puts a premium on maintaining 'face' and other forms of polite public presentation that constitute literal falsehoods, or at least fictions, so it is a natural instinct for the Japanese to tell the West what it wants to hear about Japan's economy. Japan's government is heir to a Confucian tradition in which the public is told only what the rulers deem it should know. Journalists and academics, who in America or Europe would have challenged its version of the economy by now, are loyal collaborators of the system, not its critics. So from a Japanese point of view, there is nothing immoral, unusual, or terribly difficult about misrepresenting Japan's economic performance. In fact, because it is in the national interest, it would be unpatriotic not to do so.

A crisis invented to fit a theory

The idea that Japan is thriving is not so different from the received wisdom as one might think. The Western press has over the last few years been full of stories about Japan's deep gloom, but in point of fact, the *admitted* state of the Japanese economy – let alone its actual state – is simply not that bad and in any other country would be producing mild expressions of concern, not brazen crowing about a crisis sufficient to force change in the fundamentals of the system.

Even the Japanese government admits that Japan is not actually declining economically, but rather growing at about 1 per cent a year (which has ticked up to 2 per cent since these words were first written). This is a better performance than many other nations in recent years. So even if one accepts the official statistics, Japan is not in anything like the death-spiral that *laissez-faire* mythology supposes. It is, at the *absolute* worst, accepting all the public mythology, stuck in a gentle stagnation of slow growth. And that it may now be emerging from this simulated rut (partly because the truth was getting too hard to conceal between the cranes on the Tokyo skyline) only reinforces this argument.

And this stagnation, even if one believes in it, is (or was) at the top of a very high plateau of aggregate and per-capita GNP, so Japan is hardly suffering by any reasonable international standard. *Even according to the official figures*, it is the second richest country in the world. It is doing far better than other economies that get better press because they conform more closely to the globalist model of what an economy ought to be. It is a vastly richer nation, for example, than Britain, which globalist magazines like *The Economist* like to depict as an economic leader because it genuflects, at least in theory, to the right neoliberal principles.

Furthermore, the Japanese system is deliberately designed to contain the usual forms of economic stress that produce shocks to the political system, like inflation and unemployment, so Japan's (quite mild) economic problems are miles away from having the political consequences needed to cause the radical revision of the system that 'see-what-they-want-to *laissez-faire*' ideologues suppose. Is 5 per cent unemployment, in the context of a family structure more intact than in any Western nation, a crisis? In what other nation would 5 per cent be considered a crisis level?

Nevertheless, we are fed a neoliberal fantasy that Japan is in a state of economic crisis and that this crisis is forcing her to revise her economy to conform to the world-conquering American version of capitalism.

Penetrating the illusion of a failing Japan

It is not hard to see through the illusion of a failing Japan if one knows where to look. The key is to look at indicators not susceptible to manipulation by the Ministry of Finance in Tokyo. First among these are export statistics, which are hard to conceal as they show up as imports in the statistics of other nations. Some key facts, not denied by the mainstream media, that make clear that Japan's economy is thriving:

1. Japan's net exports for the decade of the 1990s, when she was supposedly in decline, were 240 per cent of those in the decade of the 1980s, when everyone admits she was booming. How is this possible if her economy is falling apart? We are being asked to believe that in an export-centered economy, exports are booming and yet the economy as a whole is failing.

2. The standard of living in Japan rose significantly during the supposedly stagnant 1990s, so that the Japanese are now among the world's greatest buyers of high-end consumer goods of all kinds, a fact visible in the shopping districts and parking lots of every Japanese city.

3. Japan's foreign assets have continued to grow rapidly. IMF figures indicate they nearly quadrupled in the 11 years to 2000, an inevitable consequence of her relentless trade surpluses.

4. Although a declining Japanese economy would imply a declining yen, the reverse has been the case.

5. Japan is the world's largest exporter of capital, enabling her to play the leading role in shaping the development of other nations. Americans ideologues who crow about the 'spread of capitalism' ignore the fact that in large areas of the world, including its fastest growing region, East Asia, it is Japanese-style capitalism that is spreading, largely through the subsidiaries and suppliers of Japanese corporations.

6. Japan's supposed problems with its government budget are in a category all their own when it comes to misunderstanding. First, Japanese government accounting is very different from European or American government accounting, and that what has sometimes been reported as deficits are in fact surpluses. Second, although Japan's ratio of national debt to GNP is indeed somewhat large, it is not grossly out of line with other nations whose economies are not characterized as being in crisis, and given Japan's higher savings rate, she can finance this debt easily.

7. Western press reports about the supposed crisis in the Japanese banking system are based on the false assumption that Japan's banks are similar to banks in the US and Europe. Because of their complex structural relationships to Japanese industry and to government, explained below, they are nothing of the kind. They have sources of stability to tide them over temporary difficulties that Western banks do not, and their rare failures cause far less disruption.

Japan's economic system only makes sense as a whole

The Japanese economic system does not make sense when viewed in parts, as the significance of any one part of an economy is determined by its relations with the other parts. Westerners naturally assume, when looking at one part, that it exists in a context similar to the one it would inhabit in the American capitalist economy. But in Japan, it frequently does not.

For example, the Tokyo stock market, unlike the New York one, is economically a minor sideshow to the real action, because most capital is allocated by banks, even when they use the stock exchange as a forum to execute this. Its failure to be a real capital market is made clear by the fact that the Ministry of Finance has on occasion forced the shares of individual companies to hover at arbitrary levels for various reasons.

The key to understanding the Japanese economic system is that it is not just a system of economics, but a system of *political economy*. This term – Adam Smith never used the word 'economics' – is an older one and enjoys the key advantage of not covertly implying that the economic system is an autonomous sphere of human activity operating, at most, within a loose cage of politically-enforced property rights. This erroneous conception tends to further the *laissez-faire* delusion that state power is something alien that intrudes upon economic activity from without, and that the only important economic choice is between more and less state control.

A non-socialist centrally planned economy

Japan is something that is virtually impossible by definition within the frame of reference of neoliberal economics: a non-socialist state-directed system. To over-simplify a bit, it is a centrally-planned capitalist economy.

Neoliberal economists are dimly aware of the fact that fascist and Nazi economics were centrally-planned but not socialist, but they tend to dismiss these economic systems because of the attendant political horrors and have made precious little effort to develop rigorous theoretical accounts of how they worked. As we shall see, the Japanese system has achieved many of the things the fascists wanted.

Modelling the Japanese system

The best way to model the Japanese system is to start from the conventional models of free-market capitalism and centrally-planned socialism and discuss how it differs from both.

In order to grasp what the Japanese have done, it is worth comparing it to Western attempts to achieve the same thing. For example, the Japanese have understood that the ambition of the advocates of the 'mixed economy,' like Hugh Gaitskell in the UK, to socialize the 'commanding heights' of the economy, has some rational basis, in that it embodies the desirability for some government direction of the economy without a total Gosplan-style takeover.

But this aspiration was misinterpreted in classic socialism, which understood the commanding heights to be basic industries like coal, steel and railways. The problem with this, however, is that these industries do not *command* anything. Important though they are, they do not constitute a lever by which the economy as a whole can be controlled; they do not issue orders to the rest of the economy that determine how it behaves. The supply of capital to business, however, does, and this is under state control in Japan. One way to think of the Japanese system is as a capitalist economy with socialized capital markets.

Capitalism without plutocracy

Another case in point: does capitalism require plutocrats? The classic capitalist answer is that somebody has to own productive assets with a view to maximizing their profit, some of those who do will succeed brilliantly, therefore somebody must be rich.

But the Japanese see this as wasteful, so their system is designed so that corporations, in essence, largely own themselves. Even when there are nominal outside owners, corporations are managed so that the bulk of the wealth generated by the corporation flows either to the incomes of present workers or to investment in the future competitive strength of the company, making the workers and the company itself the *de facto* or beneficiary owners.

Most corporate capital in Japan is owned by banks, and the banks are principally owned not by shareholders, but by other companies in the same *keiretsu* or industrial group. And who owns these companies? Although there are some outside shareholders, majority control is in the hands of the *keiretsu's* bank and the other companies in the group. So in essence, the whole thing is circular and private ownership of the means of production has basically been put into the back seat.

Actually nationalizing the means of production would produce all the problems that led to the wave of privatizations in many nations in the last 20 years, and is unnecessary anyway. The Japanese system makes a sly mockery of both capitalism and socialism.

Forcing growth by forcing the accumulation of capital

One key way in which the Japanese system differs from American capitalism is that it squarely faces a fact that neoliberal economists admit, but tend to do nothing about: *the rate at which any economy – capitalist, socialist, feudal, fascist or what have you – can grow depends on how much of its production is saved and invested, rather than consumed.*

America does almost nothing to increase its very low savings rate. Japan has a very high savings rate and this is a result of deliberate government policy and the lynchpin of the entire system.

How do they do it? The architects of the Japanese system understood that the socialist and communist way to produce high savings, i.e. outright confiscation of wealth, is destructive of people's incentive to work (not to mention its other problems) so they did not implement it. They understood that by definition, savings equals production minus consumption, so they focused on repressing consumption.

This means, for example, deliberately restrictive zoning policies that keep Japanese houses small, and it means not having the various devices in place by which America subsidizes borrowing and makes debt easy to assume. As a result, the populace of Japan is forced to save a far higher percentage of its earnings than Americans do.

It is a mistake to attribute Japan's savings rate, or many of its other key aspects, to 'culture,' as Japan had the same culture before the Second World War, when her savings rate was low. It is the interaction of culture with deliberate state policies, *not* culture itself, that is key. The use of 'culture' as a catch-all explanation by foreign analysts of Japan is an evasion of serious analysis.

Controlling the economy by controlling the accumulation of capital

The Japanese government deliberately channels savings into a limited number of financial institutions under its control simply by making sure there is nowhere else to put the money. For example, it has seen to it that the Japanese cannot just open a brokerage account at Merrill Lynch and invest their money in the American stock market.

This huge torrent of savings flows to a handful of major banks, which the government has under its thumb because banking is extremely regulated in Japan, enabling regulators at the Ministry of Finance (MOF) to crack down on any bank at any time they see it doing something they don't want it to. So the banks are subject to the whim of the government, which then controls the economy by controlling how the banks allocate all this capital.

The net result is that the world's second-largest pool of private investable capital is subject to the control of a few hundred elite bureaucrats in Tokyo. The leverage they exert by controlling where this capital goes is the key to all their power.

How Japan avoids the problems of Soviet-style central planning

The real genius of this system is that it is so indirect. These MOF bureaucrats are not stupid. They have read von Hayek, watched the Soviet Union struggle and understand perfectly well that classic Gosplan-style central planning is unworkable. So they do not even remotely attempt this.

They understand quite well that the day-to-day detailed operation of the economy is best left to the invisible hand, just like Adam Smith said. They do realize, however, as Adam Smith didn't, that it is possible to manipulate an economy that is 99 per cent capitalist into being, essentially, a centrally-planned economy *if* the state controls the right 1 per cent. And this 'right 1 per cent' is the allocation of capital, especially big capital.

The MOF uses its stranglehold on the allocation of capital to make the banks into willing servants of its mission to control the Japanese economy. The banks, which in this respect (but not others) function similarly to the classic universal banks of Germany, handle almost all the detailed work of figuring out which companies should be loaned money and for which projects. The MOF essentially sits back, audits their performance, and rewards or punishes as appropriate.

This elitism in the MOF's control of the Japanese economy explains why so many outside observers fail to see it at all, though if one approaches the literature on Japan with this in mind, one quickly sees which observers have grasped the game.

In the early days of the Japanese system, the government had to be more involved in the details of deciding which industries to finance, because the banks had not developed the necessary sophistication, and so a far larger role was played by the Ministry of International Trade and Industry, the famed MITI, which actually did perform the classic industrial-policy functions of picking winners, and so on. But as Japan's private-sector banks have become more sophisticated, the need for this has diminished, and the MOF has become the key to the system. (The MITI is still around, because there are some more speculative parts of the economy that the banks are not expert in and so the government still needs it sometimes.)

What is all this capital seeking?

As noted above, the MOF's key role is to audit the performance of the banks in allocating capital. But what counts as performance? In a conventional capitalist system, that's an easy question: maximizing return on capital. But in the Japanese system, this is not so.

For a start, the capital in question, although nominally privately owned, is 'captive' capital in that it has nowhere else to go if it is unhappy with its return. This seemingly minor fact changes the whole dynamic of the entire economic system, because it means that capital, rather than chasing the highest return, can be made to obey political directives. Obviously, from the point of view of enriching individual investors this makes no sense, but this is not the MOF's objective. The investors don't have their money stolen from them – Japan is not a Marxist society – and they certainly get *some* return, but they do not get the maximum possible return.

What the MOF *does* want is to supply huge quantities of cheap capital to Japanese industry to build up its long-term productive capacity. The MOF *wants* capital to be paid a low return so that Japanese companies will enjoy the competitive advantage of access of cheaper capital than their European, Asian and American competitors. In capital-intensive industries like the advanced manufacturing in which Japan specializes, this is a huge advantage.

From the MOF's point of view, neoliberalism is designed to selfishly benefit the investors at the expense of the nation as a whole. And the investors themselves lose in the long run as their greed for high returns bleeds industry by imposing on it a high cost of capital, undermining these industries in the long run. In the Japanese analysis, the return to society as a whole of having strong industries (high wages paid, secure employment, a strong balance of payments) is more important than returns to individual investors, though these must be respected to some extent.

A successful planned economy

The natural question a neoliberal economist asks at this point is, how can the MOF make rational capital-allocation decisions? Isn't it an article of faith, vindicated by years of experience, that governments are bad at this and markets good?

Well, yes, which is why the MOF intervenes at only the very highest levels of this process, most of the work being done by banks and the large corporations beneath them in this hierarchical system. Banks in Japan are attached to large industrial groups called *keiretsu,* meaning that they are both tied into sophisticated networks of industrial expertise and have several layers of administration below them to do the detailed work.

Much of the Japanese system operates similarly to similar corporate structures in the West, though it faces a deliberately altered set of incentives. Because these incentives are just a fact of life to most of the corporate managers facing them, they don't even have to know where they came from or why. Most of the system doesn't even know that it's centrally-planned, and doesn't need to.

If there is any question as to whether they have been able to make these high-level decisions correctly for the last 50 years, one has only to look at Japan's relative economic performance, which has made her by all accounts the second-richest nation in the world and possibly soon to be the richest.

Simply put, *laissez-faire* theory is just plain empirically wrong: a planned economy can work. Period. Empirical facts trump abstract theories.

Unfortunately for the political left, Japan's success equally makes a mockery of socialism, which may explain why her system has attracted so little affection in the West. It does not flatter anyone's ideological religion, left or right.

Wall Street Works, but isn't it awfully expensive?

Essentially, the architects of the Japanese system looked at the classic capitalist economy and reached the exact same conclusion as the average member of the Western world: that most of it is rational, but that an absurdly high proportion of national income is wasted rewarding the tiny elite that performs the capital-allocation function. Wall Street types do their jobs reasonably well, but why not replace them with elite bureaucrats who will perform the same function for $90,000 a year apiece, rather than people who earn ten, or even a hundred, times that? After all, one can teach bureaucrats the same technical skills of economic analysis.

In the Japanese view, investment banking is a business which, because of its structural monopoly on extremely valuable information, tends to produce grossly excessive returns for those engaged in it. The capital allocation function is irrationally priced because the intrinsic bottlenecks of information make it impossible for new entrants to drive down returns. Therefore the market cannot be relied upon to rationally price it. Capitalism, paradoxically, is rational except at its very pinnacle.

But aren't all bureaucrats idiots?

At this point in the argument, neoliberal ideologues object in one of two ways:

1. *By making some snide comment about the rule of elite bureaucrats.*
    An acceptable point, but one should not confuse the effectiveness of economic bureaucrats with the cultural and social mischief perpetrated by bureaucrats in other areas of government. The cold fact is that even the economies of those nations that most closely conform to neoliberalism, like the United States, are regulated by elite bureaucracies such as the Federal Reserve Bank, the Financial Accounting Standards Board, the Treasury Department, and the Interstate Commerce Commission.
2. By claiming that without paying the elite bureaucrats at the MOF huge returns directly proportional to the performance of the businesses they allocate capital to, they have no incentive to do their jobs well.

This is just empirically false. The performance of the Japanese economy shows that they do their jobs very well, and the key to this is something the architects of the Japanese political economy have understood that American economics tends to lose sight of: *Economic rewards are not the only effective incentives for economic action.*

Exploiting the power of non-economic incentives

The Japanese are well aware that a successful economy requires the motivating effects of pay differentials and opportunities to accumulate private wealth. They are not living in a hippie socialist fantasy. But they have understood, as neoliberal economists, with their purely economic view of the economy, have not, that economic rewards operate in a social context and that social rewards for economic achievement can be as effective as cash.

In fact, because of the diminishing marginal utility of money, it is *irrational* for an economic system to rely on purely economic incentives. If all you pay people in is money, it gets awfully expensive to maintain their motivation as you go up the income scale. How much money does society have to dangle in front of a billionaire to get him to allocate another five hours a week from leisure to the work needed to run the part of the economy he owns?

That is to say, money is an efficient motivator (measured in terms of what society has to pay relative to what it gets for its money) under some circumstances, which is why we have capitalism, but inefficient under extreme conditions, which is why the Japanese deliberately limit it. It is no accident that Japan has one of the lowest levels of economic inequality of any major nation at the same time as it has one of the most hierarchical cultures. The incomes of the top fifth of the Japanese population are only 2.9 times that of the bottom fifth, compared to 9.1 times in the US.

The income differential between a Japanese CEO and an assembly-line worker in his company is much less than in America, but the social-status difference is much greater. This does not consist of a system of static class differences that are different from economic differences, as in Britain, which the Japanese rightly see as producing class antagonisms that harm social cooperation. It consists in a *dynamic* social status system embodied in such oddities as the fact that Japanese grammar itself expresses the difference in status between the interlocutors, the Japanese reverence for hierarchy, and much else.

The Japanese have understood that what people are largely pursuing in the workplace is not so much money as the respect of the people around them, and therefore maintain a sophisticated – indeed, bizarrely over-elaborate to the Western eye – economy of *respect* in addition to the economy of money. They have understood that a large part of what money-seeking individuals really want is just to spend that money on purchasing social respect, though status display or whatever, so it is far more efficient to allocate respect directly.

Did you really think people as obviously intelligent as the Japanese were doing all those odd-looking bows for nothing? Sure, these behaviours are derived from tradition, but there's a reason they kept these traditions and the West hasn't. Interestingly, this understanding on their part of the need for unapologetic status differentials contradicts the emphasis in Western socialism on a *culture* of equality.

It also follows that if society is to maintain status differentials without suffering withdrawal of social cooperation due to the resulting resentment of low-status individuals, society must contain these status differentials within strong overarching sentiments of social unity. Naturally, the Japanese are famous for this, too. It all fits.

Platonic guardians of an eternal Japan

Why are Japan's bureaucrats so effective? Well, an American can start by looking at those American bureaucrats who are generally conceded by most people outside the far left to be effective: the military. The two salient characteristics of the military hierarchy in the US are that it has a governing ideology of nationalism and it is motivated by non-economic rewards. Japanese bureaucrats at the MOF are the same. Like five-star generals, they are no more than reasonably paid, but their real reward is in the form of status: they are recognized everywhere as outranking people hundreds of times richer than they are. They can demand to be recognized as equals by anyone in their society and as superiors by all but a few.

Plato would have recognized such men as Platonic guardians, who were produced in his *Republic* by a process the Tokyo University men who run Japan would recognize: an elite education, followed by long apprenticeship and combined with relative material asceticism, ruthless scrutiny by the other guardians, a tight in-group *esprit de corps*, and a guiding ideology of nationalism. Anyone who knew the pre-1960s Jesuits will also understand what is going on here.

The long time horizon

One of the key advantages of Japan's system is that it enables the imposition of an exceptionally-long time horizon on economic decision-making. Few American corporations think more than five years ahead; the Japanese routinely think 15 years ahead and the architects of the system obviously thought 50 years ahead. There is no pressure for short-term returns because at the end of the day capital is allocated by MOF bureaucrats and not impatient shareholders and mutual funds. MOF bureaucrats know they will be judged by whether they succeed in building up Japanese industry in the long term, so this is what they aim for.

What does it mean to build up industry?

The key thing the Japanese have understood, which America, among others, has forgotten, is that a nation's long-term ability to pay high wages to its citizens depends on its having a strong position in monopoly industries. Monopoly industries have the strongly entrenched competitive positions that enable them to charge superior prices on the world market. Boeing and Microsoft are the classic examples in the USA.

The core Japanese belief is that the benefits to society at large – in the terms of classical economics the positive externalities – of having these industries are so large that the free market on its own will mis-price their value and not produce enough of them. Therefore it is rational for government to artificially direct capital into them, whether or not they produce the best short-term return to investors.

The usefulness of cartels

If one's objective is a strong competitive position for the industry as a whole, cartels immediately recommend themselves as a means to this end. Cartels are a device of industrial policy that has essentially been repudiated by neoliberal economics, for two reasons:

1. Within a neoliberal framework, profits from a cartel will just be captured by private interests, so there is no public interest in allowing them.
2. Neoliberal economics has an *a priori* obsession with vindicating free competition as the best policy.

Because the Japanese system, as noted above, forces the profits of monopoly industries into either paying its workers well or building up the industry so it can do so in future, the first reason is inoperative, and the second simply never interested them. Once one has these two factors out of the way, the many benefits of cartels can be tapped into:

1. They enable the individual firms in a monopoly industry to avoid fratricidal competition that would only benefit foreign customers, not the Japanese producers.
2. They enable the extraction of additional investment capital from the domestic consumer market by imposing higher prices.
3. They enable scale economies in research and development and standard-setting, which are crucial advantages in high technology.
4. They enable Japanese industry to avoid bidding wars in buying foreign technology and raw materials.
5. They enable Japanese industry to share out scarce sales in times of recession, avoiding bankruptcy of weaker firms. Naturally, these firms will pay a price in terms of losing control and will be whipped into shape, but they, and their workers, will not incur the traumas and layoffs of bankruptcy.
6. By enabling government-led control of prices and profits, they enable the government to pump subsidies into favoured industries with the confidence that these will go to building up the industry and not simply 'wasted' as private profits to the shareholders.

Naturally, the Japanese are wise enough to the benefits of some competition that they don't simply agglomerate entire industries into 'national champions,' as several European nations have sometimes tried to do. A regulated cartel delivers the best of both worlds.

Manipulating corporate behaviour through corporate structure

Japan's key banks each sit at the apex of a pyramid of cross-shareholding companies called a *keiretsu*. This has a number of important consequences, and each coordinates with the overall aims of the system.

1. Because each *keiretsu* links companies with their upstream suppliers and downstream customers, this biases customer–supplier relationships towards the long-term relationship-based, rather than the short-term transaction-based, profit-seeking. The former is a key advantage in high-tech industries in which companies must make huge irrecoverable investments in research and development that will only pay off if they can count on stable relationships with customers and suppliers. Compare this to the American bias in favour of short-term business relationships – a bias that then leads to short-term business thinking that is mutually reinforcing.

2. The *keiretsu* system helps force companies to select their suppliers from within the *keiretsu*, not from foreign companies who may offer lower bids. Although this is superficially inefficient, because it deactivates the 'exit' option American-style companies have in their dealings with their suppliers, it is in the long term efficient because it enhances the 'voice' option Japanese companies have to enlist the aid of the entire *keiretsu* in whipping an under-performing supplier into shape.

3. Because each *keiretsu* contains within itself companies in a wide range of industries, the bank at its apex can draw on a wide range of reliable and proprietary expertise concerning appropriate allocations of capital.

4. Because each company in the *keiretsu* is on a leash to its bank, the bank (a puppet of the Ministry of Finance) can impose policies that it wants: for example, policies to keep desirable high-value-added jobs in Japan. When Japanese jobs move to China, they are jobs that the MOF wants Japan to shed so her workforce can move up into ones with higher value-added and thus higher sustainable incomes. Naturally, pressure from the bank alone isn't enough to bring this about, and this policy depends on all the other policies that combine to make it economically feasible to pay Japanese wages for these jobs.

5. Because the *keiretsus* in effect create a monopsony for the purchase of elite executive labour, they can avoid the problem that American companies have of getting into expensive bidding wars for executive talent. This helps drive down economic inequality without all the problems of redistributing income through taxation. The emphasis in Japan on teamwork and consensus decision-making also helps prevent the accumulation of valuable proprietary knowledge inside any one head, which would then have excessive leverage to extract wealth.

Taking state capitalism seriously

State capitalism (of one degree and structure or another) is not unique to Japan. What is unique to Japan, or taken to its greatest extreme there, is serious thinking-through of what state capitalism means and what is required to make it work.

The French government, for example, would dearly love to be able to order companies to keep their plants in France open to serve its full-employment goals. But, consciously or unconsciously infected with a socialist class-struggle mentality, it considers the cost of doing this 'the company's problem,' not its own, with the predictable result that it barks orders at companies that simply cannot afford to do what the government wants them to.

The Japanese government, by contrast, understands that if it expects companies to provide full employment, it must provide them the wherewithal to achieve sustainable competitive advantage, and it does so by guaranteeing them a supply of cheap capital, as explained above, by protecting them from foreign competition, and by other means.

Sustainable competitive advantage in hard industries

I have thus far only described Japan's economy in the abstract. The concrete consequence of her policies is an emphasis on advanced manufacturing as a sector, because:

1. it is the sector which is most able to pay sustainably high wages to ordinary workers;
2. it is the sector which is most susceptible, because of the proprietary know-how involved, to the acquisition of sustainable competitive advantage;
3. it is the sector whose produce is most exportable, a key consideration for a nation that must import most of its raw materials and energy.

Lifetime employment aligns incentives

Japan's famed lifetime employment system for core workers seems to the neoliberal eye inefficient, as it supposedly interferes with efficient hiring and firing. But it has a key benefit in a system designed around maximizing long-term rather than short-term success: it aligns the interests of the worker and the company to a much greater degree than under a hire-and-fire system. (Of course, Japanese companies have ways of disciplining bad employees short of firing them.) And since their long-term orientation leads to an emphasis on maintaining sales, not profits, in slack times, they tend to avoid the layoff cycles that Western companies endure.

Lifetime employment also gives companies an incentive to invest in giving their workers expensive technical training, since they know the workers won't just jump to a competitor once they have it. Since a highly trained workforce is one of the absolute keys to success in any advanced sector of the economy, this is very important. And lifetime employment forces *executives* at the company to care about its long-term success, rather than just to pump the company for quick profits during the few years they are there.

Furthermore, the architects of the Japanese system understand that as a sociological and political matter, providing lifetime security to a core group of male 'breadwinner' workers confers stability to society as a whole, especially when combined with a traditional male-dominated society that has stronger inter-generational obligations (to care for the old, for example) than most contemporary Western nations.

Ending the Marxist curse of alienation

Lifetime employment helps nourish the emotional bond between the worker and the company, which is also expressed by such things, which seem silly to Western eyes, as company songs. These make perfect sense within the context of Japanese culture.

Americans tend to forget that Marx wrote so much about alienation (which we tend to associate with teenagers with purple hair, not with serious economic questions) for a reason: he saw this as the key *psychological* phenomenon, in the head of the individual proletarian, that makes him a revolutionary. Alienation is an important consideration.

The Japanese were acutely aware of the Marxist challenge to capitalism, and they internalized this problem by taking seriously the elimination of alienation. The West has not, choosing to smother it with consumerism while doing nothing about the phenomenon itself, resulting in the central weirdness of Western culture since the 1960s: the fact that our culture, from rock music to academia, is centered on the institutionalization of rebellion.

Unsurprisingly, Japan had no '1960s' on our scale, and maintains levels of traditional morals (their traditions, remember, not ours) and deference to authority that remind most Americans and Europeans of the 1950s. This achievement is under certain stresses, as Japan is not immune to the corrosive forces of modernity any more than any other society, but it remains intact to a remarkable degree.

Fascism without the fascism

If the use of non-economic incentives sounds familiar, it is because the last time this issue was seriously addressed in the West in the context of a modern economy was by Peter F Drucker in his 1940 book *The End of Economic Man*, which discussed how the Nazi system was based on creating a non-economic power structure to resolve the social conflicts that had been irresolvable within capitalist European society. This, in his view, was the sick genius of Nazism and the reason it had been able to come within a hair's breadth of creating a world-conquering social system.

The political economy described above is the product of thinking that originated among Japan's colonial bureaucrats entrusted with the industrialization of Japan's colony of Manchuria in the 1930's. They published their *Economic New Structure Manifesto* in 1940 as a result of their experience of the inefficiency of traditional capitalism as a development strategy. In the short run, the elite *Zaibatsu* capitalists of Japan vetoed their ideas, but in the long run, partly as a result of the American occupation's assault on the big property owners, a product of their New Dealers' conviction that industrial concentration was an abettor of fascism, they were able to triumph.

One way to describe the Japanese achievement is to say that they have achieved what the Nazis wanted to achieve but didn't, largely of course because they were mad serial killers obsessed with many things other than economics. Ironically, Asiatic Japan comes closer than any nation on earth to what Hitler wanted. It is a socially conservative, hierarchical, technocratic, orderly, pagan, sexist, nationalist, racially pure, anti-communist, non-capitalist and anti-Semitic society.

Of course, it would be unfair to describe contemporary Japan as Nazi-like in any of the senses that are notorious (though one cannot help observing that she has never been contrite about her actions of the Second World War in the way Germany has.) More correctly, the architects of the Japanese system learned from their disastrous Second World War experience that the kind of society they wanted could not be achieved through a totalitarian predator-state and they calculated that it could be achieved through the forms, though not the content, of liberal democracy, which is how Japan presents itself.

The Japanese model makes democracy (almost) irrelevant

One of the consequences of Japan's long-term orientation that is least palatable to the Western liberal mind is that it has the effect of making democracy almost superfluous. The reason is simple: if the objective of the government is the long-term well-being of the nation, the means to this end have already been figured out, and execution has been entrusted to a bureaucracy with a track-record of success, then *there is very little for democracy to do*. What is there for the elected representatives of the people to debate? Particularly since serious debate about these questions turns on economic expertise they do not possess.

As a result, the Japanese Diet is essentially relegated to the 'Tammany Hall' functions of a democracy: interceding with the bureaucrats on behalf of individual citizens and co-opting potential troublemakers by dispensing corruption. In fact, the bureaucrats, who control the spigot that dispenses the grease, like to keep the elected officials corrupt so that they can be disciplined at any time by the threat of running to the police. As a result, the supposed 'democracy' in Japan is a trivial and compliant rubber stamp for the bureaucratic elite, which operates under enabling laws that give them the legal basis to do as they see fit. Since anyone seriously interested in running the country went into the bureaucracy long ago, there are few representatives in the Diet with any inclination to challenge this system, which gives them the perks and popularity that elected officials really want.

Japan is not really a liberal democracy

In terms of the fundamentals of contemporary political philosophy, the key issue this all raises is whether Japan has refuted the idea that running an advanced society requires freedom. This assumption, which is not without evidence, is the absolute cornerstone of the contemporary Western assumption that the increasing economic development of the world may be presumed to have an ultimately benign political outcome. It impinges on a whole host of crucial issues too numerous to discuss here.

Japan has preserved, of course, the nominal forms of liberal democracy. But she has systematically drained them of content, just as she has drained capitalist institutions like the stock exchange of content. But if these forms are not necessary to the system, then both Peter F Drucker, who has argued that an advanced society must be a free society, and Francis Fukuyama, who has argued that liberal democracy is the ultimate state of human ideological evolution, are wrong. The significance of this is incalculable.

Japan is thus a far more important example of the famous Asian 'soft authoritarian' model made famous by Singapore, and the challenge of this model is far more profound than people realize. This is particularly so given that China is desperately trying to construct a sustainable regime without risking the national disintegration that she quite reasonably fears attempted democracy would cause.

Theoretical implications

Not only has economic history not stopped, but the range of alternatives exceeds the conventionally assumed one between capitalism and socialism. Perhaps the Japanese system is capitalism of a sort, but if so, it is a kind of capitalism in which private capital is not the dominant organizing principle of the economy, so I would dispute this.

As nationalists, the Japanese only want their system to serve them and have no interest in winning ideological arguments. They will not make significant efforts to disabuse foreigners of their economic theories, especially when these theories make foreign nations accept their trade surpluses.

Japan's economic achievement refutes the proposition that neoliberalism is the only route to economic success. This does not mean, however, than all neoliberal theory is false. Clearly, within rationally-defined limits, much of it is true.

Practical implications

Neither does it all mean that nations setting economic policies can ignore neoliberal prescriptions willy-nilly and expect not to pay a price. The Japanese system is a sophisticated construct that requires some of the world's most skilled economic managers. Outsmarting capitalism is not a game for amateurs.

The Japanese system is a *system*, so one cannot just copy any piece of it and expect it to work outside its original context. But some pieces depend upon things that are sufficiently similar in other economies that they are plausibly imitable. For example:

1. Any nation can usefully increase its savings rate, not necessarily by

Japan's means.

2. Any nation can prop up working-class wages by not importing cheap foreign labour.
3. Advanced nations can benefit from carefully relaxing anti-cartel laws to allow cooperative R&D, as in the Sematech consortium in the US.

Other policies, like lifetime employment and cartel price-fixing, would clearly be a disaster if simply imposed, because they need constraints supplied by the rest of the system to ensure that the benefits are socially diffused and not just captured by narrow interests.

The lynchpin of the system, politicized capital allocation, probably cannot work in a democracy, as it would just result in plants being built in the districts of powerful parliamentarians and would not make investments whose payoff exceeded one election cycle. Naturally, kleptocratic oligarchies wouldn't be good at it either; politicized capital allocation is only likely to work under highly platonic systems like the MOF. And even then, there is no guarantee: power still corrupts and one can easily imagine such a system becoming inbred and perverse. Japan's achievement is an empirical fact, not a guarantee to all eternity.

Other policies fall in between the imitable and the inimitable, like the emphasis on advanced manufacturing, an extremely complex topic.

Still other policies, like protectionism, can only be rationally evaluated in the context of a general debate on the topic of which the Japanese case is but an important part.

Notes

1. Ozaki, Robert, *Human Capitalism: The Japanese System as a World Model.*
2. Fallows, James, *Looking At The Sun: the Rise of the New East Asian Economic and Political System.*
3. Kenrick, Douglas, *Where Communism Works: the Success of Competitive Communism in Japan.*
4. Gerlach, Michael, *Alliance Capitalism: the Social Organization of Japanese Business.*
5. Fingleton, Eamonn, *Blindside: How Japan Won the Race to the Future While the West Wasn't Looking.*
6. Wade, Robert, *Governing the Market: Economic Theory and the Role of Government in East Asian Industrialization.*
7. Fruin, Mark, *The Japanese Enterprise System: Competitive Strategies and Cooperative Structures.*
8. Calder, Kent, *Strategic Capitalism: Private Business and Public Purpose in Japanese Industrial Finance.*
9. Johnson, Chalmers, *MITI and the Japanese Miracle: the Growth of Industrial Policy 1925–75. & Japan: Who Governs? The Rise of the Developmental State.*
10. Drucker, Peter F, *The End of Economic Man.*

29.

LIBERALISATION AND SOCIAL STRUCTURE: THE CASE OF LABOUR INTENSIVE EXPORT GROWTH IN SOUTH ASIA

Matthew McCartney

Introduction

Neoclassical theorists argue that discrimination is impossible in a competitive market economy. Any firm or individual with a 'taste for discrimination' will be driven out of business by lower cost competitors who employ, trade and produce according to the criteria of profit and productivity maximization. By this logic, free markets and free trade will allow a developing country to exploit a comparative advantage in labour-intensive manufacturing and agro-processing. Such labour-intensive growth will inevitably draw women for the first time into employment outside the home. Employed women will achieve an independent income and higher social status.

Neoclassical economics forgets economics is a branch of social theory. The outcome of liberalisation will be crucially dependent on the social structure of values and institutions in which it occurs. Where there is a pre-existing ideology of gender subordination (India and Pakistan) business has utilized this social structure to cut costs and fragment formal labour institutions. More egalitarian Sri Lanka has witnessed women being drawn into the formal employment sector and receiving the benefits of independence, mobility and independent income.

Liberalisation, efficient growth and labour markets

In Neoclassical economics growth in a free market will reflect the preferences of rational individuals: growth must then by definition be efficient,[1] as each exchange will reflect mutually beneficial gains by optimising economic agents. 'Getting the prices right' will allow developing countries to exploit a comparative advantage in labour-intensive production and exports. Overvalued exchange rates discriminate against labour-intensive agro-exports and reduce the cost of imported capital goods. Minimum wage and other labour 'rights' raise the cost of labour and reduce the elasticity of employment with respect to output growth. Sometimes synonymous with removing 'urban bias', liberalisation could be better described as removing capital bias.

Numerous authors have highlighted labour market rigidities as being a key factor in explaining poor developmental outcomes in India.[2] Employment protection[3] has hindered restructuring in union dominated public sector enterprises. It became more costly and time consuming for firms to adjust to changing market conditions and absorb new technologies, and legislation encouraged firms to remain small and informal,[4] trading off access to formal credit and scale economies in order to avoid the strictures of labour legislation. Firms in declining industries were prevented from shedding excess labour and piled up losses; those in expanding industries were reluctant to hire new workers and so substituted labour for capital. The jobless growth in the 1980s is cited as evidence for this proposition. Minimal expansion of formal sector employment between 1980 and 1989 coincided with an increase in annual earnings per worker of 3.5 per cent and large-scale substitution of labour for capital.[5]

The supposed potential of labour-intensive growth in South Asia is demonstrated by post-Mao China. China's labour markets have proved highly flexible in the non-state sector. Formal sector employment increased rapidly from 95 million in 1978 (9.7 per cent of the economically active population) to 148.5 million in 1994 (19.2 per cent). In India by contrast formal sector employment has increased from only 22.9 million in 1978 (6.8 per cent) to 27.4 million in 1994 (5.4 per cent).[6]

Labour intensive export growth and gender

The crucial 'optimistic' Neoclassical assumption is that markets reflect mutually beneficial voluntary exchange. The spread of markets is thus by assumption proof that the economy is becoming more efficient.

Discrimination in the sense of paying workers of identical productivity different wages will not persist over the long term in a capitalist economy. Any employer refusing to employ workers on the base of colour, creed, gender or caste will be less profitable than a non-discriminatory rival. Over time the dynamics of competition will drive out those with a 'taste for discrimination', the logic of the market will separate discrimination from the process of production. In a broader sense the dictates of the market separate society from the economy.

> The bourgeoisie, wherever it has got the upper hand, has put an end to all feudal, patriarchal, idyllic relations. It has pitilessly torn asunder the motley feudal ties that bound man to his 'natural superiors', and has left remaining no other nexus between man and man than naked self-interest, than callous cash payment.[7.]

'Female employment intensive' growth

Historically, labour-intensive export growth has been associated in many instances with a disproportionate increase in the employment of women. In the textile mills of nineteenth-century Britain, silk weaving in 1920s Japan, and electronics factories in the post-war Tiger economies. Wood[8] found a strong relationship between increased exports and increased female employment in manufacturing, the largest increases occurring in Mauritius, Tunisia, Sri Lanka, Malaysia and the East Asian Tiger economies. In export processing zones (EPZs) most labour is female, (80 percent in the Caribbean and the Philippines); this bias is especially strong in the garments sector.[9]

Drawing women into the formal labour market will improve their economic status and social position. The relative respect and regard of women is strongly influenced by their ability to earn an independent income, being employed outside the home and having ownership rights. These factors are linked by the positive impact they have on strengthening women's voice and agency through independence and empowerment. With independent waged employment, a woman's contribution to the family's well-being is more visible, she is less dependent on others, the exposure to ideas outside the home makes her agency more effective.[10] An ability to seek employment outside the home can contribute to the reduction of women's relative and absolute deprivation.

Really existing markets

Neoclassical economists are quick to generalise this optimistic scenario to support an exclusive focus on liberalisation. However, re-rooting economics as social theory reveals such outcomes to be context dependent. Markets as they really exist do not accord to this hypothesised ideal, rather, they are embedded in wider social structures of values and institutions.

> Real markets are permeated by power relations of various kinds; they are embedded in social processes which may, for example, involve class exploitation or gender subordination; and they are saturated by divergent institutions, ideologies, ethical and cultural values.[11]

The idea that liberalisation will remove politics from the economy and lead to a more rational and efficient allocation of resources is false. Markets are not politically neutral but are embedded in social structures. Just as government intervention can be distorted by an underlying political economy so too can markets. There is no neat dichotomy between state-regulation and markets: rather both are meshed into existing social structures of (among others) caste, religion and gender[12] in South Asia.

Liberalisation can remove market constraints but not structural constraints such as patriarchal values that prevent equal access of men and women to markets. These are not just imperfections of the market but deep-rooted characteristics of society.[13]

Social construction of gender in India

In India, employers have utilized a pre-existing and intensifying ideology of gender subordination to undermine male unionised labour and replace it with low cost ruralized, casualized, and informalized female labour. In 1985, 250,000 people were employed in the Bombay textile mills, by 1996 this had declined to only 54,000. Women then constituted only 0.01 per cent of the cotton mill workforce while accounting for more than 45 per cent of the unorganized cotton handloom sector.[14]

The social environment in which 'labour intensive' growth occurs is a crucial determinant of its net impact on women's agency. The missing factor to be controlled for is the pre-existing social structure of gender relations. The experiences of Sri Lanka and Pakistan offer sharply contrasting responses to liberalisation.

Sri Lanka and Pakistan: Empowerment and Exploitation

Sri Lanka has had traditionally good human development indicators, a 90 per cent-plus literacy rate and, compared with other developing countries, minimal gender disparity in education.[15] There has been a persistent upward trend in the educational attainment of males and females. Female literacy in 1995 was 87 per cent, only marginally lower than that of men. In this context, of relatively equal gender relations liberalisation has had an empowering impact.

Liberalisation policies were initiated in 1977. By the early 1980s there was economic growth of slightly under 6 per cent per annum. The fastest growing sectors since 1977 have been unskilled labour intensive manufactures, mainly garments and textiles. The structure of exports has indeed shifted towards Sri Lanka's comparative advantage. The institution behind this growth has been mushrooming export processing zones (EPZs),[16] set up in 1978, 1984 and 1990. Eighty per cent of the employment in EPZs is female. The female–male ratio in manufacturing has increased from 25 per cent to 80 per cent between 1963 and 1985, and the total employment of women in manufacturing increased by 50 per cent between 1977 and 1995.[17]

In Pakistan by contrast, gender relations have historically been highly unequal, the sex ratio at 910 women for every 1,000 men being even lower than that of India. Literacy, school enrolment and a persistently high fertility rate all point to the low status of women. Female primary school attendance is around 35 per cent, among the lowest in the world. Female labour force participation is only 3.5 per cent and represents severe crowding into low pay, low-skill occupations.[18] The labour market is also highly segmented, especially in urban areas where there is also widespread segregation between sexes.

The structure of modern industry in Pakistan is similar to that of Sri Lanka, consisting mainly of labour-intensive processing of agricultural products as well as textiles and clothing. In 1992/3 textiles and garments accounted for 64 per cent of total export revenue.[19] However, on a pre-existing base of gender discrimination the gender composition of employment in textiles and garments is very different. In Pakistan it is a male-intensive sector: 88.3 per cent of urban textile manufacturing workers are men. As in India, there is evidence of widespread contracting-out by garment enterprises that employ poor and young women. Most of this work is done in informal sector workshops or home-based work. Such work by itself will have little impact on bargaining strength or increasing the social status of women. In fact there may be a contradictory impact by implicitly devaluing the implied worth of unpaid domestic employment and further marginalising those women without paid external employment.

[I]n South Asian countries, women are rarely able or willing to work outside the marital home. In that case, wage work outside the house increases her work load because she is not in a position to bargain with others about sharing her housework.[20]

Gender and fragmentation of labour in India

Structural adjustment in the 1990s has given impetus to the long-term trend of increasing market relations in South Asia. There has been no long-term improvement in the status of women in Pakistan or India. The logic of capital is not dissolving discrimination but working within the social structure of a pre-existing gender ideology and intensifying female disadvantage.

Female–male (population) ratios have been declining in India since the beginning of this century. The 1991 census showed a further decline in this ratio, to 927 women for every 1,000 men.[21] Mortality levels of women are abnormally high from birth until the mid-30s. Increased urbanisation, modernisation and economic growth have not improved these trends. In fact the lowest ratios are recorded in the richest states, Haryana and the Punjab. Using the ratio for Sub-Saharan Africa, Dreze and Sen[22] calculated there were approximately 37 million missing women in India in 1986.[23]

Economic change is working within a social structure of female disadvantage. The north Indian pattern of anti-female discrimination is spreading southwards by means of cultural assimilation, and is not being undermined by economic change. Even in North India there is a pronounced process of Sansrikisation.[24] The dominant castes in the north are the martial and patriarchal Rajputs and Jats. Traditionally they have a pronounced gender division and obsession with honour. Honour is to a large extent a function of the conservative behaviour of women.[25] Lower castes in the north have been traditionally more equal, female–male ratios among tribes and scheduled castes having long been significantly higher. Over time lower castes have been emulated, rather than opposed, the ideology of dominant castes. Practices such as restrictions on widow remarriage and dowry have been diffusing down the caste hierarchy. The fall in female–male ratios has been generated by a convergence of ratios in lower castes to those of dominant castes.[26]

Conclusion

Liberalisation is a context-dependent, not a neutral and deterministic process. The social structure within which liberalisation occurs has a crucial impact on outcomes.

Despite having levels of female disadvantage of a similar if not worse magnitude to India and Pakistan, throughout the 1990s Bangladesh has enjoyed rapid labour (female) intensive employment growth in the export-orientated textiles sector. There is evidence to support the proposition that a prior restructuring of social relations (by NGOs among others) has enabled this favourable outcome.[27]

Economics is social theory. Neoclassical theory forgets social structure at the cost of relevance.

Notes

1. For a longer exposition see Matthew McCartney, 'Driving a car with no steering wheel and no road map: Neoclassical discourse and the case of India', *Post-Autistic Economics Review*, 21, 13 September 2003, article 5, http://www.btinternet.com/~pae_news/review/issue21.htm (Chapter 1. this volume).

2. See for example Peter R Fallon and Robert Lucas, 'Job security regulations and the dynamic demand for labour in India and Zimbabwe', *Journal of Development Economics*, 40, 1993, pp. 241–75; Roberto Zagha, 'Labour and India's economic reforms', in J D Sachs, A Varshney and N Bajpai (eds) *India in the Era of Economic Reforms*, Oxford University Press, 1999, pp. 160–85; Montek S Ahluwalia, 'Economic reforms in India since 1991: has gradualism worked?', *Journal of Economic Perspectives*, 16 (3), 2002, pp. 67–88; Timothy Besley and Robin Burgess, 'Can labour market hinder economic performance? Evidence from India', LSE: STICERD working paper no.33.

3. The 1976 amendment to the Industrial Disputes Act required state government permission to carry out any retrenchments in a firm of more than 300 employees. An amendment in 1982 reduced this figure to 100. The constitutional validity of this change was challenged and the second reform reintroduced as a constitutional amendment in 1984, Zagha *Labour and India's Economic Reforms*,.

4. Only 7 per cent of a labour force approaching 390 million are in the organized sector subject to social security and labour laws.

5. R Nagaraj, 'Organised manufacturing employment', *Economic and Political Weekly*, 35 (38), 2000, pp. 3445–8.

6. Nirupam Bajpai, 'Sustaining high rates of economic growth in India' *Harvard Centre for International Development*, working paper no. 65, March 2001.

7. Karl Marx and Friedrich Engels, *The Communist Manifesto* Penguin, 1967, p. 82.

8. Adrian Wood, 'North–South trade and female labour in manufacturing: an asymmetry', *Journal of Development Studies*, 27 (2), 1991.

9. Martin Rama 'Globalisation and workers in developing countries', World Bank Development Research Group, working paper no. 2,958, 2003, p. 15.

10. Amartya Sen, *Development as Freedom*, Oxford University Press, 1999, Chapter 8.

11. Gordon White, 'The political analysis of markets: editorial introduction', *Institute of Development Studies Bulletin*, 24 (3), 1993, p. 1.

12. Barbara Harriss-White, *India Working: Essays on Society and Economy*, Cambridge University Press, 2003.

13. Indira Hirway, 'Economic reforms and women's work', in *Employment*, in T S Papola and A N Sharma, *Gender and Employment in India*', Vikas, 1999, p. 356.
14. Ushma Upadhyay, 'India's new economic policy of 1991 and its impact on women's poverty and AIDS', 6 (3), *Feminist Economics*, 2000, p.108.
15. Marzia Fontana, Susan Joekes and Rachel Masika, 'Global trade expansion and liberalisation: gender issues and impacts', *Briefings on Development and Gender*, report no. 42, University of Sussex 1998, p.23.
16. An EPZ is a geographical location where foreign and/ or local investors are allowed to set up 100 per cent export-orientated facilities, and usually an array of incentives are granted such as tax holidays, access to duty free imported inputs and superior infrastructure.
17. Wood, 'North–South trade and female labour in manufacturing: an asymmetry', pp. 168–89.
18. Shahid J Burki, '*Pakistan: fifty years of nationhood*', 3rd edn, *Westview, 1999, Chapter 4.*
19. Fontana et al, *Global Trade Expansion and Liberalisation: Gender Issues and Impacts*, p. 25.
20. Nirmala Banerjee, *How Real is the Bogey of Feminisation?*, in T S Papola and A N Sharma, *Gender and Employment in India*, Vikas, 1999, p. 314.
21. Satish B Agnihotri, 'Missing females: a disaggregated analysis', *Economic and Political Weekly*, 19 August 1995.
22. Jean Dreze and Amartya Sen, *India: Economic Development and Social Opportunity*, Oxford University Press, 1995, p. 141.
23. There are a number of explanations for these disturbing trends, see Harriss-White, *India Working: Essays on Society and Economy*.
24. A process whereby lower castes emulate the practise and rituals of higher castes.
25. See Jean Dreze and Haris Gazdar, 'Uttar Pradesh: the burden of inertia', in J Dreze and A Sen (eds), *Indian Development: Selected Regional Perspectives*, Oxford University Press, 1996, pp. 33–128.
26. The female–male ratio among the dominant Rajput caste has remained stable at 890 for most of this century, and there has been a general convergence among lower castes to this 'standard'.
27. See Petra Dannecker, *Between Conformity and Resistance: Women Garment Workers in Bangladesh*, University Press, 2002).

30.

POLICY RELEVANCE IN THE LATIN AMERICAN SCHOOL OF ECONOMICS

Ana Maria Bianchi

As I understand it, one of the main goals of the post-autistic movement is to stimulate the economics profession to transcend autism and communicate with the rest of the world, non-economists included. One of the ways of attaining this goal is to look back at the history of economic ideas, which is full of interesting episodes that can help us to understand what happened in the past and what is going on today. Historical reconstruction may attract our attention to some currents of thoughts which developed outside the mainstream of the profession and were never made part of the academic textbooks, although they brought up significant new perspectives on the functioning of economic systems.

In this connection, it is worth recalling the episode that concerns the building of the Latin American School of Economics in the mid-twentieth century. This school of thought originated in the United Nations Economic Commission for Latin America and Caribe (ECLAC), founded in 1948. Its best-known leader is the Argentinean economist Raúl Prebisch. After holding important executive positions in the Central Bank of his country, Prebisch taught economics at the University of Buenos Aires and soon after joined the ECLAC staff, where he stayed for 15 years. His conception of the growth processes in Latin America was developed in several essays published by the ECLAC[1] and became the basis of what is now known as the Latin American school. Under the leadership of Prebisch, the institution became a think tank for a whole generation of heterodox economists and social scientists in general, the so-called *cepalinos*, whose ideas provided theoretical justification for the economic development of Latin America countries during the second half of the twentieth century.

The main thesis advocated by the Latin American School was that the 'peripheral' countries, which specialized in exporting raw materials and primary products in general to the 'central' industrialized countries, suffered from a long-term decline in their terms of trade. The benefits of external trade were unequally shared by these two groups of countries, the producers of manufactures, on the one hand, and the producers of raw materials and primary goods, on the other. Owing to this asymmetrical relationship in their foreign trade, peripheral countries faced a vicious circle of low productivity and low rate of savings. Regarding the central countries, market imperfections such as rigidity of wages and monopolistic conditions were such that the gains in productivity derived from technological improvements did not result in decreasing prices for industrial goods exported to Latin America and peripheral countries in general. The balance of payments deficits were detrimental to Latin America's economic growth, as receipts deriving from exportations did not create the import capacity needed to provide the region with the capital goods that it required in order to develop its industrial sector.

In order to overcome this situation, it was argued that Latin American countries should protect their foreign trade and concentrate on the production of an array of formerly imported manufactured goods. Import substitution was a necessary condition for peripheral growth, in association with structural reforms in the economy. The focus should be placed on the strengthening of the domestic market, which was seen as the crucial element of an inward-looking model of development. Exports were still necessary because they would guarantee the foreign exchange needed for importing capital goods, but the hallmark of the *cepalinos'* conception was its focus on the domestic market. Within Latin America, economic integration between countries would allow them to take advantage of economies of scale, in the sense of providing larger markets and favouring the dissemination of modern technologies.

These were, in a nutshell, the main theses defended by the *cepalinos*, who worked hard to gather statistical data about Latin American countries and their patterns of foreign trade. It is important to notice that this was not a widespread procedure in the 1940s and 1950s. On the contrary, in many economic texts, mostly those meant for a lay audience, there was no systematic concern with the role of statistical evidence in economic analysis. The *cepalinos* prompted a break from the prevalent discursive style. Concern with the empirical support of economic theses was present in the very spirit that presided over the conception of the ECLAC. The entity's staff was put in charge of assembling statistical data about Latin America, in order to compensate for the chronic deficiency, and they did the best they could do in this area.

Another important point about the *cepalinos* is the fact that they were severe critics of the conventional theory of international trade, both in its Ricardian and neoclassical versions. In a late interview, Prebisch (1987) stated that, although he was raised in the neoclassical tradition, the Great Depression forced him to review his ideas. Already in his writings as a member of the ECLAC staff, he argued that the main mistake of neoclassical economics was to attribute a general character to something that was geographically circumscribed. From the viewpoint of the periphery, conventional economics suffered from a 'false sense of universality', as its general laws did not apply to the world economy as a whole. The international division of labour which this theory pictured as a 'natural' outcome of the world system of trade was of much greater benefit to central than to peripheral countries. A new investigative effort was thus necessary for a correct interpretation of Latin American problems, one that would bear in mind the need to tailor the neoclassical theory to the specific conditions of peripheral economies. This did not mean, however, that the new generations of Latin American economists had to start all over again, building a completely different economic theory. On the contrary, they had to learn neoclassical economics before being able to make the necessary adaptations.[2]

Prebisch and the *cepalinos* were influenced by the German Historical School, especially its forerunner Friedrich List, from whom they borrowed the 'infant industry' argument. According to this argument, a potential manufacturer in a developing country, faced with an initial period of high costs, should be put under state protection. Temporary intervention would make entry into the new industry profitable provided that, on the longer term, its production costs would decline below the imported cost. This argument was combined with an appeal for import-substitution industrialization as the only way out of poverty and underdevelopment. Although not an end in itself, industrialization was the principal mechanism at the disposal of peripheral countries to obtain a share of the productivity gains achieved through technological progress. In this scenario a major role was attributed to the state, which should provide protection for the newborn domestic industries.

The *cepalinos* also placed great emphasis on economic programming and planning techniques. The development process should follow an orderly strategy, and it could not be conceived as the spontaneous process that characterized it during the nineteenth century.

On the empirical counterpart of this ideological and institutional movement, the *cepalinos* succeeded in mobilizing the energies necessary to give a new impulse to the state-led industrialization process. Industrialization through import substitution had begun earlier in countries such as Brazil, Argentina and Chile, but it gained a new momentum with the diffusion of structuralist ideas and policies. Burger (1999) claims that with the ECLAC industrial policies came to represent a logical continuation of this early process, systematized into a more coherent body of ideas.

All in all, this industrialization model worked in Latin America, if by 'working' we mean driving the per capita output for quite an extensive period of time. During the three decades that followed the Second World War, Latin America saw a continuous growth of its industrial product, its gross domestic product and its per capita income. Between 1950 and 1978, Latin America´s gross domestic product grew at an annual rate of 5.5 per cent, a rhythm that far exceeded the world average. The Latin American industrial product was multiplied by six in the same time period, growing at rates far superior to the population growth, which grew 2.8 per cent a year. The continent as a whole exhibited a persistent growth of its GNP per capita of about 26 per cent a year.

Yet the import-substitution industrialization model had shortcomings and the *cepalinos* quickly came to acknowledge this fact. In a book published in 1971, called *Change and Development*, Prebisch pointed out the limitations of this model as it had actually evolved. Latin American economies, he claimed, could no longer continue to rely on import substitution alone. Rather than concentrating on the production of basic goods for general consumption, the newly created industries had tended to concentrate on the production of consumption goods that benefited a small portion of the urban consumers. The industrialization model adopted by the Latin American countries produced growth but failed to produce equity, as it was unable to absorb the excess labour force, marginalizing large masses of people from its benefits.

In this sense, the import-substitution model adopted by Latin America after the Second World War was inefficient in achieving a significant reduction of poverty and income concentration in the continent. Latin America became less poor in the second half of the twentieth century, and this is something to be applauded, but its indices of inequality, which were already comparatively high in 1950, remained so throughout the period 1950–80. The costs of this process included high inflation levels – a further object of concern of Prebisch and the *cepalinos*, which accelerated at an unprecedented rate near the end of the century. These costs also included a growing foreign debt and a bloated, inefficient and corrupt public sector. The integration of the continent itself, a dream nurtured by ECLAC from its very beginning, moved at the speed of a turtle.

From the academic point of view, the Latin American School of Economics did not acquire many followers outside the continent. There are very few mentions of it in the international literature of the history of economic thought, macroeconomics and growth economics. One exception is found in Thirlwall and McCombie (1994, pp. 256–7), who refer to the importance of Prebisch in the construction of center-periphery models of growth and development. (The authors build an equation, which would later be adopted in post-Keynesian growth models.)

Be that as it may, the most important feature of the Latin American School is the fact that its authors were thoroughly concerned with the practical relevance of their writings. This is not a prerogative of this school, as we learn from Milberg (1996), who claims that in the field of international economics, researchers have been persistently concerned about the relevance of policy. Nevertheless, this is something to be praised, in times when ultra-formalism tends to dominate a significant part of the academic scene. Influenced as they were by the German Historical School, the *cepalinos* fully recognized the prescriptive nature of economics. Their writings show an explicit commitment to values such as economic development, social welfare and equity. The *cepalinos* wanted to learn the relevant theory and to assemble the relevant statistics, but they also wanted to say something important and true about their Latin American world. In this sense, they mobilized some broad-based economic expertise in order to propose economic and social changes, thus bridging the gap between what they learned in the textbooks and the outside world.

Notes

1. Among these writings two were specially path-breaking: the essay called 'The economic development of Latin America and its principal problems', presented for the first time in June 1949, during the ECLAC general assembly held in Havana, Cuba; and the introductory part of the *Economic Survey of Latin America 1949*, presented during the ECLAC general assembly held in Montevideo, Uruguay, in May 1950.

2. This is what Hodgson (2001) would call the neglected problem of historical specificity, which he considers to be a problem of vital significance for the social sciences, fully recognized by all the leading members of the German Historical School. It addresses the limits of explanatory unification in the social sciences, in the

sense that they must build theories that are sensitive to historical and geographical variations. In the author's own words:

'... differences between different systems could be so important that the theories and concepts used to analyse them must also be substantially different, even if they share some common precepts. A fundamentally different reality may require a different theory. This, in rough outline, is the problem of historical specificity.' (Hodgson, 2001, p. xiii)

References

Burger, Hillary, 1999, *An Intellectual History of the ECLA Culture, 1948 to 1964*. Boston, MA: Harvard University Press.

Hodgson, Geoffrey, 2001, *How Economics Forgot History*. London and New York: Routledge.

Milberg, William, 1996, 'The rhetoric of policy relevance in international economics', *Journal of Economic Methodology*, 4 (2), 199–200.

Prebisch, Raúl, 1948, 'Desarollo Económico de América Latina y sus Principales Problemas'. Santiago: CEPAL, E/CN.12/0089, 87 pp., (published in English as 'The economic development of Latin America and its principal problems.' UN E/CN. 12/89 Rev.1.

Prebisch, Raúl, 1971, *Change and Development: Latin America's Great Task*, New York: Praeger.

Prebisch, Raúl, 1987, 'Cinco Etapas de mi Pensamiento sobre el Desarrollo'. *Comércio Exterior*, 37 (5).

Thirlwall, A P and McCombie, J S L, 1994 *Economic Growth and the Balance of Payments Constraint*, St. Martin's Press.

United Nations, Economic Commission for Latin America, 1951. *Economic Survey of Latin America 1949*, Santiago: United Nations.

31.

DRIVING A CAR WITH NO STEERING WHEEL AND NO ROAD MAP:NEOCLASSICAL DISCOURSE AND THE CASE OF INDIA[1]

Matthew McCartney

Neoclassical economics is based, as is any school of economics, on certain assumptions. It is my contention here that too often these assumptions have served to narrow its analytical perspective. In particular the analysis of economic liberalisation has been limited to accounts chronicling its implementation. Analysis is very seldom concerned with the practical impact on issues such as productivity, employment, social stability, etc. This is examined here with particular reference to India in its 'liberalising' period after 1991.

Economics and assumptions

Assumptions make life easier. In partial equilibrium analysis *ceteris paribus*[2] allows a researcher to turn his attention from a bewildering array of possible general equilibrium interactions and reach a commonsense conclusion. A demand curve slopes downwards; a higher price of apples will reduce the quantity consumed. There is no pressing reason to explain the endlessly complex interactions with markets for oranges, bananas, guavas ... Assumptions in economics offer simplification; they give to a question a parsimonious structure, enabling the researcher to focus on the heart of the problem. Altering the assumptions and gauging the impact on the conclusions enables the robustness of the model to be analysed. Even in a patently unrealistic abstraction, such as the Walrasian general equilibrium model, assumptions provide a benchmark. Once we drop the assumption of perfect information we can analyse the impact on welfare of asymmetric information in exchange; of externalities and imperfect competition in production. Properly utilized, the Walrasian general equilibrium provides us a gateway to the rich analysis of Stiglitz, Akerlof et al.[3]

In neoclassical economics assumptions obscure underlying economic processes. Results may be totally contingent on an assumption included for mathematical convenience. Ultimately assumptions may serve to distract the researcher from the heart of the issue.

> Theories can therefore be judged by their assumptions to some extent, if one has an intelligent taxonomy of assumptions. A theory may well draw power from 'unrealistic' assumptions if those assumptions assert, rightly, that some factors are unimportant in determining the phenomenon under investigation. But it will be hobbled if those assumptions specify the domain of the theory, and the real world phenomena are outside that domain. (Keen, 2002, p. 153)

Efficient Growth (By Assumption)

By assumption individuals are rational and exchange is voluntary. Under perfect competition, consumption will be distributed inter-temporally efficiently. Profit maximizing firms will utilise these available resources and optimise investment decisions. The growth path over time reflects preferences of individual agents, hence by assumption it must be efficient.

Economic reform (comprising stabilization and structural adjustment) is based on this assumption of efficient growth. The two components are intrinsically linked. Stabilization ensures that growth will be sustainable, reducing inflation, government budget deficits and any trade imbalance.[4] Once stabilization is achieved, the reform process (synonymous with liberalisation) is simply an accelerator.

Structural adjustment comprises all those policies that may interfere with optimising decisions by consumers and firms. Tariffs must be reduced to align domestic with world prices. Privatization will ensure that decisions are made by rational profit-maximizing entrepreneurs. Removal of minimum wage legislation enables agents to make voluntary and hence mutually beneficial exchanges in the labour market. There is no question of steering the economy, simply of speeding up (deepening is the typical metaphor) or slowing down the process of transition from dirigisme to a free market.

Neoclassical analysis typically focuses nearly exclusively on the depth, pace and implementation of reforms. A typical example is the slowdown in economic growth in India after 1996. There is a broad consensus among neoclassical economists on the need for a 'second generation' of reforms to deepen those launched in 1991, to liberalise those areas hitherto neglected – especially the labour market and privatization. Growth has stalled, and hence the accelerator needs pressing.

Liberalisation, Means and Ends

Much of the intellectual artillery for the neoclassical counter-revolution in economics was derived from close study of the experience of countries that had pursued strategies of import substitution in the post-war period.[5] Industry was found to be high cost, capital intensive and hence generating little employment. Far from achieving self-sufficient industrialization, such countries continued their dependence on imports of capital goods and inputs. The counterpart of industrialization was a general discrimination against agriculture.

This type of analysis provided important antecedents for the shift to strategies of outward orientation often as intrinsic parts of structural adjustment programs from the 1980s onwards.[6]

However the widespread adoption of the neo-liberal agenda has not seen a complementary pattern of analysis. The success of 'reform' is not typically measured in terms of employment, inequality, and growth. Rather:

> The problem was that many of these policies became ends in themselves, rather than means to more equitable and sustainable growth. In doing so these policies were pushed too far, too fast, and to the exclusion of other policies that were needed. (Stiglitz, 2002, p. 53)

A good example of the neoclassical evaluation of liberalisation in India is provided by Ahluwalia[7] (2002) and Bajpai[8] (2002). Ahluwalia makes the claim that,

> … we consider the cumulative outcome of ten years of gradualism to assess whether the reforms have created an environment that can support 8 percent GDP growth, which is the government's target. (Ahluwalia, 2002, p. 69)

Ahluwalia retreats into a typical twofold analysis, considering first whether growth is sustainable – examining as a consequence trends in the fiscal deficit, current account deficit and foreign exchange reserves; and then cataloguing how far liberalisation has been implemented – tariff reductions, degree of integration with the world economy,[9] removal of price controls, deregulation.[10]

Bajpai (2002) follows the same track. He compiles a review of liberal policy reforms – devaluation, current account convertibility, trade liberalisation, encouraging FDI inflows, opening the capital market to portfolio investment, permitting domestic companies access to foreign capital markets. Bajpai does not even make passing reference to the impact of these 'reforms' in any other context than the change in integration with India and the world economy. He notes, over the course of the 1990s that the weighted average tariff fell from 90 to less than 30 per cent, foreign investment increased from 0.1 to 1 per cent of GDP and the share of trade increased from 18 to 30 per cent of GDP.

The underlying assumptions of voluntary exchange and rational optimising individuals mean that it must by definition be the case that the level of growth reflects individual preferences and hence maximizes welfare in a free market. The successful outcome of reform and the degree of implementation of liberalisation are collapsed by a priori assumption into the same meaning.

There is, it is assumed, no need to examine the impact of liberalisation on the productivity and level of investment, the degree of social cohesion, political and social stability, the level of spending on R&D or the diversification of exports into more dynamic industrial sectors.[11]

Liberalisation, reform and a roadmap

There is no roadmap because by assumption neoclassical economics does not admit the possibility of an alternative.

Rodrik (2000) argues to the contrary that integration with the world economy cannot substitute for a development strategy. Development is increasingly viewed as synonymous with global integration and with trade and investment being used as yardsticks for evaluating government policy. In actual fact 'integration' may crowd out alternatives. Rodrik suggests globalization should be evaluated in terms of the needs of development, not vice versa.

It is clear, that although there exists a near consensus on the positive relationship between openness and growth,

... there is a dirty little secret in international trade analysis. The measurable costs of protectionist policies – the reductions in real income that can be attributed to tariffs and import quotas – are not all that large. (Krugman, 1995, p. 31)

And there is another fact often forgotten. Liberalisation and integration are not concerned solely with the removal of controls and unwinding of government intervention. They also have demanding institutional requirements. Rodrik notes that to comply with the full panoply of WTO obligations (customs, phyto and sanitary, intellectual property rights, etc.) would cost the typical LDC $150m. The small gains from trade noted by Krugman are undoubtedly offset by the potentially enormous gains from an alternative – such as basic education for girls.[12]

Liberalisation, Implementation and Crisis

The neo-liberal discourse has not reacted to crises by evaluating their underlying assumptions, but instead adding layers of complexity to preserve them. To the concern with the pace and depth of implementation have been added other considerations.

Liberalisation in the Southern Cone countries of Latin America in the early 1980s saw rapid capital account liberalisation and large budget/trade deficits. This generated huge capital inflows, consequent currency overvaluation, deindustrialization, debt accumulation and inevitable collapse. There was no fundamental attention to assumptions in response, no puzzling that in the case of Chile at least the vast bulk of the accumulated debt was private[13] so could not by definition be considered a problem. The concept of *sequencing* of liberalisation emerged, specifically that a fiscal deficit should be corrected before the capital account is liberalised. With a similar crisis in Asia in 1997, sequencing implies prudential regulation of the banking sector before capital account liberalisation.

The economic disintegration of Russia in the years following 1989[14] despite a bold pursuit of liberalisation (price reform, privatization, abandonment of planning) and rapid democratisation generated much discussion of the relative merits of *gradualism* over *shock therapy* and the importance of *institutions*. An evident example is that privatization without a functioning legal system in the midst of an economic collapse will generate compelling incentives for asset mining among managers and workers.

Analysis of liberalisation can be likened to driving a car with no steering wheel – there is only one path of reform (from dirigisme to a free market), the only item of control is the accelerator (the speed and depth of implementation), and there is of course no road map (there is no alternative). To extend the analogy (too far), even at its worst moments, when neoclassical theorising careers through red lights – in the Southern Cone countries in the 1980s, in Russia in the 1990s – there is no critical evaluation of underlying assumptions, only ever more convoluted refinements to preserve them.

Notes

1. Grateful thanks to Ashwin and Alan for invaluable comments.
2. Other things being equal.
3. See for example Stiglitz (1986).
4. Private sector induced trade deficits, representing an excess of (optimal) private sector investment over (optimal) private sector savings reflect efficient decisions of optimising consumers so do not represent a macroeconomic problem.
5. For the case of India see Bhagwati and Desai (1970), Bhagwati and Srinivasan (1975).
6. The experience of East Asia may have been wrongly interpreted as one of 'outward-orientated' free trade rather than a strategy of export promotion. The latter may imply an increase in government intervention through a mechanism such as export subsidies.
7. Finance Minister in 1991–6, working in the Congress Government which launched the first generation of liberalising reforms.
8. One of the famously influential American-based non-resident Indian economists who have done so much to promote the agenda of liberalisation in India over the 1990s.
9. Exports plus imports as a share of GDP and level of Foreign Direct Investment.
10. There is momentary concern with other potential determinants of growth, infrastructure provision and education, but this does not detract from the primary thrust which is concerned not with 'an environment to support eight percent growth' but the sustainability and implementation of liberalisation.
11. See variously Athukorala and Sen (2002, Chapter 7), Rodrik (1999), Fosu (1996), Barro (1991), etc for discussions of these issues and their positive role on economic growth.
12. See Sen (1999).
13. Unlike Argentina the public sector budget was in balance.
14. Under IMF tutelage in the 1990s industrial output declined by a larger share than during the whole of the Second World War.

References

Ahluwalia, M S (2002), 'Economic reforms in India Since 1991: has gradualism worked?' (*Journal of Economic Perspectives*, 16:3).
Bajpai, N (2002), 'A decade of economic reforms in India: the unfinished agenda' – (Centre for International Development, Harvard University working paper no. 89).

Barro, R (1991), 'Economic growth in a cross section of countries' (*Quarterly Journal of Economics*, 106).

Bhagwati, J N and P Desai (1970), 'India: planning for industrialisation, industrialisation and trade policies since 1951' (Delhi, Oxford University Press).

Bhagwati, J N and T.N.Srinivasan (1975), 'Foreign trade regimes and economic development: India', (Delhi, Macmillan).

Fosu, A.K (1996), 'Primary exports and economic growth in developing countries' (*World Economy*, 19:5).

Keen, S (2002), 'Debunking economics: the naked emperor of the social sciences', (New York: Pluto Press).

Krugman. P (1995), 'Dutch tulips and emerging markets' (*Foreign Affairs*, July/August).

Rodrik, D (1999), 'Where did all the growth go? External shocks, social conflict, and growth collapses', (*Journal of Economic Growth*, 4).

Rodrik, D (2000), 'Can integration into the world economy substitute for a development strategy' (World Bank EBGDE European Conference, 26–8 June).

Stiglitz, J E (1986), 'The new development economics', (*World Development*, 14:2).

Stiglitz, J E (2002), 'Globalisation and its discontents', (London: Penguin).

32.

DYNAMIC VERSUS STATIC EFFICIENCY: THE CASE OF TEXTILE EXPORTS FROM BANGLADESH AND THE DEVELOPMENTAL STATE

Matthew McCartney

This chapter begins by outlining the neoclassical theory of efficiency, using international trade in Bangladesh as a case study. This notion of efficiency is extremely narrow, and concerned only with the allocation of a given quantity of resources. Competition is better modelled as a dynamic process. This difference is considered in the context of Bangladesh. The phase-out of the WTO's Multi-Fibre Arrangement (MFA) quota regime will lead to intensified international competition for textile exports. Dynamic efficiency can be defined as a virtuous circle of increasing productivity, output and wages (the high-road). Likewise a vicious circle of reduced wages, longer hours and intensified working conditions is possible (the low-road). Neoclassical economics has no means to distinguish between these two processes, if all returns are equalized at the margin it is perfectly possible for both to be considered efficient. Dynamic efficiency is argued here to be an alternative paradigm to neoclassical economics. The implications for economic analysis and policymaking are briefly considered. The principal conclusion of this chapter is that the narrow view of efficiency has restricted the relevance of neoclassical economics. A more realistic interpretation of how economies function as dynamic rather than static entities is important in properly evaluating the conflicting and complementary roles of government intervention and the free market. The most important implication of dynamic efficiency is in setting a theoretical basis for the economic analysis of the developmental state.

Neoclassical theory: liberalisation and comparative advantage

The explicit theoretical rationale of liberalisation according to neoclassical economics is to achieve an efficient (static) allocation of resources. The link to economic growth is implicit, rational individuals will save according to criteria such as the life-cycle hypothesis, and profit maximizing firms will utilise these available resources to invest efficiently. In a free market there is no such thing as growth that is too slow – growth reflects the time preferences of individual agents. Price signals link the short and long run, and there is no need to consider the two separately.

In international trade neoclassical economics offers a strong theoretical prediction. The theory of comparative advantage states that a country will export goods intensive in its abundant factor, and import those intensive in its scarce factor. For South Asia with a relatively low area of land per person[1] and abundant labour, exports should principally comprise labour-intensive manufactured goods rather than primary sector products. Structural adjustment should see a shift in the composition of production from capital-intensive import substituting industries[2] to export-orientated labour-intensive industries. A well-documented and lauded example of such growth[3] is the phenomenal expansion of the ready-made garment sector (RMG) in Bangladesh. Exports were negligible in 1979/80, by the late 1990s Bangladesh had become the twelfth largest apparel exporter in the world, and the RMG sector accounted for about 76 per cent of total export earnings. By the late 1990s the industry employed 1.5 million people, 90 per cent of them women. The change is efficient from a neoclassical perspective, the abundant resource (unskilled/female labour) has been re-allocated (rural–urban migration) in a rational response to price incentives.

Efficiency in neoclassical Economics

The neoclassical concept of efficiency is extremely narrow: this is revealed with striking clarity by an examination of four well-used microeconomics textbooks.[4] In general 'efficiency' gets only a passing mention and is entirely subsumed by the concept of Pareto efficiency.

In Gravelle and Rees (1992) and Kreps (1990) efficiency is solely a static concept concerned with the efficient level of output of public and private goods, efficient risk sharing, solution to bargaining, the Edgeworth Box and Walrasian equilibrium.[5] In Mas-Colell (1995) efficiency gets six entries in the index, while the Pareto concept appears 76 times. Kreps (1990) doesn't bother to separate them: 'Efficiency, see Pareto efficiency' (p. 824) notes the index; Pareto efficiency in its various forms appears 26 times. Also in Varian (1992) efficiency appears only as Pareto efficiency (p. 225).

The necessary requirements for Pareto efficiency (Gravelle and Rees, 1992, pp. 479–85) are 'efficient consumption', 'efficient input supply' and 'efficient input use' (production efficiency) and 'efficient output mix'. Theses are the 'three types of efficiency embodied in a Pareto optimal exercise' (Mas-Colell, 1995, p. 564). The first is *consumption efficiency*, where consumers have allocated their budgets to maximise their own well-being (utility maximization). The marginal rate of substitution between any two goods equals their price ratio. The second is *production efficiency*, where producers cannot alter the ratio of inputs to raise output or reduce the cost of a given volume of production. The marginal rate of technical substitution between any two inputs equals their price ratio. The final measure is *aggregate output efficiency*, where resources are allocated simultaneously to achieve both production and consumption efficiency, for example in a society of bipeds equal numbers of right and left shoes are produced. Utility and profit maximization will ensure consumption efficiency and the efficient use of inputs and composition of outputs.

Glancing again at the index in Gravelle and Rees (1992) at 'dynamic' reveals only a set of references that give more mathematical rigour to the concept of static equilibrium. By 'dynamic efficiency', neoclassical economics means the existence, stability and uniqueness of equilibrium. Dynamic analysis is shorn of any substance and asks simply whether an economy in equilibrium (existence) subject to an exogenous shock will return (stability) to its original position (unique). There are a few cases such as the cobweb model, which has a unique equilibrium but any deviation from it can produce an explosive divergence of price and output: such cases are given passing attention at best.

Imperfect information and market failure: a radical departure?

Theorising on imperfect information and markets failures appears to be a radical departure from the neoclassical paradigm. However this analysis implicitly accepts efficiency as being a static concept, Pareto efficiency as the benchmark and government policy as a means to make the world look more like the neoclassical theory.

If there exists a wedge between social and private costs (an externality), a taxation, subsidy or regulation can push the economy towards the overall social optimum. An optimal Pigouvian tax can replicate efficient allocation (see Mas-Colell et al., 1995, p. 355). Similarly government policy may help solve the preference revelation problem for public goods (see Varian, 1992, p. 425). There may be some problems government policy is unable to overcome such as moral hazard and asymmetric information in the market for bank loans. The market is then constrained to allocate resources in a second best world (see Stiglitz and Weiss, 1981). The very notion of 'second best' illustrates the striking normative preference for Pareto efficiency

It is not the analysis of market and information imperfections that force us to confront the implications of an alternative paradigm. The crucial assumption is an economy that is static, where efficiency is measured at a moment in time. In an alternative world, when we consider the dynamics of competition, investment and growth, what we mean by efficiency takes on a radically new meaning. An implication of this proposition is introduced in the context of future prospects for the Bangladeshi textile industry.

Competition is a Dynamic Process

As of 31 December 2004, with the final abolition of the MFA,[6] textile and clothing products will be subject to WTO rules. When the MFA was implemented in the 1970s Bangladesh was not considered to be a viable exporter, and consequently it was never subject to its strictures. Other potentially competitive exporters such as Sri Lanka, India, Pakistan and China have been subject to binding MFA quotas on apparel and textile exports. Bangladesh has been able to export into an open niche in world markets since the late 1970s, but after 2005 Bangladesh will face intensified competition on world markets.

There are broadly two potential outcomes, the low- and high-roads of competition. The latter is 'dynamically efficient', leading to rising wages and productivity over time. The concern of neoclassical economics with efficient allocation has no theoretical means to distinguish these two processes: as long as marginal equalities are retained according to neoclassical criteria even the low-road of competition could be judged efficient.

Dynamic efficiency and the low- and high-roads of competition

Bangladesh is currently most competitive in price sensitive, low-value, low-priced items.[7] Bangladesh has two options to compete after 2005, namely raising productivity or reducing costs.

a) The low-road of competition

Bangladesh could react to intensified competition by trying to enhance its price competitiveness within its existing niche by extending hours, reducing overheads (subcontracting) and intensifying work conditions (a low-road of competition). There is some evidence this path has already been pursued in the Indian textile industry.

The fragmentation, ruralization and casualization consistent with a low-road of competition has already had a profound impact in India. As early as the 1960s textile mills in Ahmedabad and Bombay began putting out weaving work to centralized power-loom units. Pharmaceutical firms in Bombay passed on work to smaller units located away from the high-wage industrial belt. From the 1970s there was a general increase in the use of contract, temporary and casual workers. The share of casual workers in large factory employment rose from 4.6 per cent in 1980/81 to more than 12 per cent in 1993/94.[8] Subcontracting was not a significant activity prior to 1970, but by 1978 it was a prominent activity in large factories with a share of 21 per cent of total employment.[9] In India the decline of large urban cotton mills and ruralization of the industry has been especially sharp.[10] This ruralization of labour is reflected in the fall in the average size of industrial units from 3.2 to 2.5 workers between 1961 and 1991. The fall in average employees per factory had occurred in most industries and has persisted throughout the 1970s and 1980s.[11]

b) The high-road of competition

A high-road of competition could consist of remaining in an existing production niche and raising productivity, or upgrading to a less (price-) competitive market niche to capture rents. In the RMG sector Bangladesh may compete by capacity building to enhance skills in fashion, design, cutting and technology upgrading, developing backward linkages to suppliers to shorten lead times, and improving the skills and training of management and workers.

Good policy can be defined as that which helps achieve a high-road response to competition. Dynamic efficiency is a situation characterised by a virtuous circle of higher productivity, output growth and higher wages rather than having a rigorous mathematical definition.

Dynamic efficiency, rents and learning

Dynamic efficiency is an alternative paradigm to neoclassical efficiency. In fact there is likely for various reasons to be trade-offs between static and dynamic efficiency. When considering dynamic efficiency, good policy cannot be mechanically judged in terms of whether it liberalises the economy, encourages competition or expands the freedom of decision-making. Policy is a far more nuanced process that has to be carefully evaluated in terms of its effect on the dynamics of investment, growth and competition.

a) Static and dynamic efficiency

One neoclassical assumption immediately disposed of when we consider dynamic efficiency is that no allocation or industrial structure is preferable to any other. In fact, while many allocations may be efficient, some are more (dynamically) efficient than others.

   Neoclassical theory argues that export structures are simply a product of comparative advantage and factor prices. The composition of exports does not matter; no set of activities is more desirable than any other. There are no externalities, so returns are equalized at the margin (efficient allocation). Lall (1999, p. 1,775) notes that spillover benefits for the whole economy are positively related and competitors' ease of market entry is negatively related to the technological complexity of a product. Dynamic efficiency creates the potential for the government to make industrial policy, rather than market or information failures. We can broadly define industrial policy as a deliberate action by the state to shift the structure of the economy away from its static comparative advantage to a structure offering more dynamic potential. We generate the first strong implication of our alternative paradigm: there may exist a trade-off between static and dynamic efficiency.

b) Profits and Efficiency

Profits in the neoclassical model are a temporary aberration of the market. Profits may exist temporarily before resources and factors flow into a sector and compete them away. In a dynamic world, profits (or more correctly rents) are useful to induce and reward learning in order to raise productivity or upgrade to higher value-added and fewer price-sensitive sectors. Learning is much like patents that reward innovation in a developed country.

Neoclassical economics assumes innovations in advanced countries and learning in less developed countries (LDC) are simply a matter of selecting the most appropriate. Innovation (shifting the production frontier) is distinct from mastering/adapting technology.[13] In truth, though much technology is tacit, experimentation and learning are necessary to understand the tacit elements and adapt them to local conditions. In practice, there is less difference between innovation in developed countries and industrialization based on learning already commercialized technology.

Investment in learning by one entrepreneur in discovering a commercial niche that can be profitably exploited is likely to lead to rapid imitation.[14] If such learning requires investment, the returns to which cannot be fully appropriated, entrepreneurs in LDCs face similar problems to innovators in developed countries. While neoclassical economics subscribes to the need for patent protection to generate an incentive for innovation, it advocates complete freedom of market entry in all other scenarios. LDC investors should not get patent protection no matter how high the (external) social return. Entrepreneurial learning is likely to be under-supplied. Profits/rents that reward and motivate learning may lead to a more dynamically efficient economy even if they are a sign of resource misallocation according to considerations of static allocative efficiency.

How do we evaluate policy?

Analysing policy intervention in the static neoclassical model is easy – anything that increases the scope of the free market and free decision-making is a good thing. When we consider our alternative paradigm, that of dynamic efficiency, analysing policy is much harder. Policy needs to increase the expected payoff to learning, hence it is important to distinguish firms that are engaged in costly learning and those who simply imitate the results of others' learning. The parallels with innovation and patent protection are evident.

Temporary trade protection may increase profits from learning but only for firms producing for the domestic market.[14] Trade protection does not discriminate between innovators and imitators. This will promote early entry and lower the expected return to learning. Export subsidies avoid the anti-export bias of trade protection but also fail to discriminate between learners and imitators. Export subsidies can be relatively good at discriminating between successful and unsuccessful performers ex-post.

Providing subsidies or government credit contingent on exporting can allow policy makers to discriminate between firms.

Dynamic efficiency and liberalisation

Neoclassical analysis of efficiency pre-supposes that good economic policy consists of removing constraints on the operation of the free market. Individuals are rational, so any constraints on voluntary options and mutual exchange can only reduce welfare and efficiency. One exception is that of game theory, or more precisely the 'prisoners dilemma'. This illustrates a situation in which individuals acting in their own self-interest generate a socially sub-optimal outcome. Some sort of constraint is necessary to prevent individuals rationally defecting to maximise the social return. The literature has typically analysed this in terms of extra-economic factors such as trust, culture or coercion. For example:

> ... an economy can perform well only to the extent that it is embedded in a well integrated society, and that a society exists only to the extent that it is capable of imposing normative constraints, or social obligations, on the pursuit of individual interest.[15]

This kind of analysis has not closely informed macro-economic policymaking, which remains heavily imbued with a liberalising bias. Once we consider efficiency in a dynamic rather than static perspective it is easy to generalise this finding from game theory: good economic policy cannot be reduced to removing constraints on rational actors. The pressure of competition may generate a counter-productive temptation of short-termism. Constraining obligations may on occasion increase productivity. Employers who are permanently prevented by high labour standards from being competitive as low-wage mass producers may be compelled to produce high-quality customised products. Constraints can open up otherwise unknown opportunities by making learning unavoidable. Having fewer choices may foreclose short-term remedies and stimulate strategic creativity beyond present interests and structures. The argument is sometimes made in the case of minimum wages, a form of intervention that it is impossible to support in a static neoclassical world.

This question is of immediate relevance to Bangladesh. Currently unions are forbidden from operating and organizing in export promotion zones where many of the RMG factories are located. Japanese and Korean foreign investors are threatening to withhold FDI should the law be amended.

Concerned institutions in the US motivated by 'fair trade' rhetoric are pressing for this to happen under threat of countervailing import duties. Placing a floor under the process of cost-cutting, longer hours and intensified working conditions may force producers to pursue a high-road to international competition.

Conclusion

Successful policy cannot simply be judged in terms of the degree to which markets are liberalised. Once we consider economies as dynamic rather than static entities and evaluate policy in terms of achieving dynamic not static efficiency, what we conceive of as good policy becomes far more nuanced. The impact of policy on learning and imitation is relatively clear, but the relative merits of trade protection, export and government subsidies are more subtle and complex. Certainly we can say liberalisation has to be carefully compared and evaluated against other possible policies; certainly liberalisation can only ever be a policy means to achieve a given end; it certainly cannot be judged an end in itself. Beginning with a benchmark of 'dynamic efficiency' we have arrived at the theory of the developmental state, and this is the archetype of a dynamically efficient economy. The developmental state is an alternative to neoclassical efficiency, not an occasional aberration and second best-solution to allocative inefficiency[16].

Notes

1. A Wood and M Calandrino, *When the Other Giant Awakes: Trade and Human Resources in India* (2000), University of Sussex, IDS mimeo.
2. These were prominent parts of the domestic industrial structure in India especially before liberalisation.
3. Y W Rhee, 'The catalyst model of development: lessons from Bangladesh's success with garment exports', *World Development*, (1990), 18:2, pp. 333–46. This paper argues that this growth was not due to liberalisation but to the Korean firm Daewoo providing a catalyst, in the form of FDI in the RMG sector, with a very heavy emphasis on developing indigenous capabilities in Bangladesh.
4. These are H Gravelle and R Rees (1992), *Microeconomics* (2nd edn) London, Longman (1992); H R Varian, *Microeconomic Analysis*, (3rd edn) London, W W Norton (1992); D M Kreps, *A Course in Microeconomic Theory*, London, Harvester Wheatsheaf, (1990); A Mas-Colell, M D Whitston and J R Green, *Microeconomic Theory*, Oxford, Oxford University Press (1995).
5. The nearest to an exception is repeated games (Game Theory).
6. The Multi-Fibre Arrangement, which places quotas on the exports of apparel and textiles from LDCs to developed countries.

7. All data from M Muqtada, A M Singh and M A Rashid (eds) et al, *Bangladesh: Economic and Social Challenges of Globalisation*, (Dhaka, University Press Limited, 2002).

8. K V Ramaswamy, 'The search for flexibility in indian manufacturing: new evidence on outsourcing activities', *Economic and Political Weekly*, (1999), 34:6, pp. 363–8.

9. B.Harriss-White, *India Working: Essays on Society and Economy*, Cambridge, Cambridge University Press (2003).

10. T Roy, in S Uchikawa (ed.), *Economic Reforms and Industrial Structure in India*, New Delhi, Manohar (2002), pp. 85–111.

11. R Nagaraj, 'Organised manufacturing employment', *Economic and Political Weekly*, (2000), p. 3446.

12. S Lall, 'Technological capabilities and industrialisation', *World Development*, 20:2, pp. 165–86; A H Amsden, 'Editorial: bringing production back in – understanding governments role in late Industrialisation', *World Development*, (1997), 25:4, pp. 469–80.

13. Y W Rhee (1990) notes that the number of export-orientated RMG factories in Bangladesh exploded after the single firm Desh proved it was a profitable proposition at the end of the 1970s: by 1985 there were 700 such firms.

14. R Hausmann and D Rodrik, 'Economic development as self-discovery', *Journal of Development Economics*, (2003), 72, pp. 603–33.

15. W Streeck in J R Hollingsworth and R Boyer, *Contemporary Capitalism: The Embeddedness of Institutions*, Cambridge, Cambridge University Press (1999), p. 199.

16. See H-J Chang, in M Woo-Cumings (ed.) *The Developmental State*, New York, Cornell University Press (1999).

PART 7:

IS ANYTHING WORTH KEEPING IN MICROECONOMICS?

33.

IS ANYTHING WORTH KEEPING IN STANDARD MICROECONOMICS?

Bernard Guerrien

The French students' movement against autism in economics started with a revolt against the disproportionate importance of microeconomics in economic teaching (Appendix I). The students complained that nobody had really proved to them that microeconomics was of any use; what is the point of going through "micro1", "micro2", "micro3", etc, using lots of mathematics to speak of fictitious households, fictitious enterprises and fictitious markets?

Actually, when one thinks about it, it turns out that microeconomics is simply "neoclassical theory". Realizing this, I agree with the French students when they say that:

1) In a course on economic theories, neoclassical theory should be taught alongside other economic theories (classical political economy, Marxist theory, Keynesian theory, etc) showing that it is just one among several other approaches;

2) The principal elements and assumptions of neoclassical theory (consumer and producer choice, general equilibrium existence theorems, and so on) should be taught with very little mathematics (or with none at all). The main reason being that it is essential for students to understand the economic meaning of assumptions made in mathematical language. As they study economics, and not mathematics, students must decide if these assumptions are relevant, or meaningful. But, to this end, assumptions must be expressed in clear English and not

in abstruse formulae. Only if assumptions, and models, are relevant, can it be of any interest to try to see what "results" or "theorems" can be deduced from them.

I am convinced that assumptions of standard microeconomics are *not at all* relevant. And I think that it is nonsense to say – as some people do (using the "as if" argument) – that relevant results can be deduced from assumptions that obviously contradict almost everything that we observe around us.

The main reason the teaching of microeconomics (or of "micro foundations" of macroeconomics) has been called "autistic" is that it is increasingly impossible to discuss real-world economic questions with microeconomists – and with almost all neoclassical theorists. They are trapped in their system, and don't in fact care about the outside world any more. If you consult any microeconomic textbook, it is full of maths (e.g. Kreps or Mas-Colell, Whinston and Green) or of "tales" (e.g. Varian or Schotter), without real data (occasionally you find "examples", or "applications", with numerical examples – but they are purely fictitious, invented by the authors).

At first, French students got quite a lot of support from teachers and professors: hundreds of teachers signed petitions backing their movement – specially pleading for "pluralism" in teaching the different ways of approaching economics. But when the students proposed a precise programme of studies, without "micro1", "micro2", "micro3" ... without macroeconomics "with microfoundations" or with a "representative agent" – almost all teachers refused, considering that it was "too much" because "students must learn all these things, even with some mathematical details". When you ask them "why?", the answer usually goes something like this: "Well, even if we, personally, never use the kind of 'theory' or 'tools' taught in microeconomics courses (since we are regulationist, evolutionist, institutionalist, conventionalist, etc) – surely there are people who do 'use' and 'apply' them, even if it is in an 'unrealistic', or 'excessive' way."

But when you ask those scholars who do "use these tools", especially those who do a lot of econometrics with "representative agent" models, they answer (if you insist quite a bit): "OK, I agree with you that it is nonsense to represent the whole economy by the (inter-temporal) choice of one agent – consumer and producer – or by a unique household that owns a unique firm; but if you don't do that, you don't do anything!"

There are also some microeconomists who try to prove, by experiments or by some kind of econometrics, that people act rationally. But, to do that you don't need to know envelope theorems, compensated (Hicksian) demand or Slutsky matrix! Indeed, "experimental economics" has a very tenuous relation with "theory": it tests very elementary ideas (about rational choice or about markets) in very simple situations – even if, in general, people don't act as theory predicts, but that is another question.

Microeconomics: "unrealistic" or "irrelevant"?

Most of the time microeconomics is criticized because of its "lack of realism". But "lack of realism" doesn't necessarily mean "irrelevance"; the expression is usually understood to mean that the theory in question is "more or less distant from reality", or as giving a more or less acceptable proxy of reality (people differing about the quality of the approximation). The idea is implicitly this:

> If we work hard, relaxing some assumptions and using more powerful mathematical theorems, microeconomics will progressively became more and more realistic. There are then – at least – some interesting concepts and results in microeconomics, that a healthy, post-autistic, economic theory should incorporate.

That's what Geoff Harcourt implicitly says in the *post-autistic economics review*, no.11, when he writes:

> Against this macroeconomic background, modern microeconomics has a bias towards examining the behaviour of competitive markets (as set out most fully and rigorously in the Arrow–Debreu model of general equilibrium), not as reference points but as approximations to what is actually going on. Of course, departures from them are taught, increasingly by the clever application of game theory. Moreover, the deficiencies of real markets of all sorts are examined in the light of the implications, for example, of the findings of the asymmetric information theorists (three of whom – George Akerlof, Michael Spence, and Joe Stiglitz – have just (10/10/01) been awarded this year's Nobel Prize. From Amartya Sen on, the Nobel Prize electors seem to be back on track).

What is Harcourt saying? He is telling us that the Arrow–Debreu model has something to do with "the behaviour of competitive markets"; he is saying that game theory can be cleverly "applied"; he says that there are "findings" made by Akerlof, Spence and Stiglitz. If all this is true, then students have to learn general equilibrium theory (as giving "approximations to what is actually going on"), game theory, asymmetric information theory, and so on. That means that they need micro1, micro2, micro3... courses (consumer and producer choice, perfect and imperfect competition, game theory, "market failures", etc).

I don't agree at all with Geoff Harcourt because:

1. The Arrow–Debreu model has nothing to do with competition and markets: it is a model of a "highly centralized" economy, with a benevolent auctioneer doing many things, and with stupid price-taker agents;
2. Game theory cannot be "applied": it only tells little "stories" about the possible consequences of rational individuals' choices made once and for all and simultaneously by all of them.
3. Akerlof, Spence and Stiglitz have no new "findings", they just present, in a mathematical form, some very old ideas – long known by insurance companies and by those who organize auctions and second-hand markets.
4. Amartya Sen, as an economist, is a standard microeconomist (that is what he was awarded the Nobel Prize for): only the vocabulary is different ("capabilities", "functionings", etc.).

But, perhaps, not all "post autistic" economists will agree with me.

It would be good then that they give their opinion and, more generally, that we try to answer, in detail, the question: *Is anything worth keeping in microeconomics – and in neoclassical theory? If there is, what is it?*

34.

IN DEFENCE OF BASIC ECONOMIC REASONING

Bruce J Caldwell

In the previous chapter, Bernard Gurrien poses the provocative question, "Is there anything worth keeping in standard microeconomics?" His answer seems to be, "not much." Gurrien complains about the highly formalized nature of modern microeconomic theory, about the use of assumptions that describe neither the world nor the actions of the people that populate it. He finds much formal theory useless and irrelevant for helping us to understand how the world works.

I agree with many of Gurrien's criticisms of formal, highly mathematicized microeconomic theory. I disagree, though, with his conclusion that the irrelevance of the theory undermines microeconomics. In my opinion, there is a body of economic reasoning, something that might be called "basic economic reasoning" that can and should be separated out from what might be called "formal microeconomic theory." Much of basic economic reasoning is in fact microeconomic in nature, but it preceded the latter temporally in terms of its development and it does not depend on formal economic theory for its validity or usefulness. It is my contention that basic economic reasoning is truly important. My fear is that if we take Gurrien's advice, we will throw out the standard economic reasoning "baby" with the formal economic theory "bathwater."

I will elaborate on these claims by citing some personal examples. In recent years I have taught both a one-semester "everything you want to know about economics" course as well as the principles of microeconomics course to American undergraduates. I use very little mathematics in either course. With the exception of a little algebra for calculating elasticities, all other concepts are handled graphically, with production possibilities curves and supply and demand diagrams being the chief graphical tools employed. Even with this elementary set of tools, by the end of the course students have learned a lot about how the world works. Their education is a practical one, one that allows them better to read a paper and to understand economic issues that are discussed in the news. Of course what I am doing in the classroom is not unique; many other economists do the same things in their own principle courses.

Basically, I use graphs to tell stories about the world. The graphs alone are useless without the stories, and similarly, the stories lose all focus without the graphs. So, for example, in discussing price fixing we use a supply and demand diagram to distinguish between price ceilings and price supports. When price ceilings are binding, one can expect to see excess demand, or shortages, and one also often encounters such things as non-price rationing, deterioration in product quality, and black markets. With these general concepts, we can then explore such diverse phenomena as rent controls in New York City, black markets for tickets to the theater and sporting events, the use of ration coupons during times of war, queues at gasoline stations in the US in the 1970s (when gas prices were controlled), and the ubiquitous queues that one used to observe in East Bloc countries under communism. The price support diagram is useful for analysing current policies (like agricultural price supports or the minimum wage law) as well as those that have been proposed (comparable worth policies).

Once the concept of elasticities has been introduced, the diagrams can be used to analyse everything from the incidence of taxation to the "paradox of plenty" in agriculture (good growing seasons can lead to a reduction in farmer's revenues if demand for their product is inelastic) to the reason why a successful "war on drugs" that managed to reduce the supply of illegal drugs would put more revenue into the pockets of drug dealers. (If the demand for drugs is inelastic, a rise in the price of drugs causes a less than proportionate fall in quantity demanded, so total revenue increases.) Production possibilities curves can be used whenever the discussion focuses on opportunity costs and the necessity of making trade-offs.

Basic economic reasoning and simple diagrams can also be used to tell stories that go beyond economics to what might be called political economy. The recent history of agricultural price supports in the US provides numerous insights into how politics and economics interact. In 1996 a law was passed that was supposed to phase out agricultural price supports gradually, so that they would be gone by 2002. In order to induce farm interests to accept the law, payments in the initial years were quite generous. But as we got closer and closer to 2002, and prices for agricultural products began falling (this was exactly what was supposed to happen, of course), farm interests declared a "crisis" in their industry. For the past few years, "emergency" farm legislation was passed by Congress to help agricultural interests survive their "crisis." The recurring crises have in turn prompted calls for a "comprehensive" farm bill to deal with the problems on a permanent basis. And sure enough, after September 11 some have begun referring to the new proposed legislation as a Farmland Security Bill. A few years ago, a dot.com at the end of a company name was supposed to ensure that investors would love it. Now in Congress putting the word "Security" into a bill's name will help to ensure its speedy passage.

Many other examples could be given. The recent decision by the Bush administration to place tariffs of about 30 per cent on steel imports was analysed in one newspaper under the wonderful byline, "In big steel states, the Bush democrat may be born." Ohio, West Virginia and Pennsylvania are major steel-producing states, and the outcome of mid-term elections there may be crucial in deciding who controls Congress. So again steel has had help, even though it is one of the most protected of all American industries: past studies have estimated that it costs American consumers about $750,000 (in terms of higher prices paid) for every steelworker's job saved. That number will need to be updated in the light of this recent event, especially given that other nations have begun retaliating with tariffs of their own that will further raise the prices that consumers face.

Though basic economic reasoning is simple, it is not simplistic, and indeed, it often leads one to results that are not at all obvious. For example, the idea that the incidence of taxation depends on the elasticities of supply and demand, and not on whether a tax is initially paid by a buyer or a seller of a good, is not at all intuitive, but is crucial if one wants to understand who actually bears the burden of a tax. Similarly, the idea that there can be gains from trade even when one country has an absolute advantage in the production of goods – the fundamental idea of comparative advantage – is not one that many non-economists have mastered.

Some will say that basic economic reasoning is not valid because it rests on faulty foundations – one must assume that agents are perfectly rational, with complete information, trading in perfectly competitive markets to get its results. This simply confuses formal mathematical theory with basic economic reasoning. In my opinion, basic economic reasoning does not depend on formal microeconomic theory for its validity. Now, to be sure, economists have not been very good at identifying just what it does depend on. That is a topic for economic methodology, and over the years various contending views have been advanced. My own intuition is that there may well be multiple "foundations" that help to explain why different parts of the theory may work. In any event, my own confidence in basic economic reasoning has less to do with the fact that I know why it works, then with the fact that it does work: as my examples should demonstrate, it can prove to be extremely useful in organizing and understanding various and often very diverse social phenomena. The proof of the pudding is in the eating, and in this regard basic economic reasoning seems to me to provide much upon which to feast.

There will of course be the complaint of those who believe that basic economic reasoning is simply ideology dressed up as science. For them, to say that "we live in a world in which scarcity makes choice necessary" is an ideological statement; or to assert that "producing goods for which one has a comparative advantage permits gains from trade" is a not-so-covert defence of globalization; and so on. To this I would reply that I think of the statements of basic economic reasoning as being positive rather than normative claims. (This is not to say that they are easily testable claims.) I would further rejoin that those who think that basic economic reasoning is simply a defence of capitalism should look once again at the socialist calculation debate, and in particular at the positions articulated by the defenders of market socialism, or for those who would like to go back further, at the Austrian economist Friedrich von Wieser's *Natural Value*. These economists recognized that an understanding of economic reasoning was necessary even if one was in favour of organizing a socialist economy. As one wag put it on the recent television production of the book *Commanding Heights*, ignoring how markets operate is much like ignoring the winds and the tides – you do so at your peril.

In conclusion, I join with Bernard Gurrien in lamenting the turn of the profession towards microeconomic models of ever increasing formal complexity. Explaining why the profession has gone down this road is something that has increasingly captured the attention of our (ever diminishing number, alas, of) historians of economic thought. But we should not conclude that microeconomics is of no value. Basic economic reasoning was there before the advent of such modelling, and it remains a powerful tool today for understanding how the world works.

35.

DOCTRINE-CENTRED VERSUS PROBLEM-CENTRED ECONOMICS

Peter Dorman

Bruce Caldwell's response to Bernard Guardian illustrates exactly what is wrong with mainstream economics as it is taught and applied: it is doctrinaire. He believes that he has made an advance over more typical teaching approaches by scaling down the math, but I can see no change in the overall project of imposing a dogma in the name of an academic discipline. It is sad to have to conclude this, given Caldwell's large contributions to economic methodology, but there it is.

His examples of "economic reasoning" for the improvement of undergraduate minds are worth a closer look. I could take up all of them, but I will confine myself to the two that are given the most attention, the role of price supports in agriculture and the advantages of free trade over protection.

Agriculture

Agricultural policy has many dimensions. It is a social policy that can support, change or weaken rural culture. It is certainly an ecological policy, whether by intent or not. It influences food security in the face of ineradicable uncertainties in supply. It is competition policy, favouring either centralized or decentralized market structures. And, or course, it has a political economic dimension, responding to the various interest groups that have a stake in the choices made by government.

What do Caldwell's price-ceiling diagrams tell us? If they are like all the other price-ceiling diagrams I have seen, they announce that, as a first-round effect, price supports are economically inefficient, sending false signals to the marketplace and incurring deadweight loss. The second-round effect, alluded to by Caldwell, is political: rent seeking that further absorbs resources and distorts policy.

It seems obvious to me that the price-ceiling analysis, while it has some value, is hopelessly inadequate as a primary guide to what to do about agriculture. The role of uncertainty and time, of environmental externalities and public goods (such as a healthy rural culture) ought to be central to any serious analysis of this topic, and to short-circuit the process in the way Caldwell describes is to abandon higher-order for lower-order thinking. In practical terms, it also silences students, because their common-sense intuitions about agriculture (many of my own students have rural backgrounds) often have no standing amid the supply and demand curves.

Trade

Caldwell would have students learn the theory of comparative advantage as a guide to making sense of globalization and combating the naive belief that interference with trade can ever be a good idea. He talks in precise dollar terms about the cost per job saved by tariffs on steel, as though the complex effects of such a policy can be perfectly known and calculated. Yet trade policy is complex, and it is fair to say that economists have not yet put together a convincing model of how the system works. In particular, comparative advantage depends on the assumption of balanced trade at the margin – that every extra dollar or euro of imports will be automatically and simultaneously balanced by an equivalent additional value of exports. If this were true in the real world, of course, we would have a simpler, more pleasant life: no country would experience balance of payments crises, there would be no pressure on countries to be "competitive", and one policy alone – free trade – would be all we would need to follow. (For a more extended critique of this sort of cost-of-protectionism analysis, see Dorman, 2001.)

Unfortunately, life is not like that. Laid-off steel workers will not automatically find jobs in exporting sectors, and not only because they have the wrong skills or live in the wrong cities, but also because the effect of more steel imports may simply be that the trade deficit increases. (Yes, I know, there is also a theory that says that this can't happen because it would require investors to change their already-perfect international allocation of asset positions. No comment!) This doesn't mean that protective tariffs are a desirable policy response, just that an a priori dismissal of them contradicts the creative, disciplined thinking that teachers ought to encourage in their students – and that denying the legitimacy of reasonable ideas that might occur to students pushes them into passivity or out of the door altogether.

Conclusions

I have two concluding thoughts. First, the level of math is not the issue. One can be dogmatic with blackboard diagrams and open-minded with reams of equations. In general, less math is generally better, because it lowers the barrier to critical thinking, but simply getting rid of math is not the point. Second, the solution is not to replace one dogma by another or even by a menu of competing dogmas, but to redefine, for our students and ourselves, economics from being a doctrine-centered to a problem-centered enterprise. Instead of agreed-upon theories dictating simplified or completely fictitious examples (with their widgets, perfectly behaved functions, etc), real-life cases in all their messiness should be the measure of any theories we throw at them. Such an economics would not only be post-autistic, but also a lot more fun.

Reference:

Dorman, Peter, 2001, *The Free Trade Magic Act.* Economic Policy Institute briefing paper. For details visit: http://www.epinet.org/briefingpapers/dorman-bp2/dorman-bp2.pdf.

36.

YES, THERE IS SOMETHING WORTH KEEPING IN MICROECONOMICS

Deirdre McCloskey

Bernard Guerrien is severe on Messrs (no Mesdames, I note) Varian, Schotter, Kreps, Mas-Collel, Whinston and Green, and I think he's quite right to be so. The usual idea of "microeconomics" is, as Guerrien avers, formalism useful only for the generation of articles in the *American Economic Review* and worse. It's scandalous that game theory and GE and overlapping generations and other mere existence theorems are taught as "tools." As we say in American English (with thanks to Yiddish): tools, schmools. No physicist would consider such stuff scientific. She would want tools that can measure.

The problem comes partly from a terminological confusion. "Theorist" has come to mean in economics "guys trained in mathematics-department math." (I note again that this Hilbert/Bourbaki style has nothing, nada, rien, to do with the sort of math that physicists and engineers actually use to investigate the world; go have a look at *The Physical Review* and you'll see what I mean.) Since the "theorists" so defined can't do anything else (like give a substantive course in economic history or in urban economics), they get assigned to first-year graduate courses. It's their comparative advantage, considering that the department has made the mistake of hiring them in the first place.

The result has been a catastrophe for economic education. Most economists arrive on the job without knowing how to think like economists. In fact they've been specifically and elaborately trained by the "theorists" *not* to think like economists, but to think like Hilbert/Bourbaki mathematicians, though of course to a childishly simple standard. (By the way, a distinguished committee of the American Economic Association was some years ago on the edge of doing something about the catastrophe; Bob Lucas vetoed the proposal, since he wants economics to carry on being unscientific.)

So I agree. I highly recommend a pamphlet just published at the University of Chicago Press, *The Secret Sins of Economics*, which shows how thoroughly I agree.

My disagreement with Guerrien is merely this: if microeconomics were properly taught it would be obvious that it *does* indeed have numerous scientific uses. Not the Whinston and Green stuff, on the whole. Most of that is useless, unless you think "useful" means not "good for grasping the world in a quantitative way" (called "science") but "good for generating publishable articles."

Yet there is tons of really useful stuff in, say, (the lamentable George) Stigler, *The Theory of Price*, or in Steve Landsburg's or David [sic] Friedman's similar books; or (if I may) in a wonderful but neglected book published last in 1985, *The Applied Theory of Price*. (It's available free in its entirety, diagrams and all, on the web site www.uic.edu/~deirdre2; David Friedman's is available free on his web site, too.) If graduate courses taught "micro theory" in this sense – namely, ideas about how to show this or that effect in an economy, quantitatively – economists would be good scientists instead of bad philosophers. Some of the economists, admittedly, survive the first-year courses and go on to actually think about economic ideas and to measure their impact on the world. But so do some children survive households with beatings and sexual abuse.

It just won't do, therefore, to say as Guerrien does that price theory (as we Chicago types prefer to call it) "obviously contradicts almost everything that we observe around us." Really? When OPEC (viz, Saudi Arabia) cut the supply of oil in 1973, didn't the relative price of oil rise, just as a simple supply-and-demand model would suggest? And when the population of Europe fell by a third in 1348–50 didn't the ratio of wages to rents double, just as a simple production-function-and-marginal-productivity model would suggest? The point is that both of these can be made as quantitatively serious as you want. They are real scientific ideas. If you want to see hundreds upon hundreds of such examples, see *The Applied Theory of Price* – or, indeed, the serious scientific work of any serious economic scientist, someone actually trying to measure the impact of an effect: Robert Fogel, say, or Moses Abramowitz, or Simon Kuznets (their teacher).

Let me put down the following challenge to the people who think they hate, just hate, neoclassical price theory. Go work through a serious book about it – not the "theoretical" micro that Guerrien and I both think is silly – and *do the applied problems*. If you can't get inside the hundreds of empirical exercises in, say, my book, or in the applications of price theory as they occur (obscured by nonsensical existence theorems) in the neoclassical literature then you don't really know what the tradition of Marshall-Wicksell–Friedman–Coase–Alchian is about, and you are not qualified to sneer at it, right? Doesn't that sound fair? I think so, and I would apply it to my own understanding of Marxian or institutional economics.

37.

RESPONSE TO GUERRIEN'S ESSAY

Jacques Sapir

Bernard Guerrien's provocative paper in *Post-Autistic Economics Review* no. 12 raises some important issues. Along with other heterodoxical French economists I am greatly indebted to Guerrien's frequently illuminating work about neoclassical economics. However, I feel that this particularly recent contribution was ill-conceived and perhaps pointless.

I agree with Guerrien that standard microeconomic assumptions are not relevant. I too criticized them in my *Les Trous Noirs de la Science Économique*. In addition, I agree that the Arrow–Debreu model has nothing to do with a decentralized economy. However, part of Guerrien's argument reveals an unhelpful bias against abstraction itself. One of Spinoza's famous arguments is helpful here. Spinoza taught us that the concept of 'dog' doesn't bark nor bite but the concept of 'dog' is nevertheless necessary to understand a world where real dogs can do both.

Guerrien's misplaced bias against abstraction is very clear when he states that Akerlof, Spence and Stiglitz have no new findings and have simply restated old ideas. Actually what these Nobel prizewinners did was to restate certain ideas at a higher level of abstraction. To return to Spinoza's argument, real dogs may have predated the concept of 'dog', but such a concept was still necessary and useful in the development of human culture. Unfortunately, the way Guerrien orients his quest for reality throws us back to the nominalism which pertained pre-Ockham.

In addition, rejecting Stiglitz's contribution to the future demise of the current orthodoxy in economics, be it his theoretical one or his political economy one, will not help to achieve the needed breakthrough. The post-autistic economics movement would probably not have been possible without Stiglitz's theoretical and political work in the last decade.

To acknowledge the positive effect of Stiglitz's work does not mean agreeing to accept it as offering the limits to change. What is needed is a shift from the information paradigm – plainly positivist – to a new knowledge paradigm. The best way to move forward on this path is probably to destroy old microeconomics step by step, and not just to forget it. We now have the possibility of opposing new arguments to every argument voiced by the neoclassical traditionalists. This is particularly true when we compare the traditional way of thinking about individual preferences to what we have learnt during the last two decades (Slovic's preference reversal or Tversky's framing effect). It is also true of our thinking about rationality and, last but not least, about the necessity of making a distinction between signals and information. Actually the information Stiglitz is so fond of does not exist as such. Information is always a processed signal, which means that knowledge predates information and that knowledge is at the center of the paradigm, not information. And don't think that this is just a matter of terminology. If we acknowledge the centrality of knowledge, then trying to collect as many signals as possible can be as detrimental to decision-making as being starved of information. Increasing competition, which is Stiglitz's cure for most of our problems, would then mean a considerable increase in signal gathering that could overwhelm our signal processing ability and lead to bad decisions and imperfect resource allocation.

It is probably important for me to state explicitly that I do not belong to the methodological individualism school. I think we have to reclaim holism but in a non-deterministic framework. To understand that the individual agent is part of a whole does not tell us how and why this agent is making specific decisions. And, if we need and want to understand how agents decide to understand interactions and transactions, then we need to devise some radically new kind of microeconomics. Guerrien's nihilistic stand here does not help us to move forward.

Neoclassical microeconomics has to be taught (in an abbreviated form of course) to allow students to move forward, but also to equip them to understand the language the autistic economist uses. After all, you could never understand history of the twelfth to the fourteenth centuries without a good knowledge of the Catholic dogma, which does not mean you have to believe in it, or even in God.

38

THEORETICAL SUBSTANCE SHOULD TAKE PRIORITY OVER TECHNIQUE

Geoffrey M. Hodgson

Essentially, neoclassical theory involves actors who are rational in that their behaviour is consistent with the maximization of utility with a given preference function. Two other features follow. The concept of maximization points towards equilibrium outcomes and a disposition towards equilibrium conceptions and solutions. Furthermore, the concept of capable preference involves a more or less well-defined choice set, involving either certainties or calculable probabilities. As a result, chronic information problems such as radical uncertainty, ignorance or interpretative ambiguity are excluded.

I would prefer to define neoclassical economics in this way, and not in terms of any ideology or predisposition towards competition or markets. I agree entirely with Bernard Guerrien on this point. Theorists have attempted to apply the neoclassical approach to socialist planning and capitalist monopoly, as well as to competitive markets. Just as we have individualistic, pro-market neoclassical economists (such as Milton Friedman) we have liberal or social-democratic neoclassical economists (such as Kenneth Arrow and Paul Samuelson) and also 'Marxist' neoclassical economists (such as Oskar Lange, John Roemer and Jon Elster). The essential core of neoclassical theory involves rationality, equilibrium and adequate information. This theoretical core is quite adaptable, and has served a variety of ideological positions, from left and right.

Having defined neoclassical theory, we can now attempt to answer Guerrien's question. What is 'worth keeping'? Many mainstream economists today, especially in the last 20 years, accept some of the limitations of the neoclassical core theory. For example, Herbert Simon's concept of bounded rationality is now acknowledged. Many experimental economists are sceptical of the neoclassical axioms. Yet still the core neoclassical assumptions still dominate the journals and textbooks.

When we ask 'what is worth keeping?' there are really two questions here. One concerns what should be taught on the economics curriculum. The second concerns the adoption, application or development of a theory by a researcher. I'll deal mainly with the first question and touch briefly on the second.

There are several reasons why the curriculum is still dominated by the neoclassical approach. Among these, economics has almost turned into a branch of applied mathematics, where the application and development of the technique has become more important than the explanation of the (economic) phenomena involved.

A second reason is equally important: heterodox critics of neoclassicism have failed to develop a substantial alternative theory that addresses the questions of individual agency and choice that should be part of the core of any viable analysis. The development of such a theoretical alternative is a major priority. There is progress, but it is frustratingly slow, and it is discouraged by the prevailing incentive structures of modern academic economics.

So, where do we go from here? The first injunction is: concepts have first priority, mathematical techniques second. Those that complain that it is necessary to devote an entire curriculum to neoclassical theory, on the grounds that there is 'not enough time available' to teach anything else, are typically driven by techniques, not by concepts. They stress the paraphernalia of technique rather than core ideas. They are often ignorant of the theoretical alternatives that do exist.

Pedagogic economies can and must be made. The core ideas of neoclassical theory should not be excluded from the curriculum but placed alongside alternatives. For example, the psychological assumptions that underlie 'rational economic man' should be made explicit and compared with other psychological approaches. Just as much emphasis should be placed on the conceptual limitations of game theory as on its techniques. Students should be encouraged to identify, compare, contrast and criticize key ideas.

One of the problems now is that teachers of economics have been trained in a technical fashion and are ignorant of where the key concepts come from. Economists should regain and enhance the capacity to scrutinize concepts, and give those abilities more weight than mere competence with techniques. The awful truth is that the reform of economics may now require the retraining of a whole generation of teachers of economics.

An important first step in revitalising economics would be to give more space and prestige to the methodology of economics and the history of economic thought, where greater understanding of the meaning and historical evolution of concepts and ideas can be obtained. Conceptually minded and critically able economists will once again be attracted to the profession.

Another vital step would be to introduce a plurality of theoretical approaches. Overall, in the curriculum, neoclassical theory should be just one approach alongside institutional, evolutionary, behaviouralist and other alternatives.

Turning to the second question: what use is neoclassical economics as a theoretical approach? This question is very complicated and an adequate answer would take much more space than I have available here. But I would like to stress the following points. First, for all their defects, the different versions of neoclassical theory have enormous heuristic power. It is a good intellectual work-out to read and criticize some parts of neoclassical theory. Second, neoclassical theorists such as Alfred Marshall, Leon Walras and Vilfredo Pareto were subtle and powerful thinkers and it is still worth reading their texts. Third, and above all, neoclassical approaches are deeply flawed but we have not yet developed an adequate alternative.

The development of an alternative to neoclassical theory must involve adequate answers to a number of key questions. For example: how are market prices formed? I do not believe that Marxian or Sraffian theories are sufficient here because they both lack an adequate conceptualisation of the human agency and decision-making processes. Evolutionary and institutional approaches may provide an answer, but as yet one has not emerged.

Of course, a new economics will create new questions, as well as providing new answers to old questions. But it will not replace neoclassical theory unless it can show overall superiority in both respects. The task of developing a new theory is an urgent priority. What is required is a new generation of theorists, with a broad and critical training in economics, which is lacking in the modern curriculum. Dealing with the first 'what is worth keeping?' question may well provide a solution to the problem raised with the second.

39.

TWO PERSPECTIVES TO GUERRIEN'S QUESTION

Steve Keen

There are many perspectives from which Guerrien's question "Is there anything worth keeping in standard microeconomics?" can be answered. I will consider two: the empirical and the mathematical.

The empirical perspective

There is little doubt that the conventional theory of the firm and of consumer behaviour are bad empirics.

On the former front, there are now numerous surveys in economic literature which establish that what neoclassical economics teaches as "the" behaviour of the firm – profit maximization by equating rising marginal cost to falling marginal revenue – applies to at best less than 5 per cent of firms and 5 per cent of products. Research into the actual cost structure facing most products, have routinely found that in 95 per cent or more of cases, marginal costs remain constant or fall across the relevant range of output. Research into the actual behaviour of firms shows similarly that, in 95 per cent or more of cases, firms chase the maximum possible level of sales without any consideration of declining marginal revenue (Fred Lee is the modern chronicler of this literature, with his book *Post Keynesian Price Theory*, 1991, being the ultimate reference).

Similarly, the vision of consumers deciding what to purchase by working out the point of tangency between the budget hyperplace and indifference hypercurve has failed miserably in experimental work. The latest and best reference on this, Sippel 1997, concludes very honestly with the observation that the theory failed to predict students' behaviour in a very well designed controlled experiment, and that as a consequence economists "should therefore pay closer attention to the limits of this theory as a description of how people actually behave".

The fact that despite these empirical failures, economists continue to teach the standard theory of the firm and consumer theory is perhaps the strongest indictment one can give against standard microeconomics. It has acted as a barrier to an honest confrontation with the real world, and deserves to be dropped on that ground alone.

But of course, it won't be: because ever since Friedman's defence of the "as if" approach to economic methodology, economists have felt justified in ignoring the real world since whatever firms and consumers think they are doing, they must be behaving "as if" they were doing what economists say they do, otherwise they wouldn't be profit maximizers or rational consumers.

The mathematical perspective

Well, if economists can't be persuaded to consider reality because it conflicts with their mathematics, we're going to have to turn our attention to the mathematics itself. And it turns out that there are good mathematical reasons to reject standard microeconomics.

Let's take first of all the theory of consumer behaviour. The standard presentation – of a consumer making a choice between two commodities – makes the exercise appear simple. But whoever heard of a consumer living on just two commodities? Yet each additional commodity considered involves an additional set of axes – three for three commodities, four for four – and each axis increases by an order of magnitude the number of choices facing the consumer.

Once we get anywhere near the number of commodities and number of units per commodity that a typical Western consumer buys on a monthly basis, the number of choices explodes to such a level that simple "rational" utility maximization is inconceivable. For example, if we simply consider a purchase of less than ten items each from a set of 30 commodities, the number of combinations to be considered is 10^{30} (to put this number in perspective, the age of the universe is under 10^{18} seconds).

This "curse of dimensionality" is a well-known phenomenon in computer science, and it is well known that an exhaustive maximization approach is simply impossible with such problems. Instead, consumers have to be following algorithms that drastically reduce the choice space: letting their choices be guided by custom, convention, habit, income-constrained tastes, etc. The conventional, simplistic vision of consumers as rational utility maximisers is a positive hindrance to serious study of the interesting question of how consumers manage to make consumption decisions in the face of overwhelming choice. By not honestly considering the mathematical implications of their theory of consumer behaviour, economists are practicing bad mathematics.

The same applies in the theory of the firm, where students start off being taught bad mathematics. All economists know the "perfect competition" assumption that the derivative of the market demand curve with respect to the output of a single firm is zero. Too few know that George Stigler – hardly a radical there – pointed out in 1957 that this is mathematically invalid: if the market demand curve is negatively sloped with respect to market output, it is negatively sloped with respect to the output of a single firm. This is a simple application of the chain rule for a continuous function (and also a product of the assumption of atomism).

A minority of economists appear to know Stigler's attempt to get around this by redefining marginal revenue for the individual firm as market price plus market price divided by the number of firms times the market elasticity of demand, coupled with the assertion that "this last term goes to zero as the number of sellers increases indefinitely" (Stigler 1957: 8). Too few realise that this was a sleight of hand: the term is a constant if there is a minimum firm size, and therefore the firm's marginal revenue is always less than price.

So-called mathematical economists have attempted to evade this by assuming that each industry consists of an infinite number of firms each producing an infinitesimal output (not an infinitesimal fraction of total industry output, but an infinitesimal output!). But this makes a mockery of the theory of exchange – how can consumers buy a single unit of anything if they have to go to an infinite number of producers to buy a single unit? – and of the theory of production itself – how can diminishing marginal productivity apply (the foundation of the proposition that marginal cost rises) if the minimum firm size is zero?

All these nonsense propositions have been put forward to defend the indefensible concept of perfect competition, and *they are propositions that any decent applied mathematician would reject outright.*

Yet this kind of behaviour – proposing decision processes that are empirically impossible, making assumptions that are absurd in order to preserve an initial proposition that has been shown to be fallacious – is a direct consequence of adherence to the conventional theory of microeconomics. It is bad, unscientific behaviour, which should have no place in a serious discipline.

References

Lee, F (1998), *Post Keynesian Price Theory*, Cambridge University Press, Cambridge.

Sippel, R (1997), 'Experiment on the pure theory of consumer's behaviour', *Economic Journal*, 107, 1431–44.

Stigler, G J (1957), 'Perfect competition, historically considered', *Journal of Political Economy*, 65 1–17.

40.

SUPERIOR ANALYSIS REQUIRES RECOGNITION OF COMPLEXITY

Anne Mayhew

Neoclassical microeconomic theory is, both in its simple and in its more rarified forms, a theory of how a unit will respond when faced with the commercial logic that says buy cheap, sell dear, and if you don't cover your costs over some reasonable period of time, you will cease to exist. It does not matter whether the prices to which the unit responds are changed through competitive or uncompetitive markets or by an auctioneer; the analysis is of response to price.

The question to ask, in answering Guerrien's question, is whether or not the commercial logic is applicable to units whose behaviour one wishes to analyse. The sleight of hand performed at the beginning of most introductory economic textbooks, and assumed thereafter in more advanced work, is that given conditions of unlimited wants and limited resources, the logic does apply widely. The wants can be wants for revenue for firms, utility for consumers, benefits for recipients of government services. If the wherewithal to get those wants (costs of inputs for firms, work or disutility for consumers, tax revenues for governments, resources for all of society) are limited then commercial rationality is assumed to be the only possible rationality. The alternative is assumed to be irrationality.

The power of economic analysis described by Bruce Caldwell in his defence of the use of microeconomic theory (*Post-Autistic Economics Review* no. 13; Chapter 34, this volume) is the power to explain the impact of price ceilings or floors, price supports, and the like *given that the units involved react to price according to the commercial logic.* I would agree with Caldwell that if this condition is met, then microeconomic theory does have wide applicability.

However, there is a large issue that requires further exploration, and it has nothing to do with the contestable assumption that wants are unlimited and resources finite. I am quite prepared to grant these assumptions for short-term analysis of many economic issues. What I am not prepared to grant is that two additional conditions for application of the commercial logic are in fact met by most of the economic units with which economic analysis must deal if such analysis is to be useful in thinking about economic issues.

The first condition is that there must be a *numeraire* that can be used to perform the double-entry bookkeeping that is core to the commercial logic. A numeraire, or common measurement for otherwise diverse elements, is required to know if you are buying cheaply and selling dearly, and, in fact, is required if the commercial logic is to have any meaning at all.

From this observation follows the second condition that must be met if commercial logic is to apply: the goals of the units being analysed must be the goal of having commonly measured inflows at least equal to or in excess of outflows. However, as is widely recognized the goals of many social units, such as families and even large commercial corporations, are multiple and cannot be toted up as a simple double-entry bookkeeping exercise. To take a simple example: children are not produced in accord with variation in the current, or even projected, price of labour, so that even if the amount of labour offered from an existing stock of people varies with price (a doubtful assumption), labour markets will also be rendered slightly odd by virtue of the failure of the model of commercial logic to capture the full array of relevant variables. For large firms with political, social and market power, long-term strategies of location, survival and other goals are likely to outweigh and obscure the simple application of commercial logic.

Where both numeraire and the simple commercial goal exist, microeconomic theory *can* be a useful way of describing probable action and outcomes. Many of Bruce Caldwell's examples of the power of economic reasoning probably meet these requirements. If new rental housing is added in response to expected revenues from rent, and if apartment rental rates weigh heavily in consumer demand, then rent control may reasonably be expected to result in shortages. If, however, as is apparently the case with minimum wages, there are other factors that weigh more heavily than price on behaviour of units involved (relatively fixed staffing requirements, number of unskilled people in the labour force, and so on) then neoclassical price theory becomes less useful. It is certainly less useful in exploring the behaviour of large, international corporations with multiple goals, and of families with a variety of lifestyle options, than it is in explaining the behaviour of small firms that operate in markets consisting of other such firms.

The answer to Guerrien's essay, therefore, depends on what you are analysing. There is certainly something worth keeping in standard microeconomics, but we should not be deluded by the fancier ways of articulating what remains a simple model, a model so simple that it cannot capture the complexity of interaction in economies. Superior analysis requires recognition of this greater complexity.

41.

WHAT SHOULD BE RETAINED FROM STANDARD MICROECONOMICS

Julie A Nelson

Bernard Guerrien's question, "Is there anything worth keeping in standard microeconomics?" is one that I have been thinking a lot about recently. In working with colleagues on writing an alternative *Principles of Microeconomics* textbook, we've had to address the question of what it is that we actually want students to know.

My co-authors and I come from a variety of backgrounds – ecological, social, feminist, institutionalist and radical. While, to have a chance at adoption in most departments, a textbook must cover a number of neoclassical concepts, we've given ourselves some leeway in putting these "in context," and in deciding which to stress, and which to downplay.

We certainly don't think that the number one priority is to inculcate students into adopting a free market ideology, which is the apparent goal of many of the currently available textbooks. Nor should it be to teach students about the elegance of mathematical and graphical modelling. Even if that were to remain a priority at more advanced levels (which we would debate), the vast majority of principles students will use their knowledge for citizenship, not further study. Lastly, we don't think, given the pressing nature of real-world economic problems, that our number one priority should be to tell beginning students about our internal professional debates about philosophy and methodology. So what should we teach?

We've rejected the usual emphasis on models of "producer and consumer choice," with all its focus on technique and all its bizarre assumptions (e.g. that efficiency is the only goal, that households are not productive, that

perfect competition is the default scenario). But – and here we differ from
Guerrien – we *do* see value in teaching some parts of the standard
introductory microeconomics toolbox. For example:

- The general notion of choice. Choice behaviour is one facet of human
  economic behaviour – though not the only one. Putting choice in
  context means also recognizing the roles of habits or customs (as stressed
  by institutionalists) and power (as stressed by radical economists) in
  explaining behaviour. Certain traditional microeconomic concepts like
  opportunity cost, and "rational" (read "reasonable") economic decision-
  making, in the sense of weighing both costs and benefits in coming to a
  decision, we have concluded, are worth teaching.
- Supply and demand curves. We introduce these as mental constructs
  that can give us some insight into real-world price variations, not as
  curves that exist "out there" in the world. While we also expose students
  to marginal cost curves and utility theory (for adoptability of the book),
  we demonstrate that the usefulness of supply and demand analysis does
  not depend on identifying supply curves with marginal cost curves, nor
  with identifying demand curves with the result of indifference curve
  analysis. In fact, our central example in the supply and demand chapter
  is a highly politicized national market for petroleum. Further
  elaboration introduces students to the relevance of elasticities for
  business and government policymaking.
- Gains from trade. Ricardo's old England-and-Portugal story is the basis
  for the neoliberal push for globalization today, so it is important that
  students understand the argument. However, we also complement this
  story with a discussion of the drawbacks of trade. In addition, we
  include transfer as an important form of distribution right alongside
  exchange, bringing discussions about intra-household and government
  transfers into the core of analysis.

Our book, *Microeconomics in Context*, takes well-being as the goal of economic
activity. Teaching from it will probably feel less "secure" for many
instructors in that it will hold fewer cut-and-dried answers and subjects for
chalk-and-talk lectures, and more opportunities for discussion. But, we
believe, such teaching will be considerably more intellectually challenging
and socially responsible.

Of course, much of Bernard Guerrien's criticism might more aptly be
taken to apply to advanced graduate work and professional research –
Slutsky matrices and general equilibrium theory are not usually the stuff of

principles classes. I would attribute much of our profession's fascination with mathematical elegance, over understanding of the real world, to warped notions of "rigour" and a misguided attempt to achieve certainty and absolute control (see Nelson essay in *post-autistic economics review*, issue no. 9, 20 October 2001). By keeping our eyes on the more pragmatic goal of developing and disseminating economic knowledge in the service of promoting well-being, I think we can keep what is useful in existing bodies of work – even neoclassical – while working towards developing new and more adequate forms of research and teaching.

42.

COMMENT ON BERNARD GUERRIEN'S ESSAY

Geoff Harcourt

May I comment on Bernard Guerrien's chapter, in which he has some disagreement with what he alleges I argued in Issue 11 of *Post-Autistic Economics Review* (2002)? There I set out what I think is happening in modern mainstream microeconomic theory, for example, that the general equilibrium model is the basis for descriptive analysis of competitive markets instead of being *at best*, a reference point, as is conceded by the most thoughtful general equilibrium theorists, such as Frank Hahn. Guerrien says I agree with this. If he had any knowledge at all about what I have argued for many years now, he would not have advanced such a canard. In fact, like Joan Robinson, I do not even accept the distinction between micro and macro as valid or useful; and I have doubts about whether general equilibrium is a reference point and certainly it is not descriptive analysis.

I also tend to think that game theory may not be very much use in thinking about non-competitive market structures. But I am re-examining this long held view, following re-reading Ken Arrow's masterful obituary of John Harsanyi and his contributions (*Economic Journal*, 111, 2001, F747–52). Minds should never be closed even in your seventy-first year! (I do not know how old Bernard Guerrien is.)

Guerrien quibbles with my (implicit) description of Akerlof, Spender and Stiglitz's findings as "new", arguing that they are just presenting some very old ideas in a mathematical form. He is right about the latter; but then I never claimed the findings were new. Mainstream economists think it is helpful to establish rigorously by maths, if at all possible, the arguments for conjectures, old and new. I think that there is a limited place for this approach in economics. Moreover, if it helps to illuminate the understanding of people who find thinking in this way useful, no harm is done, provided that this way of proceeding is not regarded as the *only* way of proceeding, and its advocates do not insist on a monopoly. I argued this in my first essay in *PAER* (issue 6) and in many other places. Finally, Amartya Sen is a real force for good in our discipline and the award of the Nobel Prize to him is a positive signal, to be embraced, not belittled.

43.

FOR GUERRIEN … AND BEYOND

Gilles Raveaud

When reacting to Guerrien's essay "Is there anything worth keeping in standard microeconomics?", one must not forget that he is among the world's best (and perhaps the best of all) specialists of neoclassical theory, in particular in all its technical details and difficulties. This is why listening to what he says is, I think, imperative (and why his best-selling French books need to be translated into English). It is mainly due to his work that many French students know that the general equilibrium theory (GET) describes a highly *centralised* economy, and not a decentralised one as far too many economists, orthodox and not, believe. This is not a trifling detail, but a major point, as it means that GET fails to give an account of how our (decentralised) economies and societies work. The debates on Lange's thesis in the 1930s made this point clear, but apparently it has been forgotten.

Now what is Guerrien saying? He is saying that if one starts studying neoclassical economics *as it is taught today*, one simply never gets beyond it. Any economics student can confirm this. Hence the obvious conclusion: one must teach it differently. Exactly how to do it remains a matter for debate, as indeed it should because a plurality of viewpoints must be taken into account. But what is certain is that, to start with, one must sharply reduce the amount of time dedicated to neoclassical theories so as to make room for the others. Second, neoclassical theory, like any other theory, should be taught *for what it is* (a depiction of a perfectly transparent and centralised economy where economic agents do not look at or talk to one another, but look only at the prices indicated by the auctioneer) and not taught for what it *seems* to be (a "simplified" picture of a decentralised modern market economy). Approached in this way, the place of maths and "technique" is immediately reduced, as the maths not only do not allow such a presentation but actually prevent it.

There is, therefore, a need to break from the very start (i.e. in first year) from current practices. Indeed, it is a shame for all economics teachers that neoclassical economics is taught in the first year. Why? There are two major reasons. Firstly, this particular persuasion in economics developed *after* many others, and so ought to be taught *after* them (and surely not in first year, where one should present Smith, Ricardo and Marx). Secondly, by covering neoclassicalism first, teachers send the following message to students: "economics has nothing to do with reality. Here we draw curves and manipulate equations that have no counterpart in reality. And this is not going to change." So students either do something else (exit) or stay in economics, but do not involve themselves any longer in their studies (descend into passivity). Just ask your students how they make the link between what they are taught and what they read in the newspapers.

So what then? Things being what they are, it is hard to think of ways to bring about such a fundamental change. It requires a total re-direction of current curricula. One step in this direction would be to start with *problems* – not with theories, which would be presented only in so far as they are able to explain these problems. Isn't this a very common definition of any "scientific" activity? Doing this, one would of course dramatically reduce the place of neoclassical economics teaching and research, as Guerrien proposes to do.

But we – the students in France who started this now world-wide movement for reform – have frequently pointed out that teachers who define themselves as "heterodox" (in their past or present research) devote most of their teaching time to neoclassical economics, because, as they put it, it is the "core" of the discipline, its "base", etc. But I appeal to them: please ask yourself and tell us, as we have asked everybody in the economic community for nearly two years now, with not a single answer yet: what is the scope of relevance of this theory for analysing current problems, such as, say, the crisis in Argentina or the level of unemployment in France? And please devise your curriculum in consequence. Reality is so complex that no time should be lost by teaching again and again those silly stories about Robinson and Friday. Time hurries on, and room has to be made for intelligence to gain ground on the repetition of empty exercises. In fact, as the recent political events in France indicate, your responsibility in devising sensible curricula (i.e. ones that give the students clues to understanding the society and world they live in) is not merely a pedagogical and "scientific" one. It is also a moral imperative. And I cannot prevent myself from thinking that those who do not give their students a sensible account of the economic and social realities of our time, so that they can make informed individual and collective choices, bear some responsibility for the ills of today and of tomorrow.

Please let me believe that this is just a temporary error, due to a stupid fascination for the "great theory" of the general equilibrium – and not the consequence of ignorance of the realities and debates of our time on the part of those who are supposed to light the way for the future adults of our societies.

44.

TEACHING POST-AUTISTIC ECONOMICS TO STUDENTS OF POLITICAL SCIENCE

Poul Thøis Madsen

Teaching economics to students who are not intending to be economists poses pedagogical questions that are central to the post-autistic economics movement. Most especially, a thoughtful teacher in this situation must ask: *What exactly should I teach?* This question, although arising from a situational context, addresses an even broader field of choice than does Bernard Guerrien's question: 'Is there anything worth keeping in standard microeconomics?' As a case study, I want to share with you my most recent experience in dealing with this question when in the autumn semester of 2001 I co-ordinated the teaching of economics to 132 second-year political science students at Aalborg University, Denmark.

Choice and use of textbooks

It was very difficult to choose an appropriate textbook for this target group. Currently, my preferred choice is *Economics* by Mulhearn and Vane (Macmillan, 1999) because it is explicitly targeted at non-economist students. Many economics textbooks, even very basic ones, intentionally or unintentionally address students who are pursuing a degree in economics. For our target group, these textbooks rely too heavily on mathematical and graphical representations of economics and focus on the current (or often even rather out-dated!) economic *theoretical* debate rather than the debate on *actual* economic problems.

More importantly, in standard textbooks – intended or not – the students are drawn into an *autistic* world for the sake of being there and not much else. Somehow, teachers and authors of textbooks seem to believe that students who stay within this universe long enough will gradually learn how to analyse actual economic problems and the related debates (which is the basic intention of our teaching). Neither standard textbooks nor standard teaching really addresses the acute and difficult problem of *linking* the models presented to reality (defined as the actual economic development, the actually applied economic policies and the real life debates on economic issues). In essence, the occasional real-life examples in textbooks serve as mere illustrations of the often very abstract arguments presented, thus, serving as some kind of entertainment without becoming an integrated part of the argument. The partly implicit and partly explicit working assumption in text books is that the more formal models presented to the students, the more they will – somehow – be able to understand of the working of the real economy. This is doubtful, to say the least, for many reasons. One important reason is that the assumptions in many models do not survive the meeting with 'reality' as defined above.

What kind of economics to teach?

After years of discussion, the teachers participating in our study have agreed that our students need to learn a few of the basic models (the simple Keynesian model, the Phillips-curve and the Aggregated Supply and Demand curve) but not necessarily by heart. I have argued that it is of central importance to complement this with conscious efforts to teach the students how to apply the models to 'reality'. But applying models to reality is difficult, and attempts to do so all too easily become too abstract. Teachers and the weaker students run the risk of losing the distinction between the model and reality. Most students, however, have an intuitive understanding of the problems of confusing model with reality and, hence, also of the dangers of assuming reality to behave like the model. But although possessing this awareness may make the students very critical, it does not equip them with any tools to cope with the newly discovered complexity.

A preliminary conclusion to be drawn from our experience is that we can help the students by organizing our teaching more consciously and directly around *basic economic causalities* (such as: expansive fiscal policy, increased economic activity, increased employment, increased imports). These causalities should be discussed at length. What are the basic assumptions?

What is kept ceteris paribus and why? How certain are these causalities? What do different economic theories tell us about these causalities? Do the causalities work in any kind of society, for example, whether industrialised or developing? What are the assumptions concerning the institutional setting? And so on.

The next logical step is to introduce (economic) politics and discuss what possibilities exist for them to manipulate or intervene in economic causalities. This is another obvious occasion for introducing different theoretical perceptions – in this case the limits and possibilities of economic policy.

What would we like the students to learn?

As a consequence of our reforms, we have also changed the way we *examine* the students. Years ago one extreme but common practice during examinations was to make the students derive the simple Keynesian model right from scratch (and, provided the students were very clever, they were asked to do the same exercise with the ISLM model). For most of our students this took up most of their examination time. And the weaker the student, the more he or she stumbled on their road to – what? More often than not students would not have time to discuss actual economic policy or the limits of the models (usually teachers claimed that this was the ideal intention underlying this type of examination). In recent years examinations have become much more human (traditionalist economists would say 'lax'), the examination being based on the papers produced by the students. In these papers they apply and discuss the economic causalities most likely to be of actual economic relevance. For example, in a recent semester the students discussed the possible consequences of the economic policies of the new Danish right wing government.

This focus on real life economic causalities, at the expense of time spent on formal models, creates uncertainty for the students and to a lesser extent for the teachers. Despite the shift of emphasis, the models still tend to be seen as 'state of the art' to be taught by teachers and learned by the students. Consequently, the students expect to be examined on the formal models and they become a bit frustrated and surprised when in the main they are asked to relate the learned causalities to real life instances.

It is also seen by many as easier and fairer to the students to tell them that they will be examined on the formal models. In this way economics becomes one of the few fields within social science at university level in which we are able to state very precisely what is required. Personally, I see this as a weakness – not a strength. To quote Keynes: 'It is better to be vaguely right than exactly wrong'. Seen from my perspective, teaching the students how to make 'vaguely right' analyses and conclusions should be the basic goal of teaching economics.

My view is that the teaching and learning of models should take up at most 10 per cent of our time. Our students, but also students in general, should learn how to 'think' and in this case to 'think economics'. What does this involve? First of all this is much more diffuse and more difficult than handling rather simplified formal models. Basically, it means learning how to make realistic assumptions and to discuss the possible causalities within the field defined or framed by these assumptions. Moreover, the clever students should also be able to question these basic assumptions. And of course they should learn to consider both the implications of relaxing the assumptions and to discuss the degree of realism of the different assumptions made. Hereby, economics becomes just like any other social science and henceforth also loses its aura of infallibility. This is a very important and not at all hidden part of the agenda underlying the reforms.

Suggested basic content

Summarising, I believe that we should try to teach the students:

- the basic economic concepts;
- the basic economic causalities;
- the basic economic policies;
- the basic features, firstly of their own national economy – secondly of the international economy (in this order and priority for pedagogical reasons). These features concern the institutional set-up, the kind of economic policies practiced, etc;
- the national debate;
- the international debate;
- basic economic theories in relation to actual causalities and politics;
- and finally introduce them to the world of models.

This sequence turns the usual way of doing things upside down.

But – and this is important – they should not be taught models for the sake of models. They should be taught models for two reasons:

- to get a distanced and critical idea of how economists think ...
- ... as a first to step to gaining a critical understanding of major

econometric macro-economic models, which could be seen as extended versions of the simple models.

Reactions from the students

According to the most recent evaluation in which 78 of the 132 students responded, we have had some success in our efforts. First, the students have become much more satisfied than previous students. Almost all of the students rate the course as being 'good'. More importantly, almost all of these non-economic students say they have gained an increased interest in the subject of economics. Teachers of economics with experience in teaching students not intending to become economists will know how hard it can be to reach this group.

We have also asked them what they have learned. Here are three examples (my translations):

1. 'I have learned a lot. I can follow the economic political debates.'
2. 'I feel better equipped to understand economics, as it is in the real world.'
3. 'I can read a newspaper article and relate it to an economic causality. It feels good.'

This is what I understand by post-autistic economics!

45

CAN WE PLEASE MOVE ON? A NOTE ON THE GUERRIEN DEBATE

James K Galbraith

Gentlemen, ladies, comrades ... Your contributions to the Guerrien debate have been reflective, even wise occasionally. But even where points were most deftly made, as they were (to my taste) by Peter Dorman and by Steve Keen, something about the discussion troubles me. There is here the flavor of a certain type of social activist, earnest and dedicated, honourable in every way, yet so caught up in the problems of the poor that one comes finally to understand they would be quite lost if poverty were ever made to disappear.

In other words, aren't we wasting our time? Isn't there more important work to do? In the immortal words of Thorstein Veblen:

> If we are getting restless under the taxonomy of a monocotyledonous wage doctrine and a cryptogamic theory of interest, with involute, loculicidal, tomentous and moniliform variants, what is the cytoplasm, centrosome, or karyokinetic process to which we may turn, and, in which we may find surcease from the metaphysics of normality and controlling principle?

Critics of the neoclassical doctrines have penned, over more than a century, millions of words – though few as good as those just cited. But how many have devoted themselves to new and alternative theory, to an economics that was not merely a variant or a gloss on neoclassical doctrine? Keynes. Robinson. Schumpeter. Ayres. Simon. Leontief. Galbraith *père*. Georgescu-

Roegen. Sraffa. Minsky. Davidson. Nelson and Winter, too tentatively. Pasinetti. Peter Albin. And since then? *Yes, I know* there are others, including some readers of these very words. But aren't you tired of embedding your originalities in critical restatements, however elegant, of what is already clear to thousands of bright undergraduates on the second day of class?

It is time to get on with it. We need a replacement for neoclassical economics. A new curriculum. Let's build it. Let me suggest a few key characteristics of what should follow.

1. The micro/macro distinction should be abolished. It exists in principle to separate irreconcilable doctrines. The new classicals have recognized this, and have abolished macro. (As Evelyn Waugh said of Randolph Churchill's surgeons, it was a miracle, they found the only part that was *not* malignant, and removed it.) We should take the opposite tack: toward a theory of human behaviour based on principles of social interaction.

2. Empirical work should be privileged. Real science does not protect bad theory by concentrating on unobservables. It is, rather, a process of interaction between conjecture and evidence. In the history of science, new technologies for measurement have often preceded new ideas. Believe it or not, this could happen in economics too.

3. Mathematics should mainly clarify the complex implications of simple constructs, not obscure simple ideas behind complex formulae. Dynamical systems (as Steve Keen rightly insists), fractal geometries, cellular automata all help us to understand the principles underlying evolutionary social dynamics. They are also fascinating. They help students learn to think. Mathematics should lie, in other words, at the essential core of a new curriculum; it should not be deployed defensively, as the protective belt.

4. Our economics should teach the great thinkers, notably Smith, Marx, Keynes, Veblen and Schumpeter (to restrict myself tactfully to a few of the honoured dead). We need not reinvent the field; nor should we abandon it. Economics over the sweep of history is not mainly about scarcity (which technology overcomes), nor about choice (which is generally neither free nor the defining characteristic of freedom). Rather, economics is about value, distribution, growth, stabilization, evolution. The great ideas in these areas, and the history in which they were embedded, are fundamental. They should be taught, and not as dogma but rather as a sequence of explorations.[1]

5. Pop constructs derived from neoclassical abstractions (social capital,

natural capital ...) are not part of our canon. While they are noteworthy as efforts to reconcile neoclassical ideas and policy commitments to real social problems, these constructs also extend, rather than attempt to overcome, the logical defects of the neoclassical system. From the standpoint of post-autism, therefore, they represent a dead end.

6. Nor should we accept the reconstruction of economics as an amalgam of interest-group politics. This approach – popular these days at the American Economic Association – has become a way of isolating certain dissenters who cannot conveniently be suppressed. But the fact that race, gender and the environment are important social constructs does not mean that economics requires a separate branch for the economics of race, another for the economics of gender, and another for 'sustainable development'. It should instead mean that the core of what we teach should handle these questions (which relate to power, discrimination, entropy, and so forth) in a way that is central to the discipline we espouse.

7. An economics of modern capitalism should study the actual, existing features and behaviour of our system. Households, business enterprises of all the types (including some characterized by diminishing and others by increasing returns, some with monopoly power and others without), money and credit systems, governments and their budgets, and the international system are all parts of a nested, hierarchical structure of rule- and convention-setting institutions, of interacting and sometimes conflicting sources of power. Their behaviour is characteristically unstable and sometimes violent. To have reduced the subject to shapeless households, firms and markets, all linked by a uniform conceptual structure of supply and demand curves (labour market, capital market, goods markets ...) – and in equilibrium! – that was the original neoclassical mistake, already analysed by Keynes in the first pages of the *General Theory*.

8. Accounting matters. We should work with and teach from the full spectrum of information sources, not merely sample surveys (with their obsessive focus on personal characteristics such as years of schooling) and the national accounts, but also credit, trade, industrial and financial data. Not to mention linking economic measurements to other information: political events, the environment, quality of life, demography and health.

9. A focus on social structures and the data that record them requires new empirical methods. The study of dispersions, of inequalities, is intrinsic to the study of power. Neoclassical economics with its bias in favour of

the sample survey, the gini coefficient, and the assumption of normality in the distribution of errors has neglected the mathematics and statistics of dispersion measures. There are large gains to be had here, for small investments of effort. Likewise the study of social structures cannot be done properly with parametric techniques held hostage to the dogma of hypothesis and test. There is no single formula for empirical learning. Numerical taxonomy, discriminant analysis, multidimensional scaling, and many other techniques are available for studying the phenomena of real economic systems, and we should learn, use and teach them.[2]

10. Finally, our economics is about problems that need to be solved. There remain before us the pursuit of full employment, balanced growth, price stability, development, a sustainable standard of life. That is why students once were attracted to our field. That is why they abandon it now. That is also why, if we develop a coherent research programme, and a teaching curriculum derived from it, that broadly respect the principles outlined above, we *will prevail* in the long run.

Notes

1. I thank Pedro Conceição for his characteristic insightfulness on this point.
2. In my view, the study of inequalities and social formations provides the linkage between Keynesian macro principles and the behaviour of smaller social formations – but I will not try to persuade you of that right now.

46.

ONCE AGAIN ON MICROECONOMICS

Bernard Guerrien

I am happy to see that my paper on microeconomics[1] has provoked so many reactions: that was one of its main purposes. I cannot answer everyone – it would take too long.

It is clear that several contributors to this discussion clearly disagree with me: Deirdre McCloskey,[2] Bruce Caldwell[3] and Julie Nelson,[4] for example. As for Jacques Sapir,[5] I confess that I did not understand most of what he wrote – perhaps because I never read Spinoza. All of the participants I just mentioned believe that there is something worth keeping in microeconomics, something they more or less identify with "economic reasoning".

Two obvious remarks before answering on the substance of the matter

First of all, *I am not against "theory"* or "abstraction" as Jacques Sapir suggests ("... part of Guerrien's argument reveals an unhelpful bias against abstraction itself"). On the contrary, I am in favour of teaching a lot more theory. When French students who are revolting against their *curriculum* say "no more micro1, micro2, micro3 ...", they mean that they want to be taught more theories, in the plural (including neoclassical theory), more history of economic thought, more moral philosophy (even Spinoza), more sociology, and so on.

You can explain neoclassical "abstract" theory in a very simple way, because it consists of a set of "stories" or "parables" – and with a lot of mathematics, but if you think that these stories are not relevant, then insisting on proofs of existence, on comparative static results and other refinements, will not make them relevant; all this has no interest (except, perhaps, for mathematicians).

Second remark: I am not against "economic reasoning". When I say that neoclassical theory is not "relevant", I am not at all pointing to the obvious fact that "economic men" do not resemble "actual men" but mainly to the fact that "the relations" these economic men entertain among themselves (in neoclassical theory) do not resemble the relations that exist in any known economy, past or present.

I am not against reasoning about abstract men (whose self-interest is grossly exaggerated, becoming almost their only motive) as long as the relations they enter into (firm–wage labourer, landowner–tenant, banker–industrialist–merchant, etc) resemble relations that exist in the real world. I may not entirely agree with him, but I find John Stuart Mill's economic reasoning "relevant" although, as he says himself, it is based on "an *arbitrary definition of man*, as a being who invariably does that by which he may obtain the greatest amount of necessaries, conveniences and luxuries, with the smallest quantity of labour and physical self-denial with which they can be obtained in the existing state of knowledge" (*System of Logic*, p. 326, his italics). Probably, neoclassical economists agree with this, too. Then, the difference between us is not that I reject "economic reasoning".

The logical flaw in micro theory

Now, after these two remarks, I remind you that the principal bug in microeconomics – as you find it in all textbooks (including McCloskey's – see appendix) – is not in the use of mathematics, or in the "unrealistic" preference relations, and so on, but in the very simple fact that, if you suppose, as micro theory does (at least, "at the beginning"), that *everyone* is a price-taker, then you *logically* need an auctioneer-type institution to set prices. Then, *and only then,* can you legitimately speak of supply and demand *curves* (or *functions*) and so on. Without an auctioneer, you need at least some *price-making* agents, and if you introduce such agents you find yourself in a completely different theory. You can, for instance, imagine people wandering around, bargaining and so on ... as David Kreps suggests in his *Microeconomic Theory*, pp. 196–7, saying that these kinds of models are in their "relative infancy" (how is this so, when there are so many people all around the world producing all kinds of models?).

I don't think that I need to remind you that the founders of neoclassical theory were perfectly aware of the logical problem concerning the origin of prices in a model in which everyone is supposed to be a price-taker. Jevons tried to avoid it with his "trading bodies" metaphor, Walras by assuming that prices are "barked" or "barked out" ("les prix sont *criés*") and that there are no exchanges (nor production) outside of equilibrium. Edgeworth, perhaps the most clever of them, clearly criticized these illegitimate assumptions and saw the logical flaw or circular reasoning implied in them – a flaw that you find in all microeconomic (or "price theory", or "economics") textbooks, Stiglitz included – which consists in deducing supply and demand curves (functions) from the behaviour of *price-taking* agents and then explaining that the prices they take are determined by these supply and demand curves (see appendix to this chapter for two examples).

So, if you insist on keeping a neoclassical or individual-based theory about the world around us, you should at least be consistent and not skip necessary steps: you have to suppose that there are (at least, some) price-making agents, and that they bargain. You cannot escape the problem, as is so often done by saying that "the market does this" or "the market does that" and by speaking of "market forces", "the law of supply and demand", "equilibrium point", which are just words or metaphors that suggest some mysterious "mechanism" that constantly engenders prices. Worse still: these prices are supposed to be efficient if they are not hampered by rent controls, agricultural subsidies and trade barriers, as in Caldwell's examples.

You may give the impression of rigour by drawing supply and demand schedules on the blackboard (they give this impression to people who have been brought up on them); but you don't escape the logical flaw. If you want to draw something, then draw Edgeworth's box: at least it allows you to introduce some of the more elemental problems of bargaining.

Deirdre McCloskey gives an example of "applied microeconomics" (sorry, "price theory"): the rise of oil prices in 1973. This is exactly the kind of important historical event that it is silly to explain by using nice supply and demand curves. This is a very complex case of multilateral bargaining (with price-makers involved)! There are OPEC and non-OPEC countries, quotas decided by some of them and not by others, strategic and political problems between countries, expectations of traders about what will happen in the future (see what is happening now, with the US–Iraq affair). Even Cournot's model (where there *is* an auctioneer) is of no use here.

I am sure that a certain type of student is very happy when we use "applied price theory" to explain the oil crisis (and the French Revolution and the decline of Spain, as is so often done) – it's so nice to understand without studying. But I doubt if we are able to do it, even though there are a lot of people publishing papers on the oil question.

Caldwell and Nelson give the Ricardo comparative advantage example of microeconomic reasoning – but where are supply and demand curves in this case? Do they think that Ricardo is a "micro-economist"? I have never seen his name in microeconomics textbooks.

There is also the (inevitable) question of elasticities and of the impact of taxes – a normative question, for sure. It is obvious that if you take general equilibrium prices (with an auctioneer, etc) as a benchmark, then *every change in prices* is sub-optimal (in the sense of Pareto) – because Arrow–Debreu general equilibrium is a Pareto optimum. As Samuelson remarked a long time ago, you don't need the "surplus" concept, and the demand and supply schedule, to explain that. That's for the abstract theory. If you want to study the problem in practice, you start from the fact that agents are more or less sensitive to the price movements of different goods; if you want to know just how sensitive, you can ask them, make polls or use different kinds of econometric methods to evaluate this sensibility (approximately); then you have an approximate idea of the effects of varying taxes (elasticity, in the mathematical sense, is a local notion that only gives information about small "movements" around a given – observed – point).

I also don't agree with Ann Mayhew[6] when she says that "explaining the behaviour of small firms that operate in markets consisting of other such firms" is a "simple problem" for which "there is certainly something worth keeping in standard microeconomics". It is "a simple problem" only if you suppose that there is an auctioneer with price-taking firms (and consumers). But does anyone consider that these are "simple", or relevant, assumptions?

En résumé, and again: if you want to be a consistent neoclassical theorist (starting from individuals, tastes, technology and endowments), you have to start from the beginning: generalized bargaining between individuals. Unhappily, you cannot go very far in this direction; you can perhaps say something about Nash (normative) solutions, about Salop–Rubinstein models with complete and perfect information, about the core of the economy (without production), and about its "shrinking" when the numbers of agents of each type increase. But nothing more. I suppose that's why microeconomic textbooks don't start with bargaining, and prefer the (invisible) Walrasian auctioneer.

Now, in practice, what do we observe around us? With the exception of the stock market and commodities prices, most (relative) prices are quite stable: why? That is a very interesting question. We are constantly teaching that prices adjust with supply and demand; but, in fact, it is quantities (stocks) that adjust, and most relative prices don't move, or move slowly. And this is a very important and happy fact: if prices were moving constantly and everywhere, as in the Stock Exchange (the famous "volatility"), then no middle- or long-term calculation could be made, and there would be no investment – and, finally, no production. People would spend most of their time bargaining, searching "the lowest price", and so on. A long time ago, John Stuart Mill – who didn't use "supply and demand" curves (and not because he was intimidated by elementary mathematics) – explained that competition could not be separated from custom. He tells us of competition (supply and demand) that "it rather acts, when it acts at all, as an occasional disturbing influence; the habitual regulator is custom modified from time to time by notions of equity or justice ... when competition does exist, it often, instead of lowering prices, merely divides the gains among a greater number of dealers".

I think that you cannot study economic relations if you don't pay attention to institutional arrangements, customs and traditions, mass psychology, class conflict and so on. Obviously, this is very difficult, and you have to be very modest when you teach these things (it is much easier to tell our students that "theory – mathematical models – show this or that; if you do this, then you will have that, etc", than to say "well, I don't really know, but in my opinion ..."

Now we come to the last, and eternal problem of the "alternative theory". Well, first we have to be cured of our inferiority complex with neoclassical theory. If we think that it is a bad, empty theory, then there is no problem: any other theory can be at least as good. Classical economists (Smith, Ricardo, Mill) say many interesting things; Marx and Keynes, too; there are some good ideas in "old macroeconomy", in the ISLM fashion. Leontieff and Sraffa models allow us to think about inter-dependencies in the economy. Economic history is quite fascinating – especially the evolution of capitalism (in the way done, for example, by the French "regulationniste" school).

Neoclassical models – with utility and production functions, and maximizing agents – have nothing to say about all this. And we have to explain why, again and again.

I don't think that we will some day "produce" a new "great theory", whether in the axiomatic way or not. But do we need it? Even without it, we can say a lot of interesting things about the world and how to change it. Economists always have something to propose.

Appendix: On McCloskey's and Friedman's "price theory"

Deirdre McCloskey gives her *Applied Price Theory* (www.uic.edu/~deirdre2) and David Friedman's *Price Theory* as examples of good economics. – but I don't see the difference between these two books and other standard microeconomics textbooks (almost all the "examples" in these two books are imaginary and made up) and I find in them the same logical fault that I pointed out in my main critique of microeconomics. Here is the proof.

Both McCloskey and Friedman start with traditional consumer choice theory and suppose price-taking agents – without this assumption it would be illegitimate to draw a "budget line", as they do. This seems to be the obvious thing to do: when a consumer goes to a shop, he takes prices as given.

Then, they both deduce the demand (and supply) curves of a household: this is standard microeconomics (Friedman, Chapters 2–4; McCloskey, Chapters 1–4).

They differ a little in the next step: Friedman treats the firm in the same way as the consumer. He always supposes price-taking agents (without saying it clearly); but this is a less obvious assumption: bosses or managers don't buy their inputs in shops as consumers do, and, when they sell, they propose a price. But, after more than 40 figures (about consumer choice), students probably don't react anymore: instead they are likely to be tired and ready to accept anything.

Both (McCloskey and Friedman) have a special chapter on exchange – Friedman, Chapter 6, "Simple trade", and McCloskey, Chapter 5, "Trade" – where, among other things, both present the Edgeworth box.

Here is the real problem: we all agree (even Marx) that there are mutual gains to be had from trade, but that this is not enough to determine prices. Friedman uses the usual *deus ex machina*: "the market". The title of his Chapter 7 tells us how he sees things: "Markets – putting it all together". Friedman says: "in Chapter 3, we saw how the behaviour of an individual consumer led to a demand curve, a relation between the price at which he could buy a good and the quantity he choose to buy" (p. 156). Then he explains "the *market demand* curve is the horizontal sum of the individual demand curves" (p. 156, his italics). But who did this "sum"? The same happens with the supply curve: "in Chapter 5, I showed how individual supply curves could be derived ... the market curve is the horizontal sum of the individual supply curves" (p. 157). Then comes the (apparently) obvious: "we are now ready to put supply curves and demand curves together". Obviously, too, these curves cross at only one point, equilibrium (E). Friedman asks: "What will the market price be and what quantity will be produced and consumed at that price?" (I suppose that "the market" is "we", as it is "we" who "put supply and demand curves together"). He then answers: "As any experienced guesser could predict (sic!), the answer is point E, where the supply and demand curves cross". He explains then that it is because "if price is too high, producers find themselves with products that they cannot sell. In order to get rid of them, the producers are willing to cut the price. Price falls" (p. 157). Elementary, my dear Watson, if you forget that demand and supply curves give the choices of *price-taking* agents! Then: *who* cuts prices? Friedman doesn't answer this question (indeed, I am quite sure that he isn't even aware of it, and he is perfectly satisfied with appealing to the metaphor of "the forces moving the system back to equilibrium", as he does on page 159).

Deirdre McCloskey is a little more subtle. She prefers to use the "many agents" Edgeworth's approach (and, implicitly, the Debreu–Scarf result). At the beginning, she accepts the indetermination of bargaining, but only when there are few people, and then she uses an "everyday life" argument: "Fortunately for someone trying to understand and predict it, most economic behaviour is not bargaining between two people" (p. 96). And she explains that it is because the situation is different when there are many people on both sides: "competition takes place among many buyers and sellers of the same item. In such circumstances each seller or buyer takes the price obtainable as given, for with many sellers and buyers no one of them can alter the market price by threatening to refuse to bargain" (p. 97). I ask: if "each seller or buyer takes the price as given", where did this "market price" that they cannot "alter" come from? Next, in a section very significantly entitled: "How the market achieves equilibrium" ("the market" does this or does that), she says: "a radical simplification in the theory of exchange is permitted by price-taking. It eliminates bargaining" (p. 97). Who "permits" this simplification? After explaining that "one can still, however, look at the behaviour of the market (sic!) in an Edgeworth box", she considers exchanges of "thousands of (farmers and consumers called) Howsons and Webbs", that form "the whole market". And she explains that "Each Webb is unable to influence the money price of wheat he faces in the market and therefore takes the price as given". The same for each Howson. Fine. But just after that, she writes: "When the price varies …" (p. 8). Do you see the bug?

No? Try again: "The market price is determined, the self interest of thousands of price-taking suppliers and demanders has led to the glorious end of the story, Equilibrium" (p. 99). Agents "determine" prices that they take as given.

Notes

1. Bernard Guerrien, "Is there anything worth keeping in standard microeconomics", *post-autistic economics review*, 12, March 15, 2002, article 1; Chapter 33, this volume.
2. Deirdre McCloskey, "Yes, there is something worth keeping in microeconomics", *post-autistic economics review*, 15, September 4, 2002, article 1; Chapter 35, this volume.
3. Bruce J Caldwell, "In defense of basic economic reasoning", *post-autistic economics review*, 13, May 2, 2002, article 4; Chapter 34, this volume.
4. Julie A Nelson, "What should be retained from standard microeconomics", *post-autistic economics review*, 14, June 21, 2002, article 8; Chapter 41, this volume.
5. Jacques Sapir, "Response to Guerrien's essay", *post-autistic economics review*, 13, May 2, 2002, article 5; Chapter 37, this volume.
6. Anne Mayhew, "Superior analysis requires recognition of complexity", *post-autistic economics review*, 14, June 21, 2002, article 7; Chapter 40, this volume.

Part 8:

Some Big Ideas

47.

TWO FEASIBLE FUTURE SCENARIOS: A HIGH-TECH UTOPIA AND A HIGH-TECH DYSTOPIA

Trond Andresen

Introduction

The current political and ideological climate does not encourage the launching and discussion of truly long-range societal goals (in this chapter "long-range" means "a century or two"). Such topics are discouraged for several reasons:

1. the dramatic and complete collapse of attempts at socialist societies.
2. related disillusionment because of revealed theoretical and ideological weaknesses of socialism and communism;
3. the increasing "post-modernist" belief in many academic and intellectual circles that (even) hitherto uncontroversial programmes as enlightenment and progress are simply not possible.

This chapter holds that the baby is being thrown out with the bathwater. If utopias – grand visions for qualitatively better societies – do not play a part in public debate, this has detrimental effects on political choices made today, even when the visions in themselves are maybe not feasible and can never be completely realized. In this context the metaphor of an asymptote may be useful. An asymptote in mathematics means a straight line that a given graph approaches with an always-diminishing gap, but which it will never reach completely. The utopian society to be presented is feasible in an asymptotic sense.

Another important concept for this paper is *the self-fulfilling prophecy*: Political processes, as opposed to natural or "physical" processes, are subject to this mechanism. If some new view or proposal for big change is disseminated only by some individuals or fringe groups, and only mentioned occasionally in the media, it may easily be disparaged as "crackpot". But attitudes and ideas that are repeatedly disseminated and talked about will after a while, seem feasible and "realistic" even if they were initially met with scepticism – what was controversial becomes conventional wisdom by repetition. An example of the latter is how public opinion of what constitutes a "realistically" achievable level of employment has (been) changed since the early 1970s, and how this change in opinion has made possible political reforms that disadvantage the unemployed. But the mechanism of the self-fulfilling prophecy should also give grounds for optimism, since it can work the opposite way: It indicates that unconventional or "grand" ideas should not necessarily be considered crackpot because they are initially derided.

In this spirit, with the (somewhat pretentious) notion of contributing to self-fulfilling prophecy processes, this chapter will present both a utopia and a dystopia. The first should be strived for, the second avoided (the author brashly assumes that most readers will agree on the respective attractive and repulsive, characters of the two scenarios to be presented).

Both future visions have something in common: they presuppose that science and technology progress in a relentless manner, and may not or will not be hindered or retarded significantly by human interference. (Thus the possibility of a grand collapse of modern civilization into barbarism for some reason is not considered.)

With the assumption of progress in science and technology (I should note the term "progress" is used in a strictly descriptive way – not implying any positive value per se), it follows that employment in all types of work that can be automated will contract: in the dystopia, to increase profits without a second thought to those that lose their jobs, in the utopia as a deliberate tool to liberate labour for meaningful "service" jobs – creating, interacting, teaching, entertaining or caring for other people.

The utopian scenario

Maybe the most famous single quote describing the essence of a future utopia is this from Karl Marx:

> In a higher phase of communist society, after the enslaving subordination of the individual to the division of labour, and therewith

also the antithesis between mental and physical labour, has vanished; after labour has become not only a means of life but life's prime want; after the productive forces have also increased with the all-around development of the individual, and all the springs of co-operative wealth flow more abundantly – only then can the narrow horizon of bourgeois right be crossed in its entirety and society inscribe on its banners: From each according to his ability, to each according to his needs! (Marx, 1875)

Marx's visions for communism is (sadly) somewhat out of fashion these days, so let us turn to literary (science) fiction, which is less constrained by what is considered "realistic". The novel *The Dispossessed* by Ursula K LeGuin (1974) describes a communist society in the Marxian sense (with one important exception). In the language spoken in this society, the words for "play" and "work" is the same. But there is a separate term for "drudgery". This is an important point for the utopia to be discussed: work must be attractive in itself. LeGuin's utopia diverges strongly from the Marxian one however, in the sense that "to each according to his needs" is difficult to fulfil. Hers is an anarcho-communist society *with scarcity*. This society is realized on an arid planet with few natural resources, and is constrained by this in spite of advanced science and technology. While individuals are not restrained by rationing or the need for money (which does not exist in a communist economy), and therefore in theory may consume or take whatever and as much as they want of the output of society, they hold back voluntarily only by the (more or less internalized) fear of losing the respect of their fellow citizens, and/or their self-respect.

Another utopian novel is *Voyage from Yesteryear* by James P Hogan (1982), where a robotic expedition arrives at the abundant and pristine earth-like planet Chiron. The expedition has a cargo of the necessary genetic material to "hatch" a new generation of humans. These children grow up under benign robotic supervision, and – free from the influence of any earthly society – spontaneously create a utopia without a state, coercion, money, wages, formal authority or hierarchies. As opposed to LeGuin's utopia, this is a society with nearly limitless abundance due to technology (robotics, tamed fusion energy) and a low population in relation to the resource base. So what makes people behave in Hogan's utopia? Something similar to that in LeGuin's society: respect and self-respect. A second and much later wave of colonizers, this time consisting of actual grown-up human beings with all the conventions and hang-ups due to socialization in a competitive capitalist society (Earth) arrives on Chiron and is confronted with attitudes and values which they simply do not grasp: "When in a store, and you don't have to pay for anything, why not grab all the attractive goods you can lay your hands on, and come back for more?" "You will learn", the Chironians reply, cryptically. And most of the new colonizers do. The Chironians also have an interesting "informal command structure": Authority exists only to the degree that workers in a plant accept that a certain person aspiring to a leading or coordinating role has the talent for it. If not, the person will simply be disobeyed or ignored. But if the person is considered competent, her right to take decisions on behalf of the collective is readily accepted, and "orders" are loyally implemented.

With Marx and these books in mind, let us now discuss the material basis for a(n) (at least "asymptotic") utopia. What enables today's high living standards in industrialized countries (abstracting from exploitation of poor countries and unsustainable use of the environment) is:

- a high level of education;
- modern infrastructure (communications and transportation);
- automated manufacturing, process industry, and information-technology mediated services.

The last factor is underestimated and will therefore be discussed. Let us begin with the question: what sort of work *can* be automated, and what sort of work cannot – or should not – be automated? A former Norwegian conservative prime minister once replied in an interview that it was the government's goal to "increase the productivity in our day-care centres", which demonstrates that he had not reflected much on this. For work where people care for, teach or entertain other people must necessarily remain labour-intensive, regardless of technological advances. One should instead pose the question from another angle: isn't the point of automation where it is technically possible and not detrimental to people or the environment, to increase our capacity to "work" instead with and for each other? Should not working with/for other human beings be less – not more – "efficient" in a throughput sense? ("Work" is here placed in quotation marks in the spirit of LeGuin). A future car assembly plant, or a paper factory, or industrial cleaning, can be run with hardly any staff. Such automation has no adverse side-effects (cars, paper, floors and other non-living things do not need human caring). The only argument for upholding such jobs is in a type of society that cannot offer alternative employment. But if "liberated" workers had (more) meaningful work to go to, shedding workers because of automation would be just the way to go.

The future utopia then has a tiny workforce (a couple of per cent) in highly automated and roboticized plants, churning out manufactured consumption and investment goods, and processing raw materials for inputs to other factories.[2] The public transport system is also highly automated and (at least for the urban stretches) free. Over 90 per cent of the workforce is employed in a few mandatory hours a day or per week (but if they like they may of course work more – most work is play anyway) with jobs consisting of interacting with other humans, or doing individual creative-type work, which also cannot and should not be automated. Tasks are:

- sports;
- cultural and creative activities;
- media;
- research;
- teaching, also in recreation activities, such as mountain-climbing, horse riding, diving, chess;
- day-care, health services, care for the elderly – with a dramatically reduced workload.

All these services are cost-free for the users.

Another type of task that also has a limited potential for automation is working with non-human living organisms, such as ecological restoration or ecological agriculture, which will be more labour intensive than today's industrialized version.

The reader may protest that not all of these tasks are purely work/play in the LeGuinian sense, but contain elements of drudgery. This is an important objection. In spite of automation and information technology, some necessary work will – due to its character – not change much, and remain boring or unpleasant. The answer to this is (even) shorter mandatory working hours for such jobs, and job rotation – which has merits in itself. In Marx's words:

> In communist society, where nobody has one exclusive sphere of activity but each can become accomplished in any branch he wishes, society regulates the general production and thus makes it possible for me to do one thing today and another tomorrow, to hunt in the morning, fish in the afternoon, rear cattle in the evening, criticize after dinner, just as I have a mind, without ever becoming hunter, fisherman, shepherd or critic. (Marx, 1845)

A bit more prosaically one could say that a small amount of drudgery (changing napkins in the nursing home) qualifies for a lot of pure work/play (hiking in the bush with the kids).

Another objection is "why should people work at all in/with factories and manufacturing plants when instead they can do all this more meaningful and/or entertaining stuff?" The answer to this is twofold:

- A minority of people are deeply fascinated by tinkering with technical processes, and gradually making them run even better. They are not very interested in interacting with people as the central point of their job.
- Pride: the select few who control the utopia's manufacturing plants and process industry are the persons enabling society as a whole to enjoy its very high living standard. They know it, and the others know it too.

This utopian scenario assumes that there is a reciprocal understanding and respect between the "producers" and "non-producers" – an understanding that is lacking in today's societies. In the author's Norwegian experience, debates on government budgets and macroeconomic choices to a large degree take the form of an entrenched conflict between two camps: The employers and some union leaders in the competitive private sector emphasize that "the rest of society lives off the values created here", and therefore public sector spending and wages should be curbed. Public sector union leaders on the other hand, hold that spending should be based on "what is needed", and their wages should track those of industrial workers. They have little interest for or understanding of the importance of an industry exposed to the efficiency demands of a world market. This is a deadlock that could be ameliorated by discussing scenarios of the type that is presented here. The solution should be to get the "warring factions" to agree that the automated state-of-the-art manufacturing and process industry is a prerequisite for affording a comprehensive free (public) service system. But manufacturing and industry is not a goal in itself. A comprehensive, free essential services sector is the goal – automated manufacturing is mainly a means.

(A note about the term "essential" used here: The utopia is organized such that the type of private services that we see on the rise today will not be very much in demand: finance, security, marketing, catering to the rich. These are here termed "non-essential"; see also the section on the "dystopian scenario" below.)

Another issue that should be discussed in the light of the utopian scenario, is whether a country *today* should do something to uphold and develop manufacturing, or should it all be outsourced to countries like China, for instance. An argument in favour of today's trend is that these countries need to export to richer countries to lift themselves out of poverty. And wages there will increase as they develop, so these countries' competitiveness will decrease correspondingly. Then automated manufacturing may be revived in those of today's importing countries that temporarily gave it up for overblown non-essential services such as finance, marketing and similar businesses. This may be an acceptable strategy, but it is not at all publicly discussed today. Seen in the time perspective suggested in this chapter, it is self-evident that any country that wants the type of near-utopian society sketched here must have its fair share of state-of-the-art automated manufacturing.

Note also that this implies a critique of today's widely publicized opinion in academia and among media pundits, that western developed societies have reached an advanced "post-industrial" stage. The reality is that these societies have simply outsourced their manufacturing to countries with low wages.

The following should also be discussed in connection with the utopian scenario: what is a "high living standard" and does this not imply environmental damage? But work consisting of interacting with other people is not ecologically unsustainable. A "high living standard" in our context does not mean a large consumption of resources and energy, and corresponding waste generation. The necessary energy may be generated from renewable sources and through efficiency improvements, particularly in end-uses. The feasibility of this even with today's technology has been demonstrated by – among others – Reddy et al. (1989). And with comprehensive use of information technology and robotics, goods may be efficiently produced and recycled, and waste minimized.

A final point in this section about a long-term utopian scenario is the question "can we get there gradually"? Ignoring the controversies on the political left about "reform versus revolution", I will here suggest that a modern market economy may (at least in theory, assuming that persons/parties with the political will for it are in power) be gradually changed in the direction of the utopia, by – among other things – carefully selecting activities that are "ripe" for being made public and cost-free for the users. Such selection can be done based on at least one of the following criteria being fulfilled for the product or service in question:

1. Limitless consumption is no problem, capacity- or environment-wise

(example: local phone calls, Internet access). (This is the sole – and therefore unrealistic – premise of Marxian "higher-stage communism".)
2. Consumption is inherently limited or rationed (example: schools, hospitals, funeral services, local public transport but not long-distance travel).
3. Neither of the above, but attitudes have changed, so that people voluntarily abstain from over-consumption of a certain good/service.

By these criteria, a fair share of modern industrialised societies are already somewhat "utopian" or "communist" ("… from each according to his ability, to each according to his needs"), in the sense that essential public services are free or with low fees (even if there are forces at work trying – to some degree successfully – to roll things back). This chapter proposes that today's developments should be discussed and evaluated in the light of the long-term utopian scenario (and alternative dystopian one – see below). If we do that, this gives an extra argument for keeping services like health and schools free and in the public sector, and this will then be an indicator that a society is advanced and modern. Note that this contradicts the current conventional wisdom that privatization and "user pays" are signs of modernity.

Having an eye for the long term also gives an incentive to look for and evaluate examples of already implemented "utopian" reforms in sectors where they are the exception to the rule. An example is the Belgian city of Hasselt, which has made all public transport free.[3]

The third criterion is the most challenging (and interesting), because it concerns change in public attitudes and behaviour. This is "LeGuinian internalisation", so that citizens automatically restrain themselves, *without experiencing this as a "sacrifice" on their part*. This is not something that could be implemented on a significant scale today: Imagine an experiment where one made basic foodstuffs free for the taking. Such a system would break down since a large share of the population would over-consume and also throw away untouched or half-eaten food. But an area, admittedly somewhat trivial, where voluntary restraint works to a fair degree even today, is littering. A large share of the population does not throw waste on the street, even if it would be more convenient for them to do so. The "sacrifice" of taking the litter with you for later appropriate disposal is not considered as such, because the action is internalized and automatic. Most people also don't leave their discarded TV sets and washing machines at the roadside, even if that is more "convenient" (and one can easily get away with it) than getting rid of such things in the mandatory manner. Such altruistic behaviour may be the exception to the rule, but gives grounds for optimism.

It gives support to those who hold that responsible socialization of new generations by schools, the media and in entertainment is not futile. Note that this is not arguing the obvious, it is taking a position that is today seen as outdated and futile among many intellectuals. I refer to 1980s' and especially 1990s' attitudes in advertising and entertainment (and even "post-modernist" aesthetic–academic circles) – deriding enlightenment and the possibility of progress, and cultivating violence, chaos and decay for "aesthetic" – or pecuniary – purposes. (A striking example of this intellectual current of the 1990s was reported in the British newspaper *The Independent* on 16 May 1995, where some TV commercials were criticized. One used a teenage suicide as a vehicle to advertise a product. Confronted with this the advertizer replied that this was not meant for the public in general. The target group were those who were "nihilistic, narcissistic and hedonistic".) The last decade has seen an unusual alliance between the powers that be ("there is no alternative"), and the cultural/media avant-garde ("working for a better society is futile – and since we can't do anything about it anyway: isn't today's world *fascinating* in all its cruelty?")

In the light of the above it seems that one must start from scratch again, to restore the legitimacy of the view that socialization towards responsible behaviour in relation to one's community is both necessary and feasible. And this does not need to be promoted on moral or religious grounds – it may (also or alternatively) be promoted on the basis of a long-range utopian vision.

The (feasible) capitalist dystopia

A school in Marxism holds that capitalism cannot sustain itself indefinitely, due to an inherent persistent decrease of the profit rate (Shaikh, 1978, pp. 232–5): Capitalists have to substitute workers with machines to keep up with the competition, whether they want to or not. This will increase their capital and mercilessly reduce their profit rate in the long run. Following this logic, as production becomes possible with only a small number of workers, conditions for creation of surplus value, exploitation and capital accumulation gradually wither. There is also a related Marxist argument that since only "productive" workers create "value", and most service and/or public sector work is considered non-productive, a completely service-dominated capitalist economy cannot uphold capital accumulation. There are, however, contradictions among Marxists (and in Marx's own writings) about how to define what is "productive" work (Hunt, 1979).

Regardless of these theories and positions, I will argue that there *is* a feasible scenario for viable "eternal" and strongly class-stratified capitalism – even when production is comprehensively automated. Such a future seems the more probable since it may be seen as an extrapolation of current trends. This dystopian society has the major share of its workers doing wage labour in capitalist service/servant ("s/s") firms. Such activity is labour-intensive, and with low capital intensity. I use the term "servant" here to indicate the presence of firms catering to the rich – such as domestic help, leisure activities, security, luxury tourism, etc. This comes on top of (mostly privatized) services for the general population like (health) care, education, entertainment, media – which are also labour-intensive activities A small minority of workers (just as in the utopian scenario above) is employed in the high-tech automated manufacturing and process industry sector. As long as a major share of the employed is in labour-intensive activities, this will ensure that the profit rate can be upheld, even if manufacturing is nearly wholly automated. And the profit rate in the highly automated manufacturing sector will be equalized with that of the s/s sector through the price mechanism. A large share of the population is unemployed, which ensures compliant labourers and high profit rates.

The prospect of chronic and very high unemployment in a capitalist future world is something that is not only described by critics of capitalist globalization. It is considered natural or unavoidable by some far-seeing thinkers among the elite. Martin and Schumann (1997) report from a conference of the world's most powerful in late September 1995:

> … 500 leading politicians, businessmen and scientists from every continent – a new "global brains trust"… which is supposed to point the way to the "new civilization" of the twenty-first century.
>
> From this point on [in the meeting], the top-class group discussing "the future of work" concerns itself entirely with those who will have none [this future scenario, having been launched at the conference, had an 80 percent unemployment rate].
>
> The expression on everyone's lips is Zbigniew Brzezinski's "tittytainment". The old Polish-born warhorse, who was Jimmy Carter's national security adviser for four years, has continued to occupy himself with geostrategic questions. He thinks of "tittytainment" ("tits" plus "entertainment") in terms not so much of sex as of the milk flowing from a nursing mother's breast. Perhaps a mixture of deadening entertainment and adequate nourishment will keep the world's frustrated population in relatively good spirits. Top

managers soberly discuss the possible dosage and consider how the affluent fifth will be able to occupy the superfluous rest. The pressure of global competition is such that they think it unreasonable to expect a social commitment from individual businesses. Someone else will have to look after the unemployed.

A future world with 80 per cent unemployment seems unrealistic. But the point of the above is that the world's power elites are willing to accept such scenarios and prepare for them. Based on today's trends, it seems more probable that employment will be higher, but in a predominantly low-wage and very insecure s/s-sector.

Investors are especially eager to take over such activities that have until now been in the public domain. Critics of this have to a large degree explained this trend as being "ideology-driven", i.e. that it is due to a strong neoliberal belief among decision makers that these activities will be run much more efficiently if privatized.

I suggest instead that the reasons are mainly material, not ideological. Consider these special characteristics of public sectors like health, caring and education:

1. They are socially necessary, as opposed to other non-essential services, so they will always be in demand.
2. The costs will therefore at least to some degree be covered by the state.
3. These services will be locally and predictably demanded – sales are not dependent on success in a risky world market.
4. They are inherently labour-intensive and cannot be automated.

These characteristics make investment especially attractive, the first three obviously so. The fourth characteristic may at first glance seem not to fit, since capitalists will always try to shed workers to reduce costs. So why is it attractive to enter a field where there are few possibilities for this? The keywords are "inherently" and "cannot". These services *will* be in demand, and they *cannot* be much automated. When these are stable and lasting conditions for all competing firms in the field, the inherent labour intensity becomes an *advantage*, not a drawback. For when a large share of capitalists' costs are for wages, and a small share for capital, the possibilities for significantly enhancing profits by a given percentage reduction of wage costs are greater than in a highly automated plant where capital costs dominate and wage costs are minimal. That said, the capitalist dystopia would also ensure acceptable and stable profits for the owners of capital-intensive automated plants, via the price mechanism: if profitability becomes low, plants will shut down and production will decrease. Demand for scarce goods will lead to increased prices, until the profit rate equals that in the s/s sector. The distribution of output between owners and workers in the large labour-intensive s/s sector – which depends on the balance of power between these two groups – then sets a benchmark for the profit rate for the economy as a whole. Hence, as long as there are plenty of workers employed by capitalists – regardless of this being in so-called non-productive jobs – strongly class-stratified and profitable capitalism may continue forever.

Conclusions

Long-term and even "unrealistic" scenarios for future societies ought to be regular topics for public debate. Both positive and negative scenarios are useful. Dissemination and discussion of such scenarios will have a positive impact on important political choices and decisions being made today. On the other hand, lack of such vision and discussion has detrimental effects.

One should be unafraid and confident about launching and supporting unconventional proposals or visions. For the mechanism of self-fulfilling prophecies is at work, for good or bad. One should work for awareness of this among those controlling the arenas for public discourse. Based on the recognition of this mechanism, one may argue that unconventional ideas should not be disparaged out of hand, but be given a fair chance in the media and elsewhere to compete with established thought.

Capitalism should not be considered a "stage in history" by its critics, but a system that may continue forever. Here it would appear that there is an element of agreement between critics and supporters (one of the latter is Francis Fukuyama with his "end of history" scenario). The difference however, is in the analysis of the probable characteristics of such a system, and whether there are better alternatives.

Notes

1.   In Proceedings of the Fifth Path to Full Employment Conference and the Tenth National Conference on Unemployment, Newcastle, Australia, December 10–12, 2003 – slightly revised here.
2.   There are also service sector jobs that can and should be automated – examples of this are the ATM and Internet banking, which dramatically reduce the need for banking personnel. So "automated manufacturing" in this paper should be interpreted in a wide sense, also incorporating a part of service sector activity.
3.   See http://www.ils.nrw.de/netz/leda/database/cities/city0100.htm.

References

Hogan, J P (1982), *Voyage from Yesteryear*, Baen Books; reprint edition 1999.

Hunt, E K (1979), 'The categories of productive and unproductive labour in Marxist economic theory', *Science and Society*, 43 (3).

LeGuin, U K (1974), *The Dispossessed*, Eos; reprint edition 1994.

Martin, H P and H Schumann (1997), *The Global Trap: Globalization and the Assault on Prosperity and Democracy*, Zed Books.

Marx, K (1875), 'Critique of the Gotha programme', *Marx/Engels Selected Works, Volume Three*, Moscow: Progress Publishers, 1970.

Marx, K (1845), 'The German ideology: part I', *The Marx–Engels reader*, New York: Norton, 1972.

Reddy, A K N, J Goldemberg and T B Johansson (1989), *Energy for a Sustainable World*, John Wiley & Sons.

Shaikh, A (1978), 'An introduction to the history of crisis theories', in *U.S. Capitalism in Crisis*. New York: Union for Radical Political Economics.

48.

THE POLITICAL ECONOMY OF DESTRUCTIVE POWER

Mehrdad Vahabi

1. Destructive power: a new field of study

From its inception, political economy has been interested in analysing the value that agents, individually or collectively, can produce or exchange at national or international levels. According to Say, political economy has to be "confined to the science which treats of wealth" and "unfolds the manner in which wealth is produced, distributed, and consumed" (Jean-Baptiste Say, [1821] 1964, p. xv). The main object of Political Economy is thus the *productive power* of human beings. But what about their *destructive power*? This latter question is not less important than the traditional central question of Political Economy, since it is easier to *destroy* than to *create*. In fact, we are able to destroy a hundred or even thousand times more than what we can create.

The *creative power* of an ordinary healthy high-school graduate may amount to no more than four or five thousand dollars of value per year. This creative or positive economic power refers to the graduate's capacity to produce or to exchange. But that is not the only economic power that he possesses. As an extortionist, for example, he can destroy a hundred times more. Furthermore, extortion can be used by a criminal, a brigand or a revolutionary. Whatever the extortionist's motive, it is *destructive power*, the power to destroy use values or exchange values, that he uses. Is the question *how much can an agent destroy* irrelevant to Political Economy? Neoclassical economists say that it is.

Neoclassical economics rejected social disequilibria and conflict, and assumed a sustainable harmony among individual agents through a market economy. Consequently, revolutions or radical conflicts undermining the social system are considered to be "unnatural" or irrational, and thus treated as actions resulting from passions and emotions and not from reason. Since by definition neoclassical economics was the study of "rational behaviour", the study of this type of irrational behaviour was, as Pareto urged, delegated to sociology, politics, psychology and history. Of course, Pareto ([1902] 1966) acknowledges that "The efforts of men are utilized in two different ways: they are directed to the production or transformation of economic goods, or else to the appropriation of goods produced by others". However, since the appropriative activity does not come within the scope of free choice, it cannot, under the neoclassical view, concern the economist.

It is true that elementary textbooks frequently introduce the production possibilities frontier between "guns" and "butter" (as Samuelson's favourite example describes the optimal allocation of resources in his *Economics*, 1948) to illustrate the nature of the economic problem and the concept of opportunity cost. It is noteworthy, however, that they never consider the question of how "guns" might be used in a *destructive* manner to appropriate resources from neighbouring peoples or states, and thus push out the production possibilities frontiers of the society.

I propose an alternative approach to Political Economy, one that considers both the *creative* and the *destructive* power of human beings. This requires that a new field of study, namely *destructive power*, be explored by economists. This field consists not of fragmented and specialized studies regarding the military sector, criminal activities or the economics of warfare. Instead it embraces the *destructive power* of human beings in all its diverse forms. Federating existing fragmented studies will not achieve a general comprehension of destructive power, because these studies are based on standard and inappropriate economic assumptions and methods, such as maximizing and rationality behaviour, and individual cost–benefit analysis. In this chapter I am going to explain what I mean, in an economic context, by destructive power.

2. Definition of destructive power

To understand destructive power, we must distinguish between destruction as an integral part of "creation" (or what Hegel calls "specific, limited or definite negation") and destruction as the antithesis of creation (or what Hegel calls "abstract negation", [1807] 1977, pp. 359–60, 567–8).

2.1 *Destruction as an integral part of creation*

In a sense, *destruction* can be considered as the very act of *creation*, since all production involves what might be called "destructive transformation", like wheat being ground into flour, or flour baked into bread (Boulding, 1989, p. 239). To produce a chair, we need to use, consume and thus *destroy* wood, and the destruction of wood in a particular way leads to the construction of the chair. Final consumption can also be viewed as a form of destruction. Destroying a product through consumption is the counterpart of creating utility. In this sense, destruction is part of creation.

In a similar way, innovative activity can be considered as *creative destruction*, as Schumpeter referred to the process of capitalist development (Schumpeter, 1951, Chapter 7). This kind of destruction is the direct outcome of innovation, namely the *destruction* of old products, past processes of manufacturing and archaic forms of organization through the introduction of new products, ways of producing and organizational methods.

The process of learning is also a kind of *self-destruction*, namely the reshaping of our knowledge framework, the rearrangement or reconstruction of our data and mental representations, through which biases can be removed or replaced by new ones. Science can be defined as a form of *destruction*, or a process of permanent destruction of certain ideas, concepts or paradigms. The negation of past knowledge is *mental destruction*, which like *material destruction*, may give birth to the construction of something new, in this case new knowledge.

The accumulation of capital involves concentration and centralisation of different forms of capital (such as industrial, financial, or commercial capital), which results in the elimination of small property owners. Property rights are not limited to *holding* things *for oneself*, since through capitalist development, they result in *withholding things from others* (Commons, [1924] 1995, pp. 53–4). Thus this process of capital accumulation generates *bankruptcy*, i.e. the destruction of certain firms and the creation of new firms, *job destruction* and *job creation*, as well as mergers and acquisitions in financial markets with their direct consequences in terms of *value creation* and *value destruction*. Competition as a natural selection mechanism of capitalism brings into play forces necessary to weed out elements that can hinder capitalist development. Budget, monetary and financial constraints provide economic sanctions through which competition exerts its full power as a selection mechanism. In all these cases, destruction is an integral part of the creative process. Overconsumption and overproduction are part and parcel of economic crisis. Karl Marx clearly speaks of the "destruction of capital" through crises (Marx, Part II [1861–3], 1978, pp. 495–6) and distinguishes two different meanings of *capital destruction* during crises, namely *destruction* of *real capital* (use-value and exchange value) and *destruction* of *capital* defined as *depreciation* of exchange values. Destruction of capital through crises constitutes a necessary moment of the capitalist reproduction process. In this respect, destruction of values is an integral part of value-creation. Nonetheless, the *destructive power* of crises is a "spontaneous" or an "unintended" destruction which does not result from strategic decisions of individuals or social groups.

2.2 *Destruction as the antithesis of creation*

To differentiate destruction from creation, we have to focus on *abstract* destruction, for which destruction is not just a moment of the creative process, but constitutes a moment in itself: it means *destruction for the sake of destruction*. This is what Boulding refers to as "the dark side of destructive power", which goes back a long way, as shown in the story of Cain and Abel (1989, p. 22). This brings us once again to *threat power*, which is different from *creative power*. The remainder of this paper will focus on this particular sense of destruction and *destructive power* rather than on destruction as an integral part of creation.

Strictly speaking, destructive power is threat power that may lead to the destruction of use or exchange values or even human beings and nature. This *instrumental* definition of destructive power is free of value judgments. I do not necessarily consider a destructive action to be a "bad" or Mephistophelian one. By the same token, a creative action is not necessarily a "good" action. In other words, my distinction between destruction and creation, as well as destructive and creative value is not based on an *ethical* criterion. It does not mean that the ethical or legitimising aspects of any recourse to destructive or creative power are denied, it simply implies that in this definition, the value has a purely *instrumental* character, and does not contain a *judgmental* value.

Moreover, destructive power should not be reduced to *violence* (revolution, civil war and war, terrorism, hostage taking or other criminal types of activities). It also includes *non-violent* activities (strikes, demonstrations or deliberate exclusion). Among different non-violent forms of destructive power, exclusion plays a key role. Exclusion is the supreme mechanism available to a dominant institution (academic, religious, political, economic or cultural) or a social group, caste or nation, enabling it to exert its destructive power against opponents.

Destructive power is both physical and moral or spiritual. The earliest civilizations were allegedly based on priesthoods. Priests established social rules and threatened disobedient people with social exclusion or divine punishments. Non-believers were told they would be punished by preternatural powers and should expect to endure excruciating pains after their death by going to an awful place like hell, while believers were promised a blissful life in a beautiful place like paradise. *Moral destructive power* can be carried out through moral threat. However, there exist other forms of this power that cannot be reduced to moral threat. For instance, gossip is not a moral threat. But it can spread scandal against certain targeted people, put them down, exclude them from collective action or groups, and even morally lynch them. In gossip, destroying one's reputation is not necessarily based on the truth, and in blackmail, the non-revelation of the truth can be a source of power.

Lying and historical forgery are other forms of destructive power that can destroy individual or collective memory or identity. This sort of behaviour cannot be reduced to a situation of asymmetrical information. It may be deployed by a dominant group that tries to impose its "truth" by any means, including destroying evidence, historical forgery and excluding non-believers. As Napoleon justly remarked: "What is history but a fable agreed upon?"

Finally, destructive power can be *individual* or *social*. When a child "cries" or "breaks things" and throws a tantrum to impose her/his desire on her/his parents, s/he is using her/his individual destructive power. Likewise the power of a community to exclude or to sanction is its social destructive power. Destructive power has a strong integrative power. Its importance in social integration is such that the etymology of "society" gives credence to the idea that "society" was historically perceived as a *military alliance*. Let us examine the etymology of "society". It derives from the Latin word *societas*. This elaborated *socius*, meaning a non-Roman ally, a group willing to follow Rome to war. Such a term is common in Indo-European languages, deriving from the root *sekw*, meaning "fellow". It denotes an asymmetrical alliance, society as a loose confederation of stratified allies. (Mann, 1986, p. 14). The recourse to destructive power is not only a symptom of crisis or disequilibrium, but a constant dimension of collective action.

3. Two different functions of destructive power

Destructive power has two different functions: *appropriative* and *rule-producing*. Although these functions are inextricable, I treat them separately for theoretical clarity. For example, the war of the Bush administration against Iraq is being waged to pirate Iraq's oil and to control its economy. In this sense, war as a form of destructive power has an *appropriative* function. But this colonialist war also has a *rule-producing* effect, since the United States is trying to establish its sovereignty over Iraq, its hegemony in the Middle East, and perhaps to draw a new map for the whole region in co-operation with Israel. These two different functions are present in other forms of destructive power. A revolution is for changing rules, but it also has an appropriative aspect. In the case of strikes, the *appropriative* function is straightforward, since their targets are usually to increase salaries, reduce working hours and so on. Nevertheless, strikes also decide on the way an enterprise should be run. For workers' trade unions, striking is a very strong tactic that allows them to negotiate with employers concerning workers' participation in the management. Even the right to strike is an important political question that involves the *rule-producing* function of destructive power. Criminal activity, as another form of destructive power, has both types of function. Its pirating or *appropriative* function is obvious, but it has a more enduring effect, namely a destabilising or *rule-disturbing* effect which implies disorder, anarchy and insecurity.

3.1 *Destructive power in its appropriative function*

The difference between these two functions is crucial. Destructive power in its *appropriative* function is a means, whereas in its *rule-producing* function, it is an end in itself. In the former case, destructive power can be defined as an alternative means of reallocating resources. It can be dubbed "rent-seeking", "predation" or "appropriative" and be integrated in a rational expectation or general equilibrium model of individual agents choosing between creative and destructive activities in accordance with their *private* costs and benefits. In a perfect world of fully informed agents with no randomness, and devoid of radical uncertainty, it can be shown that the *appropriative* function of destructive power may be realised with no real destruction or violence (see Grossman and Kim, 1995, 1996). All strands of the neoclassical approach, such as rational conflict theory, general equilibrium models of violence and socio-political instability models of new political economy, lead to this result. *Money neutrality* in a general equilibrium model of creative activity is analogous to *violence neutrality* in a general equilibrium model of appropriative activity. In both cases, money and violence are considered to be the means to achieve a particular end. In neoclassical theory, money neutrality is related to the role of money as a means of commodity circulation, or *fiat* money. By the same token, violence neutrality is related to the role of destructive power as a means of appropriation. In both cases, money and violence disappear in equilibrium. Agents are regarded as self-interested and calculating individuals endowed with *ex ante* rationality and maximizing behaviour.

3.2 *Destructive power in its rule-producing function*

Destructive power in its *rule-producing* function resembles money as a *store of wealth*. Money in its function as a store of wealth is required for its own sake, for its *liquidity* and can be regarded as an end in itself. What determines the *liquidity preference* of people? "Our desire to hold money as a store of wealth is a barometer of the degree of our distrust of our own calculations and conventions concerning the future [...] The possession of actual money lulls our disquietude; and the premium which we require to make us part with money is the measure of the degree of our disquietude." (Keynes, 1937, p. 216). Uncertainty about conventional judgements resulting from a multitude of agents' anticipation about the state of the market in the future, and their distrust about their own calculations are the sources of *liquidity preference*. Money can serve as an insurance against uncertainty because of its *social* or *universal* value. *Liquidity preference* is thus decided not by *individual* agents but by conventional judgements, which are formed through a *social* process. In this process, the dominant opinion of the leading deciders in financial markets determines the *social norm*.

Destructive power in its *rule-producing* function is most likely required for its own sake, since it is the foundation of law or legal order. Destructive power as the last resort to maintain a desired order can overcome or mitigate our distrust about the possible violations of order by others. While the *appropriative* function of destructive power may be dealt with in an individualistic framework, the *rule-producing* function of this power can only be grasped in a social context. Keynes's famous phrase "in the long run, we are all dead" reveals an important aspect of economic reasoning. Any individual is concerned first and foremost by economic interests during her/his personal lifetime. Individuals do not behave as species or dynasties with regard to their short-term economic interests. However, it is true that in war as well as revolutionary action "individualism is the first to disappear" (Fanon, 1968, p. 47). In such cases, one can observe a kind of group coherence which is more deeply felt and shared by large masses of people and shows a much stronger, but less enduring, attachment than all other varieties of private or civil friendship. Individual self-consciousness thus turns into a collective consciousness and the immortality of the species takes the centre stage of our experience. Nonetheless, it is not only in wars, revolutions, or other violent forms of action implying death that we are confronted with this sort of behaviour. In almost all protestations undermining the existing order, individuals become conscious of their role as part of a species or a dynasty. Broadly speaking, if economic reasoning leads to Keynes's motto that "in the long run, we are all dead", political reasoning results in the opposite motto "in the long run, we are all alive". The time horizon of economic reasoning is different from that of political reasoning.

Destructive power in its *appropriative* function follows economic or *private* reasoning, whereas destructive power in its *rule-producing* function complies with political, social groups' (classes) or *public* reasoning. This explains why the *appropriative* function of destructive power is consistent with an individualistic neoclassical framework, while the *rule-producing* function of this power is in contradiction with such an approach.

Conclusion

Integrating both functions of destructive power into Political Economy is a new challenge for economists who think that economics should extend its traditional frontiers as a science of creative power of human beings. My objective is to bring together the question of sovereignty with that of property, which is more in tune with what Adam Smith ([1776] 1961) considered to be the main concern of Political Economy: "The great object of the political economy of every country is to increase the *riches* and *power* of that country". In doing so, I must emphasize that my intentions are free from economic imperialism for two reasons. First, I do not find the application of the present standard assumptions of economic analysis such as rationality and optimisation appropriate for my goal. Second, the integration of destructive power in economic analysis requires economics to come closer to other social sciences, such as philosophy, political science, psychology, sociology and military science. Nevertheless, I think that in analysing the *value* of *destructive power* economists have something to say, since they have been dealing mainly with the issue of value over the last three centuries. As a student of social science, I have tried elsewhere (Vahabi, 2004), to take advantage of all social sciences that are relevant to my subject in order to contribute to the *Political Economy* of destructive power. This effort comes within the scope of an approach that regards Political Economy as a discourse both on the creative and destructive power of human beings.

Note

1. Contact address: Mehrdad.vahabi@wanadoo.fr. This article draws extensively on a book I have recently published (Vahabi, 2004).

References

Boulding, K E, 1989, *Three faces of power*, Newbury Park, London, New Delhi, Sage Publications.

Commons, J R, [1924] 1995, *Legal Foundations of Capitalism*, New Brunswick and London, Transaction Publishers.

Fanon, F, 1968, *The Wretched of the Earth*, New York, Grove Press edition.

Grossman H, and M Kim, 1995, "Swords or plowshares? A theory of the security of claims to property," *Journal of Political Economy*, 103, pp. 1275–88.

Grossman, H, and M Kim, 1996, "Predation and production", in M Garfinkel and Skaperdas (eds), *The Political Economy of Conflict and Appropriation*, Cambridge, Cambridge University Press.

Hegel, G W F, [1807] 1977, *Phenomenology of Spirit*, translated by A V Miller with Analysis of the Text and Foreword by J N Findlay, FBA., FAAAS., Oxford, Clarendon Press.

Hirschman, A O, 1970, *Exit, Voice, and Loyalty*, Cambridge, MA, Cambridge University Press.

Keynes, J M, 1937, "The general theory of employment", *Quarterly Journal of Economics*, February, pp. 209–223.

Mann, M, 1986, *The Sources of Social Power*, vol. 1, *A History of Power from the Beginning to A.D. 1760*, Cambridge, Cambridge University Press.

Marx, K [1861–3] 1978, *Theories of Surplus-Value*, 3 parts, Moscow, Progress Publishers.

Pareto, Vilfredo, [1902] 1966, *Les Systèmes d'Economie Politique*, in S E Finer (ed.), *Vilfredo Pareto: Sociological Writings*, New York, Praeger.

Say, J B, [1821] 1964, *A Treatise on Political Economy or the Production, Distribution and Consumption of Wealth*, New York, Claxton, Remsen & Haffelfinger.

Schumpeter, J A, 1951, *Capitalism, Socialism, and Democracy*, London, George Allen and Unwin.

Smith, Adam, [1776] 1961, *An Inquiry into the Nature and Causes of the Wealth of Nations*, London, Methuen.

Vahabi, M, 2004, *The Political Economy of Destructive Power*, Cheltenham, UK; Northampton, MA, USA, Edward Elgar.

49

CAPABILITIES: FROM SPINOZA TO SEN AND BEYOND

Jorge Buzaglo

Part I: Spinoza's theory of capabilities

In a recent article in the *Post-Autistic Economics Review*, Emmanuelle Benicourt (2002) challenges heterodox economists to explain why they consider Amartya Sen's theoretical approach a real force for reform in economics. I would like to communicate here what I see as a real force for change in Amartya Sen's approach to the economic dimension of human development. I would like to describe some of the genealogy of the approach, and also to show the potential that this critical tradition has for the renewal of economics.

Before I embark in my task I would like to refer to Emmanuelle Benicourt's orthodox/heterodox partition of economics, which I do not think is very useful. Both categories are too heterogeneous to be helpful. If we consider what I think is a more useful categorization, that between conventional and progressive economics (or similar characterizations, such as conservative/radical, bourgeois/socialist, and so on), we will find orthodox and heterodox economists in both categories. Amartya Sen, for instance, is an orthodox economist, as both he and Emmanuelle Benicourt point out (Amartya Sen says "mainstream economist"). He is an orthodox economist because he uses the conventional apparatus of ordinary neoclassical theory. But as I see it, he is a *progressive* orthodox economist, since he applies this conventional apparatus to the advancement of a progressive cause, namely, the cause of equality.[1] The equality he advocates is not merely economistic/utilitarian, but refers also to all other dimensions ("functionings") of human existence. A quite radical message indeed, articulated in the suave and diplomatic language of neoclassical economics. One can only speculate if this is an Aesopian strategy of telling subversive truths in covered language, or if it would be better or more effective to develop a more appropriate heterodox idiom to say the same thing. But it must be admitted that many a heterodox economist would shy away from so radical an objective for economic science and human development.

I will argue here that Sen's radical approach to human welfare is not new, and that the original source of the approach contains other important and deep insights. I will also argue that this same source inspires some present-day approaches to natural science, and could also inspire the renewal of economics that Emmanuelle Benicourt longs for.

The "hideous hypothesis" of *The Ethics*

The source I am thinking of is *The Ethics* of Baruch de Spinoza ([1670] 1951).[2] Spinoza's doctrine of capabilities in *The Ethics* prefigures rather explicitly Amartya Sen's ideas, but it does not seem that Sen was aware of it. For one thing, Amartya Sen is very open and magnanimous with his sources and credits – he refers to Aristotle's *Nicomachian Ethics*, Marx's *Manuscript of 1844* and Adam Smith's *Wealth of Nations* as sources of inspiration.[3] Also, the doctrine of capabilities, in spite of its crucial importance in Spinoza's message, if barely mentioned, is not given the importance it deserves in most of the expositions, commentaries and criticisms of *The Ethics* I am aware of.[4] This was perhaps due to the fact that the doctrine appears among what are considered the most difficult and "mystical" propositions of the last half of Part 5, which usually repulse narrowly conceived positivism. In these last propositions Spinoza explains when and in what sense the human mind can be said to be eternal.

In effect, in 5.39 (Part 5, Proposition 39), Spinoza affirms that:

> He, who possesses a body capable of the greatest number of activities, possesses a mind whereof the greatest part is eternal.[5]

Let us recall that *The Ethics* is composed in the axiomatic-deductive mode, with all propositions deduced from preceding propositions, lemmas, axioms and definitions.[6] Proposition 5.39 is demonstrated as follows.

> *Proof.* He, who possesses a body capable of the greatest number of activities, is least agitated by those emotions which are evil ([*by proposition*] 4.38) – that is (4.30) those emotions which are contrary to

our nature; therefore (5.10), he possesses the power of arranging and associating the modifications of the body according to the intellectual order, and, consequently [*5.14, missing in the Elwes version*], of bringing it about, that all the modifications of the body should be referred to the idea of God [*or Nature, or Substance; i.e. self caused, infinite, eternal being*]; whence it will come to pass that (5.15) he will be affected with love toward God, which (5.16) must occupy or constitute the chief part of the mind; therefore (5.33), such a man will possess a mind whereof the chief part is eternal. QED.

The first proposition referred to in the proof is crucial for the understanding of Spinoza's doctrine of capability. Proposition 4.38 states that:

> Whatsoever disposes the human body, so as to render it capable of being affected in an increased number of ways, or affecting external bodies in an increased number of ways, is useful to man; and is so, in proportion as the body is thereby rendered more capable of being affected or affecting other bodies in an increased number of ways; contrariwise, whatsoever renders the body less capable in this respect is hurtful to man.
>
> *Proof:* Whatsoever thus increases the capabilities of the body increases also the mind's capability of perception (2.14); therefore, whatsoever thus disposes the body and renders it capable, is necessarily good or useful (4.26, 4.27); and is so in proportion to the extent to which it can render the body capable; contrariwise (2.14, 4.26, 4.27), it is hurtful, if it renders the body in this respect less capable. QED.

That is, the proof says that whatsoever increases the capabilities of the body also increases the mind's capability of understanding. And what increases our power of understanding is certainly good.

In order to prove that whatsoever increases the body's capabilities also increases the capabilities of the mind, the proof uses Proposition 2.14, which states that

> The human mind is capable of perceiving a great number of things, and is so in proportion as its body is capable of receiving a great number of impressions.

Spinoza could also have stated that the reciprocal statement is also true; that whatsoever increases the capabilities of the mind augments also the capabilities of the body. That is, the proof could have used the often quoted

Proposition 2.7, the base of Spinoza's so called body/mind "parallelism" theory:

> The order and connexion of ideas is the same as the order and connection of things.

The Note to this Proposition further affirms this same idea, that is, that:

> [...] substance thinking and substance extended are one and the same substance [*God or Nature*], comprehended now through one attribute, now through the other. So, also, a mode of extension and the idea of that mode are one and same thing. This truth seems to have been dimly recognized by those Jews who maintained that God, God's intellect, and the things understood by God are identical.

Now, we know also from the Note to Proposition 2.1 that:

> [...] in proportion as a thinking being is conceived as thinking more thoughts [*or, what is the same, as an extended being is conceived as capable of more activities*], so it is conceived as containing more reality or perfection.

This relationship between increased capabilities and increased perfection or reality can be used for an alternative explanation of our starting Proposition 5.39, on the relationship between capability and eternity. Spinoza affirms in the same Note to 2.1:

> Therefore a being which can think an infinite number of things in an infinite number of ways [or, what is the same, which can perform infinite acts in an infinite number of ways], is, necessarily, in respect of thinking [or in respect of extension], infinite.

Infinite thoughts are timeless, eternal thoughts. A being capable of thinking infinite thoughts would be thinking eternal thoughts. Such a being would be so sharing, as to say, in eternity, insofar as it thinks infinite/eternal thoughts.[7] Also, psycho-physical identity ("parallelism") would suggest that a mind which is thinking infinite thoughts has an extended correlate which is performing infinite acts. This would be one way of interpreting the relationship between capability and eternity in Proposition 5.39.

Spinoza's demonstration of 5.39 quoted above recurs to his idea of *scientia intuitiva*. The proof says that the larger the capabilities of the body, the greater the faculties of the mind (and vice versa, we should add); in particular, the greater is the capability of the mind of rationally comprehending its emotions. The mind will thus be more able to form clear and distinct ideas; that is, ideas that can be referred to the idea of God or Nature, since whatsoever is (or is conceived in the mind), is in God or Nature. Spinoza calls this ability of the mind *scientia intuitiva*, and this *third kind of knowledge,* by which the mind conceives things under the form of eternity (*sub specie aeternitatis*).[8] Now, the mind, regarding its own power of comprehension, is affected by pleasure, this pleasure being accompanied by the idea of God or Nature (so much the more in proportion as it understands itself and its emotions). According to Spinoza, pleasure accompanied by the idea of an external cause is love. Pleasure accompanied by the idea of God or Nature is what Spinoza calls *intellectual love of God.* This intellectual love is an activity whereby God or Nature – insofar it can be explained through the human mind – regards itself accompanied by the idea of itself. Since God or Nature is an absolutely infinite being, this love of the mind is part of the infinite love wherewith God or Nature loves itself. This love, this knowledge *sub specie aeternitatis*, is possible for the mind insofar as it conceives its own body under the form of eternity. And this idea, which expresses the essence of the body under the form of eternity, is necessarily eternal.

The above ideas are indeed difficult and mind-boggling.[9] They nevertheless clearly point towards the idea of human growth or human perfection as the increasing realm of human capabilities of thought and activity, that is, of effective freedom (cf. Sen 1999). Human perfection depends on expanded domains of activity for every individual on every conceivable dimension of human existence, which implies also increased domains of knowledge and understanding in enlarged dimensions of thought. Human development does *not* depend on increased levels of "utility" derived from consumption.[10]

Part II: A Spinoza–Sen economics research programme

The Ethics and present-day science

The psychophysical identity theory in Spinoza's *The Ethics* is particularly well adapted for the analysis of the body/mind problem in the framework of present day natural sciences. In particular, evolutionary theory finds its natural foundation in the notion of immanent causation inherent to Substance (God or Nature) – that which has itself as its own cause and is not produced by anything external. Particular entities are modifications or *modes* of the Substance, produced by one another in an infinite chain of causation.

According to Henry Atlan (1998, p. 215), "[w]ith such a notion of immanent causality, Evolution can be seen as the unfolding of a dynamic system, or a process of complexification and self-organization of matter, produced as the necessary outcome of the laws of physics and chemistry. In this process, new species come into existence one after the other as effects of mutations and stabilizing conditions working as their efficient causes, whereas their particular organizations are particular instances of the whole process." The omniform complexity of the texture of matter/extension corresponds to the omniform complexity of the thought dimension of the Substance. To the chain of causes in the material domain corresponds an equivalent chain of causes under the attribute of thought.[11] It is important to remark the absence in this conception of interaction between matter and thought; both have their own, equivalent causal structures, as they are two (different) faces of the (same) coin. In his *Ethics* Spinoza writes:

[A] mental decision and a bodily appetite, or determined state, are simultaneous, or rather are one and the same thing, which we call decision, when it is regarded under and explained through the attribute of thought, and a conditioned state, when it is regarded under the attribute of extension, and deduced from the laws of motion and rest. (3.2, Note)

Or, as emphatically stated in 3.2: "Body cannot determine mind to think, neither can mind determine body to motion or rest or any state different from these, if such there be".

However, the idea that the decisions of the mind determine the actions of the body is deeply rooted in our intuitive (unreflective) view of our actions. This is due, thinks Spinoza, to the fact that, in general, we are aware of our desires and intentions, but unaware of the causes that motivate these desires and intentions (2.35, Note; 3.2, Note).[12] The belief is so entrenched that it is merely at the bidding of the mind that the body performs its actions, says Spinoza (3.2, Note), that only experimental proof may eventually induce us to change our minds.

Now, it seems that neuroscience can today supply the conditions for an experimental proof of immanent causation, and convincingly reject the hypothesis of mental causation of bodily action. As reported by Atlan (1998), Libet (1985) consistently found that a conscious decision to act corresponds to an electrical brain event that occurs 200 to 300 milliseconds *after* the beginning of action. This experimentally reproducible fact, consistent with the above "monist" model, falsifies the conventional idea of mind-determined bodily action. The action of the body is triggered by some neuronal unconscious stimuli. That is, a physical impulse determines a bodily movement. Accompanying that action there is a conscious observation with an understanding of the action. The conscious observation accompanies the action, but it is not its cause. The psychic decision and the neural impulse are identically equivalent, each within their own domain of existence/description.[13] This fact has of course important consequences for our understanding of *homo oeconomicus,* and for what can be accepted as meaningful explanation in economic theory.

Economic theory after The Ethics

The effects of the above insights on conventional economic theorising are, I think, devastating. The utility maximizing individuals of conventional theory are isolated minds commanding bodily actions. *Homo oeconomicus* is a mind with a particular preference system and a perceived resource constraint commanding a body to perform specific actions (purchases and sales) in a marketplace. This mind is conscious of its own actions, and ignorant of the causes by which it is conditioned. This idea of "rational choice" simply reflects ignorance of any cause for the agent's actions.

That is, the *homo oeconomicus* model of conventional microeconomics does not specify how the preferences of the mind have been themselves determined, and even less how the mind determines the body to perform its "optimal" decisions in the market. Microeconomics is totally silent on how and where this interaction could take place. The model of man propounded by microeconomics simply eludes the problem of interaction. The man of microeconomics should more accurately be named *homunculus oeconomicus*. In cognitive science, the *homunculus* is an implausible little man inhabiting the brain and embodying an uncaused will making choices and commanding the body to execute them.[14]

The canonical model of body/mind dualism is still that of Descartes in *Traité des Passions de l'Ame* (1.50). In Descartes, the will, located in the pineal gland, receives signals and sends impulses – by means of the bodily humours (*esprits animaux*) – to other parts of the body.[15] But, as Spinoza argues (Part 5, Preface) it is not possible to have non-physical entities acting on material objects (*deus ex machina*) as an acceptable form of rational explanation. Should an interactive mechanism ever get specified, it would absorb the non-physical antecedent into the physical consequent[16]

In *The Ethics*, individual entities are, as described in the previous section, causally interconnected in an unlimited web of modifications (*modes*) of the uncaused Substance (*causa sui*). The ideas of the mind are causally connected to other ideas, as bodies in space are causally interrelated. Yet this does not exclude autonomy and responsibility. On the contrary, individual entities endeavour to exist according to their own individual nature (3.6):

> Everything, in so far as it is in itself, endeavour to persist in its own being.

For Spinoza (3.7), the actual essence of a thing is nothing else but this endeavour to persist in its own being (*conatus*). The mind endeavour to persist in its being, and is conscious of it (3.9). An implication of conatus, as formulated in the *Theologico-Political Treatise*, is that:

> [...] no man's mind can possibly lie wholly at the disposition of another, for no one can willingly transfer his natural right of free reason and judgment, or be compelled to do so ... All these questions fall within a man's natural right, which he cannot abdicate even with consent. (Spinoza 1951, p. 257, quoted from Ellerman 1992, pp.144–5)

The freedom of the mind is, for Spinoza, inalienable, for it cannot renounce, even if compelled to, its own nature.[17] Conatus (a thing endeavouring to persist in its own being) belongs to the essence of human being, and this essence is common to all human beings. An important consequence is that slavery, even when voluntary, is inherently invalid. The same logic, applied to the modern employment contract, makes it also inherently invalid and universal self-employment or economic democracy the only "post-socialist" alternative to present day wage-slavery.[18] Spinoza (1958, Chapter VI, paragraph 12) also propounds that land – the principal source of status, power and wealth in feudal society – be the public ownership of the commonwealth, and hired to its citizens. An up-to-date radical Enlightenment reform would then imply public ownership of capital, to be hired to the producers ("labour hires capital," instead of the other way round) – along with abolition of the employment contract.

Now – what would it look like, an economic science that is consistent with the ontological scheme of *The Ethics*? As I see it, in the first place *Homunculus oeconomicus* should be exorcized. The fiction of invisible homunculi with particular (arbitrary) idiosyncrasies performing their autistic optimising calculus, and thereby shaping the economic (extended) space, should be abandoned.[19] Instead of the homunculus, we should introduce the notion of an (intersubjective) economic mental space. In my view, the most fruitful concept for representing the causal web of interconnected thoughts is the notion of *field*. Individual thoughts (perceptions, deliberations, feelings, volitions, etc) are not arbitrary or contingent, but belong to structured sets.[20] Consumption choices, for instance, characteristically change between socio-economic classes. They show also observable patterns over space. Being subjected to causal processes, individual preferences also show definite patterns of change over time – although accepting this obvious fact is anathema for conventional economics. Another obvious fact is that individual choices are influenced by persuasion (advertising, etc), which so contributes to shaping the field of preferences. Collective opinion, as reflected for instance in regulating bodies and other social institutions, also shapes the economic mind-space. Similar analysis of causal chains should be applied to the subjective dimension, or economic psychology, of production and other spheres of economic activity. All these aspects should also be embedded in the characteristic mentality or spirit of the time (and place), or dominant ideology, which influences the configuration of the whole economic mind-set. Our Spinoza–Sen objective for economic and social development is enlarged human capabilities, rather than consumption or output, but it would also be necessary to confront the additional difficulty of tracing the effects of consumption and production activities on mental capabilities. Certain types of consumption (and production) contribute to enlarging capabilities more than others; some have negative effects; some have only transitory effects, others more durable ones, etc.

I am afraid that, to many, the above research programme would look rather quixotic. However, what as a whole and at first sight can look like an overly ambitious project, might give some interesting results already at the initial stage of description, conceptualization, formalization and organization of data. Indeed, the task is greatly facilitated by the wealth of extant results from empirical research in different disciplines (marketing, experimental and industrial/economic psychology and so on). However imperfect and limited, this change of perspective, from the constricted perspective of the homunculus towards the extensive causal network of the economic mind-space, would imply a decisive movement, within the discipline of economics, in the direction of what one philosopher of science called the "great transformation," in the evolution from the ego-centered image towards a unified, scientific view of human being.[21]

Let us now leave the mental dimension, and briefly refer to the "extended" dimension of our "psychoeconomic" identity, that is, the external world of observable economic relationships. With the sortilege of the homunculus gone, big chunks of masonry – or even all of it – risk falling from the baroque façade of economics. The underlying classical structures, closely related to social philosophy and ethics, will appear in all their august beauty. The parts of economic theory inhabited by the homunculi and affected of Cartesian interactionism/dualism will lose much of their enchanting power. A case in point is the Arrow–Debreu model of general equilibrium, the central piece of conventional economic theory and the archetype of interaction between atomistic, self-caused minds and passive bodies (consumers, factory owners, firms and so on) acting in the markets. This means also that most of microeconomics should follow the same fate, for it is today conventionally conceived as variations on different aspects – in teaching, a piecemeal construction – of the general equilibrium model. Along with microeconomics should also go most of macroeconomics, since most of conventional macroeconomics has today abandoned the Keynesian paradigm, to become a kind of aggregated, policy-oriented – and often interest-group-controlled – microeconomics.

The view of the economy as a causally structured, directly observable system of relationships existing in time has deep roots and lively ramifications in economic theory. One of the oldest sources of this view is the *Tableau Économique* of François Quesnay (published in 1766). For Quesnay, the chief question for investigation was what causes the wealth of the nation, and how this wealth circulates between "*la classe productive, la classe des propriétaires & la classe stérile.*" The *Tableau* is the first sophisticated analysis of the flow of value through the economy and among social classes. This focus on value creation *and* distribution was characteristic of the classical economists, including Marx, and could be seen as the permanent characteristic of a wide strand of economics that flourishes still today. This wide current includes nowadays post- and neo- Keynesian (Kaleckian) economics, Sraffrian and neo-Ricardian economics, input–output economics, and (non-interactionist) post- and neo-Marxian economics.[22] But what is still lacking from the Spinoza–Sen perspective in all these theoretical approaches is how output and distribution relate to capabilities. These theories focus on the growth and distribution of output and income, but not on how they influence the growth and distribution of human capabilities. These theories describe production and distribution/exploitation in the system where "the accumulation of capital is God and the prophets." We should also analyse systems operating towards expanding human capabilities.

Notes

*   I would like to thank Edward Fullbrook for his suggestions during the work on this essay and the Wenner–Gren Foundation whose grant facilitated this study at an early stage.

1. There are many well known economists in this category. Serge-Christophe Kolm could for instance be mentioned, as a continental member of this class.

2. The "hideous hypothesis" of "that famous atheist" was "the doctrine of the simplicity of the universe, and the unity of that substance, in which he supposes both thought and matter to inhere" (Hume, 1911 [1739–40], p. 229). (I must say that I do not agree with the word "simplicity" in Hume's description; the reasons why will be apparent in what follows.) According to Jonathan Israel (2001, p. 159) "hideous" could had been an ironic characterization. Hume belonged in fact to the same banned category of radical Enlightenment thinkers such as Diderot, Voltaire and Spinoza himself (Israel, 2001, p.109). Curiously, Diderot's article on Spinoza in the *Encyclopédie* could be also said to be "ironic."

3. See for instance Sen (1988). By the way, the young Marx was a dedicated student of Spinoza (see Rubel, 1978). Aristotle's ideas do not exactly prefigure Sen's (or Spinoza's) notion of capabilities –see the discussion of the Aristotelian principle in Rawls (1999, section 65).

4. As an assiduous reader of Spinoza literature, I know that I am aware of only one small portion of it. According for instance to the Swedish bibliographic database (www.libris.kb.se) there are 743 Spinoza-related books in Nordic libraries – 42 of them published in 2001–2. (Journal articles must most probably be counted in the thousands. There are also several Spinoza websites.) The increasing rate of publication may perhaps be announcing the near fulfilment of Lichtenberg's famous prediction: "If the world should endure for an incalculable number of years the universal religion [ethics] will be a purified Spinozism. Left to itself, reason can lead to nothing else and it is impossible that it ever will lead to anything else" (1990 [1800–1806], p. 115).

5. I quote from Elwes's version on compact disc in *Lire l'Éthique de Spinoza*, Phronésis, Paris, 1998.

6. The title of *The Ethics* in the original is *Ethica ordine geometrico demonstrata*. Possibly Spinoza chose this mode of argumentation because of its overwhelming power of conviction. For many centuries *The Elements* of Euclid was second only to the Bible in numbers of extant copies. Also, the prominence of mathematics and natural science was rapidly growing in fifteenth-century Europe.

7. For a suggestive comparison of this insight with the insight of meditation, see Wetlesen (1977).

8. Spinoza's first and second kinds of knowledge can be succinctly described as hearsay or opinion and science respectively.

9. Spinoza's own reply in the last words of *The Ethics* was "But all things excellent are as difficult as they are rare," comes naturally to mind.

10. Increased levels of *passive* consumption or leisure, from *The Ethic's* perspective, might indeed be seen as *lessening* human perfection. Cf. Proposition 5.4: "In proportion as each thing possesses more of perfection, so is it more active, and less passive; and, vice versa, in proportion as it is more active, so it is more perfect." But of course in most cases increasing capabilities involve increased consumption and/or investment.

11. This implies that to all forms and levels of organization of matter correspond different forms and levels of organization of thought. The psychophysical identity, says Spinoza (2.13, Note), is "... entirely general, applying not more to men than to other individual things, all of which, though in different degrees, are animated." This type of theory has been named, in different contexts, monism, panpsychism, or hylozoism.

12. Or, in the words of a brain scientist and philosopher (Flanagan, 1996, p. 56): "We typically have no accurate and ongoing personal access to proximate causal antecedents of conscious acts of thought and choice, and this can produce a 'user illusion' that unmoved volitions precede and guide acts."

13. Or, in other words (Feigl, 1967, p. 79), "... the states of direct experience which conscious human beings "live through," and those which we confidently ascribe to some of the higher animals, are identical with certain (presumably configurational) aspects of the neural processes in those organisms." Or also (ibid, p. 149): "... the configurational (Gestalt) features of immediate experience are isomorphic with certain global features of our brain processes. Hence, strange as it may sound at first, it is possible that by doing introspective–phenomenological description of immediate experience, we are in effect ... doing a bit of ... brain physiology." This type of insight led Bertrand Russell (1959, p. 25) to maintain that "... the brain consists of thoughts." In the intricate language of quantum mechanics, psychophysical identity is described as follows (Lockwood, 1990, p. 191): "An n-dimensional phenomenal quality [mental] space is to be identified ... with an n-dimensional space of observable attributes, each point of which is associated with some n-tuple of eigenvalues of the spectra corresponding to the shared eigenstates (eigenvectors) of a set of n compatible brain observables." A particular (and in my view, restrictive) version of psychophysic identity theory, popular among scientists ("physicalism"), simply affirms that "there is no mind: the mind *is* the brain" □ there are no psychological facts that are incapable of being reduced to physical facts (see Humphrey 2002).

14. See Dennett (1991).

15. Descartes's *esprits animaux* became famous among economists as the unfathomable "animal spirits" of the investors in Keynes.

16. "I think we know for sure that neuroscience is not going to find any place for metaphysical freedom of the will, since that would involve neuroscientific vindication of the hypothesis that there is a faculty that initiates thought and action without itself having causal antecedents" (Flanagan 1996, p. 58).

17. See Flanagan (2002, Chapter 4) for a recent discussion of the compatibility of free human agency and moral accountability with universal causation (no Cartesian free will).

18. See Ellerman (1992). Chapter 9 of this book contains an enlightening intellectual history of this argument in the protracted struggle against slavery.

19. "The image of a decision maker that makes choices by consulting a preexisting preference order appears increasingly implausible. The alternative image is of a decision maker ... who constructs preferences in the context and in the format required by a particular situation." (Kahneman, 2000, p. xvi).

20. Kurt Lewin (1936) represents a seminal exponent of this approach. Unfortunately, it does not seem to have produced as many followers as it deserves. Another, more recent, possible structuring principle is the set theoretic dialectical psychology of

William Hoffman (1999). Kahneman and Tversky (2000) document a wealth of experimental research showing the implausibility of the homunculus, and pointing to the (intersubjective) rationality of causal structures/processes.

21. 'What happens in this "great transformation" is the replacing of most (or all) concepts of the solipsistic (egocentric) perspective as well as the manifest [dualistic/Cartesian] image (still suffused with subjectivistic features) by a completely intersubjective account. This has been seen, but expressed far too obscurely, even by the existentialists (e.g. Martin Buber), when they speak of the shift from the "I–Thou perspective" to the "It perspective" of impersonal, objective cognition.' (Feigl 1967, p. 155.)

22. Kurz and Salvadori (1995) is a concise survey of these schools. Other related schools are, for instance, the *école de la régulation*, evolutionary economics, (progressive) institutionalism, Latin American structuralism, and the SAM (social accounting matrix) approach.

References

Ellerman, David P, 1992, *Property and Contract in Economics: The Case for Economic Democracy*, Blackwell, Oxford.

Feigl, Herbert, 1967, *The "Mental" and the "Physical"*, University of Minnesota Press, Minneapolis.

Flanagan, Owen, 1996, "Neuroscience, Agency, and the Meaning of Life," in: *Self-Expressions*, Oxford University Press, Oxford.

Flanagan, Owen, 2002, *The Problem of the Soul*, Basic Books, New York.

Hoffman, William, 1999, "Dialectic – a universal for consciousness?," *New Ideas in Psychology* 17, 251–69.

Hume, David, 1911 [1739–40], *Treatise of Human Nature – Volume I*, J.M.Dent & Sons, London.

Humphrey, Nicholas, 2002, *The Mind Made Flesh*, Oxford University Press, Oxford.

Israel, Jonathan I, 2001, *Radical Enlightenment: Philosophy and the Making of Modernity 1650–1750*, Oxford University Press, Oxford.

Kahneman, Daniel, 2000, preface to D Kahneman and A Tversky (eds). *Choices, Values, and Frames*, Cambridge University Press, Cambridge.

Kurz, Heinz, and Neri Salvadori, 1995, *Theory of Production*, Cambridge University Press, Cambridge.

Lewin, Kurt, 1936, *Principles of Topological Psychology*, McGraw-Hill, New York.

Libet, Benjamin, 1985, "Unconscious cerebral initiative and the role of conscious will in voluntary action," *Behavioral and Brain Sciences*, 8, pp.529–66.

Lichtenberg, Georg C, 1990 [1800–1806], *Aphorisms*, Penguin, London.

Lockwood, Michael, 1990, *Mind, Brain and the Quantum*, Basil Blackwell, Oxford.

Rawls, John, 1999, *A Theory of Justice – Revised Edition*, Oxford University Press, Oxford.

Rubel, Maximilien, 1978, "Marx à la rencontre de Spinoza", *Économies et Sociétés*, January/February, 12, pp.239–65.

Russell, Bertrand, 1959, *My Philosophical Development*, Allen & Unwin, London.

Sen, Amartya, 1988, "The Concept of Development," in H Chenery and T N Srinivasan (eds), *Handbook of Development Economics – Volume I*, North Holland, Amsterdam.

Sen, Amartya, 1999, *Development as Freedom*, Oxford University Press, Oxford.

Spinoza, Benedict de, 1951 [1670], *Theological–Political Treatise*, Dover, New York.

Spinoza, Benedict de, 1958, "Tractatus Politicus" in A.G.Wernham (ed.), *Spinoza: The Political Works*, Clarendon Press, Oxford.

50.

THERMODYNAMICS AND ECONOMICS

Dietmar Lindenberger and Reiner Kümmel

Since Georgescu–Roegen´s statement on entropy, there has grown a vast literature on the implications of the laws of thermodynamics for economics. Most of this literature is related to the environmental consequences of the second law, i.e. that any economic activity unavoidably causes pollution.[1] This important insight could, at least to some extent, be integrated into (environmental) economic theory. Other implications of thermodynamics will probably be more difficult to be incorporated into the prevailing neoclassical framework, if this is possible at all. An example is the notion of irreversibility, which implies at least some sort of non-equilibrium. A corresponding micro-economic modelling approach was proposed recently in this journal [1]. Another example is discussed in the following. We address the issue of appropriately including the indispensable production factor energy into macro-economic theories of production and growth, and try to draw some conclusions.

In conventional neoclassical theory the production factor energy is either neglected altogether, which is inconsistent with thermodynamics, or attributed only marginal importance. The argument is that energy's share in total factor cost is small compared to the cost shares of labour and capital. However, the recessions after the oil price crises in 1973/74 and 1979/81 have posed the question how a production factor of monetarily minor importance can have such grave economic consequences.

The conventional view of the low economic importance of energy dates back to the first stages in the development of neoclassical economic theory.

Initially, the focus was not so much on the generation of wealth, but on its distribution and the efficiency of markets. Consequently, the early thinkers in economics started with a model of pure exchange of goods, without considering their production. With a set of assumptions on rational consumer behaviour it was shown that through the exchange of goods in markets an equilibrium results in which all consumers maximize their utility in the sense that it is not possible to improve the situation of a single consumer without worsening the situation of at least one other consumer (Pareto optimum). This benefit of (perfect) markets is generally considered as the foundation of free-market economics. It shows why markets, where "greedy" individuals meet, work at all. But later, when the model was extended to include production, the problem of the physical generation of wealth was coupled inseparably to the problem of the distribution of wealth, as a consequence of the model structure: since the neoclassical equilibrium is characterized by a (profit-maximizing) optimum in the interior – and not on the boundary – of the region in factor space accessible to the production system according to its state of technology, factor productivities had to equal factor prices. In the resulting production model the weights with which the production factors contribute to the physical generation of wealth, i.e. the elasticities of production, have to equal the factor cost shares. These cost shares, in the industrialized countries, are typically 0.7 (labour), 0.25 (capital) and 0.05 (energy).

Consequently, according to the neoclassical model, the elasticities of production of the factors, which – roughly speaking – measure the percentage of output growth if a factor input increases by 1 percent, would have to have these values: labour 0.7, capital 0.25, and energy 0.05. With these input weights a decrease of energy utilisation of up to 7 percent, as observed during the first oil crisis between 1973 and 1975, could explain a decrease of value added of only 0.05×7 percent $= 0.35$ percent. The actually observed decreases of economic output, however, were roughly ten times larger.

Furthermore, a substantial part of observed long-term economic growth cannot be explained by the growth of factor inputs, if these are weighted by their cost shares. Large residuals remain. In most cases the residuals play a more important role than the explanatory factors, which, according to Gahlen, makes the neoclassical theory of production tautological [2]. Solow, after noting "... it is true that the notion of time-shifts in the [production] function is a confession of ignorance rather than a claim of knowledge" [3], comments: "This ... has led to a criticism of the neoclassical model: it is a theory of growth that leaves the main factor in economic growth unexplained" [4].

As it has been shown recently, the residuals of neoclassical growth theory can mostly be removed by taking into account the production factor energy appropriately [5–11]. It turns out that the crucial point is to drop the neoclassical equilibrium assumption, and to determine the elasticities of production of the factors by purely technological and empirical considerations instead. Thereby, the previously unexplained technological progress reveals its two principal elements.

The first one is the activation of the increasingly automated capital stock by energy; and, of course, the people who handle capital have to be qualified appropriately. The second one consists of improvements of organizational and energetic efficiencies of the capital stock. The short-term impact of the first element is much bigger than that of the second element, but the reverse may be true for the long-term impact, if efficiency improvements fundamentally change the course of economic evolution [11]. The efficiency improvements are identified by shifts of the corresponding technology parameters in the production functions, whereas energy's high productive power in increasingly automated production processes is revealed by its high elasticity of production: Energy's elasticity, in industrial sectors of the economy, is typically of the order 0.5, i.e. as large as those of capital and labour together. In service sectors it still exceeds energy's low cost share significantly [7]. Both in industrial and service sectors, labour's elasticity is far below its cost share. Only in the case of capital, do elasticities of production and cost shares turn out to be roughly in equilibrium, as neoclassical theory presupposes.[2]

What are the consequences of these findings? Let us frame one selected point as follows. If wealth had been distributed according to the "marginal productivity theory", labour would have received only a share of national income much smaller than the observed 70 percent. But apparently, in the past most of the value added by energy was attributed to labour. The underlying mechanism of distribution was that of wage-negotiations in which free labour unions, powerful during times of high employment, regularly succeeded in winning wage increases according to the growth of productivity, i.e. increased production due to increased and more efficient energy utilization. This way most of the population in the industrialized countries benefited from the wealth generated by the production factors capital, labour and energy.

With increasing automation in production, however, human routine labour becomes more and more dispensable. A possible consequence is the increasing inequality in the distribution of income, as can be observed in the US, where, due to flexible labour markets, the hours worked per year have increased, but the problem of the "working poor" remains unsolved. Consequently, if society wishes to organize labour markets more competitively, while socially unacceptable distributional effects are to be avoided, the question arises how the institutional settings within market-economies have to be adapted to the changing technological conditions.

Certainly, increased investments in education and the design of appropriate labour market and social policies are crucial issues. Here, let us address the issue of how such policies may be financed in a sustainable way. In the past the financial burden resulting from social policies was mainly put on the production factor labour. This is one of the causes of the identified disequilibrium between the cost shares and productive powers of labour and energy, which, in turn, accelerates technical progress towards increasing automation. If this disequilibrium is sufficiently steep, the newly emerging and expanding sectors of the economy will no longer be able to compensate for the losses of jobs due to increased automation in the existing industries, thus destabilizing the system as a whole. Therefore, in view of social and fiscal stability, it might be worthwhile to consider a shift of taxes and levies in the industrial countries in such a way that the production factors labour and energy are burdened more according to their productive contributions to value added.

Notes

1. i.e. the emission of heat and substances into the environment due to entropy production.
2. The production systems are operating in boundary cost minima in factor space, where the boundaries, at a given point in time, are established by the state of technology in information processing and automation and prevent the system from sliding at once into the absolute cost minimum of nearly vanishing labour input.

References

1. Martinás, K, "Is the utility maximization principle necessary?", *post-autistic economics review*, issue no. 12, March 15, 2002, article 4 and references therein, http://www.btinternet.com/~pae_news/review/issue12.htm.
2. Gahlen, B, Der Informationsgehalt der neoklassischen Wachstumstheorie für die Wirtschaftspolitik, J C B Mohr, Tübingen, 1972.
3. Solow, R M, "Investment and technical progress", in *Mathematical Methods in the Social Sciences*, K J Arrow, S Karlin and P Suppes (eds), Stanford, 1960, pp. 89–104.
4. Solow, R M, "Perspectives on growth theory", *Journal of Economic Perspectives*, 8, 1994, pp. 45–54.
5. Kümmel R W Strassl, A Gossner and W Eichhorn, "Technical progress and energy dependent production functions", *Journal of Economics* 45, 1985, pp. 285–311.

6. Beaudreau, B C, *Energy and Organization: Growth and Distribution Re-examined*, Westwood (CT), Greenwood Press, 1998.
7. Lindenberger, D, "Wachstumsdynamik industrieller Volkswirtschaften – Energieabhängige Produktions-funktionen und ein faktorpreisgesteuertes Optimierungs-model", Metropolis-Verlag, Marburg, 2000.
8. Ayres, R U, "The minimum complexity of endogenous growth models: the role of physical resource flows", in *Energy – The International Journal*, 26, 2001, p. 817–38.
9. Ayres, R U and B Warr, "Accounting for growth: the role of physical work", in "Reappraising Production Theory", workshop of the Max Planck Institute for Research into Economic Systems, Jena, 2001.
10. Hall, C; D Lindenberger, R Kümmel, T Kroeger and W Eichhorn (2001), "The need to reintegrate the natural sciences with economics", *BioScience* 51 (8), 2001, 663–73.
11. Kümmel, R, J Henn and D Lindenberger, *Capital, labour, Energy and Creativity: Modelling Innovation Diffusion, Structural Change and Economic Dynamics*, 2002 (in press), http://theorie.physik.uni-wuerzburg.de/TP1/kuemmel/profile.html (fields of research, ref. 14).

PART 9:

PUTTING ETHICS INTO ECONOMICS

51.

ETHICS IN ECONOMIC THEORY

Charles K Wilber

Introduction

Economics and ethics are interrelated because both economists (theorists and policy advisers) and economic actors (sellers, consumers, workers) hold ethical values that help shape their behaviour. In the first case economists must try to understand how their own values affect both economic theory and policy. In the second case this means economic analysis must broaden its conception of human behaviour.

In this chapter I will focus on the first of these two issues – economists construct theory upon a particular world view, resulting in basic concepts, such as efficiency, being value-laden.

Values, world views and the economist

There is a substantial body of literature on methodological issues in economics (though seldom found in the 'top' journals), much of it calling into question its supposed scientific character. Part of that literature deals explicitly with the impact of ethical value judgments on economics as a science. Of this literature, a greater amount argues the value-permeation thesis than defends the idea of value-neutrality. However, value-neutrality of economics as a science remains the dominant position in the day-to-day work of mainstream economists. It seems expedient to begin by laying out its arguments.

Value neutrality. There are two pervasive tenets to the value-neutrality argument. The first is a reliance on the Humean guillotine which

categorically separates fact ('what is') from value ('what ought to be'); also
known as the positive/normative dichotomy. The second basic tenet
strongly supports the first by claiming that since we have objective access to
the empirical world through our sense experience, scientists need not
concern themselves with 'what ought to be.' This second tenet is the really
crucial point and the one that a post-positivist philosophy of science has
sought to undermine.

The value-neutral position argues that scientific economics is comprised
of three separate components: pre-scientific decisions, scientific analysis, and
post-scientific application. However, there is a difference between the value
judgments of pre-science and of post-science. Hume's guillotine is protected
by drawing a distinction in social science between two types of value
judgments. A *characterizing value judgement* expresses an estimate of the degree
to which some commonly recognized (and more or less clearly defined) type
of action, object or institution is embodied in a given instance. An *appraising
value judgment* expresses approval or disapproval either of some moral (or
social) ideal, or of some action (or institution) because of commitment to
such an ideal. Some value judgments are thus not really value judgments of
any ethical significance, but judgments that merely allow one to carry on the
scientific enterprise.[1]

In other attempts to reconcile value judgments and objective science, the
notion of 'brute fact' is often used. This is the claim that facts are in some
sense 'out there' for all to see, independent of scientific theory.
Unfortunately for the value neutral position, the idea of brute fact has fallen
on hard times in the philosophy of science literature. Today it is generally
recognized even by sophisticated logical empiricists that facts are
theory-laden and that theories are tested by those facts deemed important
by the theory.

The defence of value-neutrality still stands, but the pillars have been
shaken. Blaug conceded that both 'factual' and 'moral' arguments rest 'at
bottom' 'on certain definite techniques of persuasion, which in turn depend
for their effectiveness, on shared values of one kind or another.'[2] And, of
course, McCloskey's writings on the 'rhetoric of economics' have taken this
argument into the heart of economics – *The American Economic Review* – where
mainstream economists have studiously ignored it.[3]

Value permeation. The value permeation position argues that while science
is driven by a search for truth, it is not interested in just any truth. The
relevant truth must be both 'interesting' and 'valuable,' and thus all science
is goal-directed activity. Further, the criteria for a 'good' or 'acceptable'
scientific theory cannot be ranked in terms of its intrinsic importance, but

only in relation to the degree it serves particular goals of the scientific community.

Theory choice is not, therefore, based objectively on non-controversial criteria (e.g. degree of verification or corroboration), but on criteria that are inevitably value-laden (i.e. the extent to which each theory serves specific ends). The scientists' search for 'valuable truth' is directed by what they think society (and science) ought to do. No amount of evidence ever completely confirms or disconfirms any empirical hypothesis but only renders it more or less probable.

Another line of reasoning, Kuhnian in character, has been another line of attack. Kuhn, referring to the natural sciences, speaks of paradigms, characterized by the shared values of a given scientific community.[4] It is Kuhn's rejection of the second tenet – that we have objective access to the empirical world through our sense experience – that is important for those opposed to the value-neutrality position. He argues that the empirical world can be known only through the filter of a theory; thus, facts are theory-laden. Thus, a major argument of those who build on Kuhn's approach runs as follows: A world view greatly influences the scientific paradigm out of which one works; value judgments are closely associated with the world view; theories must remain coherent with the world view; facts themselves are theory-laden; therefore, the whole scientific venture is permeated by value judgments from the start. This world view, or *Weltanschauung*, shapes the interests of the scientist and determines the questions asked, the problems considered important, the answers deemed acceptable, the axioms of the theory, the choice of relevant facts, the hypotheses proposed to account for such facts, the criteria used to assess the fruitfulness of competing theories, the language in which results are to be formulated, and so on.

The neo-classical world view: a case in point

Let me illustrate this world view argument by applying it to neo-classical economics.[5] The world view of mainstream neo-classical economics is closely associated with the notion of the good embedded in its particular scientific paradigm. It is founded on a world view made up of the following propositions:

1. Human nature is such that humans are a) self-interested and b) rational. That is, they know their own interest and choose from among a variety of means in order to maximize that interest.

2. The purpose of human life is for individuals to pursue happiness as they themselves define it. Therefore, it is essential that they be left free to do so.

3. The ideal social world is a gathering of free individuals who compete with each other under conditions of scarcity to achieve self-interested ends. As in the natural world with physical entities, in the social world too there are forces at work that move economic agents toward equilibrium positions.

Neoclassical economists either accept the preceding empirically unverifiable and unfalsifiable statements or, barring overt acceptance, conduct scientific inquiry with methods based thereon. The first two propositions contain the motivating force in economic life (satisfaction of self-interest) and the third proposition spells out the context in which that force works itself out. It is interesting that experimental studies by psychologists indicate that people are concerned about cooperating with others and with being fair, not just preoccupied with their own self-interest. Ironically, these same studies indicate that those people attracted into economics are more self-interested and taking economics makes people even more self-interested. Thus economic theory creates a self-fulfilling prophecy.[6]

It seems fairly clear that judgments of value, of a particular notion of the good, are directly implied by propositions one and two of this world view. If the purpose of life is that individuals pursue happiness, and if they do so self-interestedly, then it certainly would be good for individuals to receive what they want. Here is the basic notion of the good permeating all neoclassical economics: *individuals should be free to get as much as possible of what they want.* There are two basic judgments required to translate this concept of the good into economic theory, such as cost-benefit analysis. The first of these is that *individual preferences are what count.* The second is a value judgment on distributional equity. But this value judgment is rather superficial, for it is external to the neoclassical paradigm. Because it is external it often obstructs our view of the more fundamental value judgments, those deeply embedded in the paradigm itself.

Other ancillary value judgments of the neoclassical paradigm either qualify what types of individual wants will be considered or are derivative from this basic value judgment. These other ancillary value judgments can be summarized in this way:

1. Competitive market equilibrium is the ideal economic situation. Therefore, a) competitive market institutions should be established

whenever and wherever possible; and b) market prices should be used to determine value.

2.   Means and ends should be bifurcated into two mutually exclusive categories.

3.   Means and ends should be measured quantitatively.

The first ancillary value judgment derives from elements one and three of the neo-classical world view and from the basic value judgment that individual preferences should count. If one takes the core ideas of individualism, rationality and the social context of harmony among diverse and conflicting interests, along with a number of limiting assumptions, it can be shown that competitive equilibrium maximizes the value of consumption and is therefore the best of all possible economic situations. This ancillary value judgment does not stand alone. Competitive market equilibrium is good, in part, because it allows the greatest number of individual wants to be satisfied. Moreover, this value judgment is also determined by the world view. Without the third proposition such a judgment could not be made, for then some other economic condition could be found to satisfy individual wants. Competitive market equilibrium is good because the world view insists that only this condition can be ideal.

The notion of competitive equilibrium carries out two basic functions: it serves as an ideal and as a standard by which to measure the real value of current economic conditions. Because it serves as an ideal for which we strive, it leads directly to the value judgment that wherever competitive markets do not exist or are weak, they should be instituted or promoted. Wherever markets do not exist, the natural competitiveness of human beings will be channelled into other non-productive directions. It is better to establish markets where this competitiveness and self-interest seeking behaviour can be channelled into mutually satisfying activities. Wherever markets are weak and distorted due to monopoly power or government interference there is sure to be a reduction in actual consumption. Therefore, perfectly competitive markets should be promoted so that the ideal competitive equilibrium can be achieved.

The second and third ancillary value judgments do not spring directly from the world view. Instead, they make the paradigm based thereon operational. The separation of means and ends is not strictly required by the world view itself, but is an operational requirement without which the paradigm could generate no meaningful research or study. If means and ends were not mutually exclusive, then neoclassical economics would be nothing more than a simple statement that humans do what they do because they wish to do it. There could be, for example, no inquiry into how satisfaction is maximized by choosing among various alternatives. If some activity (e.g. production or consumption) could be both means and end then one could not determine which part is which. This results in the value judgment that consumption is the end or 'good' to be achieved. In so doing, any good inherent in the process or means for obtaining higher consumption is ignored. For example, if the production activity of human labour were more than just a means – if work was good in and of itself regardless of the final product – then it would be impossible for the neoclassical economist to discover how much individual wants are satisfied by the activity. The ends and the means would be all mixed together and it would be impossible to speak of the value of the product and the cost of the resources independently.

The splitting of economic activities into means and ends by its very nature promotes a particular notion of the good. It may be an operational necessity, but it is also a judgment of value. With means and ends separated, it becomes convenient to measure the satisfaction given by particular ends and the dissatisfaction (costs) resulting from employing various means. It becomes possible to measure how much better one situation is than another, by comparing numbers instead of concepts or ideas. Things that are apparently incommensurable thus become commensurable. This is evident in many branches of neoclassical analysis; when money values are unavailable or inappropriate, quantified units are used in their place.

The emphasis on quantification in neoclassical economics adds another element to its particular notion of the good. While the second ancillary value judgment separates means and ends, the third ancillary value judgment tells us to focus on means and ends that can be quantified. One practical outcome of this is a heavy emphasis on 'things' over interpersonal relationships, education, cultural affairs, family, workplace organization, etc. Things are countable while the quality of these other spheres of human life is not. In the area of economic policy especially, such concerns are treated often as obstacles to be removed or overcome.[7] To the extent that this occurs, the notion of the good that focuses on quantifiable inputs and outputs is embedded in the paradigm.

Within neoclassical economics there are thus judgments of value that are rooted in a fundamental world view. There are also ancillary judgments of value which operate in concert with the world view and which allow the neoclassical approach to be operational. Together these judgments make up the neoclassical position on the character of the good, and when an economic policy is planned, implemented and evaluated, it is done on the basis of these clearly defined standards.

To conclude this discussion, the paradigm or research programme of *any* scientific community is circumscribed by boundaries laid out in a world view which, while not perhaps individually subjective, is nevertheless empirically untestable, or metaphysical as Boland would say.[8] How then do value judgments about the good, the just and the right enter into scientific analysis? Such value judgments are themselves entailed by the same world view which gives rise to theoretical and factual analysis. 'What is' and 'what ought to be' are thus inextricably commingled in the data, the facts, the theories, the descriptions, the explanations, the prescriptions, and so on. All are permeated by the a priori world view.

Economists must recognize that there is no alternative to working from a world view. Making explicit the values embodied in that world view will help keep economics more honest and useful. For example, many institutional economists see the social world as characterized by interdependence of economic actors with the result that 'externalities' are ubiquitous. The assignment of rights by the political and legal systems, therefore, determines 'who gets what.' The distribution of income, wealth, and rights that results from economic transactions and public policies becomes as important as efficiency.[9]

Furthermore, it is not sufficient to simply reject the neoclassical position that satisfying individual preferences, as expressed in the market, is the only measure of economic welfare. Alternatives must be proposed and developed. Let me sketch out one possible alternative.[10]

We must broaden our view of human welfare from that of a simple consumer of goods and services with consumer sovereignty as the goal. Rather, once biological needs are met, people derive welfare primarily from social activities such as working, dancing, theorizing, playing golf, painting, partying and so forth. In order to engage in such activities people need instruments, capacities and a social context or environment.

People need instruments (goods and services) to engage in activities – fishing poles to fish, tools to work, shoes to dance in. Traditional economics focuses solely on this need. However, the instruments are worthless unless people have the capacity to use them – training is needed to learn how to fly-fish, to use tools to repair a car, to dance the Tango. Finally, people need a social context or environment to carry out these activities – a clean river is needed to fish in, good working conditions are needed to enjoy working, clean air and safe streets are needed to enjoy jogging.

The result of such a world view is that the measure of human welfare expands from consumer sovereignty to also include worker sovereignty (do people have the jobs they want; are the jobs fulfilling; does the work enhance people's capacities?) and citizen sovereignty (do people have the communities and environments they want; do they have the power to construct the social contexts within which they can develop their capacities?). With this expanded conception of human welfare the evaluation of economic policies can be quite different.

Notes

1. See Ernest Nagel, *The Structure of Science: Problems in the Logic of Scientific Explanation* (New York: Harcourt, Brace and World, 1961).
2. See Mark Blaug, *The Methodology of Economics: Or How Economists Explain* (Cambridge: Cambridge University Press, 1980), p. 132.
3. See Donald N McCloskey, *The Rhetoric of Economics* (Madison: University of Wisconsin Press, 1985) and the voluminous literature generated by it.
4. See Thomas S Kuhn, *The Structure of Scientific Revolutions*, 2nd edn (Chicago: University of Chicago Press, 1970); 'Reflections on my critics,' in Imre Lakatos and Alan Musgrave (eds), *Criticism and the Growth of Knowledge* (Cambridge: Cambridge University Press, 1970); 'Notes on Lakatos,' in R C Buck and R S Cohen (eds), *Boston Studies in the Philosophy of Science*, vol. 8 (Dordrecht, Netherlands: Reidel, 1971).
5. This section is based on Charles K Wilber and Roland Hoksbergen, 'Ethical values and economic theory: a survey,' *Religious Studies Review*, 12 (3/4) (July/October 1986), pp. 211–2.
6. See Robert H Frank, Thomas Gilovich and Dennis T Regan, 'Does studying economics inhibit cooperation,' *Journal of Economic Perspectives*, 7, 2 (Spring 1993), pp. 159–71.
7. A classic example is the construction of public housing for the poor. Square footage per household is the key variable, not such intangibles as neighbourhood, community, or access to services. Another example is welfare policy that concentrates on levels of support and ignores the psychological impact of means testing or the prohibition of able-bodied males in the household.
8. See Lawrence Boland, 'On the futility of criticizing the neoclassical maximization hypothesis,' *American Economic Review*, 71 (5) (December 1981), pp. 1031–6 and his *Foundations of Economic Method* (London: Allen & Unwin, 1982). The recent literature on 'rhetoric' takes the argument another step – economic theory is a conversation, and different groups of economists (neoclassicals, marxists, institutionalists, et al.) have their own conversations, which are all different. See McCloskey, *The Rhetoric of Economics*.
9. See A Allan Schmid, *Property, Power, and Public Choice: An Inquiry into Law and Economics* (New York: Praeger, 1978) and *Benefit–Cost Analysis: A Political Economy Approach* (Boulder, CO: Westview Press, 1989). Also see the exchange of correspondence between Warren Samuels and James Buchanan: 'On some fundamental issues in political economy: an exchange of correspondence,' *Journal of Economic Issues*, 9 (March 1975), pp. 15–38.
10. See Herbert Gintis and James H Weaver, *The Political Economy of Growth and Welfare*, Module 54 (MSS Modular Publications, 1974); Denis Goulet, *The Cruel Choice: A New*

Concept in the Theory of Development (New York: Atheneum, 1971); Charles K Wilber and Kenneth P Jameson, *Beyond Reaganomics: A Further Inquiry into the Poverty of Economics* (Notre Dame, IN: University of Notre Dame Press, 1990); and "The ethics of consumption: a Roman Catholic view," in David A Crocker and Toby Linden (eds), *Ethics of Consumption: The Good Life, Justice, and Global Stewardship*, (Lanham, MD: Rowman & Littlefield, 1998), pp. 403–15.

52.

ETHICS AND ECONOMIC ACTORS

Charles K Wilber

Introduction

Economics and ethics are interrelated because both economists (theorists and policy advisers) and economic actors (sellers, consumers, workers, investors) hold ethical values that help shape their behaviour. In the first case economists must try to understand how their own values affect both economic theory and policy. In the second case this means economic analysis must broaden its conception of human behaviour.

In a previous article in this journal I dealt with the first issue. In this chapter I will focus on the importance of the second issue – economic theory, with its myopic focus on self-interest, obscures the fact that preferences are formed not only by material self-interest but also by ethical values, and that market economies require such ethical behaviour for efficient functioning.

Values of economic actors

It is important to recognize that though Adam Smith claimed that self-interest leads to the common good if there is sufficient competition; he also, and more importantly, claimed that this is true only if most people in society have internalized a general moral law as a guide for their behaviour.[1] This means that the efficiency claims that economists make for a competitive market system require that economic actors pursue their self-interest only in 'fair' ways. Smith believed most people, most of the time, did act within the guidelines of an internalized moral law and that those who didn't could be dealt with by the police power of the state.

One result of this recognition must be the acknowledgment that a better conception of human behaviour is needed. Thus, I argue that (1) people act on the basis of embodied moral values as well as from self-interest and (2) the economy needs this ethical behaviour in order to be efficient.

Hausman and McPherson recount an experiment in which wallets containing cash and identification were left in the streets of New York. Nearly half were returned to their owners intact, despite the trouble and expense of doing so to their discoverers.[2] It could be argued that altruistic motives – modeled as the concern for another's utility as an element within one's own utility function – ultimately are an extension of self-interested behaviour. Such an argument is substantially weakened in this case because the discovered wallets belonged to persons unknown to the finders. Hence, the personal satisfaction and pleasure stemming from the wallets' return ought to be significantly diminished, as altruistic sympathies are usually weaker with a lack of personal familiarity. The effort expended and the apparently unselfish behavior demonstrated by those who returned the lost goods may, as Hausman and McPherson assert, more likely reflect a commitment to societal norms than a reflection of egoistic desires.

Similarly, it usually is argued that the provision of such goods as public broadcasting and church services will be hobbled by the classic free-rider problem that accompanies public goods. Many consumers of these goods do indeed fail to respond to funding appeals or shirk as the collection plate passes. This, however, does not explain the motivation of the many who do give. Are we to attribute irrationality to those who contribute to public broadcasting, for example, knowing that their gift offsets the free-loading of others? In the case of public church collections, it might be argued that the anticipated approval of fellow churchgoers entices contributions and their threatened opprobrium dissuades stinginess. Masking the amount of one's gift in a closed fist or a sealed envelope are effective and relatively costless, however, and suggest that perhaps a sense of duty, obligation or gratitude might be more important in compelling contributions to church collections.

It is not only for the sake of accuracy that economists should pay attention to evidence that human actions are guided by concerns not solely egoistic, but also because there are real economic consequences to non-egoistic behaviour. Robert Solow has suggested that 'principles of appropriate behaviour' among workers may explain why labour markets are not fully clearing. Appropriate behaviour dictates that one not undercut a peer in order to get that person's position. As Albert Hirschman argues, this example of seemingly non-self-interested behaviour may entail market inefficiencies and resulting costs, but most in society (with the exception of many economists) would deem the portrait of human interaction it paints as more than worth it.[3]

A case in point: the supply of blood

An example of the problem of relying solely on self-interest is given by a comparison of the system of blood collection for medical purposes in the United States and in England. In his book, *The Gift Relationship*, Titmuss questions the efficiency of market relationships based on purely monetary self-interest principles.[4] Instead he hypothesizes that in some instances, such as blood giving, relying on internalized moral values (in this case, altruistic behaviour) results in a more efficient supply and better quality of blood. Kenneth Arrow's response to Titmuss questions the extent to which altruism or other internalized moral values may be counted upon as an organizing principle yet acknowledges that there may, indeed, be a role for altruistic giving.[5] The following covers some of the more salient points in the debate and reflects on these issues in an attempt to clarify the role that embodied moral values may play in the economy.

Titmuss focuses on the blood supply system in Great Britain and the United States. The United States system has moved toward a commercialized market system in which suppliers of blood are paid for the service while in Great Britain the supply of blood depends on voluntary and unpaid individual blood donors. Titmuss argues that the commercialization of blood giving produces a system with many shortcomings. A few of these shortcomings are the repression of expressions of altruism, increases in the danger of unethical behaviour in certain areas of medicine, worsened relationships between doctor and patient, and shifts in the supply of blood from the rich to the poor. Furthermore, the commercialized blood market is bad even in terms of non-ethical criteria.

In terms of economic efficiency it is very wasteful of blood; shortages, chronic and acute, characterize the demand-and-supply position and make illusory the concept of equilibrium. It is administratively inefficient and results in more bureaucratization and much greater administrative, accounting and computer overheads. In terms of price per unit of blood to the patient (or consumer), it is five to fifteen times more costly than voluntary systems in Britain. And, finally, in terms of quality, commercial markets are much more likely to distribute contaminated blood; the risks for the patient of disease and death are substantially greater. It is noteworthy that since the AIDS crisis started in the United States, physicians regularly recommend that patients scheduled for non-emergency surgery donate their own blood in advance.

Arrow attempts to restate Titmuss's arguments in terms of utility theory. Thus the motivation for blood giving is reduced and reformulated in the form of a utility function. One such form is (1) the welfare of each individual will depend both on his own satisfaction and on the satisfactions obtained by others. We here have in mind a positive relation, one of altruism rather than envy. Another form is (2) the welfare of each individual depends not only on one's own utility and of others but also on one's own contribution to the utilities of others. By representing altruism in this way, the incommensurability of self-interest and altruism that is crucial to Titmuss's analysis is ignored.

However, the commercialization of certain activities that historically were perceived to be within the realm of altruism results in a conceptual transformation that inhibits the expression of this altruistic behaviour. Contrary to the commonly held opinion that the creation of a market increases the area of individual choice, Titmuss argues that the creation of a market may inhibit the freedom to give or not to give. If this is true then Arrow's model, which treats apparent morally based behaviour as a simple addition to an ordinary utility function, seriously misrepresents these issues. What is only mentioned in passing and downplayed by Arrow is that market relations may often drive out non-market relations. Material incentives might destroy rather than complement moral incentives.

The supply of blood provides a clear illustration of the problem. A person is not born with a set of ready-made values, rather the individual's values are socially constructed through being a part of a family, a church, a school and a particular society. If these groups expect and urge people to give their blood as an obligation of being members of the group that obligation becomes internalized as a moral value. Blood drives held in schools, churches, and in Red Cross facilities reinforce that sense of obligation. As commercial blood increases, the need for blood drives declines. Thus, the traditional reinforcement of that sense of obligation declines with the result that the embodied moral value atrophies. In addition, the fact that you can sell your blood for, say, $50 devalues the donation from a priceless gift of life to one of a small monetary value. Finally, there is an information problem. As blood drives decline it is rational for an individual to assume that there is no need for donated blood. The final outcome is that a typical person must overcome imperfect information, opportunity costs, and a lack of social approbation to be able to choose to donate blood. The tremendous outpouring of blood donations after September 11 indicates the latent altruism available.

Economists often claim value neutrality in their analysis. But value neutrality cannot be achieved merely by focusing on the efficiency results of a policy recommendation derived from a theoretical model. The motivations on which the results are based are also important, that is, *how* we achieve these results needs to be addressed.

This problem arises because economists take preferences as given – they neither change over time nor are affected by the preferences of other individuals or society. Consequently, the process of preference formation and the nature of the preferences that people have are ignored. That the distribution of beliefs and behaviours at time t influences individual beliefs and behaviours at time $t + 1$ is, however, the single most basic finding of the voluminous research within sociology on the behaviour of groups.[6]

Beliefs and preference structures are important because they are the basis for individual motivation. An understanding of these also gives us a notion as to what are and what will encourage the continuation of certain valued feelings. When economists look to self-interest to solve social problems they are placing a higher value on and promoting their own beliefs about what is proper motivation.

Even though neoclassical economists are seldom interested in why people behave the way they do, society usually places a high value on motivation. This is readily evident if one looks at the legal system. Consider a situation in which a person shoots and kills someone else. The end result is the same but depending on the motivation the act may be judged to be murder, justifiable homicide, or even just an accident.

In short, three conclusions can be derived from our discussion of issues raised by the Titmuss–Arrow debate. First, economic policies have a direct effect on both market outcomes and individual values. Second, economists should drop their narrow approach to human behaviour and join the rest of society in giving attention to the effect that policies have upon values. How we achieve results *is* important. Finally, economists must recognize that the policy impact upon values exerts its own influence on future market activity. Thus, over time the type of values promoted by public action has significance even within the 'efficiency' realm of traditional economic analysis.

Economists are often reluctant to depend on ethics. Ethics are perceived to be a less stable attribute of human behaviour than self-interest. As Arrow states: 'I think it best on the whole that the requirements of ethical behaviour be confined to those circumstances where the price system breaks down ... Wholesale usage of ethical standards is apt to have undesirable consequences.'7

Certainly individuals, with particular needs and abilities, motivated by self-interest do create consequences that often are benevolent. But there is also a role for ethically based behaviour. In response to Adam Smith's 'it is not from the benevolence of the butcher, the brewer, and the baker that we expect our dinner, but from their regard to their own interest,' the reality is that more than half of the American population depends for their security and material satisfaction not upon the sale of their services, but rather on their relationships with others. There are many occasions on which reliance on the good will of others is necessary and more reliable.

Internalized moral behaviour vs. self-interest

I do not want to leave the impression that ethically based behaviour and self-interest are necessarily mutually exclusive. Proximity to self-interest alone does not defile morality. Moral values are often necessary counterparts in a system based on self-interest. Not only is there a 'vast amount of irregular and informal help given in times of need,'8 there is also a consistent dependence on moral values upon which market mechanisms rely. Without a basic trust and socialized morality the system would be much more inefficient.

Peter Berger reminds us that: 'No society, modern or otherwise, can survive without what Durkheim called a "collective conscience," that is without moral values that have general authority.'9 Fred Hirsch reintroduced the idea of moral law into economic analysis:

> ... truth, trust, acceptance, restraint, obligation – these are among the social virtues grounded in religious belief which ... play a central role in the functioning of an individualistic, contractual economy ... The point is that conventional, mutual standards of honesty and trust are public goods that are necessary inputs for much of economic output.10

The expectation that public servants will not promote their private interests at the expense of the public interest reinforces the argument that the economy rests as importantly on moral behaviour as self-interested behaviour. As Hirsch wrote:

> The more a market economy is subjected to state intervention and correction, the more dependent its functioning becomes on restriction of the individualistic calculus in certain spheres, as well as on certain elemental moral standards among both the controllers and the

controlled. The most important of these are standards of truth, honesty, physical restraint, and respect for law.[11]

Attempts to rely solely on material incentives in the private sector, and more particularly in the public sector, suffer from two defects. In the first place, stationing a policeman on every corner to prevent cheating simply does not work. Regulators have a disadvantage in relevant information compared to those whose behaviour they are trying to regulate. In addition, who regulates the regulators? Thus, there is no substitute for an internalized moral law that directs persons to seek their self-interest only in 'fair' ways. The second shortcoming of relying on external sanctions alone is that such reliance can further undermine the remaining aspects of an internalized moral law. The Enron case might be an example of the decline of those embodied moral values in the market place. As discussed above, by promoting only self-interest, society encourages that type of behaviour rather than ethical behaviour. The argument is not that there is no role for self-interest, but rather that there is a large sphere for morally constrained behaviour. To distinguish in which sphere self-interest should be used and in which sphere altruism should be promoted is very important and sends signals to society as to what we value.

Conclusion

In conclusion, I claim that (1) self-interest alone does not adequately explain actual economic behaviour because economic actors are also motivated by internalized moral values, such as trust and honesty and (2) self-interest does not lead to efficient outcomes in the absence of these moral values. The irony of mainstream economic theory is this: on the one hand it is permeated, despite repeated denials, with ethical values imported from its governing world view; on the other hand it fails to understand fully that economic actors are motivated by more than material self-interest *and need to be* if a market economy is to function efficiently.

Notes

1. See Adam Smith, *Theory of Moral Sentiments* (London: Henry Bohn, 1861); A W Coats, ed., *The Classical Economists and Economic Policy* (London: Methuen, 1971); and Jerry Evensky, "Ethics and the invisible hand," *Journal of Economic Perspectives*, **7** (2) (Spring 1993), pp. 197–205.
2. Daniel M. Hausman and Michael S. McPherson, *Economic Analysis and Moral Philosophy* (Cambridge University Press, 1996), p. 34. It is interesting that experimental studies by psychologists indicate that people are concerned about

cooperating with others and with being fair, not just preoccupied with their own self-interest. Ironically, these same studies indicate that those people attracted into economics are more self-interested and taking economics makes people even more self-interested. Thus economic theory creates a self-fulfilling prophecy. See Robert H Frank, Thomas Gilovich and Dennis T Regan, 'Does studying economics inhibit cooperation,' *Journal of Economic Perspectives*, **7** (2) (Spring 1993), pp. 159–71.

3. Albert O Hirschman, "Morality and the social sciences: a durable tension," in *The Passions and the Interests: Political Arguments for Capitalism before Its Triumph* (Princeton: Princeton University Press, 1977), pp. 304–5.

4. Richard M Titmuss, *The Gift Relationship: From Human Blood to Social Policy* (London: Allen and Unwin, 1970).

5. Kenneth Arrow, "Gifts and exchange," *Philosophy and Public Affairs*, **I** (4) (Summer 1972), pp. 343–62.

6. Steven Kelman, *What Price Incentives? Economists and the Environment* (Boston, MA: Auburn House Publishing Company, 1981), p. 31.

7. Kenneth Arrow, "Gifts and exchange," p. 355.

8. Kenneth Arrow, "The gift relationship," p. 345.

9. Peter Berger, "In praise of particularity: the concept of mediating structures," *Review of Politics* (July 1976), p. 134.

10. Fred Hirsch, *Social Limits to Growth* (Cambridge, MA: Harvard University Press, 1978), p. 141.

11. Fred Hirsch, *Social Limits to Growth*, pp. 128–9.

53.

SOCIAL BEING AS A PROBLEM FOR AN ETHICAL ECONOMICS

Jamie Morgan

Introduction

Orthodox economics conspicuously lacks a satisfying account of social being and is thus unable to provide a practical starting point in addressing many of the problems of being that humanity now confronts. It is theoretically impoverished and practically bereft. As post-autistic economics and previous forums have shown, the current orthodoxy of economics is neither explanatorily powerful nor is it genuinely scientific. One way of showing this is to explore how its science, its method and its power are founded on a series, a cascade, of inversions of dimensions of realisms that corrupt science and method in the name of that power. Those inversions include issues of:

- the relation between economy and being;
- synchronous behaviour;
- the ill of being;
- the alienated economist;
- alienated method.

My starting point or primary organizing principle is that economics as an explanatorily powerful (and thus scientific) discipline should account for what we live for, but that it is not economics for which we live.

What are we living for?

Orthodoxy colludes in the commodification and fetishism of capitalism. Its primary inversion is that for the orthodox economist, we live for the economy - its motors (as they are represented by the orthodox economist) are *our* motors, a stochastic ordering process that reflects our most basic 'natural' behaviours and motivations. This *homo economicus ergo sum* extracts its account of the economy from the social whole and subjugates human beings to it. The economy we are told we live for is the economy of the orthodox economist, a best of all possible worlds, insofar as we are told that it is the only world there is and we'd better get used to it. It is a world we apparently make but one that escapes us. For orthodoxy, the knowledge that has previously eluded us is not a path to emancipation but rather the tracing of our prison walls. Its invisible hand offers a seductive material utopia that arrives as a clenched fist, demanding that we conform and be disciplined by its own inevitability.

The paradox of synchronicity

For the orthodox economist, our behaviour, founded though it might be in a deep-seated 'nature' of accumulation, desire and competition, will never *quite* be our own. Our behaviour is externalised, becoming *behavioural*, an imperative. Our choice in this arid world of orthodoxy is no choice at all lest it be *non-being*, an ultimate sanction of capitalism or death. One synchronises with the system in order to survive. Indeed, synchronicity *is* the system (just as it is the non-beating heart of homeostatic equilibrating method). It is the system in so far as it denies the existence of any significant and causally efficacious rules, institutions or interventions other than this primeval behavioural imperative.

Being is thus no more or less than persistence. One persists in a system that somehow claims to subordinate the self to itself. As a consequence, the utopia at the heart of that orthodoxy is simultaneously pragmatic and deterministic, avaricious and pessimistic, human yet all too holohedral. It is a charitable cruelty that affords us, each and every one, participation, a cruelty that whispers of merit, hard work, returns, and opportunity in the name of the ever-present possibility that we may succeed and that others may fail. Failure is the collateral damage of utopia – the poor, the disenfranchised, the oppressed and the marginalized. Their failure *defines* success. Their failure is an illustration that some forms of the subjugated being of orthodoxy are more abject than others. The morality of this most 'hard-headed' of disciplines is, therefore, Nietszchean. In it, 'blood and cruelty lie at the bottom of all "good things".' Of it, morality is transvaluated in a becoming that is amoral in its methodological indifference to morality, and immoral in terms of the consequences of such amorality.

Frozen being

One cannot understand an advanced capitalist economy without understanding the constitution and consequences of the transitive values that engenders its production. The absence of moral investigation within orthodoxy is thus symptomatic of the economy's contributions to the ill of social being. Orthodox economics is part of the (il)liberating problem of technologies whose social relationality it blithely ignores. It is in this sense that if we do not (should not, cannot or will not) live for economics, the economist should at least be asking what it is we are living for, and what consequences this has for how others live and die across the world, now and in the future. This is a moral as well as a practical question. As a practical question it is, all too easily, debilitated by the deterministic undercurrents of orthodox pragmatism. Such pragmatism lends itself to a utilitarian pleasure principle that is at once too narrow and too broad, providing limited descriptions without explanations; rendering the historical eternal. This is yet another dimension of orthodox synchronicity and also another element in the inversions of orthodoxy. The dynamism of the lived life of social being is frozen. *Homo economicus* is statuesque, ignorant and selfish.

Nowhere is this lack of engagement with the dynamics of social relations of economy clearer than in the home economy of the alienated and commodified self. At the same time as technology has divorced many of the centres of advanced capitalism from hard physical labour, it has produced new forms of oppressive social relations where humans have, ironically, become once more subject to subsistence agriculture's long hours of labour (for technology is now pervasive and its relations invasive); concomitantly, reduced non-working time has increasingly become an arena of instrumental activity within the emergent leisure economy, one dominated by consumption on three fronts: food, home refurbishment, and shopping.

The relations of economy of all three subject the human at the centres of advanced capitalism to accelerated rhythms, and his/her marginalized counterparts in the majority world to greater burdens. Food has become an oral fixation, a primary sensory pleasure, a lifestyle choice and a source of fear. Affluent over-consumption, knowledge of the mortality implications of the foods of choice, and obesity, channel us to the clinic, the diet book and the gym where hours of over-consumption of the world's resources are converted into joules of isolated exertion on yet more machines that are in turn the conversion point of food into further profit. Similarly, home refurbishment has become a micro-economy of perpetual investment in the reconstruction of living space whose demands rob us of what little living time we have within it. Shopping, meanwhile, is the master category of the home economy, a centre of gravity, a principle source of leisure, status and self-esteem. It is a preoccupation, a form of activity that has attuned the human to a numbing receptivity to acquisition divorced from attainment; the introduction of lifestyle obsolescence has quickened its pace at the same time as new forms of credit have softened its short-term pressures whilst all but guaranteeing a hard landing. Shopping has become the bull market of the soul. Here, orthodoxy is denied even the defence that scarcity is a purely allocative problem.

The alienated economist

Yet one cannot simply define a problem like human social being *out of existence*. The very claim is a category mistake. One is defining it *out of theory*. Such an act of power within orthodoxy simply commits the error of burying one's head in the sand. Ring-fencing narrow and problematic fundamental assumptions about humanity with forbidding formulae that produce neat and tidy mathematical outputs (that in another inversion, that of theoretical linearity, all but select their inputs) impoverish the theoretician as it bastardises the theoretical process. There is something deeply atavistic and yet all too modern in the way that the orthodox economist has become a tool of his tools. The orthodox economist is both the high priest of capitalism and another instance of its victim. A source of cant and superstition, of such linguistic abuses as 'the needs of the market,' and 'human capital downsizing.' A master who is by his own dialectic truly a technician-slave; his thought counts the cost of production but not the value of being. Yet he knows the value of differential calculus, of indices, simultaneous equations and regression. One must ask why it is that, alone amongst the social sciences, orthodox economics has so assiduously pursued the Chicago School dictum of 1926, 'When you cannot measure your knowledge becomes meagre and unsatisfactory.'

The orthodox economist's disdain for reality is captured by the (only half joking) injunction, 'But does it work in theory?' In lauding unreality, orthodoxy commits itself to a trajectory that parodies itself. A profession whose hierarchy places the mathematical economist at its airless summit, far removed from practical considerations, may provide an economist with a clear path to maximizing his own exchange value but does so by crushing his use-value. Ironically, competence is divested from its etymological relation to the socially productive. Rather it is diverted into computation; competence becomes a technical facility rather than a contribution to society. Orthodox economics thereby becomes one of the few social realms where rational expectations genuinely apply; orthodox economics becomes a profession of calculating calculators.

The ideological value of 'facts'

Orthodoxy abstracts from fantasy to construct knowledge. Unreal assumptions conducive to the simplification of complex mathematical problems dictate what is and what is not economically significant. Thus abstraction is conjoined to abacus and absolved from its relation to appropriation from the world in order to return with knowledge *of* the world. Here one shifts to a further double returning, both to 'But does it work in theory?' and to that realm where one is a tool of tools. Perfect knowledge and instantaneously equilibrating and spontaneously clearing markets make neat mathematics but require a neat world, not the untidy one that we actually inhabit.

Here wider inversions of 'to be scientific' become clear. The rejection of use-value in the maximization of the exchange value of the orthodox economist, which is inherent in the debasing of competence, is itself a sub-set of the behavioural imperative from which its theoretical core derives. In affirming a deep-seated 'nature' where we accumulate, desire and compete, orthodoxy overwrites the needs inhering in *species being* – food, sleep, shelter, warmth, dignity, security and so on. A set of descriptive nouns become ascriptive verbs whose claim to represent the same territory, a baseline from which the cultural, the social and the human begin, takes the form of disguise.

Such ascriptive verbs are *values* of means from species-being beginnings, and thus one trajectory delimiting one possible (impoverished) end. Disguising then, takes the form of overwriting species being with values claimed as basic facts. Once the behavioural imperative is installed as fact, the possibility that things could be otherwise, as species being is pursued within the social whole (and in the constitution of social being), is sublimated. The construction of orthodox 'fact' begins from disguised value. That construction is, therefore, ideological, a necessary myth. It is ideological both in its function within the secret logic of orthodoxy and within orthodoxy's relationship to the unrelenting inevitability of capitalism.

The interface between the two secretes the statement that we are (this) nature all the way up – an insight as meaningless as that we are (that) nurture all the way down. As a consequence, unreality takes yet another guise in terms of orthodoxy's claim to authority. As a theory it inverts any commitment to the overcoming of ideology in the pursuit of truth. Its truths *are* ideological and its science *is* ideological.

Likewise, its concept of 'to do science' is also ideological. Installing the behavioural imperative as fact is not only the first step in tracing the prison walls of systemic synchronicity, it is also an act within the philosophy of method. The many dynamics by which things cannot be otherwise within orthodoxy speak to a knowledge that is ultimately waiting to be found. Since things cannot be otherwise, that 'found' is not simply a beginning in both the fallible process of knowledge of the world and the work of transforming that world, it is simply what the world is – a true reflection, founded in a debased form of materialism that knows that what it observes is, has been, and will always be. Orthodoxy is, therefore, a special kind of Empiricism; a form of Humeanism without the latter's scepticism towards the possibilities inherent in the act of knowledge. Its 'to do science' makes a God of the scientist and an idiot of man. Science finds a society that is a machine of perpetual motion, a set of wheels and gears executing the same operations in an undeviating endless closed cycle, without history, without consequences, and to all intents and purposes, without meaning. In their absence it is a science without the human, and this is surely the nadir of ideology in a *social* science.

Conclusion

Such then are the inversions of dimensions of realisms that corrupt science and method in the name of the power that is orthodox economics. They are inversions of realisms because they raise the standard of unrealism. Their paradox is that they raise that standard precisely in the name of realism – of science and of method. In doing so a claim is made on common sense action within the world that ephemeralises heterodoxy, as 'softer' social theory that may be disparaged as (once more playing out the nadir of ideology in a social science) 'sociological'.

Ironically, it requires the terminology of another form of unrealism, the post-modern, to appreciate this. Orthodoxy wears its exclusions, its constructed 'other' by which it defines itself, upon its sleeve. Its philosophical defence of its own lack of realism shows precisely this. Its instrumentalism, the claim that heuristically convenient simplifications (that are actually methodological fictions rather than abstractions) are explanatorily powerful, its contraction of method to mathematical technique, and its reduction of evidence to quantifiable data (when pressed for such), all bear this out. That orthodox economics has managed such a sleight of hand – claiming to be the disciplinary proponent of all that is practical and useful in economics, offering itself as a first port of call for policy advice and justification, claiming to represent 'how things really are', whilst also being a site of fundamental and often celebrated forms of unrealism – is itself a sociological conundrum. An exploration of that conundrum may say much about how more prosaic, yet more valid, heterodox approaches have been excluded from a ready audience for their own realist claims.

Yet beyond an organizing principle that economics should account for what we live for but that it is not economics for which we live, the exploration of the inversions of orthodoxy suggest not so much what heterodoxy should be but what it should not be and what its many forms should take seriously in order to avoid being what it should *not* be. In the very process of not being orthodoxy, the possibility of explanatorily powerful and scientific economics emerges out of a plurality that is the very antithesis of orthodox conformity. The heterodox challenge is therefore to convert inversions.

Thus methodology should not dominate its object. Economics should be empirical and relational, investigating all aspects of economies, their organization and consequences. As such it cannot but deal with the historical, the non-universal, it cannot but be social and sociological, political and politicized. As such it cannot but be moral yet need not be pejoratively *moralising*, in the sense that it confronts and explores the economic problems of conflicted forms of social being – what are the human consequences of technology, what has affluence meant for social being, local and global, is poverty a derivative of affluence, what is economic growth (for)? These are issues of the human in a material and conceptual world where we must look at ourselves from the outside in and the inside out, as constitutive of economic processes, as makers of social structures and institutions, of rules, and also as agents conforming, confronting, contesting and thinking in terms of those structures, institutions and rules; as above all carriers of values and makers of value judgements.

Economics as an engagement with a transitive social reality can therefore be scientific in a non-ideological way, precisely because the political and the social are part of the historically specific economy and a science of the human must acknowledge this and construct its research and methods on that basis. Science is about the appropriate investigation of objects, explaining their processes, thinking about what causes events, with the ever-present possibility that such knowledge provides that they may be manipulated. In a human science explanation provides the understanding that is the first step in changing a *conceptual* social world. That is the moral dynamic of non-ideological human science. This can only be acknowledged when synchronicity and the behavioural imperative are abandoned, when the economist starts to take his use-value seriously, when his competence is more than computational. Only then will the contingency of social being be more than an expectations augmented exercise in modelling – only then will species being become a realistic problem of what the economist can contribute to society.

And this is not a problem of mathematics or any particular tool or technique but rather our relationship to our tools and techniques. They should be ours; we should not be theirs. We should decide where they are appropriate rather than *appropriate* what is appropriate to them. Above all, if methodology is not to dominate its object, economics must be returned to the social whole. Yet such a returning is not to demand that economics must be *the* science of society in all its aspects; rational expectations has already taken orthodoxy down that blind alley of economic imperialism. No science can be the new metaphysics. A social whole cannot be theoretically totalised. No discipline can discipline society, bringing it to heel. To argue so entails three axes, the acknowledgement of which is also a hallmark of a genuinely *social* science:

1. Though economic theories, like any other branch of social theory, thrive on the articulation of their own coherence, they subsist in terms of their own contingence. Knowledge is always and everywhere fallible.
2. A social whole can be cut across in many ways, by an economics of aspects of economy that grasp elements of the diversity of the socio-economic experience and its processes, and by other forms of social theory that take as their remit and object some other problematic.
3. A social whole is open-ended and thus incomplete, no economic theory can totalise what is not total. Its object, the economy, is human, historical, conditional and transitive.

The challenge for heterodoxy can be located in terms of these axes. Metaphorically speaking they constitute a commitment within which heterodoxy can be grid-referenced as an ensemble of theories bridged by a family resemblance that leaves open the possibility of corrigible dialogue and commensuration. This too is a hallmark of a *social* scientific method, for what else is progress to be in economics?

54.

WHEN SOCIAL PHYSICS BECOMES A SOCIAL PROBLEM: ECONOMICS, ETHICS AND THE NEW ORDER

Juan Pablo Pardo-Guerra

In an official speech just a few weeks ago, Inacio Lula Da Silva, the polemical and ever-so intriguing President of Brazil, threw hunger and poverty into that fashionable category of "weapons of mass destruction." Mr. Lula's words were uttered not in a time of worldwide prosperity but in the midst of an international crisis of pandemic proportions: while global resources become increasingly endangered, the global governance system stands on the verge of collapse as some of the most powerful nations of the world disdain collaboration over intervention, concordance over imposition and dialogue over unilateralism. On the economic side of this dire picture, an important sector of the world's population has been driven to take to the streets to manifest its discontent with the surge in global inequality, often attributed to the malformed policies of organizations such as the World Bank and the International Monetary Fund.

In contrast and following the long tradition of economic thought that has permeated the West for generations, the heads of these same global organizations blame countries like Brazil, the home of Mr Lula, for not adapting their domestic policies to the demands of these liberal times we live in. If this were only an inoffensive divergence in world views, nothing important would be at stake. However, at the core of this discussion lies the fate of millions of people, from the marginalized citizens of Michael Moore's suburban US to the famished refugees in Sudan. The destiny of global security lies not only in the proliferation of weapons of mass destruction or in the expansion of terrorist activities; the real peril lies in the increasing gap that inexorably divides the people of our world, the rich from the poor, the informed from the uninformed, the armed from the disarmed.

But who is to blame for the constant growth of this gap? Who is ultimately right: the alterglobalists[1] that took to the streets in Seattle or the high management of the Bretton Woods offspring?

Concerning the two chief systems of the world

It is virtually impossible, if not political suicide, to identify a single cause for the widening socioeconomic gap that divides our world. The alterglobalists often blame "the system" that lies on the other side of the barricades, whilst those who work for "the system" often blame the alterglobalists for being blind to the benefits of living in a global village. The fundamental problem here lies in the fact that, in some sense, both parties see the world from different perspectives and epistemological backgrounds, therefore making dialogue among them a monologue in two voices. It is an outspoken clash of two radically different cultures.

The economists and policy-makers who work in one of the myriad institutions devoted to putting some order into the global economy grew up in a world that tagged them and their jobs as eminently rational in nature; most went to colleges where they studied the rationality behind choices; they were taught that economics is a science, specifically a science of society; they read Adam Smith, John Maynard Keynes, Paul Samuelson, John Stuart Mill and even Karl Marx. They believe they are following the right track simply because they are implementing the very things they were taught to do. Activists, on the other hand, grew up in a world where the premises that economists and policy makers defended were simply not real; they saw the demise of the economic policies of the last three decades; they've seen the poverty of those affected by an uncontrolled globalization; they understood that economics is not as scientific as it claims to be; and they know that rationality is far from being carvings on a stone. The tools they have for understanding the world, both learned from theory and from practice, are usually at odds with those of mainstream economists.

There are countless examples of this philosophical divergence in the vast literature on both activism and globalization that one can find in any average bookstore. Take, for example, one of the central referents of many alterglobal activists, Naomi Klein. Consider the following paragraph extracted from a column published during the first days of the World Trade Organization's 2003 ministerial conference in Cancun, Mexico:

[the brutal economic model advanced by the World Trade Organization is itself a form of war] because privatization and deregulation kill – by pushing up prices on necessities like water and medicines and pushing down prices on raw commodities like coffee, making small farms unsustainable. War because those who resist and "refuse to disappear," as the Zapatistas say, are routinely arrested, beaten and even killed. War because when this kind of low-intensity repression fails to clear the path to corporate liberation, the real wars begin. (Klein, 2003)

These words, even at a rhetorical level, contrast sharply with those of Robert S McNamara, former president of the World Bank, who in an interview with *New Perspectives Quarterly* mentioned:

Ninety-eight percent of the protesters are young people who are extraordinarily highly motivated, desiring to improve the welfare of the disadvantaged in the world, particularly in the developing countries, in China, the Indian subcontinent or sub-Saharan Africa. But they are totally wrong in their judgment that globalization is somehow the cause of poverty or standing in the way of reducing poverty. They are just totally wrong intellectually. (McNamara, 2003)

There is simply no immediate form of bridging the positions of the pro-globalists who believe in the predictions of the theory and the *in situ* practitioners who live the reality of the policies. And as countless news reports show, the combination of these two discursive worlds generates an explosive mix: thousands of protestors, clashes with local security enforcement agencies and – as was so terribly demonstrated during the 2001 G8 meeting in Genoa – even fatal outcomes. But despite all, there is a fundamentally simple way to defuse this deadly cocktail, one that is rather well known but seldom referred to.

Perhaps the biggest obstacle that prevents these two rather distant worlds from establishing a steady dialogue can be traced back to the way in which economists are trained. I have chosen economists as the focal point of this assessment for they, in general, occupy positions that give them a more formal and official validation than that given to alternative social movements. Focusing our attention on economists is therefore following the track of political power and the channels that have a higher impact on the construction of history. But to understand and change the practice of economists one first has to comprehend their trade and this in turn requires understanding the complex web on which the modern economic discourse was built.

Building the ivory tower

Economics has suffered a series of dramatic changes over the last 200 years. From emerging as one of the strongest arms of moral philosophy, it has now come to resemble a formal, axiomatic dictum tailored with the patterns of physics and mathematics rather than with those of sociology and culture studies. In some sense, economics became an embodiment of the positive dream of a "social physics," a discipline capable of finding the general laws that rule our societies and our lives (Comte, [1830] 2003). This is not at all coincidental. As Philip Mirowski (1989) showed, the development of modern economics was closely linked to the evolution of nineteenth-century mechanics, a deterministic and materialistic vein of thought that remains entrenched in the very fabric of many sciences.

With the dawn of the twentieth century, economics became mathematical. The fast advancements in the formalization of mathematics along with developments such as the game-theoretical construction of Von Neumann and Morgenstern set the stage for a new economic discourse designed to fit the many industrial, social and political convergences of the twentieth century. The original moral character of economics consequently became enclosed by a sea of mathematical concepts, from Arrow and Debreu's theory of value, to Stiglitz's asymmetric information. Very few escaped the mathematization of the discipline; most of the survivors were old school economists of the type of Frederick Hayek and, to some extent, John Maynard Keynes. But today, decades after Bretton Woods and the institutionalization of economics as the basis of the world order, it is rare to find an economist who conceives mathematical formality only as a limited tool and not as the core of modern economic theory.

In the process of merging economics and mathematics two fundamental things were left behind. On a theoretical level, and repeating to some degree the path taken by physics, systemic complexity became something that could not be handled *within* the mainstream theory. Economic systems, just as ideal gases, were now seen as regulated by a small set of rules (utility maximization, cost minimization, benefit maximization, informational efficiency, general equilibrium and so forth) all of which were immutable, additive and universal. Even today, in a time where complexity studies have been present in academic circles for decades in areas such as technological innovation and financial economics, standard texts such as Hal Varian's

Intermediate Microeconomics (1999) still contain deeply reductionist ideas such as the one quoted below:

> Economics is based on the construction of models of social phenomena. By a model, we understand a simplified representation of reality. [...] The power of a model comes from the suppression of irrelevant details, which allows the economist to focus on the essential characteristics of the economic reality which he tries to comprehend.

Furthermore, and on a purely discursive level, the association between economics and mathematics allowed for a quick dissociation from ethical discussions. What had originally been in the words of Kenneth Boulding a "moral science" transmuted, due to the force of positivist influences, into a "hard science" (Averly, 1999). Along with compacting complexity, this shift in world views allowed economists to isolate themselves from ethical issues through the same arguments of universality and value-independence that granted physicists a certain degree of immunity when they were involved in questionable research programmes. One can still find amongst many mathematical economists the same arguments of beauty and cognitive purity that were seen in the physics community during the development of atomic weapons in the Cold War. From the time economics became fortified with the tag of "being scientific", the global economic agenda was set beyond the boundaries of ethics, from a domain where the only acceptable dictums were those of the factual laws of our societies.

Living in a pluricultural world

We now start to see a familiar terrain. The "ethics and science" debate is part of an important tradition that criticizes the administration of scientific resources and the consequences of research on our lives and the future in general. However, and for the most part, this debate has been concentrated on the role of hard sciences. Physicists are seen as the creators of nuclear weapons; chemists are seen as the developers of mustard gas and other deadly agents; and biologists and biochemists are associated to a vast array of bioweapons that pose a great danger to all of humankind. But rarely does anyone mention the other "weapons of mass destruction," namely poverty and hunger, overall far more critical than any of the weapons used so far in armed conflict. If we are to blame economics for this construct, then how should we confront the challenge of the "ethics of economics"?

The answer is not necessarily simple, though as a first step we could think of using the same strategies as the ones used in other disciplines (such as physics) but adapted to a primordially social context. This can be done by means of two different though not contradictory paths:

1. By strengthening the debate on the theoretical limits of economics and the impossibility of existing mathematical techniques to describe with no uncertainty or loss of complex phenomena, therefore opening an avenue for an "economic precautionary principle".
2. By eroding the division between theory and practice in such a way that ethics becomes a necessary tool for coping with complex economic issues. In this sense, cultural environments should be thought of as the key element in the ethical debate: is it ethical to export economic structures to regions of the planet that have a different cultural background? How do we deal with inequality from an ethical perspective? This is, in itself, an educational pathway, one that is not present in most of the current curricula in economics.

The reason for establishing these two paths is simple. Firstly, they both have a certain degree of appeal that might draw important groups of non-economists into the debate, for example activists, politicians and the general public. Hence, it is important to see that, if incorporated into the educational process of economists and policy-makers, ethics could potentially serve as a bridge between the two worlds in which our planet is divided. Additionally, ethics serves as a conveyer of the local needs of a specific population, being capable of translating the local reality onto a variety of perspectives. This results in a better communication between groups, one that might help alleviate the problems of a vast sector of the world's population. Secondly, they open new areas of research and expand the current possibilities of theoretical studies. Though complete awareness of our social universe is impossible, such a shift in views might create the need for new methodologies and analytical techniques not considered in the past. This is, in itself, an immensely valuable expansion of economic theory.

Independently of the choice, it is important to remember that ethics has the potential of being the ideal communication scheme across cultures and borders, including between the advocates and the opponents of the current economic model. Therefore, it is important to incorporate the "ethics and economics" discussion into the "ethics and science" debate.

A final note

How does all this affect the post-autistic economics movement? For one, it opens the possibility of collaborating with a whole new set of movements, that is to say, with those involved in the study of ethics and science. But more importantly, it presents itself as a concise policy recommendation: economics cannot be without ethics if our real objective is to help the world evolve into a better, more equal state, and not to perpetuate the divide that segregates our citizens, keeping them eternally confronted.

Note

1. The term alterglobalist comes from the Spanish word "altermundista" which categorizes all the movements that are against the current mainstream economic trend. However, it is a much broader term than "anti-globalists." For example, the Pugwash Conferences are an alterglobalist organization because they believe in a world free of nuclear weapons (something far from being the global trend over the past 50 years). However, Pugwash is not against globalization *per se*; instead it is seen as a potentially beneficial force.

References

Averly, J, 1999, *An introduction to economics as a moral science*. The Independent Institute.

Comte, A, 2003, 1830, *La filosofia positiva*. Mexcio: Editorial Porrua.

Klein, N, 2003, Free trade is war. *The Nation*, September 11.

McNamara, R, 2003, *New Perspectives Quarterly*, **7**, September, 2001.

Mirowski, P, 1989, *More heat than light*, Cambridge: Cambridge University Press.

Varian, H, 1999, *Microeconomia intermedia*, Barcelona: Antoni Bosch.

55.

THE ECONOMIST'S LONG FAREWELL

Robert E Lane

'Farewell! A long farewell to all my greatness.'
(Cardinal Wolsey, *Henry VIII* (III, ii))

Introduction

Adam (an economist named after Adam Smith [1723–90]) and Desiderius (a humanist–social scientist named after Desiderius Erasmus [1466–1536]) are having lunch in a local restaurant while discussing the merits and social costs of materialism. They are friends, of a sort. We find them in the midst of an argument. Of course, Adam calls Desiderius "Dessie" and we shall do the same.

"So what is wrong with materialism?" asked Adam, wiping his material lips with a material napkin – or at least a modestly material paper napkin.

Dessie knocked on wood to invoke the gods of chance to protect him from violating the laws of nature. "I want to talk about materialism as a set of beliefs and values, the source of economic man's alleged behaviour, not the metaphysical or historical variants."

"Please get on with it," said Adam as though he were asking an executioner not to delay any further.

"Good economists," said Dessie, "have always believed that the bundle of goods people demand changes as their income levels rise: e.g. a smaller proportion of their income is spent on food and shelter and a larger proportion on travel and entertainment and education – and saving. The only thing that economists, except for Tibor Scitovsky,[1] have not already noticed is that the goods people in a rich society want are those that are not to be purchased in the market, like family felicity and friendship.

"So" asked Adam, "why is your dinner less important than family felicity and friendships?"

"We can't compare them until we know whether or not you have had your dinner. Your namesake, Adam Smith assumed it was dinner time when he talked about the dominance of material self-interest,[2] and for many people in the eighteenth century dinner time came more often than did dinner. I am only reciting economists' theory of declining marginal utility. In capsule form, if you are hungry, dinner has a higher priority; if (after dinner), you are lonely, friendships are more desirable." By comparison, he thought, explaining why two and two make four would be a deep exercise.

"All right," said Adam somewhat mortified, "but you are not talking simply about a change in the goods people prefer; you are talking about a systematic shift in values; what do you call your new system? 'The New Humanism'? And you want to contrast this new system with an old one, one that economists call a 'market economy' and that you call, much less precisely, 'materialism'. Aside from substituting a preference for people over commodities, as you might say, what is the difference between the two systems?"

"You brush aside the crucial point – but one thing at a time," said Dessie. "You chaps are always talking about margins, so now I propose a marginal decline in materialism with the slack taken up by a marginal increase in the humanistic motives and activities such as friendship and an intrinsic interest in work. Because the data suggest that further increases in GDP per capita in rich countries do not contribute much to happiness,[3] a strict utilitarian analysis suggests this marginal change from pursuit of money to pursuit of companionship or other intrinsic goals. But note that this marginal change is utility-efficient only after that point where the utility of one more dollar is the same as, say, one more friend. We have passed that point in the US: number of friends is a better predictor of happiness than is number of dollars possessed."[4]

"If materialism is necessary for growth," Adam said, "then the lack of materialism implies a static economy and more poverty. It is you who seem to favour a loss of well-being."

"The set of meanings I want to explore," said Dessie ignoring the criticism, "lie in a measure of materialist attitudes in a consumer society. We are not pioneers creating our own maps of unexplored terrain. Others have been here before us. For example, Marsha Richins and Scott Dawson have developed a measure of materialism that deals with three aspects of the concept: (1) 'acquisition centrality,' meaning that 'materialists place possessions and their acquisition at the center of their lives.' (2) acquisition and possession of things as the central route to happiness, that is, materialists 'see possessions and acquisition as essential to their satisfaction and well-being;' and (3) success is defined in terms of material things: 'Materialists tend to judge their own and others' success by the number and quality of possessions accumulated.' Technically, these three elements represent three independent factors in their factor analysis of a broad range of eighteen questions. To measure the first factor, they ask, *inter alia*, whether the following is generally true for the respondent: 'Buying things gives me a lot of pleasure.' To measure the happiness dimension they invite responses to: 'It sometimes bothers me quite a bit that I can't afford to buy all the things I'd like.' And to test the third dimension dealing with success they ask agreement or disagreement with the proposition: 'Some of the most important achievements in life include acquiring material possessions.'[5]

"You're stacking the deck by your definitions – a formal rhetorical error," said Adam. "Here is young Albert starting out in life; he is married and has two small children; he has to pay for shelter, food, clothing and medical care for his family; he should save something lest his job fail and, in any event, for his children's education. Because he cares a lot about money, you call him a materialist and put him down. It isn't fair." Adam seemed to suffer vicariously for Albert.

"We are not talking about the priority of needs,"[6] said Dessie. "I agree with you and, as it happens with Marx who said someplace: 'We must eat before we think.' But that is true of people with a variety of motives and points of view. It will be more fruitful if we focus on Richins and Dawson's conceptualization of materialist beliefs and motives."

"All right," said Adam, "but I still don't see what's wrong with emphasizing material acquisitions. Albert, our young father just starting out, did. And what is wrong with agreeing with the vast majority of Americans: those who 'make it' financially have, indeed, succeeded?"

"As a matter of fact," said Dessie wearing his social science hat, "what Americans think of when they think of materialism is: 'status display,' seeking 'wealth for its own sake;' and people who are 'predisposed toward money, wealth, innovations, and the possessions of others.'[7] So Albert and the rest of us working stiffs may or may not be a materialist, but an interest in earning a living is neither here nor there." Dessie felt things were going better.

"So now you have a definition and a measure; how does this help us understand the costs of the materialism that makes us rich?" asked Adam, weary of distinctions in what had always seemed like a straightforward natural preference for a fungible currency that bought so many pleasures. But Dessie was off on another tack.

The dark side of materialism

"First, materialists are less generous than others," said Dessie, counting on his fingers. "Richins and Dawson offered their subjects a hypothetical $20,000 windfall and asked them how they would spend it. As it turned out: 'materialists would spend three times as much on themselves, would contribute less to charity or church, give less than half as much to friends and family.' Materialism scores were negatively correlated with support for a specific environmental charity. Compared to others, materialists also reported that they do not like to lend things to their friends and that they do not like to have guests in their homes.[8]

"Second, materialists are more invidious than others, especially but not exclusively when they compare themselves with those who are richer than they are.[9] 'Materialists tend to judge their own and others' success by the number and quality of possessions accumulated.' They value these things more than they value their relationships to other people.[10] This may be because of lack of interest in people, a matter of taste – or because of the lack of social skills that haunts these thing-minded people.

"Third, materialists seem to be more difficult to satisfy; they report that they need higher incomes than those low in materialism.[11] More than others, they are dissatisfied with their lives. As Durkheim prophesied, empirical studies find that: 'Although materialists expect acquisition to make them happy, ... the lust for goods can be insatiable: the pleasures of a new acquisition are quickly forgotten and replaced with a desire for more.'[12]

"The consequence of all this," said Dessie, using his hands to wield his fork instead of for counting the points he was making, "is that materialists are significantly less happy than are nonmaterialists: in the Richins and Dawson study, materialism was negatively related 'to satisfaction in all the aspects of life measured:' amount of fun you are having (note they are not hedonists), income and standard of living, friends, and even (modestly) with satisfaction with family life.'[13] These findings are not idiosyncratic; another study including young people drawn from outside college life found the same thing.[14]

"The invisible hand is thumbing its nose at you, Dessie," said Adam in a jocular tone. "As you might have guessed, it isn't the fact that people want money but *why* they want it that influences their happiness. From a study of 260 business students, we know that economic motives include security in old age, current family support, charity (sic!), and personal motives such as relieving self-doubt. Those who sought money for its own sake or because of pride and vanity were, at you might expect, unhappier than others. Those who sought money for such purposes as family support and charity were as happy as anybody else, normally happy.[15] I just can't believe," he continued, "that the hard working people that brought us this wealth (he looked around at the restaurant's imitation leather and Coca Cola clock – and looked away) can have created so much prosperity while suffering the pains of the materialism you describe."

"Remember," said Dessie, that we are not talking about Frank Knight's 'most noble and sensitive characters,' who are condemned 'to lead unhappy and futile lives'[16] because they are non-materialists; we are talking about the unhappiness of perfect fits: materialists in a material civilization. Moreover, 'placing money high in the rank ordering [of personal goals] was associated with less vitality, more depression and more anxiety.' For adolescents, 'high ratings of the importance of financial success was related to lower global functioning, lower social productivity and more behaviour problems.'[17]

"Are you sure you are not letting your distaste for economic man (or is it economist men?) bias your account of materialism?" asked Adam who was used to criticisms of the market on ethical grounds but never on hedonic grounds. "If it is the materialists who have brought prosperity to the world, why do people think it is an amoral set of attitudes and beliefs?"

Does materialism crowd out moral and intrinsic motives?

"I always thought materialism was the butt of criticisms by moralizers," Adam continued, "not hedonists. But I should remind you that moral economics in its incarnation as Christian economics did not rescue the developing countries of Europe from their poverty and, well, their 'backwardness' in the Middle Ages."

"OK," said Dessie, "will you agree that if people's material self-interest dominates choices in the presence of monetary appeals and wanes when community service or other 'intrinsic' appeals are made salient, that materialism can be said to 'crowd out' non-material, often moral appeals?

"We are back to Stigler's proposition that in any test, material self-interest will win over non-material appeals,"[18] said Adam.

"Ah ha, but this time the research is by economists!" said Dessie, triumphantly. "Consider why people pay taxes under circumstances where the chance of being caught cheating is trivial. Will you agree that the only plausible explanation is that they are responsive to community ethical norms, that is, that ethical norms dominate material self-interest in these circumstances?"[19]

"Economists never claimed that material self-interest dominates *all* other interests, such as maternal love, under *all* circumstances. They are talking about market situations," said Adam, slightly annoyed.

"OK, then," said Dessie, "consider the case of attitudes toward depositing nuclear waste in a person's own commune in Switzerland: When *not* offered a collective payment, a majority supported it as a civic duty even though they knew the hazards in such waste in their own backyards, but when offered a subsidy, far fewer people accepted the risk. This was not because the offer of money changed the perception of the risk.[20] Incidentally," he continued, "this redefinition of the situation has been found to occur in individual cases in the United States, as well. Experiments find that people are more likely to volunteer to give blood if they are *not* paid than if a payment is offered."[21]

"OK, so ethics and identification with community may sometimes crowd out material motives and material motives can crown out ethical and intrinsic motives," said Adam, hoping to limit the damage to a few extraordinary situations. "What does that prove?"

"Well," said Dessie, "this Zurich crowding out research certainty suggests that as a dominant *gestalt*, materialism shapes motives and values and crowds out competing ones wherever the competition is less forceful. If you will allow me to personify and dramatize, I see an eternal struggle between THE MATERIALIST seeking gratification of various acquisitive wants, and THE HUMANIST seeking competing gratification of a different set of wants. In a relatively unrelieved materialist culture it is not surprising that MATERIALISM wins. We stack the cards in its favour". Dessie hardly noticed the mixed metaphors.

Adam was tempted to say that nature stacked the cards and that this was what Darwin was saying in different terms, but the Darwinist defence of the market was not one he wanted to try against Dessie. He could see that he was not making any progress on this theme of competing material and nonmaterial motives. He knew that the next step was an inquiry into how much economists had to be paid to publish in the better journals[22] or, worse, whether economic students were more selfish than others (he was familiar with the Marwell and Ames study showing that they were),[23] and decided it was time to leave this topic. He remembered that wicked little verse aimed at an English professor by Hicks – not John, but Granville – at Harvard so long ago:

When some men achieve a mild success
They think of spirit more, and matter less.
And as they wiser grow, wiser and fatter,
They scold the common herd who worship matter.

"I have satisfied my material needs," he said looking at his empty soup bowl, "and my friendship needs" He paused as he put his jacket on. "But intellectually, I need more nourishment."

Notes

1. Tibor Scitovsky, 1977, *The Joyless Economy: An Inquiry into Human Satisfaction and Consumer Dissatisfaction*, New York: Oxford University Press.
2. Adam Smith, 1937 [1776], *An Inquiry into the Nature and Causes of The Wealth of Nations*, Edwin Caanan, ed., New York: Modern Library/Random House, p. 14.
3. Ed Diener and Robert Biswas-Diener, 2002, "Will money increase subjective well-being? a literature review and guide to needed research," *Social Indicators Research*, 57 119–69.
4. Angus Campbell, Philip E Converse, and Willard L Rodgers, 1976, *The Quality of American Life*, New York: Russell Sage, p. 380.
5. Marsha L Richins and Scott Dawson, 1992, "A consumer values orientation for materialism and its measurement: scale development and validation," *Journal of Consumer Research*, 19, 303–16 at 308–9.
6. See Abraham H Maslow, 1970, *Motivation and Personality*, 2nd edn, New York: Harper & Row.
7. Susan Fournier and Marsha L Richins, 1991, "Some theoretical and popular notions concerning materialism," *Journal of Social Behavior & Personality*, 6 403–14 at p. 403.
8. Richins and Dawson, "A consumer values orientation for materialism," pp. 312–3.
9. Russell W Belk, 1985, "Materialism: trait aspects of living in a material world," *Journal of Consumer Research*, 12, 265–80.
10. Richins and Dawson, "A consumer values orientation for materialism," pp. 304, 308.
11. Ibid, p. 311.
12. Ibid, p. 308.
13. Ibid, p. 313.
14. Tim Kasser and Richard Ryan, 1996, "Further examining the American dream: differential correlates of intrinsic and extrinsic goals," *Personality and Social Psychology Bulletin*, 22 280–87 at p. 280.
15. Abhishek Srivastava, Edwin A Locke, and Kathryn A Bartol, 2001, "Money and subjective well-being: it's not the money, it's the motive," *Journal of Personality and Social Psychology*, 8: 959–71.
16. Frank Knight, 1935, *The Ethics of Competition and other Essays*. New York: Augustus M Kelley, p. 66.
17. Tim Kasser and Richard M Ryan, 1993, "A dark side of the american dream: correlates of financial success as a central life aspiration," *Journal of Personality and*

Social Psychology, 65, 410–22 at pp. 417, 419.

18. George J Stigler, 1981, "Economics or ethics?" In S McMurrin, ed., *Tanner Lectures on Human Values,* vol. 2, Cambridge: Cambridge University Press, p. 176.

19. Bruno S Frey, 1998, "Institutions and morale: the crowding out effect." In Avner Ben-Ner and Louis Putterman, eds, *Economics, Values, and Organization,* New York: Cambridge University Press, 437–60.

20. Ibid, pp. 448–54.

21. W Upton, *Altruism, Attribution, and Intrinsic Motivation in the Recruitment of Blood Donors* (Doctoral dissertation, Cornell University, 1973). Reported in John Condry and James Chambers, "Intrinsic motivation and the process of learning." In Mark R Lepper and David Greene, eds, 1978, *The Hidden Costs of Rewards: New Perspectives on the Psychology of Human Motivation,* Hillsdale, NJ: Wiley/Erlbaum, p. 71.

22. Stigler does not report the effect of payment on economists' behaviour but he does say that they cultivate ideas which find a market (pp. 32–3), producing what people desire (p. 63), and preach what society wants to hear (p. 33). See George J Stigler, 1982, *The Economist as Preacher and Other Essays,* Chicago: University of Chicago Press.

23. Gerald Marwell and Ruth Ames, 1981, "Economists free ride. does anyone else?" *Journal of Public Economics,* 15, 259–310. Apparently Adam was not familiar with further contrary evidence in T D Stanley and Ume Tran, 1998, "Economics students need not be greedy: fairness and the ultimatum game," *Journal of Socio-Economics,* 27 657–64; Amanda Bennett, 1995, "Economics students aren't selfish; they're just not entirely honest." *Wall Street Journal,* January 18, 1995, B1.

PART 10:

STUDENT VOICES

56

POLITICS VERSUS ECONOMICS: KEEPING IT REAL

Daniel Gay

For someone who previously thought of duality as part of the Kama Sutra and the business cycle as an environmentally-friendly way of getting to work, the last year has been a struggle – a struggle not foremost in understanding complicated mathematical techniques and learning theory (although these tasks were far from easy), but a battle to understand why otherwise clever people devoted so much time to limiting their horizons.

Following my British undergraduate education in politics, philosophy and economics I completed a mainstream masters degree in political theory. After a few years as a journalist trying to decode the pronouncements of the dismal science, I returned to university to study a masters in economics. But if I hoped for a clearer understanding of how real people share out scarce resources, I was maximizing the wrong function. If I thought I would gain a better understanding of real economies, I was sorely mistaken. If I believed I would at last hear the God *Oikonomos*, I was surely beyond redemption.

Here, I would like to compare my experiences of learning politics and economics as a postgraduate. I found that three features of mainstream economics teaching made it less helpful for understanding real life than political theory: its shortage of rigour, the dogmatic way it uses concepts and its lack of usefulness.

Rigour not figures

Rigour, according to the latest edition of the *Oxford English Dictionary*, means "the quality of being extremely thorough, exhaustive or accurate". Usually someone is considered rigorous if they have delved into an issue and thought about every angle, arriving at a conclusion that attempts to tie up loose ends.

Mainstream economics, as is well known, prides itself on its rigour. Applying a general equilibrium approach requires showing with numbers how demand and supply interact simultaneously in several markets to produce prices for all goods. The practitioners of mainstream economics castigate those in other social sciences for "hand waving" and failing to quantify variables. Political theory, like sociology, is particularly vulnerable since many strands of the discipline openly dispute the idea of measuring society. For instance much of Marxism denies the possibility of reducing human society to individuals that can be added or subtracted.

But if political theorists are idle gesticulators, then mainstream economists are invisible hand-wavers. Their version of economics is, in fact, unrigorous because it leaves out so many possibilities. It is not thorough because it mostly analyses only things it can measure. It isn't exhaustive because it is implicitly bound by an uncritically positivist and strictly utilitarian world view that precludes uncertainty. It is inaccurate: economists themselves endlessly repeat the mantra that they are no good at forecasting levels – only directions – and often even these are wrong.

And if accuracy is judged by explanation rather than prediction, then many important parts of economics only appear rigorous insofar as they assume their results. For example that jewel in the crown of the new classical tradition – real (surreal?) business cycle theory – simply assumes a close approximation of real economic fluctuations and therefore produces similar predictable output movements to the data. Nelson and Plosser's well-known test disputing predictable trends in GDP over time might be one part of the argument against government intervention but it surely shouldn't be considered a conclusive piece of evidence when teaching the theory of economic fluctuations.

If I had handed in a politics essay containing within its argument only the blind empiricism of econometrics, it would have been graded a 'D'. In politics, years are spent drumming in the need to combine facts, theory and values in the correct combination to achieve a compelling syllogism. Simply pointing out a historical relation between several variables, however complicated the maths, is considered insufficient to prove a case. True, rigour is achieved only through a combination of argumentative forms and evidence; empirical, theoretical, epistemological, ontological. To misquote Paul Krugman: a half-hearted cheer for formalism, and reserve the other two for broad-mindedness.

Creative concepts

The analytical pretensions of economics derive in large part from the dogmatic way it uses concepts. Where politics frequently strays into the never-never land of creativity, economics steadfastly sticks to its tried and badly tested tools. In political theory we read the creative writing of Hilaire Belloc and GK Chesterton for their espousal of community values, or the novels of Jean-Paul Sartre for their subjectivist approach to existentialism, concepts that couldn't be communicated through standard philosophical works. But in economics we paced the well-worn treadmill of Samuelson, Solow and Sargent – geniuses no doubt, but hardly the freethinkers of their generation.

Economics sticks to prefabricated concepts because it thinks it is gradually improving its grip on the world. But what it fails to recognize is that the real world is dynamic and elusive, and that understanding it requires an ever-changing and nuanced approach. A variety of human activities that can be described as economic cannot be understood by strictly analytical tools. Does it clarify matters to label the Indonesian exchange rate between 1997 and 2000 – a period during which it swung between 2,500 and 15,000 to the US dollar and back again – by an ageing metaphor borrowed from physics? Or would it make more sense to question and redefine the concept of equilibrium in crisis situations?

Because economics builds up an edifice of analytics, it is simply hard to understand. That is why so many undergraduates drop out early on and take up more intuitive subjects. It is easier to grasp subjects that obviously relate to changing, everyday life. Most of the physical sciences change their views of the world around us, as do the humanities and social sciences. Economics is almost alone in the way it clings so tightly to past ideas. If it was open to wholesale re-evaluation – like physics accepted the quantum revolution – it would be much easier to understand and more popular.

Most students can see straight through the attempts of economists to present the subject as a seamless whole. I remember countless post-lecture whinges: about how if Akerlof et al. say that information is distributed asymmetrically then why does general equilibrium theory assume that it isn't? Or about why many Brander–Spencer type arguments for strategic trade think that assumptions should be realistic, while the rest of macroeconomics argues precisely the opposite.

Not that there's anything wrong with contradiction. Reality is contradictory. The point is that economics would be much more honest explicitly to admit its points of difference, and would arrive at better conclusions if it was creative in its use of concepts. The only compulsory course on my political theory MSc was entitled: "Methods and controversies in the history of political thought." Method, controversies and history are all practices studiously avoided by conventional economic thought. But arguing about and redefining concepts is part of good science.

Useful or toothless?

A lack of rigour and rigid use of concepts might be excusable if economics was useful. It isn't. Even though many students study economics to postgraduate level instrumentally – usually to gain a career in finance – they rarely use the tools they learn. Nobody would become an investment analyst if the strong form of the efficient markets hypothesis were true. Many financial professionals carry at the back of their minds a vague intuition that supply and demand are supposed to equilibrate, and so on, but much more useful is a practical understanding of how real exchange rates move, and of how stock and bond markets work in different countries.

Even some students academically interested in economics grumble about its uselessness. It is an oft-heard refrain that microeconomics is a cosy exercise easily performed in an exam, but trying to pin it down in research is much harder because reality starts to intrude. For me, microeconomics asserted a kind of Stockholm syndrome – in the end I grudgingly indulged my imprisoner. But it was less useful than the techniques learnt in politics.

You might think that political theory was about as abstract as it is possible to be. How can a discipline whose sole intent is – by definition – theory, have anything to offer everyday life? But because political theory is self-critical and pluralistic, it offers tools that are much more useful. Economics may purport to get down to the nitty-gritty details, but because of its rigidity it remains hopelessly stuck in its own nether world of axioms, lemmas and symbols.

Reading the business pages of a newspaper becomes a lot more informative if you have studied Marx's theory of ideology, whereas much of academic financial economics is irrelevant. Michel Foucault's definition of power relations says more about the behaviour of actors within the capitalist firm than does microeconomics. The Weberian theory of legitimacy offers a broad and adaptable understanding of the political state because it doesn't depend on unusual assumptions and can therefore be applied in a variety of situations. As a number of authors have shown, using unrealistic assumptions as an heuristic device often robs economic concepts of real world validity. Students often accuse academics of being out of touch, but it is university economics above all that refuses to engage with the ordinary world.

Conclusions

Of course a lot of economics is realistic. As I have suggested, applying some models from the new trade theory requires realism of assumptions. John Maynard Keynes gives a nod to real people by making uncertainty central to the general theory; the more uncertain agents are, the more likely they are to hold money and the higher the interest rate. Critical realists identify the existence of a deeper level of economic reality of which we can gain open-ended knowledge.

Political theory is only more realistic than economics because of certain features common to all broad-minded sciences – including pluralism and disagreement over certain basic issues. It has no inherent superiority. Parts of political theory can be woolly, distant and difficult to use. It is plainly harder to apply the knowledge of a diverse discipline. The so-called analytical thinking of economics at least has the merit of being able to supply answers, albeit in a limited sense.

But therein lies the problem: reality is messy and difficult to grasp. Usefully comprehending messiness and difficulty requires intuition, an open mind and common sense. And just because a discipline is hard to apply, it doesn't mean we shouldn't try. What are we doing, if not trying to understand real life? Are our ivory-tower proclamations aimed at constructing a cosy scheme that holds internal consistency, or are we highlighting and explaining useful features of real life with a view to changing them?

Rigour, flexibility and usefulness are linked. A discipline must at least show willingness to comprehensively rethink its use of terms if it is to remain objective and rigorous. If it doesn't, it is not as useful as it could be. If it can't incorporate a number of different tools then it is neither fully rigorous nor useful. If it isn't useful, it should surely think again about the concepts it uses. Avoiding rigour, dogmatically adhering to old concepts and forgetting that knowledge must be useful, all ultimately deny realism.

Economics could easily rise from the status of idiot, to idiot savant of the social sciences. And elucidating economics could be at least as rewarding as pontificating about politics. But only when economists remove their blinkers.

Bibliography

Akerlof, G (1970), 'The market for lemons: quality uncertainty and the market mechanism', *Quarterly Journal of Economics*, 84, 488–500.

Brander, J and B Spencer (1985), 'Export subsidies and international market share rivalry', *Journal of International Economics*, 18: 83–100.

Foucault, M (1980), *Power/Knowledge* (London, Harvester Wheatsheaf) (ed. Colin

Gordon).

Keynes, J M (1936), *The General Theory of Employment, Interest and Money*, (London, Macmillan).

Krugman, P (1998), 'Two cheers for formalism', *The Economic Journal*, 108 (Autumn): 1829–36.

Lawson, T (1997), *Economics and Reality*, (London, Routledge).

Samuelson, P (1947), *Foundations of Economic Analysis*, (Cambridge, Harvard University Press).

Sargent, T (1987), *Macroeconomic Theory*, (Boston, Academic Press).

Solow, R (1956), 'A contribution to the theory of economic growth', *Quarterly Journal of Economics*, 70 (1), February, 65–94.

57.

FORM AND CONTENT IN NEOCLASSICAL THEORY

Asatar Bair

I find it fascinating that those of us who are critical, in one way or another, of neoclassical economics would accept uncritically a defence of the theory offered by one of its most famous modern proponents. I refer to Milton Friedman's essay on methodology, where he basically argues that the theory should not be judged on the basis of whether or not its assumptions are realistic, but whether it is practical.

This is like saying, since supply and demand analysis explains prices, we can forget about the excesses that are so easy to find in the stringent assumptions necessary to obtain perfect competition and general equilibrium. For example, the omniscient Auctioneer who oversees the exchange of commodities in the general equilibrium model of Arrow and Debreu.

If we accept the terms of this argument, it becomes very simple for the proponents of neoclassical theory to defend it, such as Deirdre McCloskey's defence of the criticisms of Bernard Guerrien in *Post-Autistic Economics Review*, issue no. 15 (Chapter 36, this volume):

> It just won't do, therefore, to say as Guerrien does that price theory (as we Chicago types prefer to call it) "obviously contradicts almost everything that we observe around us." Huh? When OPEC (viz., Saudi Arabia) cut the supply of oil in 1973, didn't the relative price of oil rise, just as a simple supply-and-demand model would suggest?

Isn't this is a bit like saying "Supply and demand works, so the theory must be correct"? (By the way, I am not attributing this position to McCloskey, a sophisticated and original thinker, who, although committed to the *small-s* science of microeconomics, is also in her own way one of its most ardent critics. This is evinced by her writing not just in the *Post-Autistic Economics Review*, but many other places, including the recent volume *Postmodernism, Economics and Knowledge*, edited by Cullenberg, Amariglio and Ruccio. It is not against the McCloskeys of the world that we must primarily debate, for I believe that if she had her way, the terms of the debate would in fact be much more open.) The point is, there are so many ways to criticize neoclassical theory – why use the criticisms that are the easiest to brush off, simply by reference to already existing arguments?

The issue is not whether supply and demand analysis can be used to explain the movement of prices. Even Marx uses supply and demand analysis to make certain points about the movement of prices. (See, for example, his 1865 work *Value, Price and Profit*).

The issue is, what are the assumptions that form the basis of the theory and what are its conclusions? This is deeper than merely criticizing the form of the theory, for neoclassical theory can be formulated without math – see *The Economist* or *The Wall Street Journal* – or with a lot of math – see any graduate programme in economics or *The American Economic Review*. To me, the debate in these pages and elsewhere about formalism only scratches the surface. Sure, it's a problem that neoclassical economics tends to be dry as dust because it relies on abstract, formal mathematical proofs, and indeed, sometimes the emphasis on technical minutiae means that even its advanced practitioners can't communicate (or maybe even don't fully grasp themselves) the big philosophical ideas of neoclassical economics.

These are the ideas that have been around for a long time. Such as, how can a society maximize its wealth? What is the relationship between economic categories of production, consumption and distribution and the fulfilment of human happiness and human potential? How should we produce things? Does capitalism involve exploitation? And perhaps, the newer question: is there only one correct answer to each of these questions? I will go out on a limb and label these as interesting questions. Unfortunately, they are not often discussed in economics, despite the appearance of some of them on page 2 of most introductory textbooks. Could this absence have something to do with many students' hatred of economics? The proofs and formulae of modern neoclassical theory have not made the questions go away, merely elaborated one position out of many that are possible.

What about pluralism? Is neoclassical economics the truth, and the other theories false? This would be the only position that justifies the exclusion of other theories from economic discourse, but as so many have pointed out, including McCloskey in *The Rhetoric of Economics* or Wolff and Resnick in *Economics: Marxian versus Neoclassical*, such a position is untenable. There simply is no external standard by which to judge the veracity of contending theories.

Instead of looking at the form of the theory, we should look at its content. Any theory can be formalized. Take for example, one of my favourites: Marxian theory. This approach to economics is sometimes formulated in terms of proofs and theorems. What is produced is merely a mathematized version of Marxism. Of course there are many kinds of Marxism, sharing some points of agreement and differing on other points. But despite being formal in the mathematical sense (which may make it rather dry, for those not mathematically inclined), it will still be quite different in its content from neoclassical theory.

My sense is that debates over form and content have been collapsed because many students find both the form and content of neoclassical economics to be objectionable. For example, let's consider one of the central assumptions of the theory: human beings behave in their own narrow self-interest. Many of my own students find this idea repellent as a separate matter from their dislike of indifference curves. I happen to agree. There is no reason to assume that there is such a thing as human nature that exists independently of one's culture, language, politics, economic circumstances, etc. Is it not remotely possible that if people seem often to act selfishly it is at least partly owing to our societal elevation of greed to a virtue? Isn't it a kind of debasement of human beings to assume the worst of ourselves – indeed, to argue that whenever a human being seems to be acting unselfishly, sacrificing herself for the sake of another, this is really just the same old greed in disguise, charmingly called by microeconomists "warm-glow altruism"?

Of course, the amusing thing about this assumption – if we accept Friedman's formulation that we should overlook the realism and look at its predictive value – is that it turns out to have very limited value when it comes to actually predicting human behaviour. It seems that people are actually quite concerned with the welfare of others, even when it conflicts with their own pecuniary interest, as experimental results have demonstrated. By now these results are well known – perhaps the simplest evidence comes from the ultimatum game, in which one experimental subject is given a sum of money, to be divided between himself and the other player, who has the ability to veto the division, in which case both get nothing. Self-interest would dictate that the second player accept any offer, because something is better than nothing, and you don't care what the other player gets, because his utility has no effect on your own. Would you pick up a dollar on the street? Then you also wouldn't turn down an offer of a dollar, even if it meant the other player got $999. Well, it turns out people do care, and are willing to give up substantial sums of money to punish the other player's greed.

This experiment is very simple. For God's sake, why wasn't it done in the 1880s instead of the 1980s? Could it be that the assumption of self-interest was adopted in part to obtain the grand conclusion of neoclassical economics, elaborated by Adam Smith? Namely: if individuals are free to act in their own self-interest and society has established private property and competitive markets, then that society will be guided as if by an invisible hand, to the maximum wealth it can attain.

Forget whether or not this is true or realistic: this is a powerful idea. We want this idea to be true. We want it to be okay to be selfish, to pursue our own goals, and to have it work out that instead of this being inimical to the social good, it ends up being the very same thing as working for the good of society.

So this is my first suggestion: in teaching economics, we should really discuss the meaning of the assumption of self-interest, including its appeal and its limitations, rather than merely adopting it unquestioningly.

My second suggestion is that we should think about and talk about theories of distribution. The neoclassical theory of distribution says that each productive input, for example, labour, land and capital, receives a reward that is equal to its marginal productivity: wages, rent and profits respectively. We should discuss this with our students in a serious way. What does it mean? The implications are clear: provided that markets are competitive, workers, landlords and capitalists deserve exactly what they get. Each receives a reward perfectly commensurate with his or her contribution to production. You can't get anything more fair than this. Any suggestion that capitalists or landlords exploit or somehow take unfair advantage of their workers or tenants is expunged.

It does look good on paper. But it seems to go wrong somehow when applied. Say we are considering the situation of the landholders of European descent in Zimbabwe. They represent 10 percent of the population, and they own 90 percent of the land. Do they deserve the rents and profits they obtain, which in neoclassical theory came from the land and capital they contributed to production? How did they come to own this land anyway?

Pretty much the same way property rights in land were established everywhere at various times in history: theft accompanied by force.

What about the capitalists? Do they deserve to live off the profits, as my conservative students sometimes tell me, because they take risks, are responsible for workers, work hard themselves, and contribute to the economy? Or more in line with neoclassical economics, because they make the capital that they own available for production, and thus the capital receives a reward equal to its marginal product of capital? This makes sense. I guess the machines, tools, and raw materials that make up the capital really should get a reward. Throw some cash on the lumber pile! Open up the back of the machine and throw in a handful of coins! There you go – and thanks! Or do capitalists receive profits not from the productivity of the capital they own, but because of the unpaid surplus labour they unjustly steal from their workers?

This brings me to my third suggestion, that we discuss and take seriously theories of class. I admit that I am particularly interested in the Marxian notion of class defined as an individual's relationship to the surplus labour performed at a given productive site. This is fertile ground for exploring how production and the class processes therein affect individual development, social and political dynamics, economic fluctuations, and so forth – and how each of these realms in turn shapes the class processes. Not only can class help to illuminate society and the economy in new ways, most of these insights have been excluded from mainstream economics.

The issue – as McCloskey and others have pointed out – is not whether or not the theory is true, so much as does it *persuade*. Neoclassical economics prefers to hide its excesses in math, where people are less likely to understand the role of the assumptions being used. Is it embarrassment?

The dull, stifling formalism of neoclassical economics persuaded many people in its heyday, when more people believed that math equals truth. People are less apt to believe that now, so there can be no more retreating into the safety of proofs with unquestioned assumptions. Perhaps this means we will go back to debating substantive ideas rather than muddling through endless comparative statics. I hope so.

If we want economics to fulfil its promise, to be a serious scholarly field of inquiry that considers all points of view rather than excluding certain theories and approaches on ideological grounds, we must begin in the classroom, at the introductory level. To me, the post-autistic economics movement has made this clear in the most basic way: students have dramatically shown that they are not persuaded by mainstream economics.

References

Cullenberg, Stephen, Jack Amariglio and David Ruccio (2001), *Postmodernism, Economics, and Knowledge*, New York: Routledge.

McCloskey, Deirdre. (2002), "Yes, there is something worth keeping in microeconomics", *post-autistic economics review*, issue no. 15, September 4, 2002, article 1, http://www.btinternet.com/~pae_news/review/issue15.htm; Chapter 36, this volume.

McCloskey, Deirdre. (1985) *The Rhetoric of Economics* Madison: University of Wisconsin Press.

Wolff, Richard D and Stephen A Resnick. (1986) *Economics: Marxian versus Neoclassical*, Baltimore: Johns Hopkins Press.

58.

OF TEXTBOOKS: IN SEARCH OF METHOD

Nathaniel N Chamberland

> Interestingly, within the social sciences there are hierarchical views regarding the efficacy or usefulness of certain disciplines. Economics is not only much more predictive than, say, sociology, but more useful. The more scientific a discipline, the more valued it apparently is. The view of science as technology thus underpins not only the relative valuation of science versus social science, but also of the disciplines within the social sciences. It is an interesting view of the world: one that values the means (science) over the ends (society). (Henrietta More, *Anthropological Quarterly*, Summer 2002)

With four drafts already in the trash can, Henrietta More's (2002) article came to pinpoint (by its ambiguity) a question that sat with me throughout my undergraduate experience as a student: how does economics relate to other academic disciplines while assessing and influencing the economy?

According to the quote from More above, economics seems to be a popular, means driven, predictive science that takes its object of study to be different than sociology, but is nonetheless termed a social science by course catalogues. Economics is also, we are told, popularly valued for its predictive technology. Quite simply, economics is often identified as a set of tools devoted to determining price (that is, price knows a unit of measure to which all aspects of life are reducible). So why then keep up the charade of broad inquiry and explanation implied by the umbrella of 'social science'? Why not discard the chaff, that is, everything that has little to do with finance? So long as the economy is portrayed as an incredibly broad, although shallow, entity, economics, as an academic discipline, remains relatively simplistic. The mindset of financial study is maintained as a methodology (call it 'mainstream economic theory') and reproduced across a burgeoning academic and political territory.

For example, recall the opening pages of any undergraduate textbook. Faced with the task of describing economics, the author(s) relapse into an ahistorical account of *price theory*. Images of swapping apples for oranges, choosing between the production of pizza and robots, instill in the student the belief that they can derive the evolution of both society and economics from that of exchange. Exchange, here, is a pristine term. It knows no history, politics, bloodshed, or lie; exchange is marked simply by numbers and graphs, preferences and supplies. In so doing, economics lacks any kind of deep, causal realism in its account of the economy. Shirking this sort of analysis, the discipline has come to muddle its base terminology (*economy* and *economic*). An economics that reaches for more than financial accounting cannot proceed without reading its own history, accessing its method of inquiry, and articulating its object of study.

Undergraduates certainly do not read books, and rarely an article. Although students and professors alike may confide in these mediums, the thing that drives departments across the US and made a fixture of every economics course on the way to a Bachelors degree is, of course, the textbook. Where other social sciences have a timeline, *economics has simply a table of contents*. The concepts enunciated in Chapters 2 and 17 are of diverse origin and intention, but synthesized; historically anachronistic, but timeless; the result of numerous debates between authors and varying fields of study, but codified and distilled into problem sets. The titles of textbooks are simple, saying little more than *Economics* even though the most popular versions are in constant revision and flux: economics is presented as a science of grand architecture and vast consistency. It is not that dissenting pages have not been authored or that thought has gone stale across the globe, but rather that economics constructs its place within the college and within politics by institutionalizing a kind of economics that makes no home for debate.

Now, this chapter is written not to implicate ranks of teachers and cow their students, but rather to motion toward the divide between a teachers' own research and seminars with colleagues or small groups of students and the classes required by the department. Caught up in a 'non-profit' institution driven by the market and pride, departments and professors alike reserve endowed chairs and research monies for socio-economically conservative and conciliatory personages and projects. And perhaps more importantly, the jump from academia to politics is of varying length: that is, one page devoted to the mainstream economic project is not equalized by another directed toward critical realism or institutionalism or what-have-you. Liberalism and critical thought are cast as entertainment, a fantasy kept to one side of reality: Michael More tops book lists and box office ratings, and Martin Sheen plays a president from the left on the smash television programme, *The West Wing*.

It seems to me that these inequalities are propagated by the discipline's ineffectual articulation of the *economy* and the *economic* – the facet of life that has (and has had) to do with production and exchange and the thing which comes both to observe and participate in its unfolding. The 'mainstream' economic project retains its title by restraining the political and educative salience of ideologies (as well as techniques) that impugn the discipline's 'science envy' and, secondarily, a neoconservative allegiance. Simply put, the economic textbook has its finger on the pulse of the community and workplace, all else is academic, peace-nik fluff.

Now, when an undergraduate reads an article from the *Economist* or the *New York Times* as an assignment for an economics course, he or she gleans in a particular way. The graphs, equations, vocabulary, and explanations found in the supported textbook are to be conjured from the article at hand – if nothing else, *they* are there. First of all, the situation depicted is but an excerpt. The institutions, politics and histories brought to the fore are relevant *only in so far as they can be drawn into a quantifiable relationship with a particular monetary or material variable*. The narrative of the article is rewritten or read as immediately explicable by a concurrently assigned lesson from the economics textbook. Thus, economics visits the economy. Imagine an economics student reading a report detailing Ortega and Associates, an Arthur Anderson subsidiary, undervaluing the Dominican Republic's power facilities by US$ 907 million prior to the industries privatization (Enron and so on) (Vallette and Whysham, 2002). What hope is there for an economics textbook or free-market ideology here? Are we to allow a generation of budding economists to familiarize themselves with the price theory in such a light? No, of course not. For here, the *economy* is contrary, a rogue, and as a field of study, miscast by *economics*. At once, the motive for profit is depicted as coming unlatched from governmental and market regulations *while subsisting only in their assistance*: Enron could not have conquered (and fallen) without a number of national and international organizations. This line of argumentation is not defeated by the evidence of the criminalization of the white-collar crimes committed herein, but is rather vanquished by the solution which has arisen in the aftermath. As with the IMF and World Bank debacles, economics suggests measures devoted toward *improved transparency*. But what is it that we have come to see? Harvey Pitt steps down, but can the Securities and Exchange Commission institutionalize real change?

An economics that seriously attempts to relate to and progressively impact on the economy, cannot take shape simply by compiling written and jocular support against mainstream economics. There has always been debate within the discipline. That debate must be heard and harnessed. What if undergraduates read a book like Geoffrey Hodgson's *How Economics Forgot History: The Problem of Historical Specificity in Social Science* (2001) or Paul Downward's *Pricing Theory in Post Keynesian Economics: A Realist Approach* (1999)? What if undergraduates engaged with the community, both social and economic, that surrounds their school? Again, it is not high school, college or graduate-school teachers that necessarily lack the interest or education, but rather the classroom. Courage must be garnered to push toward institutionalizing community or academically heterodox orientations that already exist in students and teachers alike. As economists, we must know both humility and potency; mainstream economics and a neoconservative economy survives this chapter, yet instigates it and others like it; teachers and students have long been involved progressively and critically in the economy and in academia, yet examples of those lives and thoughts seem horribly new. The economics textbook, both as a medium and by its generally accepted contents, lacks a grasp of the economy that could be afforded by broad readings and community participation.

References and further reading

Bhaskar, Roy, 1993, *Dialectic: The Pulse of Freedom*, London: Verso.

Downward, Paul, 1999, *Pricing Theory in Post Keynesian Economics: A Realist Approach*, Cheltenham: Edward Elgar.

Fleetwood, Steve, 2001, "Conceptualizing *un*employment in a period of atypical *em*ployment: a critical realist perspective," *Review of Social Economy*, 59 (1), pp. 45–69.

Kuhn, Thomas S, 1996, *The Structure of Scientific Revolutions*, [1962]. 3rd edn, Chicago: Chicago UP.

Lawson, Tony. *Economics and Reality*, London: Routledge.

Mirowski, Philip, 1991, "The philosophical bases of institutional economics." Don Lavoie (ed.), *Economics and Hermeneutics*, pp. 76–112. London: Routledge.

Mirowski, Philip, 2002, *Machine Dreams: Economics Becomes a Cyborg Science*, Cambridge: Cambridge UP.

Moore, Henrietta L, 2002, "The business of funding: science, social science and wealth in the United Kingdom." *Anthropological Quarterly*, **75** (3), pp. 527–35.

Setterfield, Mark, 2000, "Expectations, endogenous money, and the business cycle: an exercise in open systems modeling." *Journal of Post-Keynesian Economics*, 23 (1), pp. 77–105.

Setterfield, Mark, 2002, "Critical realism and formal modeling: incompatible bedfellows?" Unpublished manuscript first presented at the Workshop on Realism and Economics at the University of Cambridge in May 1999.

Vallette, Jim and Daphne Whysham, 2002, "Enron's pawns: how public institutions bankrolled Enron's globalization game." Unpublished report for the Institute for Policy Studies.

Wolfram, Stephen. 2002. *A New Kind of Science*. Champaign, IL: Wolfram Media.

59.

CONSUMER SOVEREIGNTY RE-EXAMINED: APPLICATIONS OF THE MERIT GOODS ARGUMENT

Goutam U Jois[1]

Economic thinking has traditionally distinguished between public and private goods. Several decades ago, however, the new concept of merit goods was introduced into economic thinking. Economics has generally resisted this new concept. While public and private goods may be purchased through voluntary action (either individual are collective), merit goods are different: merit goods are those that the public authorities, through a value judgment, determine should be consumed at higher than market rates. (A demerit good is the opposite). Merit goods, by definition, aim at interference with consumer preference, and this violates the basic assumption of economics: that individual consumers' autonomy and preferences have normative value.[2] However, a survey of the writings of various authors shows that the concept of merit goods is unavoidable in economics. These writers are unable to locate their arguments within the framework of traditional economics because their prescriptions fundamentally involve interference with consumer preference.

In this chapter, I will examine articles by a variety of economists and non-economists. These articles range from economic theory to a feminist critique of philosophy, but they all involve some measure of application of the merit goods concept, implicitly or explicitly. Through this examination, I will show that the concept of merit goods must be introduced not only because it is theoretically necessary but also because it is practically unavoidable.

I begin with the article, "Fairness, hope, and justice" by economist James

M Buchanan. Buchanan is concerned with articulating a theory of economic justice that derives from a sense of fairness. To effect this fairness, Buchanan says, he will focus on "the distribution of rights and claims prior to or antecedent to the market process itself rather than on some final distribution of the product" (Buchanan, p. 53). Buchanan wants to keep his interference with market mechanisms to a minimum; this is why he proposes interference *prior* to the market process. Even still, he is forced to concede that the "justice" for which he is arguing "necessarily get[s] mixed up and intermingled with pure self-interest" (p. 55). Thus even Buchanan's very limited intervention in the market violates narrowly defined self-interest to some extent.

Buchanan argues that the primary source of "unfairness" or "injustice" in our society is birth (p. 59). Therefore, he proposes the "imposition of what we may call handicaps so as to [facilitate] … equality in starting positions" (p. 62). But while he wants to create these handicaps, Buchanan says that he does not at any point want to interfere with the market directly, either with its process or its outcome (e.g. p. 53). Therefore, he advocates the taxation of asset transfers and public financing of compulsory education (pp. 63–4). Despite Buchanan's intentions, both of these prescriptions do violate market preferences. Buchanan says as much; he admits that his policies "necessarily interfere with the liberties of those person who are potential accumulators of wealth and potential donors to their heirs" (p. 63). And the mandate of education clearly interferes with the preferences of anyone who derives a negative utility from required attendance at school. Since Buchanan wants to "interfere with the liberties" of some, his policy must be considered a merit good prescription.

Examples of merit goods are not limited to explicitly economic examples. In her article, "The need for more than justice," Annette C Baier describes the shortcomings of a system of ethics based solely on justice (Baier, 1994, p. 19). The solution, Baier says, is the introduction of "care" as an ethical system to supplement traditional liberal theories of justice. She contends that women are more likely to have feelings of care, while men generally take only the justice perspective (e.g. pp. 20, 22, 23). Baier argues that the perspective of carers fulfils people's emotional needs to be attached to something. Reciprocal equality, characteristic of contractarian liberalism, does not guarantee this attachment (p. 23).

Baier contends that this attachment (derived from care) is needed for every human being, and moreover, that it cannot be freely chosen in the traditional liberal framework. First, liberalism assumes interaction between equals. More often, care is between unequals: parent and child, doctor and patient, teacher and student (p. 28). Second, the rules of liberalism, guaranteeing basic minima, don't protect "the relatively powerless against neglect, or ... ensure an education that will form a person to be capable of conforming to an ethics of care and responsibility" (p. 29). Care is precisely *about* looking out for the powerless; it cannot be sustained at merely minimum standards. Finally, liberalism (political and economic) regards action as free choice. A moral theory, however, "cannot regard concern for new and future persons as an optional charity left for those with a taste for it. If the morality the theory endorses is to sustain itself, it must provide for its own continuers" (p. 29). Here we can see the merit goods nature of Baier's critique of liberal ethics. While Baier's argument is not directly economic, she is proposing a normative framework (of care) that necessarily interferes with individual preferences. Morality, Baier writes, must be "for all persons, for men and for women" – regardless of choice (p. 31); under her system, a mother cannot "opt out" and choose to neglect her children – the ethos is universal.

Another argument that does not facially seem to relate to economics is put forth by Nobel Prize-winning economist Amartya Sen in "More than 100 million women are missing." In this article, Sen describes the current situation in South Asia, West Asia, and China, where the ratio of women to men is less than 0.94, a far cry from the 1.05 or 1.06 ratio found elsewhere in the world (Sen, 1990, p. 61). The prevailing explanations for this phenomena are either economic or cultural: that the regions in question are underdeveloped economically or that the cultural context in those regions devalues the role of women (Ibid). However, Sen demonstrates that both explanations are inadequate – for example, some underdeveloped regions have higher gender ratios, and many countries with expanded roles for women have lower gender ratios (p. 62). Sen contends that some combination of the two is the real explanation: that women are viewed as inferior due to their lack of gainful employment and lack of education (p. 64). To remedy this situation, Sen endorses state funding of public education and public policy that can work to raise the ratio of women to men in these countries (p. 66). It is important to note here that Sen does not want to leave this situation to market mechanisms; a freely-operating market might reflect precisely the biases and social factors he seeks to change. His normative prescriptions do not allow for some society to reject the rights of women to be educated and employed. Instead, the policy (particularly of education) is to be carried out even if some derive a negative utility from the policy, even on net. Thus, Sen's argument – which seems at first to have nothing to do with economics – is a merit goods argument.

The last argument for merit goods presented here might seem strongest to classical economists. It is put forth by another Nobel laureate economist, Joseph E Stiglitz, in his article, "Whither reform? Ten years of the transition." In it, Stiglitz shows the failure of market reforms in Russia. He argues that the transition to a market economy lacked the institutional and legal infrastructure that it needed to take firm root in Russian society (Stiglitz, p. 5). This argument is important because it delineates a clear departure from classical economics. Adam Smith believed that the economic order was natural and would establish itself of its own accord. However, Stiglitz contends that the very reason market reforms failed in Russia was because Western consultants believed that the market could operate without the requisite supporting institutions (p. 3). Post-Soviet Russia lacked many such elements, presupposed in a market economy: bankruptcy laws and a judiciary to enforce them, entrepreneurship and capital (financial, social and organizational), to name a few (pp. 4–8). Indeed, Stiglitz is explicit on the need for such institutions, saying that "a market system cannot operate solely on the basis of narrow self-interest" (p. 8). The interferences in self-interest that Stiglitz argues for are merit goods: the "implicit or explicit social contract[s]" (Ibid) to supplement market mechanisms. The "credible and enforced laws and regulations" that are needed to provide the institutional framework for market economics, too, are merit goods (p. 19).

This essay began by examining Buchanan's view on economic *theory*: the fairness necessary in starting positions. From this premise, he derived a merit goods argument for taxing asset transfers and financing public education. The Stiglitz article, shows a merit goods argument deriving from economic *reality*: the harsh failures of market reforms in Russia. As Stiglitz shows, the lack of institutional frameworks to support the free market doomed reforms to failure. The economic order that was to establish itself "naturally" never materialized. The neoclassical assumption – that a fully-functioning free market would arise of its own accord – was proven wrong, because economists failed to prescribe Pareto-suboptimal remedies, even though they were necessary conditions for the functioning of the free market.

The arguments of Baier and Sen are useful to show that interference with the preference mechanism is not limited to what seem to be economics arguments. Even feminist critiques (Baier) and socio-cultural studies (Sen) require interference with consumer preferences to address the issues raised. From this diverse range of disciplines, we can see that we must, in certain cases, place normative value upon interference with consumer preferences.

As each of these authors illustrates, value judgments are unavoidable in liberal theory. Whether they are advocating the very rules that are necessary to make the market work or critiquing liberal ethics, the bottom line is the same: consumers are not sovereign – preferences are not absolute – and some degree of coercion is unavoidable. This violation of classical liberalism necessitates – theoretically and practically, economically and non-economically – the introduction and acceptance of the new concept of merit good.

Notes

1. The author is a JD Candidate at Harvard Law School, Class of 2007. This was chapter was written as an essay three years ago, when the author was a senior at Georgetown University, enrolled in the Honours Programme in Government. He wishes to thank Professor Wilfried Ver Eecke, Georgetown University Department of Philosophy, for his comments and feedback on this paper. The chapter closely tracks arguments that Professor Ver Eecke has raised, in articles and elsewhere, about merit goods. Professor Ver Eecke's work on merit goods, from which I draw liberally, includes "The concept of a 'merit good': the ethical dimension in economic theory and the history of economic thought or the transformation of economics into socio-economics." *Journal of Socio-Economics* 27 (1) (1998); "Public goods: an ideal concept," *Journal of Socio-Economics* 28 (1) (1999); and *Merit Goods: The Birth of a New Concept – The Unfinished Ethical Revolution in Economic History* (forthcoming anthology). The author's other writings have expanded the domain of merit goods into political theory, public policy, and law. See "Civic engagement among American youth: research, activism, and democracy," paper presentation at ARNOVA Conference (2005) (with Dr Chris Toppe); "Service-learning, community needs, and democratic theory," *The Generator: National Journal of Service Learning & Youth Leadership* 22 (1), (2003); "Can't touch this! Private property, regulatory takings and the Merit Goods Argument" (in development).

2. The introduction of the concept of merit good can be found in *Public Finance in Theory and Practice*, by Richard A Musgrave and Peggy B Musgrave (McGraw Hill: 1976–1984). Additional commentary on the concept (both favourable and unfavourable), can be found in Geoffrey Brennan and Cliff Walsh, eds, *Rationality, Individualism, and Public Policy*, (Australian National University: 1990), featuring selections by Charles E McClure, Jr and John G Head, to name a few.

References

Baier, Annette. "The need for more than justice." *Moral Prejudices: Essays on Ethics*, Annette Baier. Cambridge, MA: Harvard University Press, 1994: 19–32.

Buchanan, James M. "Fairness, hope, and justice." In Roger Skurski, ed., *New Directions in Economic Justice*, South Bend, Indiana: University of Notre Dame Press, 1983: 53–89.

Sen, Amartya. "One hundred million women are missing." *New York Review of Books*, 20 December 1990: 60–66.

Stiglitz, Joseph E. "Whither reform? Ten years of the transition." World Bank Annual Conference on Development Economics. Washington, DC. 28–30 April 1999.

APPENDIX:

STUDENTS IN REBELLION

APPENDIX I.
THE FRENCH STUDENTS' PETITION

(Translation of the students' petition circulated in France, June 2000)

Open letter from economics students to professors and others responsible for the teaching of this discipline

1. We wish to escape from imaginary worlds!

Most of us have chosen to study economics so as to acquire a deep understanding of the economic phenomena with which the citizens of today are confronted. But the teaching that is offered, that is to say for the most part neoclassical theory or approaches derived from it, does not generally answer this expectation. Indeed, even when the theory legitimately detaches itself from contingencies in the first instance, it rarely carries out the necessary return to the facts. The empirical side (historical facts, functioning of institutions, study of the behaviours and strategies of the agents ...) is almost nonexistent. Furthermore, this gap in the teaching, this disregard for concrete realities, poses an enormous problem for those who would like to render themselves useful to economic and social actors.

2. We oppose the uncontrolled use of mathematics!

The instrumental use of mathematics appears necessary. But resorting to mathematical formalization when it is not an instrument but rather an end in itself, leads to a true schizophrenia in relation to the real world. Formalization makes it easy to construct exercises and to manipulate models whose significance is limited to finding "the good result" (that is, the logical result following from the initial hypotheses) in order to be able to write "a good paper". This custom, under the pretence of being scientific, facilitates assessment and selection, but never responds to the question that we are posing regarding contemporary economic debates.

3. We are for a pluralism of approaches in economics!

Too often the lectures leave no place for reflection. Out of all the approaches to economic questions that exist, generally only one is presented to us. This approach is supposed to explain everything by means of a purely axiomatic process, as if this were THE economic truth. We do not accept this dogmatism. We want a pluralism of approaches, adapted to the complexity of the objects and to the uncertainty surrounding most of the big questions in economics (unemployment, inequalities, the place of financial markets, the advantages and disadvantages of free-trade, globalization, economic development, etc.)

4. Call to teachers: wake up before it is too late!

We appreciate that our professors are themselves subject to some constraints. Nevertheless, we appeal to all those who understand our claims and who wish for change. If serious reform does not take place rapidly, the risk is great that economics students, whose numbers are already decreasing, will abandon the field en masse, not because they have lost interest, but because they have been cut off from the realities and debates of the contemporary world.

> We no longer want to have this autistic science imposed on us. We do not ask for the impossible, but only that good sense may prevail. We hope, therefore, to be heard very soon.

APPENDIX II.
THE FRENCH PROFESSORS' PETITION

Translation of the professors' petition circulated in France, June 2000

Petition for a debate on the teaching of economics

This petition raises the following problems:

1. The exclusion of theory that is not neoclassical from the curriculum.
2. The mismatch between economics teaching and economic reality.
3. The use of mathematics as an end in itself rather than as a tool.
4. Teaching methods that exclude or prohibit critical thinking.
5. The need for a plurality of approaches adapted to the complexity of objects analysed.

In real sciences, explanation is focused on actual phenomena. The validity and relevancy of a theory can only be assessed through a confrontation with "facts". This is why we, along with many students, deplore the development of a pedagogy in economics privileging the presentation of theories and the building and manipulation of models without considering their empirical relevance. This pedagogy highlights the formal properties of model construction, while largely ignoring the relations of models, if any, to economic realities. This is scientism. Under a scientific approach, on the other hand, the first interest is to demonstrate the informative power and efficiency of an abstraction vis-à-vis sets of empirical phenomena. This should be the primary task of the economist. It is not a mathematical issue.

The path for "getting back to the facts", however, is not obvious. Every science rests on "facts" that are built up and conceptualized. Different paradigms therefore appear, each of them constituting different families of representation and modalities of interpretation or constructions of reality.

Acknowledging the existence and role of paradigms should not be used as an argument for setting up different citadels, unquestionable from the outside. Paradigms should be confronted and discussed. But this cannot be done on the basis of a "natural" or immediate representation. One cannot avoid using the tools provided by statistics and econometrics. But performing a critical assessment of a model should not be approached on an exclusively quantitative basis. No matter how rigorous from a formalistic point of view or tight its statistical fit, any "economic law" or theorem needs always to be assessed for its relevancy and validity regarding the context and type of situation to which it is applied. One also needs to take into account the institutions, history, environmental and geopolitical realities, strategies of actors and groups, the sociological dimensions including gender relations, as well as more epistemological matters. However, these dimensions of economics are cruelly missing in the training of our students.

The situation could be improved by introducing specialized courses. But it is not so much the addition of new courses that is important, but rather the linking of different areas of knowledge in the same training programme. Students are calling for this linkage, and we consider them right to do so. The fragmentation of our discipline should be fought against. For example, macroeconomics should emphasize the importance of institutional and ecological constraints, of structures and of the role of history.

This leads us to the issue of pluralism. Pluralism is not just a matter of ideology, that is of different prejudices or visions to which one is committed to expressing. Instead the existence of different theories is also explained by the nature of the assumed hypotheses, by the questions asked, by the choice of a temporal spectrum, by the boundaries of problems studied and, not least, by the institutional and historical context.

Pluralism must be part of the basic culture of the economist. People in their research should be free to develop the type and direction of thinking to which their convictions and field of interest lead them. In a rapidly evolving and evermore complex world, it is impossible to avoid and dangerous to discourage alternative representations.

This leads us to question neoclassical theory. The

preponderant space it occupies is, of course, inconsistent with pluralism. But there is an even more important issue here. Neoclassicalism's fiction of a "rational" representative agent, its reliance on the notion of equilibrium, and its insistence that prices constitute the main (if not unique) determinant of market behaviour are at odds with our own beliefs. Our conception of economics is based on principles of behaviour of another kind. These include especially the existence and importance of intersubjectivity between agents, the bounded rationality of agents, the heterogeneity of agents, and the importance of economic behaviours based on non-market factors. Power structures, including organizations, and cultural and social fields should not be *a priori* excluded.

The fact that in most cases the teaching offered is limited to the neoclassical thesis is questionable also on ethical grounds. Students are led to hold the false belief that not only is neoclassical theory the only scientific stream, but also that scientificity is simply a matter of axiomatics and/or formalized modelling.

With the students, we denounce the naive and abusive conflation that is often made between scientificity and the use of mathematics. The debate on the scientific status of economics cannot be limited to the question of using mathematics or not. Furthermore, framing the debate in those terms is actually about deluding people and about avoiding real questions and issues of great importance. These include questioning the object and nature of modelling itself and considering how economics can be redirected toward exploring reality and away from its current focus on resolving "imaginary" problems.

Two fundamental features of university education should be the diversity of the student's degree course and the training of the student in critical thinking. But under the neoclassical regime neither is possible, and often the latter is actively discouraged. Insistence upon mathematical formalism means that most economic phenomena are out-of-bounds both for research and for the economics curriculum. The indefensibleness of these restrictions means that evidence of critical thinking by students is perceived as a dangerous threat. In free societies, this is an unacceptable state of affairs.

We, economics teachers of **France**, give our full support to the claims made by the students. We are particularly concerned with initiatives that may be taken at the local level in order to provide the beginning of answers to their expectations. We also hope these issues will be heard by all economics students in universities everywhere. To facilitate this we are ready to enter a dialogue with students and to be associated with the holding of conferences that will allow the opening of a public debate for all.

APPENDIX III.
POST-AUTISTIC ECONOMICS NEWSLETTER, ISSUE NO. 1

sanity, humanity and science

post-autistic economics newsletter

No. 1, September 2000

To subscribe, send a blank email to pae_news@btinternet.com

FRANCE

The French economics mainstream is in a state of shock and apprehension following dramatic and unexpected events late in June.

On the 21st the influential Paris daily, *Le Monde*, featured a long article under the headline "Economics Students Denounce the Lack of Pluralism in the Teaching Offered". Economics students at the École Normale Supérieure, France's premier institution of higher learning, were circulating with great success a petition protesting against an excessive mathematical formalisation.

The petition notes "a real schizophrenia" created by making modelling "an end in itself" and thereby cutting economics off from reality and forcing it into a state of "autism". The students, said a sympathetic *Le Monde*, call for an end to the hegemony of neoclassical theory and approaches derived from it, in favour of a pluralism that will include other approaches, especially those which permit the consideration of "concrete realities". *Le Monde* found French economists of renown, including Michel Vernières, Jean-Paul Fitoussi and Daniel Cohen, willing to speak out in support of the students. Fitoussi, current head of the jury of the economics' agrégation, said that "the students are right to denounce the way economics is generally taught" and that the over-use of mathematics "leads to a disembodiment of economic discourse". Daniel Cohen, economics professor at the École Normale Supérieure, spoke of "the pathological role" played by mathematics in economics. Meanwhile, the Minister of Education, Jack Lang, assured *Le Monde* that he would study closely the appeal from the students.

French radio and television also reported the students' complaints and confirmed their legitimacy. On the 21st, BFM said that it was now recognized that "the teaching of economics no longer had any relation with the real world" and that "this discipline is going through an undeniable crisis". Also on the 21st, *L'Humanité* quoted extensively from the students' open letter, while noting that in recent years several renowned economists had expressed similar views.

On the 23rd, *Les Echos* reported that a government report on university economics teaching had reached conclusions similar to those of the students. In their lengthy article, *Les Echos* noted that it is increasingly recognized that economics' "malaise is general and of longstanding" and that "under the guise of being scientific" it has cultivated an anti-scientific environment "which leaves no room for reflection and debate".

On the 26th, the weekly, *Marianne,* carried an article about the student petition against "dogmatism" in the teaching of economics and for its replacement by "a pluralism of explanations". *Marianne* said that the petition, which was now on the Web, had 500 signatures, as well as growing support from economics teachers and interest from the highest levels of the French government.

On June 30th, *Le Nouvel Economiste,* referring to the students' petition and "mobilization", declared that economics had succumbed to a "pathological taste for a-priori ideologies and mathematical formalisation disconnected from reality". Economics, it continued, should give up its false emulation of physics and "should instead look to the human sciences".

In July, French media interest continued to fuel the mobilization. On the 3rd, *La Tribune* featured a long article titled "Why a reform of the teaching of economics". It began by saying that all concerned parties agree that economics is in crisis and that "a debate should be opened on this subject" and that the students' initiative aimed to bring this about. Economics, said *La Tribune,* had become lost in "mondes imaginaires" and "l'économie de Robinson Crusoé" and intellectually enfeebled by "the dogmatism that reigns in the teaching of the discipline." *Alternatives Economiques* carried an article titled "The revolt of the students" which noted that French Nobel Prize winner, Maurice Allais had, despite his mathematical approach, come to conclusions similar to those of the students.

L'Express, France's equivalent to *Time,* carried an article

"L'économie, science autiste?", which aired the students' analysis and complaints. It also reported that the students' petition now had more than 600 signatures, and that their teachers were now starting a petition of their own in support.

On the 22nd of July, *Politis* reported on the students' cause and on the "autism" into which economics had fallen in consequence of its "obsession to produce a social physics". *Politis* noted that student support for the petition was widespread, including not only students from the most prestigious universities, but also from the less celebrated, both in Paris and in the provinces. "Pluralism should be part of the cultural base of economists." Instead, "neoclassical theory dominates because it rests on a simple set of axioms, easily mathematized." The coming academic year, concluded *Politis*, "promises to be agitated."

We have learned that the economics students' petition now has 800 signatures and the economists' petition 147. The latter includes some of the most illustrious names in French economics, e.g. Robert Boyer, André Orléan, Michel Aglietta, Jean-Paul Fitoussi and Daniel Cohen. It concludes by calling for "a national conference that will open a public debate for all."

UNITED STATES

At last month's 10th World Congress of Social Economics at the University of Cambridge, American participants reported that in the USA the purge of non-neoclassical and non-mathematically oriented economists from university faculties continues.

Conferees spoke of the increasing "stalinization" of the profession. Unlike in France where the fight-back has begun, in the States there are not yet signs of the formation of the critical mass needed to turn economics away from 19th-century dogmas. It is agreed, however, that the number of academic economists in American universities who are out of sympathy with the orthodoxy comprise a sizeable minority. But they are fragmented, often intimidated and lack the means of joining together to exert their collective weight and moral authority. Meanwhile, it was agreed, the American economics' clock runs backwards.

American economists at the World Congress traded horror stories about the new wave of neoclassical "stalinization". History of economic thought courses are now being targeted as sources of ideas whereby students might question orthodoxy or place it in perspective. The goal is to create "history-free environments" in which students can be indoctrinated "more efficiently" into the neoclassical/mainstream belief system. For example, it was reported that from this fall the University of North Carolina is discontinuing all history of thought courses.

American participants also bemoaned plunging standards of literacy among economics graduate students and colleagues as a consequence of the mathematics fetish. The illiteracy problem is said to be particularly acute among new economics PhDs, many of whom are incapable of reading with comprehension a page of complex prose, such as one from *The General Theory*.

UNITED KINGDOM

The ideas expressed by the French students will have a familiar ring to readers of Tony Lawson's *Economics and Reality* (1997). But in Lawson's UK it is reported that economics students, although restless, are not yet rebellious. Meanwhile it is rumoured that a French translation of *Economics and Reality* is imminent.

BELGIUM

Interest in the reform campaign launched in France spread quickly to Belgium. On June 24th under the heading "Economie autiste", the daily, *Le Soir*, both reported on the events in France and offered its own analysis of neoclassical economics as a quaint political ideology masquerading as science.

A week later *Le Soir* featured a lengthy article on the crisis in economics. It draws on a recent report by Michel Vernières, commissioned by the French government to investigate the teaching of economics. Vernières emphasizes that economic theories are devices for conceptualizing reality. "Pedagogically, it is therefore essential to articulate conceptual reflection and empirical investigation ... [and] to underline the plurality of approaches and the overall coherence of these approaches."

Bernard Paulré, referring especially to neoclassical theory, said that mathematics is often used to hide "the emptiness of the propositions and the absence of any concern for operational relevance." He said that in addition to a-priori axioms, it is necessary for economics "to take account of institutions, of history, of the strategies of actors and of groups, of sociological dimensions, etc."

This newsletter aims to link people wishing to bring sanity, humanity and science back to economics. To this end, YOU may help significantly by forwarding this issue to 10 sympathetic colleagues and/or students.
YOU may also help by emailing relevant news items, thoughts and suggestions to: pae_news@btinternet.com

To subscribe to the *post-autistic economics newsletter*, send a blank email to: pae_news@hotmail.com

APPENDIX IV.
THE CAMBRIDGE UNIVERSITY
STUDENTS' PETITION

PhD students at Cambridge University support the following open letter:

Released 14 June 2001

Opening up economics a proposal by Cambridge students

As students at Cambridge University, we wish to encourage a debate on contemporary economics. We set out below what we take to be characteristic of today's economics, what we feel needs to be debated and why.

As defined by its teaching and research practices, we believe that economics is monopolized by a single approach to the explanation and analysis of economic phenomena. At the heart of this approach lies a commitment to formal modes of reasoning that must be employed for research to be considered valid. The evidence for this is not hard to come by. The contents of the discipline's major journals, of its faculties and its courses all point in this direction.

In our opinion, the general applicability of this formal approach to understanding economic phenomenon is disputable. This is the debate that needs to take place. When are these formal methods the best route to generating good explanations? What makes these methods useful and consequently, what are their limitations? What other methods could be used in economics? This debate needs to take place within economics and between economists, rather than on the fringe of the subject or outside of it all together. In particular we propose the following:

1. That the foundations of the mainstream approach be openly debated. This requires that the bad criticisms be rejected just as firmly as the bad defences. Students, teachers and researchers need to know and acknowledge the strengths and weaknesses of the mainstream approach to economics.
2. That competing approaches to understanding economic phenomena be subjected to the same degree of critical debate. Where these approaches provide significant insights into economic life, they should be taught and

their research encouraged within economics. At the moment this is not happening. Competing approaches have little role in economics as it stands simply because they do not conform to the mainstream's view of what constitutes economics. It should be clear that such a situation is self-enforcing. This debate is important because in our view the status quo is harmful in at least four respects. Firstly, it is harmful to students who are taught the 'tools' of mainstream economics without learning their domain of applicability. The source and evolution of these ideas is ignored, as is the existence and status of competing theories. Secondly, it disadvantages a society that ought to be benefiting from what economists can tell us about the world. Economics is a social science with enormous potential for making a difference through its impact on policy debates. In its present form its effectiveness in this arena is limited by the uncritical application of mainstream methods. Thirdly, progress towards a deeper understanding of many important aspects of economic life is being held back. By restricting research done in economics to that based on one approach only, the development of competing research programmes is seriously hampered or prevented altogether. Fourth and finally, in the current situation an economist who does not do economics in the prescribed way finds it very difficult to get recognition for her research.

The dominance of the mainstream approach creates a social convention in the profession that only economic knowledge production that fits the mainstream approach can be good research, and therefore other modes of economic knowledge are all too easily dismissed as simply being poor, or as not being economics. Many economists therefore face a choice between using what they consider inappropriate methods to answer economic questions, or to adopt what they consider the best methods for the question at hand knowing that their work is unlikely to receive a hearing from economists.

Let us conclude by emphasizing what we are certainly not proposing: we are not arguing against the mainstream approach per se, but against the fact that its dominance is taken for granted in the profession. We are not arguing against mainstream methods, but believe in a pluralism of methods and approaches justified by debate. Pluralism as a default implies that alternative economic work is not simply tolerated, but that the material and social conditions for its flourishing are met, to the same extent as is currently the case for mainstream economics. This is what we mean when we refer to an 'opening up' of economics.

APPENDIX V.
AN INTERNATIONAL OPEN LETTER:
'THE KANSAS CITY PROPOSAL'

To all economics departments

Released 13 August 2001

Economics needs fundamental reform – and now is the time for change

This document comes out of a meeting of 75 students, researchers and professors from 22 nations who gathered for a week of discussion on the state of economics and the economy at the University of Missouri, Kansas City (UMKC) this June 2001. The discussion took place at the Second Biennial Summer School of the Association for Evolutionary Economics (AFEE), jointly sponsored by UMKC, AFEE and the Center for Full Employment and Price Stability.

The undersigned participants, all committed to the reform of our discipline, have developed the following open letter. This letter follows statements from other groups who have similar concerns. Both in agreement with and in support of the Post-Autistic Economics Movement and the Cambridge Proposal, we believe that economic theory, inhibited by its ahistorical approach and abstract formalist methodology, has provided only a limited understanding of the challenging complexity of economic behaviour. The narrow methodological approach of economics hinders its ability to generate truly pragmatic and realistic policy prescriptions or to engage in productive dialogue with other social sciences.

All economics departments should reform economics education to include reflection on the methodological assumptions that underpin our discipline. A responsible and effective economics is one that sees economic behaviour in its wider contexts, and that encourages philosophical challenge and debate. Most immediately, the field of economic analysis must be expanded to encompass the following:

1. **A broader conception of human behaviour**. The definition of *economic man* as an autonomous rational optimizer is too narrow and does not allow for the roles of other determinants such as instinct, habit formation and gender, class and other social factors in shaping the

economic psychology of social agents.

2. **Recognition of culture**. Economic activities, like all social phenomena, are necessarily embedded in culture, which includes all kinds of social, political and moral value-systems and institutions. These profoundly shape and guide human behaviour by imposing obligations, enabling and disabling particular choices, and creating social or communal identities, all of which may impact on economic behaviour.

3. **Consideration of history**. Economic reality is dynamic rather than static – and as economists we must investigate how and why things change over time and space. Realistic economic inquiry should focus on process rather than simply on ends.

4. **A new theory of knowledge**. The positive-vs-normative dichotomy that has traditionally been used in the social sciences is problematic. The fact–value distinction can be transcended by the recognition that the investigator's values are inescapably involved in scientific inquiry and in making scientific statements, whether consciously or not. This acknowledgement enables a more sophisticated assessment of knowledge claims.

5. **Empirical grounding**. More effort must be made to substantiate theoretical claims with empirical evidence. The tendency to privilege theoretical tenets in the teaching of economics without reference to empirical observation cultivates doubt about the realism of such explanations.

6. **Expanded methods**. Procedures such as participant observation, case studies and discourse analysis should be recognized as legitimate means of acquiring and analysing data alongside econometrics and formal modelling. Observation of phenomena from different vantage points using various data-gathering techniques may offer new insights into phenomena and enhance our understanding of them.

7. **Interdisciplinary dialogue**. Economists should be aware of diverse schools of thought within economics, and should be aware of developments in other disciplines, particularly the social sciences.

Although strong in developing analytic thinking skills, the professional training of economists has tended to discourage economists from even debating – let alone accepting – the validity of these wider dimensions. Unlike other social sciences and humanities, there is little space for philosophical and methodological debate in the contemporary profession. Critically-minded students of economics seem to face an unhappy choice between abandoning their speculative interests in order to make professional progress, or abandoning economics altogether for disciplines more hospitable to reflection and innovation.

Ours is a world of global economic change, of inequality between and within societies, of threats to environmental integrity, of new concepts of property and entitlement, of evolving international legal frameworks and of risks of instability in international finance. In such a world we need an economics that is open-minded, analytically effective and morally responsible. It is only by engaging in sustained critical reflection, revising and expanding our sense of what we do and what we believe as economists that such an economics can emerge.

APPENDIX VI.
THE HARVARD STUDENTS' PETITION

Harvard University Students for a Humane And Responsible Economics Mission Statement 2003

Students for a Humane and Responsible Economics (SHARE) aims to improve economics education at Harvard by advocating for a broader diversity in the economics curriculum and by providing a forum on campus for discussion and debate on current economic issues, focusing on the social consequences of global and domestic economic policy. We believe that the field of economics plays a critical role in shaping the basic organizational structure of society and informing policies (both domestic and international) that strongly affect individual welfare. Because of the practical impact of economics, we believe economics education has important human consequences. Economic models are lenses through which students are taught to view how society should function. We believe that Harvard, by only providing one model of economics, fails to provide critical perspectives or alternative models for analysing the economy and its social consequences. Without providing a true marketplace for economic ideas, Harvard fails to prepare students to be critical thinkers and engaged citizens. We believe that the values and political convictions inherent within the standard economic models taught at Harvard inevitably influence the values and political convictions of Harvard students and even the career choices that they make. Finally, by falsely presenting economics as a positive science devoid of ethical values, we believe Harvard strips students of their intellectual agency and prevents them from being able to make up their own minds.

Despite the limited view of economics embodied at Harvard, we believe that economics poses fundamental questions about society whose comprehensive answers require an interdisciplinary approach. In order to bring to light the broader impact of economics and the intellectual possibilities of the field in a spirit of critical discourse, SHARE has three goals:

1. To diversify the curriculum of economics at Harvard. In particular, we are interested in diversifying the introductory economics course, Social Analysis 10, Principles of Economics (known as Ec 10), by amending the course and/or by providing an alternative introductory course that includes critical perspectives. We believe that diversity in an

introductory economics course is crucial, and that Ec 10 must be reformed for five reasons:

a)   Ec 10 is the only introductory course currently offered at Harvard, and it is a prerequisite for all other economics courses and a requirement for many concentrations. Thus, students who may be dissatisfied with the course have no choice but to take it.

b)   It is advertised as an introductory course, which implies a survey of various economic models. Because Ec 10 presents only the neoclassical model, however, students get the false impression that there are no other models in the field of economics. The fact that Ec 10 is often the only economics course many students will take at Harvard only makes this false impression more dangerous.

c)   Most students take Ec 10 as freshmen, when they have not yet fully learned to question what professors teach. They are therefore less likely to question what they learn in Ec 10, and more likely to accept it as fact rather than as one specific framework of analysis and interpretation.

d)   A large percentage of the articles in the sourcebook are written by Professor Martin Feldstein himself or by economists promoting similar ideological and political views.

e)   The course offers no forum for discussion. Proessor Martin Feldstein does not hold office hours for his students to ask him critical questions on his lectures or the course material. Sections are also taught uniformly and allow no official time for a deeper discussion of issues brought up in the lectures or the readings. Students are expected simply to regurgitate the information they are presented with, without questioning it.

2.   To diversify the economics faculty at Harvard. The homogeneity of the economics curriculum is mirrored in the faculty's near-unanimous acceptance of the mainstream economic model. The lack of intellectual diversity in the faculty prevents students from finding mentors who can facilitate their pursuit of critical perspectives on economics. Harvard needs to provide students with a faculty whose interests are representative of the diversity of interests within the student body and the field of economics.

3.   To educate students about economics and alternatives to the dominant model, as well as raising awareness of the social and political implications of economics. To accomplish this, we hope to provide an ongoing public forum for critical discussions around economics by inviting speakers, conducting regular discussion groups, and creating

links between Harvard students and alternative economic policy research institutes. Finally, we hope to become a center that promotes further study and research in alternative economics, and where students and faculty can engage in critical dialogue about economics.

Index